From Email to Earthquakes:
On Teaching and Learning with Technology
in The California State University

From Email to Earthquakes:
On Teaching and Learning with Technology
in The California State University

Edited by Cheryl L. Weigand

California State University Press
Long Beach CA

The California State University Press
Long Beach CA 90802
© 2003 by The California State University
All rights reserved. Published 2003
Printed in the United States of America

Original photograph by Gladys Deniz.
Cover and book design by Rachel Olivo.

Library of Congress Control Number: 2003096395

ISBN 0-974-51700-3

Contents

Preface

Cheryl L. Weigand
The California State University, Office of the Chancellor
Institute for Teaching and Learning

In the beginning, this project seemed fairly modest in scope. It started with a not unfamiliar reminder from Lorie Roth, who had become involved in conversations about systemwide academic technology initiatives, that CSU faculty have no doubt already addressed many issues facing the system. When it came to questions of academic technology and how best to use it to serve our students, she suggested that we turn to the faculty themselves. I did a quick literature review and easily came up with dozens of articles published by CSU authors. Sara Zaragoza, our talented student assistant in Academic Programs, proceeded to do the footwork—and the surfing—to produce the articles themselves. And that is how this book began to grow.

The literature review and the packet of 75 articles collated by Sara were enough to give us a taste of the breadth, variety, and energy of the CSU work on academic technology. Serving as an editorial board, Mary Allen, Jacquelyn Kegley, Lorie Roth, and I formulated a plan and issued a call for papers. We asked the provosts to forward published articles by CSU authors on academic technology, and in response we received nearly 125 articles representing almost every campus. Groups of articles, along with a clear and focused rubric, were then distributed to a panel of 29 CSU faculty volunteers who were asked to evaluate the readability and accessibility of the articles and their appropriateness for the volume. Each article was read by two faculty members, and when their views were widely disparate, the article was sent to a third reviewer. Ultimately we emerged with the 26 articles featured here.

We hope this varied collection of previously published articles will bring further recognition to these CSU authors, document their ongoing and widespread involvement with academic technology, inspire other faculty members to consider the use of academic technology in their own courses, inform administrators and other academic technology planners, provide useful "how to" advice to faculty based on first-hand experiences, inspire discussion of critical issues in the implementation of academic technology, and provide a resource for faculty development. This is no small order, but on behalf of the editorial board I am pleased to say I think the collection accomplishes just that.

Although my work as Managing Editor of *Exchanges: The On-line Journal of Teaching and Learning in the CSU* affords me the opportunity to work with faculty authors (at least through email, in any case), it has been many years since I've had the pleasure of teaching undergraduates, walking daily across a campus, and talking regularly with other faculty. Working so closely and for so long with these articles, it became difficult to see the forest for the trees. In reading through the collection once more, however, I am struck again not by any similarity in approach or viewpoint, but by how often thinking about academic technology leads directly to thinking about teaching. Thinking about teaching with technology, that is, leads to thinking not about technology nearly as much as about teaching. Rina Benmayor, for one, is explicit when she describes how the incorporation of new media tools led her to re-think just about everything—not only her course structure and its objectives but the very notion of oral history. For Benmayor, technology changes the learning environment and leads to increased collaboration and deeper learning. For Jeffrey Bell, the simulations facilitated by the Internet make it possible for students to become scientists rather than just learn about them; technology makes possible a more "authentic" learning environment, one in which students and instructors engage in scientific studies and the gap closes between the student as learner and the researcher as teacher. These are just two perspectives among many in this volume, and while the authors come from a range of disciplines and differ in their technical abilities, all are interested in advancing, deepening, and improving student learning.

What is refreshing to me about this collection is the humanity that comes across in these discussions of technology. Some of these authors are enthusiastic proponents of the potential of academic technology; others are more skeptical, emphasizing a more limited role for technology as a supplement to in-class, face-to-face interactions among students, instructors, and course material, whether books or microscopes. All, however, depict learning environments in which students and instructors continue to communicate and interact with others, and all seem energized by the pedagogical challenges posed by technological tools.

As previously mentioned, all of these articles were first published elsewhere, most in journals, some in books and other forums. We would like to thank again the many authors and publishers who granted permission for us to reproduce these articles, many of whom generously reduced or waived the usual permission fees. Except as indicated in the notes of the essays (such as when original photos could not be found), the essays have not been updated or revised. Minor obvious factual or typographical errors have been corrected; for the few essays that originally appeared in British journals, spelling and punctuation have been returned to American conventions; and notes and references have been formatted for consistency throughout the volume. Otherwise, the essays remain as they were first published.

This project has been a tremendous undertaking—had we known just how tremendous, doubt and skepticism might have outweighed enthusiasm. Luckily we didn't know, and luckily we had many hands and heads to help in the process. While most of these behind-the-scenes contributors will be thanked by name on the following pages, I would like to mention the support of the Academic Senate, CSU, represented by then-Chair Jacquelyn Kegley, and the Academic Technology Advisory Committee (ATAC), represented by co-Chairs Jacquelyn Kegley and Scott McNall. Cosponsors of this volume, both the Academic Senate and ATAC have been generous in their guidance and support. In addition, Mary Allen, Faculty Director of the CSU Institute for Teaching and Learning, has been an irreplaceable resource throughout this process, contributing everything from invaluable editorial guidance to procedural wisdom. Lorie Roth made possible the beginning, the middle, and the end of this book, conceiving its creation, guiding its development, and supporting its production. Her respect for faculty efforts and her dedication to students continually inspire all of us who work with her. Above all, we would like to thank the faculty of the California State University, without whom there would be nothing to say in the slightest.

Acknowledgments

Many people have had a hand in the making of this book, and it could not have been done without them. Every contribution (brainstorming, copying, designing, editing—the list goes on) is greatly appreciated. Those who have lent a hand include Mary Allen, Joanne Bartok, Pam Estaniel, Alex Gibson, Jacquelyn Kegley, Marsha Hirano-Nakanishi, Ed McAleer, Scott McNall, Ty Melvin, Rachel Olivo, Mindi Osowski, Ann Peacock, Kara Perkins, Sue Robb, Lorie Roth, Jo Service, Jim Spalding, Jason Stanton, Greg Steiner, Tarita Varner, Norma Warren, James Wesson, Dawn Wheeler, and Sara Zaragoza. Many of the publishers who hold the copyrights to these articles generously reduced or waived their usual reproduction fees. The faculty reviewers, whose names are listed separately, were immensely helpful in the daunting task of choosing the articles to be featured here from among so many inspiring submissions. Lastly, the support and encouragement of colleagues, family, and friends has fueled my contribution to this endeavor. My thanks go out to everyone who helped bring this idea to fruition.

ENCOURAGING ACTIVE LEARNING WITH ELECTRONIC SIMULATIONS, ROLE-PLAYS, AND TUTORIALS

Introduction

Jeffrey Bell
California State University, Chico

Gone are the days when going to college meant attending a series of lectures and taking notes. Faculty in the CSU have long been proponents of "active learning, " and throughout this chapter one sees a desire to use technology to give students more "authentic" learning experiences. While the particular approaches and methods vary widely, in every case the authors have tried to design new educational modules that engage students in activities drawn from the real world. The instructional materials described in these papers were designed by the authors to address real concerns they had with the education of their students, and while the level of support and additional resources needed for the modules vary significantly, each is clearly a labor of love for the participating faculty. Included here are descriptions of simple tutorials and Java applets to help students become better statisticians, Java applets that let students use geological data to locate an earthquake or date a rock, Java applets that let students design and interpret biology experiments, a murder mystery game in a foreign language, and a role-playing game that puts the student in the shoes of an anthropologist investigating an alien culture.

Why this desire for more "authentic" learning experiences? The problem is that most traditional course work is very different from what students will do after they graduate. Attending 50-minute lectures, poring over notes, reading textbooks written for novices, and answering multiple-choice or short-answer questions—all this is a far cry from what students will encounter after they leave the university. Students become very good at memorizing information, but they get little chance to develop many of the reasoning and interpersonal skills needed in the real world. The articles in this chapter discuss materials designed to help students develop those skills. While there are many different approaches to making the learning experience more "authentic," these authors have chosen to have students interact with computers.

There are several advantages and disadvantages to using computer modules to provide "authentic" learning experiences. The most obvious disadvantage is that students get only limited visual and auditory sensory input and usually must interact by typing at a keyboard or clicking symbols on a screen. Another frequent problem is that while the simulation or tutorial is always based on a model that the author believes is appropriate, it may be so simplified that key learning goals cannot be achieved with the simulation. Some key advantages of computer modules, many of which are illustrated in the following articles, are that they are interactive, requiring students to apply what they have been learning to solve problems; they are iterative, allowing students to get as much practice as necessary to develop the required skills and knowledge; they provide prompt and accurate feedback; and they are cheaper and safer than corresponding real-life experiences would be. Probably the biggest advantage, though, is that students actually enjoy the learning process.

Clearly, the most successful simulations are those that have been created by the gaming industry. If you want to learn how to manage a city, call plays for a football team, jump like the kids seen in skateboarding or snowboarding competitions, develop maze-solving skills, manage resources and money, fly a plane, choose the proper golf club, or name the pieces and uses of medieval armor, then there is a computer game for you. While most games do not develop any practical skills (and you would not want to ride in a car driven by someone whose experience with driving came solely from video games), many of these games do teach their players an impressive array of knowledge and skills that is easily comparable to what is covered in a typical college course. What is more, the players enjoy learning and interacting with these simulations so much that they will spend hours of their free time interacting with and learning from them.

The most successful examples of educational simulations are probably the flight simulators used to train commercial and military pilots. Medical schools and the military also have invested heavily in developing simulations to train new doctors and soldiers. The driving force behind these successful efforts has been the desire to give the students authentic learning without the risk of the real thing. The U.S. Army has even brought in game developers to teach them how to design simulations so engaging and involving that students will want to learn; the Army has now released one of their simulations as a game for the public.

The examples from the gaming industry, the government, and commercial fields make it clear that simulations and other electronic modules can be very successful tools for aiding student learning. The problem in an academic setting is how to produce, within the limited budgets and expertise available, instructional modules of high enough quality to encourage meaningful learning. Faculty from the California State University system produced the efforts described in the following articles, typically using only small amounts of seed money from local grants, although sometimes with some additional resources from the National Science Foundation (NSF) or textbook publishers. While none of these is a threat to "SimLife," all are tailored to meet the needs of students in college courses, and they illustrate many of the properties described above.

"The Biology Labs Online Project: Producing Education Simulations that Promote Active Learning" by Jeffrey Bell describes an extensive set of simulations that model various biology experiments. These simulations were produced with money from the CSU system; NSF; and a book publisher, Addison-Wesley-Longman. The simulations enable students to design their own experiments and then interpret the data produced from these experiments. The BioLab simulations illustrate how students can be given much more practice at developing critical skills than is normally possible without computer simulations: Students can design and conduct more experiments than would ever be possible in a real laboratory, as well as experiments that would be too time consuming or dangerous to do "for real." In "Multimedia Development for Cultural Anthropology: Fieldwork Simulation" Frances Berdan, Edward Stark, and Carey Van Loon show how to incorporate video into Web pages to create a very realistic simulation of anthropology fieldwork. The most game-like of the simulations described here is Terri Nelson and Walter Oliver's "Murder on the Internet," which teaches Spanish or French by having small groups of students solve a murder mystery, with all interactions taking place in the foreign language. The students learn to communicate in a foreign language by communicating in a foreign language—about as authentic as it gets. This is a good example of an inexpensive simulation, in that no expensive equipment, programs, or personnel were needed beyond extensive faculty time and expertise. Gary A. Novak's "Virtual Courseware for Geoscience Education: Virtual Earthquake and Virtual Dating" is a more elaborate simulation that is probably the most authentic of the simulations here. In Virtual Earthquake students analyze seismogram data to determine the epicenter and magnitude of an earthquake just as a geologist would. Virtual Dating likewise simulates the process by which a geologist determines the age of a rock or mineral formation. Finally, in "Teaching Statistics with Web Technology: The WISE Project," Christopher Aberson and colleagues illustrate how interactive teaching aids can be produced without extensive external support. While the learning aids used in this project are very simple Java programs that each target specific concepts in statistics, they show how instructors can slowly build up a collection of tools to help students learn better.

Readers of these papers are likely to find something they can use in their own classes, or perhaps they will be inspired to find or develop similar resources for their students. While the barriers to development are high, they are not insurmountable. In addition, there are many resources that have already been developed that can be easily accessed over the web. A good place to begin is the MERLOT site (www.merlot.org), which has a catalog of over 2,000 educational simulations—most of which are free.

The Biology Labs On-Line Project: Producing Educational Simulations That Promote Active Learning

Jeffrey Bell
California State University, Chico

Abstract

The Biology Labs On-Line Project is an attempt to create simulations of important biology experiments that students normally cannot perform in typical undergraduate laboratories. All of the simulations have enough complexity that students have the flexibility to design and interpret their own experiments. The programs generate large amounts of data and are fast enough for students to do multiple experiments, creating the opportunity for students to get extensive practice at applying scientific methods. The simulations are all written in Java and are accessed over the World Wide Web, making them easily available to students anytime and anywhere. Nine of the simulations, covering the topics of evolution, Mendelian genetics, protein translation, human population demography, protein structure-function, human genetics, mitochondrial electron transport, cardiovascular physiology and photosynthesis are already finished, with six more planned for the summer of 2000.

Introduction

Pedagogical Motivation

A major lack in much current science instruction at the university level is appropriate active learning experiences. Students in many science courses still get too few opportunities to think and reason about scientific problems. Well-designed laboratory experiments provide the best means to give students the opportunity to learn about a science subject while developing the thinking skills most instructors have as a goal of their course. However, there are many limitations on the use of real laboratory experiments in an undergraduate or high school science course. Students in educational labs are severely limited by the time required for most serious investigations. A typical laboratory for a biology class will meet once or twice a week for two to three hours each time. This time constraint is a major barrier for introductory students as they try to learn how to be a scientist. Many important biological experiments take weeks, months or years to carry out, putting them well beyond the reach of the typical teaching laboratory. Many other barriers limit the choice of experiments in teaching laboratories, including a lack of appropriate equipment, insufficient funds for expensive reagents, restrictions on the use of hazardous chemicals and radioactive materials, a lack of technical skills by the students and ethical concerns.

As a result of these difficulties, most professors either concentrate on using laboratory time to provide students with an opportunity to practice being a scientist by carrying out inquiry based investigations, or demonstrate scientific principles by having students carry out carefully controlled experiments designed by the instructor. In both cases the main mechanism for students to learn the subject is the traditional lecture. A major trend in current attempts to improve science education is to try to replace static lectures with more active learning approaches. While there are many versions of "active learning," in the sciences an inquiry approach is frequently used. One version of this is the learning cycle method in which students explore a biological phenomenon before receiving any explanation from the instructor. Other aspects of the inquiry approach include having the students propose their own hypothesis and design, execute and interpret their own experiments to test their hypothesis (Lawson, et. al, 1990, Uno, 1999). The National Research Council's Science Education Standards consider this the central strategy for teaching science (NRC, 1995). In addition to learning how to think like scientists, students learn the concepts and facts of a subject better when they have to apply the knowledge. While there are many ways to make the lecture more inquiry based, (see "Handbook On Teaching Undergraduate Courses" Uno, 1999), one very useful alternative is the use of simulations (Windschitl, 1998, Uno, 1999). To address these problems the Biology Labs On-Line Project has created several Java simulations of biological phenomena that can be used to supplement traditional laboratories and lectures, providing students with many more opportunities to learn by experimentation than is possible using traditional methods.

The Biology Labs On-Line Project is a component of the California State University System (CSU) Integrated Technology Strategy (ITS), which calls for anywhere, anytime access to information. The project initially brought together biologists from throughout the CSU system and the CSU Center for Distributed Learning (CDL) to explore ways to use technology to improve learning in introductory biology courses. Later, multimedia developers from Addison Wesley Longman were added to the development team. A major goal of the collaboration was to allow students to learn as biologists do, i.e., by actively designing experiments and interpreting their results. Eliminating the time constraints of the traditional experiment, the simulations give students the opportunity to design and interpret experiments, to learn from their mistakes, and to revise and redo their experiments just like real scientists. The simulations are not designed to replace the traditional "wet labs" found in the normal biology course, but rather to extend the laboratory experience to subjects and experiments that cannot normally be done, or not done well enough, in a traditional laboratory. The simulations are also not multi-media presentations, stand-alone tutorials or on-line courses.

A key advantage of a simulation is the potential of allowing the student to design and carry out many more experiments than would be possible with real labs. This gives the student many more opportunities to practice the skills of hypothesis creation, experimental design and data analysis than can happen in the normal lab or lecture setting. A lack of underlying complexity is a problem with many of the currently available on-line educational simulations, which frequently allow only one real experiment. Thus, one of the design goals for the Biology Labs On-Line Project was to create simulations with enough underlying complexity that students would be able to do many different experiments. For example, the FlyLab has 29 different genes on four different chromosomes, allowing the possibility of literally millions of experiments. Similarly, the Evolution Lab, which uses two islands, each with 7 independent continuously variable parameters, provides the capability of millions of different possible experiments. In addition to the complexity in the starting parameters, each of these programs operates stochastically, so that even with identical starting conditions students will get different results. The large number of possible experiments and the speed at which each experiment can be carried out, five to ten minutes per experiment, means that students can get much more practice at designing and interpreting their own experiments than is possible in the traditional laboratory. This creates new possibilities for teaching some topics as students can now figure out the underlying principle on their own, with only minimal guidance from their instructor.

The FlyLab's introduction to the topic of sex linkage illustrates how these simulations can be used in inquiry. After doing some genetic crosses that demonstrate normal Mendelian dominance and recessive inheritance patterns, students are asked to investigate one of the X-linked traits available in the simulation. The students are not told that the trait is X-linked, nor is the concept of sex linkage discussed prior to the assignment. The students can do as many different crosses as necessary to try to figure out what is going on. The ability to carry out many different experiments is a key to making this work, as that is the only way the students can eliminate many of their initial explanations for what is happening. Even for the many students who fail to solve this problem, the experience is very helpful, making them much more attentive when the genetic explanation is given in class.

Another goal of the BLOL Project was to design simulations that could be used to learn about key concepts in biology that are not normally used in traditional laboratories because of time, expense, hazards, etc. Examples of this are the Evolution Lab and DemographyLab, which simulate processes that take place over hundreds of years; MitochondriaLab, which simulates experiments that use toxic chemicals; TranslationLab, which simulates the use of radioactive isotopes; HemoglobinLab and LeafLab, which simulate the use of complicated and expensive measuring equipment; PedigreeLab, which simulates expensive mapping experiments using dozens of human families; and CardioLab, which simulates potentially lethal experiments on human subjects.

Design of BLOL and Comparison to Other Lab Simulations

Other laboratory simulation products exist, comparable in some respects to the BLOL Project. Stella, for example, is a general modeling tool, and Ecobreaker is a package that can be used to create useful simulations of ecology processes. The Bioquest Consortium sells a large number of simulations on CD, covering many of the same topics covered by BLOL. These simulations differ from those in the BLOL Project, however, in that they have certain machine requirements (Mac, PC, Unix) and distribution difficulties. Our Java-based BLOL simulations, on the other hand, are platform independent and not tied to use within the actual science laboratory.

The BLOL simulations have all been created in the Java programming language, so that they can be easily accessed over the web through any standard browser. This solves the problem of widely disseminating the applications, a common problem with most educational software. The Java application provides the user interface where students set the starting parameters for their experiment and get graphical feedback on their current settings. While each of the simulations is unique, all of them share many common interface elements and functions. In some of the simulations the Java program also calculates the results, while in others the input parameters are passed back to the server, where the real calculations take place. The students receive the results through the Java application.

The downside of using Java is that only individuals and schools with fairly new computers and software (Netscape 3 or better, etc.) and an internet connection can use the software. Another disadvantage of using Java is the inability of Java programs to save to disk or print. This limitation has been overcome through the use of a notebook that can be exported to a web page. All of the data tables, such as numbers of different types of progeny, or results of statistical calculations, can be imported directly into the notebook. After typing in their comments, students can export the notebook to a web page for printing, or to email to themselves or an instructor. The web page is temporarily stored on the server. Graphical images produced by some of the programs are also exportable to the notebook, where they can then be printed.

All of the programs share some common user interface elements, including a title bar with links to an introduction to the lab, help, sample assignments, the notebook, etc. While there is much diversity in how the different labs operate, most of them start in an input mode where the students design their experiment by adjusting different parameters, after which they run the simulation. The program calculates the results of the experiment, usually in a minute or less, and then presents the results in the output mode. In this mode there is a tabbed interface where the students choose which type of output they wish to view, a table of the data, a graph, the input values, etc. After analyzing their results they can import them into the notebook and then go back to the input mode to design another experiment. This ability to go back and forth quickly between the design of an experiment and the results is one of the powerful advantages of a simulation approach to teaching science.

Availability

For simulations to truly be useful as a primary mechanism for teaching the concepts of a course, they need to cover the majority of the key concepts in the course. The BLOL Project has produced nine different educational simulations covering the subjects of evolution, Mendelian genetics, protein translation, human population demography, protein structure-function, human genetics, mitochondrial electron transport, plant photosynthesis and respiration, and cardiovascular physiology. Current projects in progress and due to be finished by the summer of 2000 will simulate enzyme kinetics (EnzymeLab), the use of transgenic mice to study developmental genetics (TransgenicLab), phylogenetic reconstruction (CladisticsLab), population genetics (PopulationGeneticsLab), metabolism (MetabolismLab) and population ecology (PopulationEcologyLab). Thus, a significant portion of the major concepts introduced in a typical introductory biology course could be taught using a combination of real laboratories and these simulations.

Nine of the programs are currently available for beta testing and all fifteen should be finished by the summer of 2000. Descriptions of each of the labs can be found below. Current plans call for a $19.95 fee for access to all nine of the simulations and a lab manual with printed instructions and sample assignments. The fee is necessary to support the servers and for maintenance of the various programs as operating systems and computers change. Annual subscriptions to individual labs are available for $5.25 each, and there is also the option of getting the five genetics simulations, FlyLab, EvolutionLab, TranslationLab, HemoglobinLab and PedigreeLab, for $10.95. Below is a brief description of the finished simulations.

DemographyLab

The Demography Lab models human population growth for seven different countries around the world. Students can use this lab to investigate how differences in population size, age-structure, and age-specific fertility and mortality rates affect human population growth. Default values for seven countries—China, India, Japan, Mexico, Nigeria, Sweden, and the United States—have been incorporated into the program to allow comparisons between nations with very different demographics, such as Japan and Nigeria. In addition, students can change any of the parameters to create their own experiments. Initial population size can be set anywhere from two to six million. The proportion of males and females in each five-year age group can be set independently of one another. Thus, the effects of a war or a disease that affects one sex or certain age groups can be modeled. The mortality rate for males and females in each five-year age group can also be set independently so the effects of changes in health care can be modeled (by changing infant mortality rates or mortality rates for the elderly, for instance). The birth rate per female in each five-year age group can all be set for those ages in which birth rates are possible. Thus, the effects of birth control efforts or changes in marriage ages can be modeled. All of these parameters are adjusted using a simple graphical interface.

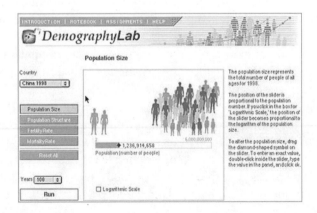

Figure 1. A thumbnail of the DemographyLab screenshot

JEFFREY BELL

After running the simulation for 100, 200, or 300 years, students get summary statistics, such as life expectancy, birth rate, population growth rate, etc. They can view a line graph of population numbers over the course of their experiment, see a graphical representation of the population structure for every five years of the experiment, or examine the number of males and females in each age group for each five-year period. With the program a variety of demographic phenomena can be demonstrated, such as exponential growth and decline, stable age structure, zero population growth, demographic momentum, dependency ratios, sex ratios and marriage squeezes.

EvolutionLab

Although evolution is the unifying theme of the biological sciences, it is perhaps one of the most misunderstood and difficult concepts to convey in a laboratory setting. The study of evolution is especially suited to computer simulations because evolution normally occurs over very long time intervals, large data sets are usually needed to understand it, and there are usually a number of important parameters that are difficult to control in real experiments. EvolutionLab is a web-based, interactive computer simulation designed to teach the basic concepts of natural selection and to convey the importance of time in the evolutionary process.

Students using EvolutionLab observe evolutionary changes in bird beak morphology in hypothetical populations of birds isolated on two islands. In the simulation, students can set the annual rainfall on island(s) containing finch populations, and then observe the effect of this environment on the evolution of the finches' beaks. Students may also change several other properties of the bird populations, such as initial mean beak size, beak size variability, beak size heritability and mean clutch size, to determine their effect on beak evolution.

While the simulation is based on Darwin's finches, changes in the species variables such as mean beak size, variability, heritability and clutch size create virtual species that can have properties similar to many other wild species. Students can investigate the parameters that are more likely to lead to the extinction of endangered species, see why some species might evolve faster than others, and examine many other facets of evolution. The program generates large data sets —one run can produce 600 data points —so students can learn how to analyze and interpret large amounts of data, unlike the situation in a typical lab. The great flexibility of the program should allow individual instructors to tailor student assignments to their particular preferences and provide students with a real opportunity to design their own experiments. Actively engaging students in exploring and studying evolution through this simulation provides another avenue for students to learn about evolution in addition to the traditional text and lecture explanations.

PedigreeLab

PedigreeLab generates a hundred pedigrees for each of the 23 different genetic diseases available, including dominant, recessive and X-linked diseases. Every student gets a unique set of pedigrees to analyze. Students can examine the pedigrees to determine the inheritance pattern of the particular disease. Once the inheritance pattern has been determined the student can choose a molecular marker, from over a dozen available markers, each with a known position on a chromosome, to study. The program will search through hundreds of randomly generated pedigrees to find 100 pedigrees meeting the criteria chosen by the student. Comparison of the presence of the disease trait to the presence of the molecular marker can be used to determine whether the molecular marker is linked to the disease trait and, if they are linked, give the distance between them. The program keeps track of the results from each pedigree they use and can determine the statistical significance of their results. They can use the molecular markers to map the disease gene to a particular chromosome or to a region of the chromosome. This is a key process in the current search for human genetic disease genes and is normally very difficult to explain to students. The program includes graphical views of the chromosomes, on which they can place a marker designating where they believe the disease gene is located. There are also graphical aids for understanding the pattern of inheritance they would expect if the marker was linked to the gene or was not linked. Having them actually go through the process of mapping a human gene can significantly improve their learning of these difficult concepts.

FlyLab

The FlyLab simulation is an update to the FlyLab originally created by Bob Desharnais. In the FlyLab, students design their own fruit flies by choosing from many different possible phenotypes for characteristics such as eye color, wing shape, body color, etc. They then mate their flies and analyze the progeny to determine the rules of inheritance for different traits. Each experiment is unique, and students can have up to 10,000 progeny produced from one mating. Offspring can also be mated, providing a wide range of different experiments. There are 29 different traits that can be studied in isolation or in various combinations so the number of possible experiments is in the millions. The traits are all represented graphically, allowing the student to observe the phenotypes directly. For instance, if the student selects the white eye mutation for the female parent, the picture of the female parent will have white eyes. After the mating, pictures of the different progeny are presented, along with numbers beside each picture to indicate the number of progeny of that type (number of females with white eyes, females with red eyes, etc.) The program includes a Chi Square calculator for doing statistical tests of the students' hypotheses, and a notebook for recording results, observations, hypotheses and conclusions. Students can import the numerical results from their crosses and statistical tests directly into the notebook.

Using this program, students can discover or study most of the important principles of Mendelian genetics, including dominant and recessive alleles, sex-linkage, lethal alleles, independent assortment, epistasis, linkage, gene order, linkage groups, and linkage maps. An advantage of the simulation is that students can discover these principles by doing the same sort of experiments as the original researchers, only much more quickly. The program is appropriate for a wide range of biology courses as the assignment determines the level of difficulty. Students can do statistical tests, but this is not required. They can do complicated crosses with multiple traits, or simple crosses with only one trait at a time. If students are confused by a complicated cross, they can always do some additional simpler crosses to try to figure out what is going on. They can also do additional crosses with the progeny from their crosses, and their progeny, etc. This ability to devise their own experiments and try many different permutations is a major strength of the FlyLab.

TranslationLab

So far, the BLOL project has produced two molecular biology simulations. The first, TranslationLab, simulates some of the original experiments used to crack the genetic code, one of the key discoveries in molecular biology. These experiments rely on radioactive materials and difficult-to-produce RNA templates, so they can't be done in the normal biology lab. Students design and create simple RNA molecules in the simulation that they then translate in a virtual in vitro translation mix. The program shows a simple animation of the techniques that would be used to analyze the products of the translation and then gives them the amino acid sequence of any proteins produced in their experiment. The student must logically analyze the results of multiple experiments to deduce the properties of the genetic code, just as the original researchers did, only with the advantage of being able to do experiments in minutes that normally take months to carry out. Various properties of the code that can be determined using this simulation are the triplet nature of the code, the non-overlapping nature of the code, the degenerate nature of the code, codon assignments for each amino acid, and the existence and identity of stop codons.

HemoglobinLab

In the second molecular biology simulation, the HemoglobinLab, students investigate various aspects of the molecular biology of hemoglobin using case studies. The goal is for the student to learn how changes in the nucleotide sequence of a gene may affect the protein sequence, which may affect the structure of the protein, which may affect the function of the protein, which may affect the properties of the cell, which may, in turn, affect the physiology of the individual. Students choose a case by selecting a patient from a pull down menu containing a list of over a dozen patients. For each case the students can examine the doctor's notes about the symptoms and medical history of the patient, the color of a vial of the patient's blood, and a microscopic sampling of the blood to determine changes in the red blood cells. They can run a sample of the blood on an electrophoresis gel to determine if there are physical changes in the globin protein, and determine the amino acid sequence of the patient's globin protein. Having determined the sequence of the protein, the student can go to the DNA sequence editor and try to alter the DNA sequence of the normal gene to see what type of DNA mutation would cause the changes found in the patient. The patients have a variety of mutations in the globin gene ranging from simple point mutations that change one amino acid, such as in sickle cell anemia, to deletions and insertions causing frameshifts, such as some of the thallasemias. The mutations cause many different patient phenotypes, such as anemia, brown blood, polycythemia (too many red blood cells), and purple skin color.

MitochondriaLab

Two biochemistry and cell biology labs have been completed, MitochondriaLab and LeafLab. MitochondriaLab simulates electron transport, proton gradients and oxidative phosphorylation in mitochondria. Students recreate the classic experiments that established the chemiosmotic theory as the mechanism for energy production in the cell. They add various substrates, such as pyruvate, succinate, etc. and inhibitors, such as malonate, cyanide, DNP, etc. to their virtual mitochondrial extracts and then measure the consumption of oxygen over time. The program produces a chart similar to what would be produced by a real oxygen electrode. Students use the chart, the known volume of the flask and the concentrations of the reagents added to determine oxygen consumed and the amounts of the substrates. From their results they can work out some of the steps in the electron transport pathway, and the mechanism by which chemical energy is converted into ATP molecules.

LeafLab

The LeafLab simulates the photosynthetic reactions in leaves. Students measure CO_2 consumption by leaves from six different plants, including both C3 and C4 plants. Students can vary wavelength and intensity of light, CO_2 concentration, air flow rate, temperature, and type of leaf and then measure the consumption of CO_2 in their simulated leaves. The program helps the student with the calculation of photosynthesis rate and has a sophisticated curve fitting function that lets students plot their data and then determine the shape of the best curve through the data. Students measure or study the light compensation point, the CO_2 compensation point, the connection between light and CO_2 consumption, photochemical efficiency, dark respiration, photochemical saturation, and the differences between C3 and C4 plants, sun versus shade plants and plants of different ploidy levels.

CardioLab

CardioLab simulates some aspects of cardiovascular function. Students can directly vary six different parameters that affect cardiovascular function, blood viscosity, blood vessel radius, heart rate, blood volume, systolic ventricle volume and venous capacity, and measure the effect of their changes on blood pressure, heart rate, stroke volume, blood volume and various nerve impulses. Concepts such as homeostasis, feedback, and compensation can be illustrated. Students can also do experiments on virtual patients with various health problems such as hypertension, congestive heart failure, mitral valvular stenosis, etc. The effects of different "real" interventions on both normal and diseased patients such as hemorrhages, exercise, dehydration, IV infusion, disruptive shock and treatment with drugs such as epinephrine, is also modeled in the simulation.

Assessment

The precursor to all of these labs is the original Virtual Fly Lab. This simulation of fruit fly genetics is now used in biology classes all over the world, and has created so much demand on the server hosting the program that there are now five different mirror servers. I field tested the FlyLab, EvolutionLab and TranslationLab in an upper division genetics course with encouraging results. 98% of the students in this course considered their FlyLab assignments useful in learning genetics; 83% found EvolutionLab to be useful; and 93% found TranslationLab useful. Some comments from the students are given below (Student comments refer to older names for the applications. Virtual Fly is now FlyLab, EvolveIt is now EvolutionLab and TranslateIt is now TranslationLab).

"Virtual Fly and TranslateIt were the assignments I got the most out of. I liked the way it made you systematically think to solve the problems."

"TranslateIt was enjoyable because it requires the student to investigate and solve the problem."

"TranslateIt gave me an excellent concept of how genes code for proteins through valuable experience. I could experiment and learn by trial and error to prove to myself that the book and what I was working on were in fact the same."

"It is a tie between TranslateIt and EvolveIt for most useful and as to how much I got out of them. They were easy to use, the help info was well defined and they both helped me see the larger concepts, 'big picture.'"

"I liked the Virtual fly and EvolveIt activities because they allowed you to do some investigation on your own and they made you think about what was really happening, which made you understand the material better."

There were only a few negative comments, usually having to do with the difficulty of getting on-line and using the programs. Students who are uncomfortable with computers are at a disadvantage when using these simulations and special care must be taken to make sure they get the most out of the simulations. The only other negative comment was, "I liked TranslateIt the least because it made my head hurt." While this is unfortunate, if the BioLabs project can produce more simulations that cause some students' heads to hurt, then the project will be producing simulations that change, for the better, the way biology is taught.

Conclusion

The purpose of the BLOL Project is to try to find ways to use technology to improve biology education. The approach decided upon was to create a team composed of biology professors, graphic artists and programmers that would design and produce simulations of significant biological processes. While this approach greatly increases the expense of producing the simulation, it is hoped that the increased quality and complexity of the simulations will make them much more useful than the typical program produced by individual faculty, which typically are used in only a small number of courses. Eventually a publisher, Addison-Wesley-Longman, was also added to provide the marketing and support that would be needed if the programs were adopted by a large number of faculty. Initial tests have suggested that the programs can be very useful learning tools. Whether significant numbers of faculty will be willing to make the changes needed to incorporate these tools into their courses remains to be seen. With the rapid increase in the computing power available to students and the increased familiarity of students with using applications over the Internet, on-line tools such as the simulations produced by the BLOL Project will become more and more useful. Simulations such as these provide new tools to increase the use of the inquiry approach to teaching science. They will not, and should not, replace real hands-on laboratories. Finding the right balance and the proper way to use these new tools is going to take some time and experimentation by instructors (Jensen, 1998). Hopefully, they will at least consider the possibilities these new tools provide.

Refererences

Jensen, M. S. (1998). Finding a place for the computer in the introductory biology laboratory. *Journal of College Science Teaching 38*(2): 247–249.

Lawson, A. E., Rissing, S. W., & Faeth, S. H. (1990). An inquiry approach to nonmajors biology. *Journal of College Science Teaching 30*(5): 340–346.

National Research Council. (1990). *National Science Education Standards.* Washington, DC: National Academy Press.

Uno, G. E. (1999). *Handbook on teaching undergraduate courses.* Orlando, FL: Saunders College Publishing.

Windschitl, M. A. (1998). A practical guide for incorporating computer-based simulations into science instruction. *American Biology Teacher 60*(2): 92–97.

Acknowledgements

The following individuals contributed to the development of these simulations. Their contributions are gratefully acknowledged: Bob Desharnais, David Caprette, Mike Palladino, Steve Wolf, Zed Mason, Ron Quinn, Terry Frey, David Hanes, Judith Kandel, Nancy Smith, Sally Veregge, Abbe Barker, Michelle LaMar, Mark Crowley, Chuck Schneebeck, Rachel Smith, David Risner, Swann Do, Lou Zweier, Scott Anderson, Peilin Nee and Anne Scanlan-Rohrer. Partial support was provided by U.S. National Science Foundation grant DUE 9455428 to Bob Desharnais.

IMEJ multimedia team member assigned to this paper: Yue-Ling Wong.

Editor's note: The following links were provided in the original online article:

- The web site for access to the labs and for current information on the labs is http://www.biologylab.awlonline.com

- A QuickTime movie (533 KB) showing how the DemographyLab works: http://imej.wfu.edu/articles/1999/2/01/demo/demography/index.asp

- A QuickTime movie (561 KB) showing how the EvolutionLab works: http://imej.wfu.edu/articles/1999/2/01/demo/evolution/index.asp

- A QuickTime movie (663 KB) showing how the PedigreeLab works: http://imej.wfu.edu/articles/1999/2/01/demo/pedigree/index.asp

- A QuickTime movie (1.46 MB) showing how the FlyLab works: http://imej.wfu.edu/articles/1999/2/01/demo/fly/index.asp

- A QuickTime movie (1.45 MB) showing how the TranslationLab works: http://imej.wfu.edu/articles/1999/2/01/demo/translation/index.asp

- A QuickTime movie (751 KB) showing how the HemoglobinLab works: http://imej.wfu.edu/articles/1999/2/01/demo/hemoglobin/index.asp

- A QuickTime movie (2.08 MB) showing how the MitochondrialLab works: http://imej.wfu.edu/articles/1999/2/01/demo/mitrochondrial/index.asp

- A QuickTime movie showing how the LeafLab (1.61 MB) works: http://imej.wfu.edu/articles/1999/2/01/demo/leaf/index.asp

- A QuickTime movie (946 KB) showing how the CardioLab works: http://imej.wfu.edu/articles/1999/2/01/demo/cardio/index.asp

Multimedia Development For Cultural Anthropology: Fieldwork Simulation

Frances F. Berdan, Edward Stark, and Carey Van Loon
California State University, San Bernardino

When students complete cultural anthropology classes, they should emerge with a clear understanding of how anthropologists collect data on other cultures—simply put, they should have a grasp of how anthropologists do fieldwork. Unfortunately, "fieldwork" is particularly difficult to convey in a classroom setting.

How can students evaluate information written by ethnographers unless they have a good idea of the conditions under which that data was collected? Lectures laced with amusing and embarrassing personal experiences lend some excitement and enlightment, readings recount a variety of ethnographic situations, and videos visually depict significant field experiences. Yet, vivid as these accounts may be, they do not directly involve the students, who still remain somewhat distanced from the fieldwork experience. One solution, of course, is to send students into local fieldwork settings, but that is usually impractical, especially when a large number of students is involved.

Another solution to actively involving students in realistic fieldwork situations is an interactive multimedia simulation of ethnographic encounters. EthnoQuest is such a simulation. In this interactive role-play, the student assumes the identity of a relatively green ethnologist who undertakes anthropological fieldwork in the fictitious Mexican village of Amopan ("Nowhere"). As the ethnographer, the student must complete designated fieldwork tasks such as finding a place to stay, taking a census, making a map, and collecting biographies. At the same time, the ethnographer becomes immersed in village events and customs, and must establish and maintain rapport with the villagers. EthnoQuest is authored in Macromedia Authorware and is currently available on CD-ROM for use in the computer labs at California State University San Bernardino. Eventually it will be more widely distributed and could be formatted for Intranet and Internet use as the bandwidth quality improves.

Multimedia and Problem-Solving Scenarios

This program was originally conceived as an adjunct to introductory courses in cultural anthropology. While it still serves that purpose, we also see the

Reprinted from *Syllabus, 12*(3), 1998: 54–57, by permission of the authors and the publisher.

value of EthnoQuest in a variety of other contexts and in a wide range of student class levels. In a general sense, this program applies multimedia technology to problem-solving scenarios in an overtly cross-cultural context, and requires users to be active participants in the learning process. As such, its format and approach can have useful applications in areas such as international business, teacher training, public administration, critical thinking, and language learning. In addition, we anticipate that with minor adjustments EthnoQuest can be effectively used in grades 7–12: the game-like format should captivate the students and the activity should enhance critical thinking skills and cross-cultural awareness. In EthnoQuest, the student travels to the fictitious community of Amopan where a variety of adventures are undertaken from the village's plaza. EthnoQuest can, ultimately, contain a great many mini-games or modules which the student accesses by clicking on designated figures in the plaza. For instance, by clicking on two children in the plaza, the student enters the module "First Encounters."

This initial module involves the establishment of rapport with selected villagers, the acquisition of some basic cultural information, and the requirement to find a suitable place to stay in the village. Subsequent modules will include, among others, "Who's Who in Amopan" (taking a census and making a map), "A Day in the Life of the Midwife" (or a farmer, or a child,

Student ethnographers must make choices about
how to best establish a rapport with villagers.

or, really, anyone), "Market Day," and "The Patron Saint's Fiesta." The value of this module approach lies in its manageability and flexibility: it focuses the student's attention on the completion of particular assignments and therefore keeps the game somewhat under control, and it allows for differ-

FRANCES BERDAN · EDWARD STARK · CAREY VAN LOON

ent modules to be applied throughout a course as specific topics unfold (e.g., in an introductory anthropology course, "Market Day" can be associated with the topic of economic anthropology, "A Day in the Life of the Midwife" with gender roles, and so on). The module format also allows for the mini-games to increase in difficulty as the student progresses through them, thus challenging the student's developing skills and testing acquired knowledge.

Embedded Learning Goals

As students interact with individual villagers and wend their way through the community, they must make frequent decisions about what to say and what to do. Some decisions are more appropriate and productive than others, and are rewarded by positive responses from the villagers; inappropriate decisions result in negative responses. In addition, a point system assigns + and – values to each decision, and student-players receive cumulative scores. Along the way, they absorb village customs and become integrated into village life. Students engaging in EthnoQuest find themselves faced with anthropologically documented culturally based dilemmas requiring realistic actions and decisions. Working singly or in groups, students achieve a number of learning goals:

1. They learn to devise problem-solving strategies in novel cultural contexts and sometimes-stressful situations. The simulation places them in a cultural setting quite different from their customary one, and requires that they interact with villagers on the villagers' terms. Since serendipity plays a part in real fieldwork, we have programmed it here: some things happen to students that are quite beyond their control (such as being accused of being a tax collector), and they must deal with those situations by choosing between alternative decision paths.

2. Students learn how to balance the costs and benefits involved in decision-making. Few decisions are cut and dried. For example, a decision to drink bottled water may safeguard the ethnographers' health but offend the hospitality of the villagers; the alternative decision to imbibe in a proffered local brew is cordial and friendly, but may have deleterious effects on the ethnographer's health. Still, they must decide. EthnoQuest does not let the players off the hook: they must make these decisions and take their consequences, as they would in the real world.

3. Students are required to evaluate why they made particular decisions and why they were appropriate or productive (or not). To achieve this important goal, a "wise man" (residing on the sidebar menu) periodi-

cally tests students on their decisions, whether good or bad. A guidebook (also on the sidebar menu) can be accessed which includes "28 good things you can do in the field" and "28 of the worst mistakes you can make in the field;" students must respond with the correct option from the appropriate category. Students also are asked questions at the end of each module which relate to the decision-making process and its consequences (such as, "Evaluate the relative merits of accepting housing at the cantina, the church, and the schoolhouse").

4. Students as ethnographers also learn how to gather accurate cultural information while not offending the villagers. Ethical issues loom large here, as much information imparted to anthropologists is given in trust and confidence. In the first module ("First Encounters") the information gathered is largely happenstance. However, beginning with the second module ("Who's Who in Amopan"), the students undertake data-gathering more directly and are faced with increasingly difficult problems: for example, informants will offer conflicting information, and female ethnographers will find they are being given different information than are male ethnographers (and vice versa).

5. The effective ethnographer records plenty of notes in the field, and student-ethnographers have to do so here. The sidebar menu contains

Students emerge from the simulation with awareness of customs and their own ability to cope with other cultures.

an icon for field notes, and students can click on this to access their fieldwork notebook at any time. Their notes are cumulative, and at the end of each module these serve as printed records of their observations and encounters. An "ideal" set of notes will be available; students can compare their notes with these ideal ones at the end of each module, assess their own strengths and weaknesses, and thus prepare better and better notes as they progress through successive modules.

6. While the students are moving throughout the village learning about people in another culture, they also become well aware of how those people view them. As villagers try to find an acceptable status for the ethnographer as an outsider, and as the students handle culture shock and become immersed in village affairs, they will discover a great deal about their own cultural selves. This is one of the inevitable outcomes of fieldwork, and EthnoQuest periodically asks players how they are feeling about aspects of their enterprise (e.g., when they discover someone has lied to them). Students also are asked such questions at the end of each module; after finishing "First Encounters," for instance, they are asked what they think the villagers think of them.

7. Ethnographers need to be alert. It is easy in the simulation to become focused on dialogues and dialogue decisions, but what about information acquired by being observant? The "wise man" keeps students on their toes with occasional pop quizzes and, after the first few, the powers of observations should improve. Furthermore, each module contains clues which assist students in successive modules; the student must be aware of the potential usefulness of these clues (such as children's pictures in the school, or notices on the cantina wall).

Learning the Culture of Village Life

In a survey of students in anthropology classes at CSU San Bernardino (Spring 1997), it became apparent that while students were very interested in "life in the field," they were also very curious about actual customs and "things" of another culture. We have responded to this interest by including informational segments throughout EthnoQuest. For instance, students may click on any of five drinks in the cantina to learn more about them, they may click on hypertext in a dialogue for more detail, or they may zoom in on a book or basket to take a peek inside. As the students progress through the game, they therefore become more knowledgeable and more comfortable with village life in the virtual world of Amopan.

In general, students playing EthnoQuest find themselves facing decisions and dilemmas based on competing values of cultural relativism and ethnocentrism. They emerge from this game-like simulation with an enhanced awareness of and sensitivity to the customs of another culture and an appreciation of their own ability to cope in novel situations. In a more subtle sense, the simulation is designed to highlight the assumptions (e.g., relativistic, ethnocentric) behind decision-making strategies. In a more directly anthropological sense, students derive, from their fieldwork mistakes and triumphs, a clear idea of the excitement, pitfalls, and frustrations encountered in the essential process of gathering data for the discipline.

EthnoQuest encourages a "you are there" mood by minimizing navigational complexity and maximizing the student ethnographer's interaction with the villagers and village activities. The virtual approach with its vivid graphics is enhanced with sound and video, and the use of the student's name throughout. And, of course, the student takes the active role of the ethnographer, must make essential decisions, may make mistakes, and must face the consequences of each decision, good or bad. This program therefore has definite pedagogical advantages over usual traditional means of teaching fieldwork. These methods, try as they may, nonetheless tend to distance the student from the actual fieldwork experience. In contrast, EthnoQuest places students at the fulcrum of their own ethnographic destinies.

Developing Multimedia—A Team Approach

The process of developing EthnoQuest has been highly dependent on co-operative teamwork. The three members of the EthnoQuest team all bring different and essential backgrounds and perspectives to this complex undertaking: an anthropological content expert, an expert multimedia specialist, and a graduate student/high school teacher. Jointly, we have faced a number of challenges in the production of this coursework. We do not hesitate to admit that we have had our share of false starts; however, each time we emerged with a new and, happily, better approach. For instance, the initial plan was to engage the student in a single long game encompassing several assignments. This proved unworkable and we then devised the module idea, one that we believe to be far superior in any event. In another arena, an on-going challenge is, quite simply, time. Progress is slow on such complex projects, and while that may be a frustration, extended periods of time also allow ideas to settle and be recast in novel forms.

A third challenge is the desire to provide a program that is at the same time academically sound, graphically appealing, educationally engaging, and a genuine learning tool. The team approach mentioned above has greatly facilitated our ability to tackle all of these dimensions and develop them into a unified program. Each team member, bringing a different perspective to the project, provides checks and balances to the others. Through consistent dialogue we have maintained sight of our fundamental idea and the learning goals involved. And the ability to look at the project from different angles has repeatedly allowed us to disentangle ourselves from rough spots and dead ends, and to generate new ideas and energy.

FRANCES BERDAN · EDWARD STARK · CAREY VAN LOON

A valuable student perspective is embedded in the EthnoQuest team, but we also have subjected the simulation to student usability testing. Students are closely observed while playing EthnoQuest, and also complete pre-test and post-test questionnaires. Such student input has encouraged us to constantly refine the program; for instance, we found we needed to provide students with more engaging and informative fieldwork preliminaries (such as budget and travel arrangements) and to include more cultural data throughout. Overall, EthnoQuest has been developed, stimulated, and sustained by the creative ideas generated through this teaching approach, and richly enhanced by usability testing.

Notes

The images shown here have been modified slightly since the publication of the original article.

EthnoQuest (CD-ROM along with a Field Guide and Workbook) is currently available through Prentice Hall. An expanded version of EthnoQuest will be available through Prentice Hall beginning January 2004.

Murder on the Internet

Terri Nelson and Walter Oliver
California State University, San Bernardino

Abstract

In this article we describe the design and testing process that resulted in the production of *Un Meurtre à Cinet* and *Un Misterio en Toluca*, two role-playing applications which ask students of French and Spanish to collaborate to solve a murder mystery using e-mail, a listserv, and a culturally rich Web site. Using our own pedagogical philosophy and our own production experience as guides, we also attempt to elaborate general guidelines for developing and adapting other materials, including other mysteries, for use in a pedagogically appropriate technology-mediated environment.

Statement of Design Philosophy/Background

Ideally, CALL software does not merely replicate textbooks and workbooks. Pencil and paper, blackboard and chalk, transparencies and screens are technological resources that support teaching and learning. CALL software, therefore, should provide "something different." We should not be using a computer just because we can and we should not be using more advanced (i.e., complicated) technologies when something simpler will do. Each technological advancement (since the paper and pen) creates different venues for learning and supports different learning and teaching styles. The computer may or may not be better than teaching on a blackboard; it all depends on what the teachers want students to learn and how they plan to teach.

In our software development, we always try to exploit the advantages and opportunities offered by computers. For example, computers more easily support different learning modalities because they can easily integrate sound, images, movies and text in an on-demand interactive environment. Computers can also expand access to learning; a well-designed Web site allows learning to occur at a time and place convenient to the student rather than merely conforming to an academic calendar. Internet technologies can "transport" students to the target culture and create new communities of learners and language users. Rather than replicating the traditional workbook exercises, therefore, we look first to what computers offer and how they enhance opportunities for language learning.

Reprinted from *Calico Journal*, *17*(1), 1999: 101–114, by permission of the authors and the publisher.

Content Constraints/Advantages

The programs—*Un Meurtre à Cinet* and *Un Misterio en Toluca* (hereafter referred to as the Murder mysteries)—are designed to promote writing for communication (see Figure 1). Writing in the foreign language classroom is rarely for communication; the student generally writes so that the instructor can assign a grade. The instructor, regardless of the exercise content, is the target audience and participates in the writing more as a coach and judge than as a true reader; there is little or no information gap. The content of the students' writing is more often associated with practice of a particular vocabulary item or structural item than with the exchange of

Figure 1. Un Meurtre à Cinet

information. Moreover, it is very difficult to create writing tasks that focus attention on communication because language learning takes place in a classroom. In a classroom, attention naturally centers on oral communication; when face-to-face, we communicate by speaking. Writing tends to be an out-of-class assignment on an individual basis.

The Murder mysteries focus attention on writing for communicative purposes. The mysteries are divided into four rounds, with a preparatory phase preceding round one. In the preparatory phase, students receive information about the character they will role-play. Each character is based upon "soap-opera like" stereotypes so that they are easily identifiable and familiar to students. Students are, therefore, immediately engaged. They recognize that these characters are not real people. Given the ludic nature of the activity, students are eager to play their role in this "fantasy" environment. In each of the four rounds, students receive specific, but not complete, information about what their character was doing on or about the time of the murder. They also receive a short list of tasks to be completed during the round (information that they must reveal). New information in the form of documentary evidence (i.e., clues) is available on the Web site with each succeeding round. Thus, the Murder mysteries are comprised of three components: (a) information individually provided to students, (b) e-mail exchanges among the students, and (c) clues provided on the Web.

DICTAMEN POLICIACO

I N C I D E N T E

SITUACION: Cuerpo de la víctima encontrado por Ramón BELTRAN ARRIAGA, bombero, después de un incendio en la empresa González y Compañía, SA. Según BELTRAN, el cadáver yacía en el despacho del presidente de la empresa, César GONZALEZ PLATA. Se limitó el incendio al despacho del presidente pero el resto del edificio se llenó de humo. Según autoridades médicas, 75% del cuerpo de la víctima se quedó seriamente quemado.

HORA Y FECHA: Alrededor de la medianoche, sábado-domingo, 3-4 de agosto de 1996.

VICTIMA: Dolores LOPEZ GALINDO, 20 años. Mesera del Café de la Posta.

DOMICILIO: 123 Calle General Ferado.

CIRCUNSTANCIAS: sin determinación ¿¿¿, accidente, suicidio, homicidio???

SOSPECHOSOS: varios, se anticipan interrogaciones.

OBSERVACIONES:

1) El sábado, 3 de agosto, alrededor de las 17 horas, se presentó la madre de la difunta, Isabela GALINDO DE LOPEZ, ante las oficinas de la Dirección de Seguridad Pública y Tránsito para iniciar el proceso correspondiente a la supuesta desaparición de su hija. La señora, según su testimonio, había sufrido un verdadero pánico cuando su hija no regresó a casa a la hora convenida como de costumbre.

2) Se encontraron $10.000 pesos en la bolsa de la difunta.

3) La víctima fue identificada por el bombero BELTRAN. Según BELTRAN, la señorita LOPEZ llevaba relaciones íntimas con su hermano de él, Alberto. Se le encontró en la bolsa también una licencia de conducir vigente del Estado de México que confirmó la identificación previa de BELTRAN.

4) Una de las dos tazas vacías encontradas en el despacho del señor GONZALEZ presentó rastros de un lápiz labial que se parece mucho a el usado por la víctima. Pizcos del lápiz han sido enviados al laboratorio federal para análisis.

5) Se inició el incendio en un basurero situado abajo de la ventana principal. El contenido del susodicho basurero fue completamente destrozado, pero las cenizas parecen ser las de un periódico.

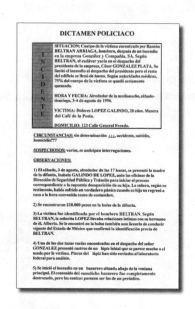

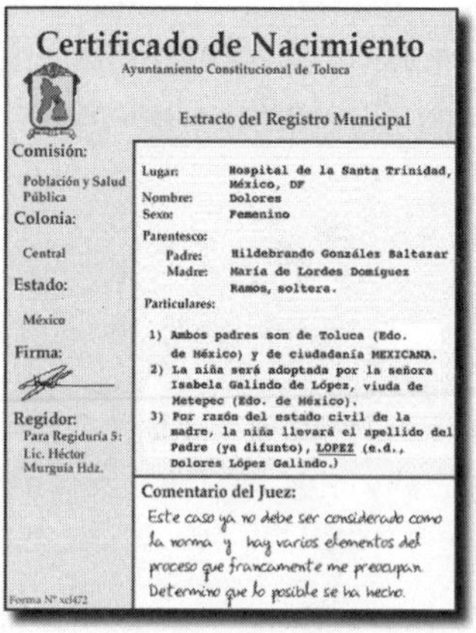

Figure 2. Police report

The structure of the Murder mysteries induces students to engage in genuine communicative behavior. At their core, the Murder mysteries utilize multiple layers of information gaps. First, students are curious about their own character because, up until round four, they do not know everything about where they were and what they were doing. All characters have a number of skeletons in their closet; students are eager to discover whether or not they are guilty of a crime. Second, the information that students must reveal in each round is designed to force other students to reveal their secrets because all students, by the rules of the game, are compelled to tell the truth (but not necessarily the whole truth) at all times and to answer all questions put to them. Finally, each round provides a number of documents written in different discursive styles (e.g., newspaper articles, police reports, birth certificates, blackmail letters, and agendas) that provide clues to the mystery (see Figures 2 and 3).

Certificado de Nacimiento

Ayuntamiento Constitucional de Toluca

Extracto del Registro Municipal

Comisión: Población y Salud Pública

Colonia: Central

Estado: México

Firma:

Regidor: Para Regiduría 5: Lic. Héctor Murguía Hdz.

Lugar: Hospital de la Santa Trinidad, México, DF

Nombre: Dolores

Sexo: Femenino

Parentesco:

Padre: Hildebrando Gonzáles Baltazar

Madre: María de Lordes Domíguez Ramos, soltera.

Particulares:

1) Ambos padres son de Toluca (Edo. de México) y de ciudadanía MEXICANA.
2) La niña será adoptada por la señora Isabela Galindo de López, viuda de Metepec (Edo. de México).
3) Por razón del estado civil de la madre, la niña llevará el apellido del Padre (ya difunto), LOPEZ (e.d., Dolores López Galindo.)

Comentario del Juez:

Este caso ya no debe ser considerado como la norma y hay varios elementos del proceso que francamente me preocupan. Determino que lo posible se ha hecho.

Forma N° xd472

Figure 3. Birth certificate

These documents either complement the information in the students' e-mail exchanges and/or provide new approaches to extant evidence. For example, in round one, a police report written in a typically telegraphic style provides preliminary information about the murder. In round two, a newspaper article takes up the same information, adds to it, and presents it in

a journalistic style. This multiplicity of evidence, when combined with the e-mail exchanges and character information, both closes some previous information gaps and opens new venues for discovery.

The most critical aspect for learning occurs through the e-mail exchanges. The students' goal is to solve the mystery without their character being implicated. To this end, students become quite adept at using the target language to carefully communicate only that which they intend to reveal. Unlike most classroom exchanges in which imprecise language use may be acceptable for communication, here students learn to pay close attention to how they use the target language. For example, if student A is directed to ask student B where she was on Saturday night, student B can truthfully answer, "At the café," even if she was also at a number of other, less innocent locations. Beyond the directions given to students within each round's message (in the "information to reveal" portion), students are motivated to ask their own questions because they want to find out as much as possible, they may not be satisfied with the responses to their questions, or they have noticed inconsistencies in another character's messages. Students are writing for communication; they care about the answers to their questions because they want specific kinds of information in these answers. They are motivated by content and not by concern for an instructor's evaluation of their work.

Context of the Project to Be Discussed

The Murder mysteries were a collaborative effort between the two authors, although each was individually responsible for the different language versions (Oliver for Spanish and Nelson for French).[1] The collaboration was an important factor in the success of the final product(s). This collaboration extended well beyond the authors to the in-class interactions among students and between students and instructors. The creative energy generated by working together allowed us to continue to add layers of complexity and resources to the project. For example, the original Web sites had a town map with only a half dozen scanned pictures attached. Students, however, were extremely enthusiastic about the photos and consistently asked for more. We are convinced that the success of the final products is due to the collaborative efforts of all involved, the extensive usability testing, and our responses to students' needs and desires.

This project was also well supported within our institution. First, and perhaps foremost, this work was recognized by our colleagues as being an important contribution to the university in terms of professional development. Because Nelson is an untenured faculty member whose tenure and promotion will depend upon developing a quality research agenda, recognition of this work is essential. Our department, college, and university have recognized the murder project to be as important as other, more traditional scholarly activities. Furthermore, we received grant funding through a Learning Productivity Grant that allowed us to obtain course releases, buy a development computer (for cross-platform development) and hire a student assistant (used for another aspect of the grant).[2]

While the involvement of Heinle & Heinle came at the end stages of the project's development (see Design Narrative below), the commercial publication of this software has allowed the authors to channel a portion of the royalties back to our department to serve as seed money for other faculty development projects. Our hope is that these projects will benefit students' learning by making an even greater range of CALL software available. In this way, too, we recognize the critical contributions of students at all stages of the Murder mysteries' development.

Technical Constraints/Advantages

The technology used in this project was chosen because each piece provides something unavailable in other, more traditional media. The initial driving force in the choice of e-mail for use in the project was directly related to the pedagogical goal of the software, that is, we wanted students to write for communication (and not for an instructor's grade). To that end, e-mail provided numerous advantages: it was easy to learn and to use, it kept students in the target language, it had convenient access (especially with a listserv), and the students stayed focused on writing rather than using whispered translations, facial gestures, and other devious signaling devices.

Our choice of the World Wide Web was initially motivated by less lofty goals. Being restricted to only 500 photocopies per quarter, we were concerned about the delivery of the documentary "evidence" or clues (see Design Narrative below). The Web provided a cheap and effective means of distributing this information. Students quickly became enamored with the few pictures provided on the Web site and demanded more. The Web sites ultimately associated with the mysteries took on a life of their own as more and more cultural information was added and thus became a secondary tool for language instruction. The final CDs include hundreds of pictures and other authentic documents that are not directly related to the murder mysteries.

When we discovered how important cultural information was to our students (publishers cannot afford to print all the pictures that students are willing to consume), we decided to adopt an open architecture in the Instructor's CDs published by Heinle & Heinle. We coded all of the documents in simple HTML with only one simple JavaScript so that the mysteries could be implemented without difficulty at any institution. Institutions who use the murder mysteries can easily customize the Web sites by adding their own materials and by adapting the materials provided. (Foreign language instructors all have treasure chests full of realia that they lug home from the target cultures.) Furthermore, the Web sites can be expanded to provide a "home" for student-generated materials such as upper-division students' writing for first-year language learners.

We firmly believe that as teacher/developers we create software that puts learning first. As teachers, we understand what learners need in order to succeed; as developers, we understand technology's advantages and disadvantages. Our retention, promotion and tenure system recognizes this work as part of our professional development. Learning to use appropriate technologies "counts." However, as advanced users of technology, we have little to no access to technical support and training. Efforts at faculty development in technology at our institution unfortunately target low-end users (e.g., helping faculty to use e-mail, PowerPoint, and Word). Advanced users are expected to teach colleagues these basic skills and to troubleshoot on an individual basis but are given no opportunities to further their own skills. Any training we received for the project was paid for out of our own pockets (e.g., conferences and workshops) or generously provided by our publisher (Heinle & Heinle paid for the AuthorWare training used in the creation of another project).

Design and Production Narrative

This project began with a number of other e-mail projects—each of which posed a number of problems. The first was a classroom exchange between students at two different institutions. The problems that arose were predictable: the number of students was not equal at each institution, the academic calendars did not coincide, students did not write or respond by the deadlines, some students dropped out after the e-mail exchange began, and students were motivated by a grade rather than communication.[3] This is not to say that the project was completely unproductive since a number of students developed correspondences that continued after the quarter ended. Another project involved writing to penpals in the target culture (using the Web site established by the French government), but students did not necessarily receive a response, and some of the responses pointed to cultural differences (one student received her letter back with copious corrections of all of her mistakes). Finally, an in-class "secret penpal" experiment involved students' sending messages and trying to determine the identity of their secret correspondent (the instructor relayed all messages and deleted identifying information). Although this task, like the others, encouraged writing for communication, once students discovered that the correct question properly posed could elicit information that (with the help of the university telephone directory) quickly established identities and brought the game to an end.

These projects established that e-mail was a good venue for writing for communicative purposes but that any project would need to be self-contained (within a class and not interinstitutional). The alpha-run of the French Murder mystery (spring 1995) combined e-mail with the idea of "Whodunit?" dinner parties in which students role-played to solve a murder. It involved very little design, however. Using a cloze exercise from a textbook, Nelson developed the characters and wrote a story outline with the help of Claude Tournier (Northwestern University). Then, as the date for each new round of the murder approached, Nelson hastily prepared informational messages for the students and provided a minimal number of clues via photocopies. The students in the alpha-group worked on the mystery in an in-class laboratory once every two weeks. Although the original mystery had design faults, problems in logic and chronology, inconsistencies, and so forth, the response of the students was uniformly positive.

An institutional change brought a partner in crime to the scene. Oliver translated the mystery to Spanish and introduced the Internet as a useful component to the project. This collaboration was, as we stated above, fundamental to the project's development and success. Once the decision was made to codevelop the murder project, the design process became more systematic. As we began to change and add materials, we developed a consistent and thorough evaluation process that allowed us to collect student input and measure the project's effect on student learning.

In winter 1996, the Murder mysteries were used as ancillary activities in third-quarter Spanish and French classes. The Web was used to deliver the evidence. We decided to use a map to represent the town where the characters lived. We scanned photocopies of the documents and linked them to the buildings where they would logically be found (see Figure 4).

For example, the census is found in the *ayuntamiento* or *mairie* 'townhall.' For fun, we scanned a couple of photos of French and Mexican buildings (e.g., restaurants, stores, houses) and linked them to the map. The reaction to the photos was unexpected; students wanted a photo linked to each of the buildings on the map.

The next phase of design involved adding and changing materials based upon the previous evaluations (spring 1995, winter 1996). We added as many pictures as we could to the Web sites and made plans to take more photos that summer. We also spent a number of days thoroughly reviewing each character; students all wanted to have secrets to hide. (A particularly telling comment was, "You've got to let Rosario have some affairs or something.") The role of all characters was developed such that each one played a significant role in the mystery. Moreover, we verified each clue (whether included in the information messages provided by the instructor to each student or in the Web documents) to insure that they were consistent and that each appeared in some context or another at least twice.

Figure 4. Town map

Given fluctuating enrollments, we needed to develop a mechanism to allow the participation of as few as six or as many as 12 students. We needed flexibility in the assignment of roles based upon students' relative abilities in the target language. We also decided to create a "core" group of six characters who are essential to the murder mystery and an additional set of six characters who, although not essential to the murder mystery, added complexity to the story line. Testing proved that 12 characters had to be the maximum because of the volume of e-mail generated by the students. (A typical group of 10 students generates 200+ messages in round four.) The designation of core and ancillary characters allows implementation of the murder mystery with any number of students, as long as there are at least six. For example, a class of 24 students could be divided into 2 groups of 12, 3 groups of 8, or 4 groups of 6, with the same character being played by 2, 3, or 4 students, respectively.

We implemented these changes in spring 1996. Rather than an ancillary activity, the Murder mysteries became the primary organizing principle of the class because students in previous evaluations had asked to spend more in-class time doing the Murder mysteries. We felt justified in doing so because we had seen how much learning took place within the context of the Murder mysteries. We supplemented the Murder mysteries activities with a grammar instruction program. During that quarter, it was not uncommon for students to start to work before the class period began and remain long after class ended. This increase in time on task was significant and self-motivated. In Spanish, only half of the students worked in the language lab during class hours; the others worked off-site—proving that the Murder mysteries were a viable option for foreign language instruction at a distance. All students came to class for the biweekly oral "interrogations." Again, these students completed detailed evaluations about the course, the murder, and their characters. They were also interviewed and videotaped by our department chair (so that follow-up questions could be asked).

In the summer of 1996, we implemented a number of changes for the courses to be offered in the following fall term. We took hundreds of pictures that we then scanned and linked to the Web sites, captioned the pictures with culturally relevant information, added extensive links to other internet resources in the target language, redesigned the grammar portion of the course for self-paced instruction and distance learning, and developed a "Detective's Manual" to help orient students to the game and the Web site. At this time, we also rewrote the newspaper articles that accompanied each round of the Murder mysteries so that they were immediately accessible from the town map and were linked to all the evidentiary documents (with new clues highlighted). Students in spring 1996 stated that they loved all of the pictures but that they wanted more help in finding the evidence as it became available.

From this point on, all changes made to the Murder mysteries were for publication purposes. The e-mail messages were recopied into text documents (rather than Eudora messages), an Instructor's Manual was written, and, a number of demonstrations were created.[4] We also had to change the names of the Spanish characters. Originally, names from a competing publisher's product were used to tie the Murder mysteries to our textbook. The Spanish murder, originally called *Homicidio en Toluca*, was renamed *Un Misterio en Toluca* to respond to concerns from reviewers that the word *homicidio* created the wrong impression of Mexican culture. Finally, there were a number of editorial changes in terms of vocabulary choices, typographical errors, and so forth. The story line, by previous agreement with Heinle & Heinle, remained unchanged.

The production process did not change: Nelson and Oliver each continued to write the Web pages in simple HTML. A student assistant, supported by funds from the Learning Productivity Grant, scanned photos for us. The rest of the work was completed by us with editorial assistance provided by Wendy Nelson and Beatrix Mellauner at Heinle & Heinle. The final publication, slated for September 1997, occurred in October of that year.

Conclusions

It is not possible to design an effective project a priori; usability testing is a must. Formal and informal evaluative processes are integral to creating good learning environments. Pedagogy should determine the technology, and users should be given a voice in the process. Often instructors impose a pedagogy (or technology) without asking for students' opinions. If, instead, students' comments, ideas, and preferences are brought into the development process, the final product is not merely determined by need; students will want to use it. If students are self-motivated to learn (i.e., if they are not simply taking classes to fulfill the language requirement), they will.

The same principle should apply to the commercialization of pedagogical software. Publishers often, for a number of financial, legal, and philosophical reasons, publish expensive products that are overly proprietary—thus imposing a pedagogy on users. We were fortunate in that Heinle & Heinle understood our belief that this product should be affordable and delivered with an open architecture. Heinle & Heinle also respected our wish to preserve the original, somewhat politically incorrect, story line; they understood that the soap-opera nature of the Murder mysteries motivated students.[5]

The most often asked question when we give presentations about the Murder mysteries is "How much time did you spend developing this?" Frankly, we do not know. Unlike commercial software developers, we have numerous other responsibilities that often take precedence. Time spent on software development is often fragmented and highly irregular. What we can say is that we work six- or seven-day weeks, our cars are generally the first in the faculty parking lots and the last to leave, and we love what we are doing. What we learned is that software development takes a lot of time and energy. Working independently (i.e., without a development team) has advantages; we had complete control over what we produced. Working independently also has disadvantages. With the exception of help with scanning photos, we had to do all of the work—the fun stuff and the not-so-fun, agonizingly mundane, tedious, frustrating stuff. Clearly, software development is a labor of love.

Notes

1. In 2002, Christine Goulding (Associate Professor of German) and Cindy Jorth (Multimedia Language Center Director) at California State University, Chico, developed a German version of the Murder mysteries.

2. This grant fund annually supports viable, high-quality projects on a competitive basis. Although modest in size, it demonstrates California State University, San Bernardino's commitment to research in technology.

3. See Barson, Frommer, and Schwartz (1993) for a description of a successful interclass e-mail project.

4. These demonstrations, to be used by the Heinle & Heinle sales force, demanded a significant amount of time and effort.

5. A more G-rated version of the Murders intended for high school students was considered but rejected for this same reason, however.

Reference

Barson. J., Frommer, J., and Schwartz, M. (1993). Foreign language learning in using e-mail in a task-oriented perspective: Inter-university experiments in communication and collaboration. *Journal of Science Education and Technology 2*(4), 565–584.

Virtual Courseware for Geoscience Education: *Virtual Earthquake* and *Virtual Dating*

Gary A. Novak
California State University, Los Angeles

Abstract

Virtual courseware developed for introductory-level, on-line geology labs is an interactive teaching/learning model that has an enormous pedagogical potential for making Web sites places where students learn by doing. *Virtual Earthquake* and *Virtual Dating* are modest examples of the "virtual courseware" paradigm. *Virtual Earthquake* helps students explore the techniques of how an earthquake's epicenter is located and how its Richter magnitude is determined. *Virtual Dating* models the theory and techniques of the radiometric age determination of rocks and minerals.

Virtual courseware applications offer several advantages over traditional floppy disk or CD ROM-based courseware, the most significant being the ease of dissemination. The author's experience with bringing these two virtual applications on-line suggests that there is a need for interactive geology labs on-line and that the approach will be received with enthusiasm by the educational community. The widespread implementation and adoption of virtual courseware can bring meaningful educational content and interactivity for the geosciences that goes beyond multimedia on the World Wide Web.

Introduction

As recently emphasized by the National Science Foundation in its *Shaping the Future Report* for 1997 (George et al., 1996), science educators are becoming aware that the traditional lecture developed during the19th century may not be the most effective method of teaching today's students. Johnstone and Su (1994) in a study of chemistry lectures, concluded that, for two thirds of the students, lecture was an inefficient medium. Doyle Davies, science dean of Rensselaer, wrote, "As the tools of the information, communication, and technology revolution become integrated into the educational process, the traditional classroom reliance on the lecture format becomes increasingly anachronistic" (George et al., 1996).

In greater numbers, science instructors are looking for ways to involve students with so-called "active" learning methods and Astin (1993) suggests that these efforts are paying off. As instructors of the geological sciences, we are fortunate that many of the lab activities for our students are naturally "hands-on" and we believe that this interactivity enhances learning. But now we are faced with the new challenges of the "Information Age" and the associated claims for computer-aided instruction and Internet technology as the answers to the problems of effective teaching and learning.

One consequence of the perceived benefits of using the tools of technology for teaching is that many faculty are trying to implement active learning by incorporating the resources of the World Wide Web. Unfortunately, in the rush to embrace the Web, many educators may be overestimating its effectiveness for learning (Clark, 1994). Web documents mostly represent one-way transfer of information, from author to reader. There are dozens to perhaps hundreds of accessible Web sites that contain materials that may be appropriate to the teaching of geology. However, "visiting" Web pages by pointing, clicking, reading and viewing can only engage learners superficially (Schick, 1995). Most instructors know first-hand that well designed interactive lessons have proven to be successful learning techniques because they involve the student in the discovery process (Barry and Presti, 1996; Friedman et al., 1996). In a good hands-on activity the student observes, measures, records, synthesizes and hypothesizes. More importantly, inquiry-based activities promote understanding, discovery, and creative thinking. The Web in its current manifestation is wonderful as an information resource (Owston, 1997), but so is the traditional encyclopedia. To be an effective tool for learning, the Web must move beyond hypertext/multimedia documents that are archives of an instructor's course notes or supporting materials. "Multimedia" on the Web is fine, but where are the challenging problems? Where are the opportunities to observe, measure, record, synthesize, hypothesize and experiment? Where are the inquiry-based activities that promote understanding, discovery and creative thinking? Where is the "doing" that leads to learning?

The Web doesn't have to be a passive environment for learning and teaching. Over the last couple of years, Web browser and server software has evolved to the point where meaningful interactivity can be achieved (Fischman, 1996; Kaplan, 1997). Server software can be linked to other computer programs (called common gateway interface or CGI scripts) that create new documents "on the fly" in response to remote requests from the user. Distributed Java "applets" and Javascripts can empower the student with dynamic content within a Web page. These Web-based, interactive multimedia capabilities present an enormous pedagogical potential that has yet to be exploited. This paper explores a unique use of this technology as an instructional resource for geoscience education: "virtual courseware" for on-line geology labs that actively engages learners through discovery processes.

The author has developed two examples of Web-based, interactive applications as models for additional on-line geology labs: *Virtual Earthquake (VEQ)* and *Virtual Dating.* (Find *VEQ* and *Virtual Dating* at http://www.sciencecourseware.com)

Each has been designed as an activity for introductory college classes at the general education level. *Virtual Earthquake* is also appropriate for high school earth science classes. *VEQ* helps students explore the techniques of how an earthquake epicenter is located and how its Richter magnitude is determined. *Virtual Dating,* in a beta release, models the theory and techniques of the radiometric age determination of rocks and minerals. The rest of this article covers the implementation of *VEQ* and *Virtual Dating* and the advantages and disadvantages of virtual applications over the more traditional "diskette" or CD ROM-based courseware.

Virtual Earthquake

Virtual Earthquake introduces earth science students to seismology, the instrumental study of earthquake waves. A fundamental component of seismology involves determining the location of the epicenter of an earthquake, the point on the earth's surface directly above its origin. A second aspect involves evaluating the Richter magnitude, an estimate of the amount of energy released during an earthquake. *Virtual Earthquake* is modeled after a NEXTSTEP application, *Earthquake.app,* written by the author in 1992. General education students in physical geology classes at California State University of Los Angeles (CSULA) are frequently assigned a traditional lab exercise of locating an epicenter of an earthquake and determining its magnitude. Students measure S–P intervals on photocopied seismograms, read graphs, draw circles on maps and then answer a few questions. This activity, although informative, is messy and not always well received by students. A different approach was needed, one that was both instructive and fun.

The NEXTSTEP operating system, new on the scene at that time, had a powerful set of objective-oriented programming tools that was used to write the graphical, user-friendly courseware, *Earthquake.app,* that proved successful in engaging students. An instructor could customize the activity for any earthquake with a location map (in the PostScript format). They could also fix the locations of the earthquake's epicenter and the seismic recording stations and specify the quake's magnitude. The program generates realistic looking seismograms which the student uses to determine epicenter and magnitude. Although, this activity was popular with CSULA students and a few other universities did adopt it, the Next computer and its OS failed to gain market share. Further dissemination of *Earthquake.app* as a tool for learning was not realistic. Following the lead of Professor Robert Desharnais of CSLA and his popular implementation of *VirtualFlyIab* (http://www.sciencecourseware.com), the concepts behind *Earthquake.app* were used to develop the *Virtual Earthquake* interactive Web-based site.

After some introductory material on the *Virtual Earthquake* home page, students select a map of one of four different geographical areas and are presented with a set of three simulated seismograms from three different seismic stations. On each seismogram the student must measure the difference in arrival times between the "primary" and the "secondary" wave. This difference, the S–P time interval, is empirically related to the distance these waves have traveled from the earthquake's epicenter. Using on-screen travel-time curves, modeled after the data of Jeffreys and Bullen (1967), the student converts the S–P intervals into distance, enters these distances into on-screen HTML form fields and "submits" this data to the Web server. A CGI script on the server uses the epicentral distances to generate circles of appropriate radius around each station. The resultant PostScript map is converted to a GIF image, combined with some explanatory text into a new HTML document "on the fly" and returned to the user as the next Web page. Assuming the student was careful in S–P interval measurement and in reading the time-travel curve, the epicenter location will be at the "triangulation" point of the three circles, Fig. 1 (A), (B) and (C) illustrates some of the steps in the process.

In a manner analogous to the location of the epicenter, the student can determine the Richter magnitude of the earthquake by measuring the amplitude of the waves on the seismograms. As Richter (1935) proposed, the magnitude for California-type earthquakes (nearby, shallow, and of moderate magnitude) can be related to seismic phase amplitude and the corresponding epicentral distance. *VEQ* has the student measure the amplitude of the S-wave on each seismogram and again use HTML forms to submit the data to the server. A CGI script generates the lines of magnitude on a model of the Richter nomogram for each station. The student who successfully completes the activity by accurately locating the epicenter (within a few kilometers) and by correctly estimating the Richter magnitude (within a few decimal points), receives a personalized "Certificate of Completion as a Virtual Seismologist." Fig. 2 shows the resultant Richter nomogram and the student's certificate of completion. The certificate page also contains the data the student collected.

The four sets of seismograms that accompany *Virtual Earthquake* are modeled after four recent earthquakes: Loma Prieta of 1989, Northridge of 1994, Kobe of 1995 and a small earthquake off the coast of Baja in 1973. The certificate page has links to additional information about each of these earthquakes as well as links to other seismology-related sites. Furthermore, CGI scripts are used throughout the activity to test the reasonableness of a student's answers. If the numbers submitted are not realistic (for example, a negative S–P interval or numbers that are out of reasonable limits) the program sends the student back to re-measure and re-submit. Finally, once a student satisfactorily finishes the activity, a "Certificate of Completion" is awarded. Many instructors will accept the printed copy of this certificate as evidence that the student has as least participated.

Virtual Earthquake Usage

Virtual Earthquake, placed on-line in July of 1996, has become popular with educators. Fig. 3 shows usage over the 8 quarters since *VEQ* first was made available. As of May 1998, users have induced over 100,000 virtual temblors.

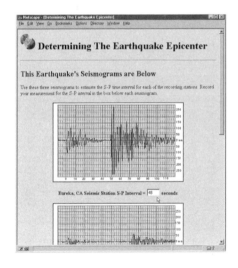

(A)

Figure 1. In (A) and (B) student makes measurements: S–P intervals from three seismograms are measured in (A) and epicentral distances equivalent to an S–P interval are read from a travel-time curve of (B). In both instances, HTML forms are used to submit input back to CGI scripts executing on Web server. Once the student clicks "Find Epicenter" button of (B), these server-side scripts generate circles of appropriate radius on PostScript map, convert this file to one with GIF format, assemble new html document and return this final map construction with its overlay of epicenter circles (C), to the student. If the epicenter has not been accurately triangulated, student is not given opportunity to continue, but is returned to page of seismograms to re-measure and re-submit.

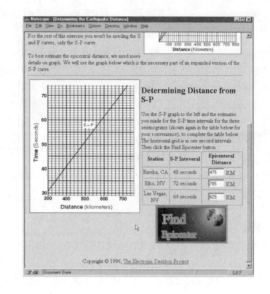

(B)

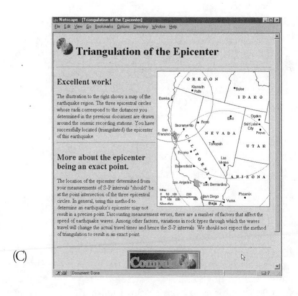

(C)

Figure 1, continued

GARY A. NOVAK

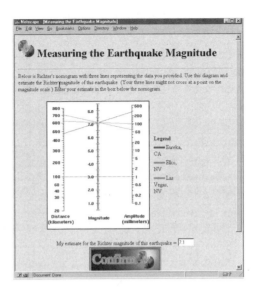

(A)

Figure 2. Richter's nomogram (A) and student's certificate of completion (B)

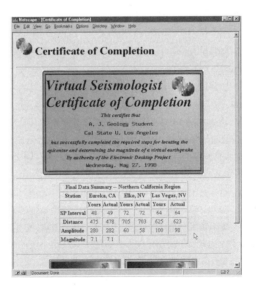

(B)

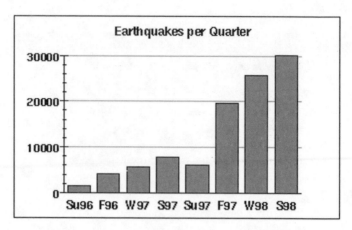

Figure 3. Simple histogram of the number of certificates issued for users of *VEQ*.

Usage is growing. During the Spring quarter of 1998 over 10,000 students per month requested a certificate of completion. Since *VEQ* first went public, students from about 100 of the nation's universities and colleges and a larger number of high and middle schools have accessed *VEQ* at least 10 times within a given month.

User Satisfaction and Assessment

A formal assessment of the effectiveness of *VEQ* in helping students learn about locating epicenter and determining Richter magnitude of an earthquake has been completed by the Center of Usability in Design and Assessment (CUDA) of California State University, Long Beach. The evaluation is based on about 40 responses from instructors who use *VEQ* as part of a course. It concludes that between 75 and 90% of the instructors say that using *VEQ* improves teaching, improves learning, speeds up learning and makes learning more fun. All (100%) of the instructors indicated that they would use more on-line interactive Web-based labs like *VEQ* if they were available. CUDA also reports about two areas of dissatisfaction: the first is that some of the seismogram images are of a poor quality and that this interferes with student learning. The second major complaint is some of the Web pages require too much scrolling.

Another type of evaluation of *VEQ*, from numerous unsolicited e-mail messages from instructors and users, suggests that the impact of *VEQ* is positive. The quote (edited for brevity) that follows is from an anonymous high school "home school" student, "... I learned more from this interactive site than I could have ever from a regular text document. It also seemed like I learned on a different level, on which I remember the info for longer periods of time afterwards. . . . this site has been the most informative I have seen yet (fun too!)" (Fall, 1997).

Most user feedback has been complimentary. Some of it has been constructive so that "bugs" in the activity could be corrected. The few negative comments received have been from instructors with complaints that the *VEQ* site is down or slow to respond.

Virtual Dating

A second virtual courseware application, currently under development and in a beta release, is *Virtual Dating*. Whereas *VEQ* relies on HTML forms for I/O to the CGI scripts on the Web server for student interaction, *Virtual Dating* utilizes a number of Java applet and Javascripts to facilitate this interaction. For example, the first page of *Virtual Dating* (Fig. 4) begins with an applet that carries out a "least squares" data reduction of a rock's isochron in order to determine its age. A student can manipulate sliders to change both slope and intercept of a "best fit" regression line to minimize the "errors" term. In this case the Rb-87 decay constant is built into the applet and the age of the rock is determined from the isochron's slope. Figs. 4-9 illustrate some of the interactive Java applets of *Virtual Dating*. Fig. 6 shows the use of Javascript to evaluate a set of student responses. The introduction of some concepts of *Virtual Dating* is accompanied by a set of questions which require either a multiple-choice response or input of quantitative answers. These question pages have built-in Javascripts which will evaluate student responses. If answers are incorrect, the student is given the option to go back and make the needed corrections.

The currently released version of *Virtual Dating* focuses on the Rb/Sr method of age determination. Students may select one of three different rocks to age-date: the Sudbury, Ontario gabbro (1843 + / - 133M.Y.), a Scottish granite (584 M.Y.), or gneiss (3660 + 1-99 M.Y.) from Greenland. Under development is an option which will emphasize the radiocarbon technique.

Advantages and Disadvantages of Virtual Courseware

Virtual courseware offers several advantages over traditional courseware. First, there is no need to reproduce software on CD-ROMs or floppy disks and mail the media to potential users. Second, in the situation of server-side scripts, one can take advantage of the processing power and storage capabilities on the server to compute results and create images. Third, there are relatively few hardware compatibility issues in the development of courseware. Finally, bug fixes and upgrades are instantaneous. Once the new CGI scripts, Java applets, or Web pages are installed on the server, everyone can take advantage of them.

There are some drawbacks to the development and use of virtual courseware. First, a number of versions of Web browsers are now in use with differing capabilities. Many users and institutions are reluctant to upgrade to the latest browser releases because of the investment of time and resources required. Far more serious at this time, the two most popular Web browsers, Netscape and Internet Explorer, implement different versions of Java, scripting languages and Dynamic HTML, a source of much frustration to developers and users. A second drawback is that learners must have Internet access to use virtual courseware. This is still a limitation in some educational institutions, especially at K-12 levels. A third disadvantage is that using virtual courseware may be slower than running software on the client machine, especially where competition for limited bandwidth is a problem. Lastly, server problems can affect everyone. If the power is lost or the server crashes, no one can use the software until the problem is resolved.

The crashing of the Web server has been a problem for users of *Virtual Earthquake*. Occasionally, during periods of high demand, multiple simultaneous requests to execute a CGI script for *VEQ* can crash the Web server.

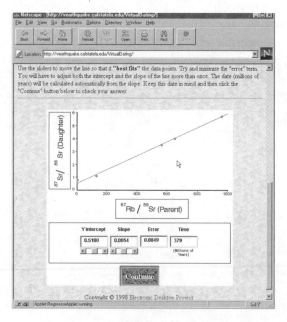

Figure 4. Intercept and slope of an isochron's "best fit" line can be adjusted in this least squares applet until "error" term is at a minimum. Corresponding age, displayed in "time" field, is calculated for student.

GARY A. NOVAK

To overcome this problem, *VEQ* is now installed on four mirror servers with identical functionality: three at CSULA on different subnets and one at Sonoma State University in northern California. During periods of peak demand, a simple Javascript can be implemented to pass users to a machine under a lighter load.

Support and Sustainability

Another concern in developing virtual courseware is that of maintaining and sustaining a Web site for activities such as *Virtual Earthquake* and *Virtual Dating*. What initially began as a simple in-house activity for CSULA students has grown into a project that requires a significant commitment in hardware and faculty time. There is funding to be secured for additional hardware and network needs, e-mail from instructors to be answered, and site upgrades to be planned and implemented. To develop, maintain and sustain over the long run more geology on-line lab activities, a long-term partnership with a textbook publisher will likely be necessary.

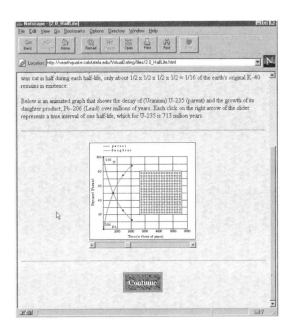

Figure 5. In this animation applet, student clicks through sequence of illustrations of decay of parent isotopes and corresponding growth of daughters during radioactive decay. Each click corresponds to passing of one half-life of time.

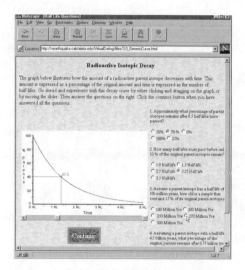

Figure 6. Students interact with this applet which shows relationship between time and amount of remaining parent material. A Javascript evaluates student responses to accompanying multiple-choice questions.

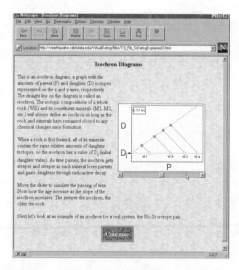

Figure 7. Relationship of slope of rock's isochron to its age is demonstrated with this animation applet. Each click on right arrow of slider represents passage of one half-life of time.

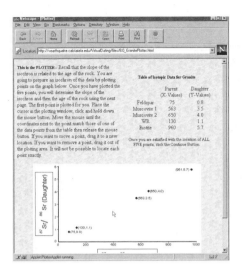

Figure 8. One final step in determining age of a rock is to construct isochron diagram. Slope of the isochron is related to rock's age. In this applet students plot (using click of mouse button) coordinates of points that are ratios of parent to daughter isotopes.

Conclusions

Virtual Earthquake and *Virtual Dating* are modest examples of the "virtual courseware" paradigm model. This model has an enormous pedagogical potential for making Web sites places where students learn by doing. Virtual applications offer several advantages over traditional courseware, the most significant being the ease of dissemination. The author's experience with bringing these two virtual applications on-line suggests that there is a need for interactive Web sessions and that the approach will be received with enthusiasm by the educational community. The widespread implementation and adoption of virtual courseware can bring meaningful educational content and interactivity for the geosciences that goes beyond multimedia on the World Wide Web.

Acknowledgements

This work was supported in part by grants DUE-9455428 and DUE-9752603 from the National Science Foundation, the Academic Opportunities Fund of the California State University system and the Innovative Instruction Program at the California State University, Los Angeles.

Figure 9. After plotting isotopic data and determining rock's age using least-squares regression applet, student will be awarded "certificate" verifying completion of exercise. This can be printed and submitted to instructor as "proof" of completion.

References

Astin, A. W. (1993). *What matters in college? Four critical years revisited.* San Francisco: Jossey-Bass.

Barry, J. M., and Presti, D. E. (1996). The World Wide Web as an instructional tool. *Science, 274,* 371–372.

Clark, R. E. (1994). Media will never influence learning. *Educational Technology Research and Development, 42,* 21–29.

Fischman, J. (1996). Working the Web with a virtual lab and some Java. *Science, 273,* 591–593.

Friedman, E. A., Baron, J. D., and Addison, C. J. (1996). Universal access to science study via the Internet. *Technological Horizons in Education, 23,* 83–86.

George, M. D., Bragg, S., de los Santos, A. G., Denton, D. D., Gerber, P., Lindquist, M.M., et al. (1996). *Shaping the future: New expectations for undergraduate education in science, mathematics, engineering and technology.* Washington DC: National Science Foundation.

Jeffreys, H., and Bullen, K. E. (1967). *Seismology tables*. Burlington House, London: British Association for Advancement of Science.

Johnstone, A. H., and Su, W. Y. (1994). Lectures: A learning experience? *Education in Chemistry, 31*, 75–79.

Kaplan, H. (1997). Interactive multimedia: A new paradigm for university teaching and learning. *Educom Review, 32*, 48–51.

Owston, R. D., (1997). The World Wide Web: A technology to enhance teaching and learning? *Educational Researcher, 26*, 27–33.

Richter, C. F. (1935). An instrumental earthquake magnitude scale. *Bulletin of the Seismological Society of America, 25*, 1–32.

Schick, J. B. M. (1995). On being interactive: Rethinking the learning equation. *History Microcomputer Review, 11*, 9–25.

Teaching Statistics With Web Technology: The WISE Project

Christopher L. Aberson
Humboldt State University
Dale Berger, Michael R. Healy, and Victoria L. Romero
Claremont Graduate University

The Web Interface for Statistics Education (WISE) aims to enhance student learning and understanding of core statistical concepts. The project includes a comprehensive World Wide Web site with links to electronic journals, archived discussion lists, datasets, and interactive tutorials. The statistical concepts addressed by the WISE tutorials are relevant to undergraduate and graduate instruction in any field—such as psychology, economics, or biology—that uses statistical methodology.

Teaching Statistics

Traditionally, the teaching of statistics emphasizes working through problems in a "cookbook" fashion. This approach tends to emphasize computation while ignoring the relevance of statistics as a tool for enhancing the understanding of data. That is, students are encouraged to learn the "how" but not the "why" or "what for." It is our belief that traditional approaches often fail to produce effective learning of critical statistical concepts and often are not conducive to creating a continuing interest in statistics. WISE was created to help faculty and students overcome these difficulties of learning core concepts in statistics.

Using Web Technology

The WISE project provides Internet-based tutorials to supplement the teaching of a variety of statistical concepts. Tutorials include interactive JAVA applets, guided demonstrations of topics, multiple-choice questions with feedback, and "thought" questions to test student understanding and shape classroom discussion. WISE tutorials are unique in that they provide detailed assignments that allow faculty to integrate technology into instruction easily. Interested faculty can simply plug in one of our tutorials as a laboratory exercise or a homework assignment.

Our tutorials focus on core statistical concepts that are essential to a detailed and complete understanding of statistical procedures and

Reprinted from *Syllabus, 14*(1), 2001: 43–45, by permission of the authors and the publisher.

reasoning. For example, null hypothesis testing procedures (such as t-test, Analysis of Variance, and Chi-square tests of independence) are a primary focus of most introductory statistics courses. These procedures are often learned by rote; students learn a step-by-step approach to drawing correct conclusions. The student is taught to reject the null hypothesis if a computed value is larger than a comparison value and not to reject the null hypothesis if the value is smaller than the comparison value. Unfortunately, teaching hypothesis testing by rote does little to establish an understanding of the procedure; rather, it allows for correct answers without an appreciation of the logic behind decisions. Such misunderstandings are the basis for much of the misapplication of null hypothesis significance testing, which has recently attracted strong criticism.

Several of the WISE tutorials address hypothesis testing in greater depth than is practical with traditional methods. One tutorial teaches concepts related to the Central Limit Theorem and sampling distributions, concepts essential to understanding why we can draw statistical conclusions based on hypothesis testing procedures. Another tutorial examines the logic of hypothesis testing and discusses the meaning of conclusions based on these procedures. A third tutorial teaches concepts related to the power of a statistical test (the ability to reject false hypotheses). There is a discussion of some of the limitations of hypothesis testing procedures while at the same time understanding the reasoning behind statistical conclusions is enhanced.

Impact on Teaching

When we first used WISE tutorials in the classroom, we needed to spend class and laboratory time instructing students in how to use a Web browser and the applets contained in the tutorials. Most students in our classes now have experience with Web browsers and applets.

In addition to the learning that occurs in the lab, the Web-based tutorials contain "follow-up" questions that often spark class discussion. Although leading discussion in a statistics class is often more difficult than structured lecturing, we find that the high level of student engagement generates especially productive exchanges, often focused around the need to consider multiple issues. Contrary to the perceptions of most students, there is not always a single correct answer for statistics problems. Discussions comparing statistical results to practical real-world concerns can be useful. Once this connection is explored and better understood, presentation of topics necessarily becomes more complex, multi-faceted, and challenging to both students and professor.

Barriers to Computer-Based Learning

The self-paced, independent nature of online tutorials offers great flexibility to students. However, this flexibility has the potential to magnify study skill problems. In the traditional classroom environment, instructors can pace their lectures to fit students' progress. When students are left on their own with an online tutorial, they may not have the skills needed to pace themselves appropriately. Research from the field of cognitive psychology tells us that self-regulation of learning is an especially important consideration with online tutorials, where students work independently and at their own pace. Without guidance, students may move too quickly through assignments, and as a result, may fail to learn.

We gave careful attention to principles of learning as we designed the WISE tutorials, and the tutorials have benefited. Each tutorial forces students to stop and answer questions before proceeding to more detailed material. Reflective exercises are used to ask students to explain the concepts that they are learning and to discuss how concepts apply to the problems at hand. Students answer multiple-choice questions throughout the course of the tutorial. Each question is structured so that students cannot proceed until they answer correctly. Each wrong answer corresponds to a common misconception or misunderstanding. The choice of a wrong answer leads to feedback that addresses the student's misconception. The choice of correct answers reinforces student learning and allows students to gauge how much they are learning. In this manner, students must think about the topics and demonstrate understanding before moving on to new material.

Impact on Student Learning

We have made a concerted effort to evaluate the impact of the WISE tutorials on student learning. In a test of the effectiveness of our Central Limit Theorem tutorial, we conducted a study with students enrolled in several introductory statistics classes who used the tutorial or attended a lecture on the topic. The group that used the tutorial performed as well as those who attended the lecture.

Evaluations of our tutorials indicated that most students rated the presentation style as useful, found the instruction easy to understand, and rated statistical explanations as clear. Additionally, most students indicated an interest in using tutorials to learn other topics.

To use the WISE tutorials, visit http://wise.cgu.edu on the Web. What you'll find is only a beginning. We have yet to take full advantage of the Internet's capability for delivery of highly interactive and effective personal instruction.

2

USING ELECTRONIC TOOLS TO IMPROVE STUDENT LEARNING

Introduction

Beth Chance
California Polytechnic State University, San Luis Obispo

A peek inside a classroom throughout the CSU would show a scene that has been familiar for decades: faculty and students discussing, reading, listening, scrawling on the blackboard, conducting experiments, lecturing, writing, looking at the clock. In the 21st century, however, at least one thing is different: The rooms regularly feature an array of technological devices, including TVs, VCRs, computer workstations, laptops, PDAs, and cell phones.

New technologies have had a tremendous impact on the educational environment—on instructors, students, classrooms, curricula, schedules, and more. The five articles in this chapter highlight a variety of technological tools that instructors use to enhance student learning in a broad range of disciplines, including statistics, science teacher preparation, construction management, nursing, and business. Topics discussed range from changes made in individual courses to implementations made at the college level to a survey of the impact of technology across a discipline. In each setting, the ultimate goals were to provide students with more hands-on, more visual, more dynamic, more inquiry-based, and more relevant student-driven learning experiences.

Technology enables students to be immersed more directly in the practice of their disciplines, to have improved access to alternative modes of learning, to focus more deliberately on the conceptual underpinnings and connections of what they are learning, and to acquire skills that will be immediately useful after graduation. These possibilities mandate new thinking about the types of pedagogy that are feasible, and the articles in this chapter provide examples of the changes that have been made and the inherent difficulties that arise. These problems include issues of portability, financial and personnel constraints, sustainability, maintenance of cutting-edge technology, and security. These authors have been striving to make the transition for students as seamless as possible in order for the technology to be a learning tool that does not overshadow the subject matter.

In "Technology in College Statistics Courses," Joan Garfield, Beth Chance, and J. Laurie Snell survey the many ways technology has enhanced the teaching of statistics, probability, and quantitative literacy. The authors provide an overview of several types of resources, such as software packages, graphing calculators, on-line resources, and multimedia available on CD-ROM. They discuss how the integration of technology has accompanied changes in the curriculum and now spurs further changes. They also discuss the need for additional research studies that assess learning outcomes when these technologies are incorporated into the curriculum; such studies will help instructors evaluate the effectiveness of these tools and how best to take advantage of them to promote student learning in the classroom.

The second article, "Utilizing Digital Video to Expand Prospective Science Teachers' View of Science" by Randy Yerrick, describes how student teachers use digital videos to record actual elementary classroom lessons. Prospective science teachers thus are able to observe many more lessons and child-teacher interactions than they could previously. They can watch and hear, analyze, and discuss children's misconceptions about scientific phenomena. These future teachers not only record lessons but also produce video autobiographies in which they discuss their own preconceptions about science. This has enabled the student teachers to better reflect on their own strengths and weaknesses in their knowledge and experiences.

Paul A. Weber and William C. Epstein, in "An Innovative Approach to Teaching Software Utilizing Computer Screen Recording Technology," point to the difficulty of teaching students how to use commercial software packages in a construction graphics course. Students cannot simultaneously watch the instructor illustrate how to use a program, take notes, and try the program themselves; they learn to use software at different paces; and instruction on software use can easily overwhelm course content. To solve this problem, Weber and Epstein have designed animated computer tutorials for students learning to use AutoDesk's AutoCAD software. These tutorials are more student-driven because they allow students to stop and rewind as needed and to focus on key aspects of the software instead of becoming "bogged down with the specific intricacies" of the program. This process has freed students to focus on learning and has improved the instructors' productivity.

Productivity and communication—as well as patient care—have also been improved through the Nightingale Tracker project at San José State. In "Using Information Technology in Community-Based Psychiatric Nursing Education: The SJSU/NT Project," Phyllis M. Connolly and Victoria L. Efrink describe an IT project that provided nursing students with handheld computers allowing them to communicate with their instructors while they themselves are in the community with mental-health patients. The computers allow the students to "access, document, and communicate care while at the point of service." The article discusses the implementation of the project, its effect on the education of the nursing students and the quality of care provided to the patients, and the implications for the future of managed health care.

The final article by Gail Corbitt and James Mensching, "Integrating SAP R/3 Into a College of Business Curriculum: Lessons Learned," focuses on CSU Chico's implementation of an Enterprise Resource Planning (ERP) system into its College of Business curriculum. The faculty worked together to decide how to integrate an ERP into the curriculum in order to provide students with experiences directly tied to the marketplace, with the overarching goal of providing students with a deeper understanding of the entire business process and how it works. Corbitt and Mensching describe not only how the large-scale software was integrated, but also how the department struggled with its own success. The integration was so successful that it proved difficult to keep headhunters, recruiters, and potential industry partners at bay and to keep faculty with SAP experience from being wooed away from academe.

While all of these articles highlight the many benefits of using technological tools in teaching, they also address many of the implementation difficulties. In addition to the financial costs involved and the constant struggle to maintain sufficient support and currency, there is also a cost to the instructor. The increased demand on an instructor's time and energy cannot be overlooked. Students often struggle as well to find the additional time to become comfortable using these tools, even as they call for more such experiences.

The possession of information skills, data management capabilities, and communication skills will be essential for the future success of our graduates. These articles highlight the direct impact these technologies have on course content and pedagogy and the need to think very carefully about the best ways to incorporate videos, multimedia systems, programming languages, and standard packages into individual courses and across the curriculum. These efforts need to be accompanied by on-going evaluation and collaborative reflection on their effectiveness—and by the flexibility to make midstream adjustments.

Technology in College Statistics Courses

Joan Garfield
University of Minnesota
Beth Chance
California Polytechnic State University, San Luis Obispo
J. Laurie Snell
Dartmouth College

Overview

Although software has long been available for doing statistical analysis, the role of technology in teaching and learning statistics is still evolving. Computers and calculators reduce the computational burden and allow more extensive exploration of statistical concepts. The availability of powerful computing tools has also led to newer methods of analyzing data and graphically exploring data. During the past 20 years, since personal computers became available in homes and schools, the developments in educational technology have progressed at an accelerated pace (Ben-Zvi, 2000).

The types of technology that are now being used in statistics instruction fall into one or more of the following categories:

- statistical packages and spreadsheets for analyzing data and constructing visual representations of data;

- multimedia materials to teach, tutor, and/or test students' statistical knowledge and skills;

- Web or computer-based tools, including simulations, to demonstrate and visualize statistical concepts;

- graphing calculators for computation, graphing or simulation;

- programming languages that students can use to set up more complicated simulations or numerical analyses.

As the capabilities of technology have increased and more software tools have become available, it has become important to consider the most appropriate uses of technology in facilitating students' learning of statistics in different situations. Ben-Zvi describes how technological tools are now being designed to support statistics learning in the following ways (2000, p. 128):

Reprinted from Joan Garfield, Beth Chance, and J. Laurie Snell, "Technology in College Statistics Courses," in *The Teaching and Learning of Mathematics at University Level: An ICMI Study*, Eds. Derek Holton, et al., 2001: 357–370. © 2002. Reprinted with kind permission of Kluwer Acacdemic Publishers.

1. Students' active construction of knowledge, by "doing" and "seeing" statistics.
2. Opportunities for students to reflect on observed phenomena.
3. The development of students' metacognitive capabilities, that is, knowledge about their own thought processes, self-regulation, and control.

Moore (1997) sees a reform of statistics instruction and curriculum based on strong synergies among content, pedagogy, and technology. He cautions statisticians to remember that we are "teaching our subject and not the tool" (p.135), and to choose appropriate technology for student learning, rather than use the software that statisticians use (which may not be pedagogical in nature).

This paper examines the ways technology is being used in a variety of college-level statistics courses: introductory statistics, probability, mathematical statistics, and intermediate statistics. Although there is some overlap in the types of technological resources being used in these different courses, an attempt is made to isolate the particular types of technology or software that are most appropriate or most used in each type of course. Because of the large number of Web sites referenced in this paper, a Web version of the paper with links to all the sites mentioned can be found at www.dartmouth.edu/~chance/technology.html.

The Introductory Non-Calculus Statistics Course

Like the calculus reform movement in college mathematics programs, a statistics reform movement has called for changes in the introductory statistics course. Changes are recommended in course content (e.g., more emphasis on real data, less emphasis on formal probability and mathematical formulae), pedagogy (use of active learning, cooperative groups, and real data) and student assessment (use of alternative approaches including student projects, reports, and writing assignments). In addition, instructors are urged to incorporate more technology in their courses, to represent, analyze, and explore data, as well as to illustrate abstract concepts (Cobb, 1992).

The 1990 Mathematics Undergraduate Program Survey (CBMS) showed that the enrollment of students in statistics courses taught in departments of mathematics in four-year colleges and universities and in two-year college mathematics programs, more than doubled from 1970 to 1990 (from 76,000 to 179,000 students). Recently, many institutions have added the requirement of a data-oriented, or quantitative-literacy course in their core curriculum, increasing the statistics enrollment, so that now more sections of statistics courses are offered than calculus courses in colleges in the USA.

The 1995 CBMS study reported 3530 sections of elementary statistics taught in mathematics departments, 820 in statistics departments, and 2566 sections taught in two-year colleges. Numerous elementary statistics courses are also taught in other disciplines, such as psychology, business, education, sociology, and economics.

In a recent survey of the introductory statistics course, Garfield (2000) found that most students in these courses are required to use some type of technology, and most of the faculty surveyed anticipated increasing or changing the use of technology in their courses. The type of technology is often different depending on the type of institution. Students in two-year college courses are more likely to use graphing calculators (for computations using small data sets). Students in four-year colleges or universities are more likely to use a statistical software or spreadsheet program.

Statistical Software Packages

A variety of different software packages are used in introductory statistics courses, several of which are reviewed by Lock (1993). The most widely used statistical software program in introductory statistics courses is Minitab (Joiner and Ryan, 2000), which is perceived as easy to learn and use, and is available on both Mac and PC platforms. Data are entered in a data window and pull-down menus allow students to easily graph or analyze data. In addition, "macros" are small programs that instructors or students can create to generate data or run simulations. Minitab is incorporated into over 250 textbooks directly or as a special supplement and has been used in over 2000 colleges and universities around the world (Shaughnessy, Garfield, and Greer, 1997).

Data Desk (Velleman, 1998) offers a strong, visual approach to data exploration and analysis, integrating dynamic graphics with tools to model and display data. The intent of this program is to allow students to explore data with an open mind, no preconceptions, and no formal hypotheses, in the spirit of detective work. Users are asked to consider the question: "Can I learn something useful?" Data Desk provides many unique tools that allow students to look for patterns, ask more detailed questions about the data, and "talk" with the program about a particular set of data. Despite the many unique features of this software, it has not been widely used in introductory courses. Data Desk is sometimes difficult for students who are accustomed to a spreadsheet system for data entry, and some instructors do not like the non-standard method of manipulating data.

A newer software package, developed to help students explore and learn statistics, is Fathom. Originally called "Dataspace," Fathom is described as a dynamic computer learning environment for data analysis and statistics based on dragging, visualization, simulation, and networked collaboration (Finzer

JOAN GARFIELD · BETH CHANCE · J. LAURIE SNELL

and Erickson, 1998). Although originally aimed at middle school and high school level students, Fathom is beginning to be used in college level statistics classes as well.

Although not actually a statistics program, the Excel software, produced by Microsoft, is widely available in most computing labs and on many personal computers. This spreadsheet software has add-ons that allow the software to perform some statistical analyses. However, concerns have been expressed about using this software instead of more authentic statistics software (e.g., McCullogh & Wilson, 1999).

World Wide Web Resources

In addition to graphing calculators and statistical or spreadsheet software, technology resources available on the World Wide Web are increasing daily. Several Web sites have been established that make links to other sites to assist instructors of introductory statistics courses as well as their students. For example, Robin Lock's Web site organizes and links Web resources by categories and awards medals to the ones he finds most useful or of the highest quality. His categories include:

- On-line Course Materials (e.g., course syllabi and materials for particular instructors);

- On-line Textbooks (some are free and some are available for a fee);

- Java applets (a platform-independent Web programming language which is used to develop interactive demonstrations that can be accessed via any Java-capable browser). Examples include randomly generated scatterplots from which students are asked to guess correlations, dynamic regression-lines that change when points are added or removed, graphical visualizations illustrating the power of a statistical test when different parameters are varied, and histograms where students manipulate the bin width to see the effect on the overall pattern;

- Data sets or links to repositories of data (such as the Data and Story Library that contains data sets and accompanying stories along with analyses, and government agencies such as the Census bureau, that collect and store data);

- Miscellaneous sites (such as the electronic *Journal of Statistics Education*, sites that consist of links to sample test and quiz questions, or collections of links and resources for teaching an introductory level course).

The development of the World Wide Web has produced unprecedented means for instructors to easily share their ideas on ways to improve the teaching of statistics (Lock, in press). The links on Robin Lock's Web site represent just a sample of resources that are currently available. He encourages faculty not to be daunted by the volume of on-line materials but to search and try out resources that may greatly enhance students' learning.

An example of a statistics course that is based exclusively on the World Wide Web is The Visualizing Statistics project which has developed an on-line introductory statistics course, *CyberStats* (Kugashev, 2000). This course, consisting of over 50 modular units, includes several components: text material, case studies, Java applets, self-assessment questions for students, exercises, and a glossary. This commercial product is designed to be flexible and can be adapted to different educational settings and courses. In some cases, using these materials has enabled instructors of even large statistics courses to spend more time in class on group work or computer activities (e.g., Harkness, 2000).

Another example of an integrated set of Web materials is the Rice Virtual Lab in Statistics, which is freely available to students. This Web site contains an online statistics textbook (HyperStat Online), links to Java applets that demonstrate statistical concepts, case studies that provide examples or data, and some basic statistical analysis tools. This is a dynamic set of resources, and instructors are invited to contribute links to appropriate pages of the Web site.

Multimedia Materials

Velleman and Moore (1996) define multimedia as a computer-based system that combines several components such as text, sound, video, animation, and graphics. Since their article appeared, which described the "promises and pitfalls" of using multimedia in statistics courses, several types of multimedia materials have been developed and are being used in various ways in statistics courses.

ActivStats (Velleman, 2000), is a multimedia resource for students to learn basic statistics. It can be used by itself or along with a textbook. This CD-ROM, which runs on either Mac or PC platforms, contains videos of uses of statistics in the real world, mini-lectures accompanied by animation, tools similar to Java applets to illustrate concepts interactively, and a student version of Data Desk. Lessons on the CD-ROM instruct students in how to use the software, and many homework exercises are included that have data sets formatted for analysis with Data Desk. Other versions of *ActivStats* may be used with software programs such as Excel or SPSS.

Cumming and Thomason (1998) describe *StatPlay* as multimedia designed to help students develop a sound conceptual understanding of statistics and to overcome misconceptions. These materials consist of dynamically linked simulations and microworlds, "play grounds" and estimation games, along with recorded mini-lectures or directions on analyzing data or using the software tools.

Another unique CD-ROM is the *Electronic Companion to Statistics* (Cobb and Cryer, 1997). In contrast to *ActivStats* and *StatPlay*, this is a study guide for students that provides interactive illustrations and exercises to present examples of the different topics covered. It allows students to explore the relationships between statistical concepts using concept maps, and includes a variety of self-assessment items and animations to help students review or better understand important concepts.

Many other multimedia resources are currently being developed around the world, several of which were described at the Fifth International Conference on Teaching Statistics (Pereira-Mendoza, 1998).

Stand-Alone Simulation Software

Some concepts in statistics are particularly challenging for students to learn, such as the idea of a sampling distribution and the Central Limit Theorem. The Tools for Teaching and Assessing Statistical Inference project (Garfield, delMas and Chance, 2001), has developed some simulation programs that are easy for students to use, and are accompanied by structured lab activities and assessment instruments. Although there are other simulation tools on the Internet or on CD-ROM (such as ActivStats), this software is unique in that it provides more detail and flexibility. It allows students to manipulate a variety of populations (based on discrete or continuous data), and draw samples from these populations for different sample sizes. Templates are provided to compare the sampling distribution to the population and to a normal distribution, as well as to calculate probabilities. The tool can be used to illustrate confidence intervals and p-values as well.

The RESAMPLING STATS Software (Simon and Bruce, 1991) is a software package that offers an easy-to-use, powerful tool to conduct repeated simulations (including the bootstrap), calculate test statistics, and analyze and view the results.

Other Technological Resources

Two other types of technological resources that are used in introductory statistics classes are video and email. Moore (1993) discusses strengths and weaknesses of using videos in statistics classes. The *Against All Odds* video series produced by COMAP is an excellent set of videos that illustrate real-world applications of statistical topics. A shorter series of segments of these videos were produced and distributed as *Decisions Through Data*. Some of these videos are now included in the multimedia materials described above. Additional videos are described in the section on quantitative literacy courses.

Email is a technological tool that is impacting all courses, including statistics courses. For example, Chance (1998) reported on the use of email in introductory statistics courses to foster outside-of-class communications between the student and instructor and between students. This type of support network appears to be especially relevant in a course such as statistics, which students often enter with much trepidation and unease. Hyde and Nicholson (1998) extend this communication to intercontinental collaboration by linking statistics classrooms in different countries, allowing students to collect and analyze data comparing themselves to their international peers.

The Role of Technology in a Probability Course

As described earlier, the arrival of the computer in the classroom and the ability to analyze real data in the elementary statistics course has completely changed the way this course is taught in many colleges and universities. This has resulted also in a change in the way probability is taught in these statistics courses. The types of technology now used in these courses simulate simple experiments such as coin tossing, rolling dice, and choosing random samples from a population. Minitab has the ability to write macros to simulate any kind of chance experiment. The new statistical package Fathom can also simulate a wide range of experiments.

Statistics courses have taken advantage of this by having their students learn the basic probability ideas such as the Binomial distribution, the law of large numbers, and the Central Limit Theorem, through simulations. This means that the statistics teachers do not have to spend time on the mathematics of probability associated with the study of combinatorics, sample spaces and formal properties of probability measures. A separate probability course still develops the mathematics of probability but instructors in these courses also take advantage of simulation to help the students better understand theoretical results and to solve problems which do not lend themselves to mathematical solutions.

Software and Programming Languages

Teachers of probability courses are beginning to take advantage of powerful symbolic mathematical software such as Mathematica, Maple, and Matlab. However, those who have tried using these packages have had mixed success.

Simulating a chance experiment or solving a combinatorial problem to calculate a probability often requires writing a procedure, and students find this difficult. They may spend so much time trying to write the procedure that they end up feeling that they did not learn enough from this effort to justify the time they put in.

One area where the students can appreciate the value of these packages is in the study of Markov Chains. The ability to raise matrices to powers and to solve equations saves the students an enormous amount of work and makes Markov Chains come to life. Of course the teacher can use these packages to write procedures to illustrate basic probability results. Elliot Tanis shows on his Web site how this can be done for the Central Limit Theorem.

Traditional probability courses rarely deal with real-life data in their courses. Perhaps the success of statistics reform will convince probabilists that it is very natural and rewarding to show students how their probability models fit real data. Technology facilitates the introduction of real data into probability models, helping students become more aware of the role of variation in the real world.

World Wide Web Resources

The World Wide Web should play an important role in the future of the probability course. The Web has been particularly successful in leading to the development and dissemination of interactive text materials. An interactive probability book by Siegrist at his "Virtual Laboratories in Probability and Statistics" has applets to go with each topic. Several of the on-line interactive statistics books also have chapters on probability and make good use of applets (e.g., HyperStat by David Lane at Rice University). Individual applets that are particularly useful in teaching a probability course are Binomial probabilities, Normal approximation to the binomial distribution, Central Limit Theorem, and Brownian motion.

Probability is full of surprises, and Susan Holmes has a Web site titled "Probability by Surprises." This site includes applets related to interesting probability paradoxes and problems such as the birthday problem, the box-top problem, the hat-check problem and others. Alexander Bogomolny also provides a discussion of a number of puzzling probability problems illustrated with applets at his Web site. His list includes Benford's law, the Buffon needle problem, Simpson's paradox, and Bertrand's paradox.

More traditional probability books are also available on the Web. *Introduction to Probability* by Grinstead and Snell (1997) is an example of such a book. This book includes applets as well as Mathematica and Maple programs illustrating basic probability concepts. Waner and Costenoble have an on-line probability book, *Calculus Applied to Probability and Statistics for Liberal Arts and Business Majors*, which deals exclusively with continuous probability.

One of the greatest strengths of the Web is the ability to find very current information on probability theory that cannot yet be found in textbooks but might be good to use in a probability course. The classic example of this is David Griffeath's "Primordial Soup Kitchen." For the past ten years David has provided each week a new beautiful colored picture showing how simple cellular automaton rules create fascinating structures from random initial states. Another good example of this is the "Web Site for Perfectly Random Sampling with Markov Chains," which provides the latest information on the use of Markov Chain simulations which have recently found numerous applications in physics, statistics, and computer science. As in the case of Griffeath's site, the fact that, unlike publishers, the Web has no trouble with colored pictures makes the Web a wonderful way to transmit the current progress in these fields.

Finally, Phil Pollett maintains a Web site called "The Probability Web" that provides a comprehensive resource for links to various probability resources on the Web.

Technology in Quantitative Literacy Courses

Over the past 10 years a new course is increasingly being offered in mathematics and statistics departments, often referred to as Quantitative Literacy or Statistical Literacy. This course typically attempts to help students develop an understanding of quantitative information used in the world around them, including basic concepts in statistics and probability. Gal (2000) describes what a course on statistical literacy should be and how it differs from a standard introductory statistics course. He argues that such a course should be aimed at consumers of statistics rather than producers of statistics. The basic statistical concepts taught are not different, but the emphasis should be different. For example, a much broader discussion of types of experiments is essential to understanding reports in the news on medical experiments. Students need to understand different interpretations of probabilities (subjective and objective) and risk (relative and absolute) etc. than would normally be taught in a first statistics course. Gal has started a Web site, "Adult Numeracy: Research and Development Exchange," which provides information on statistical literacy for adults and students.

The course called "Chance" at Dartmouth, developed with several other colleges in 1992, is an example of this new type of quantitative literacy course. This course was designed to help students understand statistics used in the media and utilized articles from the current news to focus class discussions each day. The Chance Web site provides resources for teaching a Chance course or a standard course enriched with discussion of news items that include reference to ideas of chance. The Chance project produces a monthly electronic newsletter called *Chance News* that abstracts, and provides discussion questions for, current issues in the news that use probability or statistics concepts. This newsletter is sent out by email and archived on the Chance Web site.

Many major newspapers have Web versions and are a good source of articles to use in a quantitative literacy course. Search engines such as Lexis-Nexis may be used to locate articles on particular topics such as DNA fingerprinting, weather forecasting, polls and surveys, and lotteries. Articles in science and medical journals are also available on Web sites where the full text of the articles may be accessed.

Another source of information on how probability and statistics is used in the real world is provided by the videos of the lectures from the Chance Lecture Series available on the Chance Web site. In this series, experts in areas of probability and statistics that are mentioned regularly in the news provide lectures on their topic. Some of these are David Moore from the Gallup Organization on problems in polling, Arnold Barnett from MIT on estimating the risk of flying, Bruce Weir on the use of DNA fingerprinting in the news, etc. The lectures are also available on a CD-ROM for those with slow Internet connections.

The Web site "Chance and Data in the News" maintained by Jane Watson is a useful resource for quantitative literacy courses. This is a collection of newspaper articles from an Australian newspaper grouped according to the five topics: Data Collection and Sampling, Data Representation, Chance and Basic Probability, Data Reduction, and Inference. Each topic starts with general questions for articles related to this topic. In addition, each article has specific questions pertaining to it and references to related articles.

National Public Radio (NPR) also covers the major medical studies as well as other chance news. They keep all of their programs in an archive that students can access and listen to with free RealAudio software. Their reports are usually in the form of questions and answers from the researcher who did the work or other experts in the field or both. These questions often anticipate questions readers of the newspaper report might have and so often make a significant contribution. NPR has a good search engine to look for discussions of older articles. The Chance Web site has a number of these interviews under "Video and Audio."

Technology in Other Statistics Courses

This section focuses on more "advanced" introductory statistics courses. By this we mean introductory courses with a calculus prerequisite (often serving students majoring in statistics, mathematics, science, or engineering) as well as second-semester introductory courses. Similar to the statistics reform movement in the introductory course, a slower movement has addressed the content and pedagogy of these courses, with technology again playing a central role. While progress has been slower there is also tremendous potential for innovative uses of technology in these courses.

Web applets and computer packages now allow a greater emphasis on the conceptual ideas underlying the statistical methods. For example, students can use Minitab or a Java program to simulate the sampling distribution of the least squares regression slope or the chi-square statistic. This expands the types of simulations students use in other statistics courses to study more complicated techniques. Students can use Excel to graph and numerically estimate the maximum likelihood estimator, while easily changing parameter values to see how the maximum likelihood function updates. Students are therefore able to focus on the function and less on the calculus involved.

SPlus is another computer package that allows students to program routines and perform simulations. Similar to programming in the C language, students can be asked to write simple scripts for performing analyses. SPlus also offers exemplary graphical techniques for exploring more complicated data sets. A similar, but free, student version, R, can be downloaded from the Web.

These more advanced courses have also seen an increase in the number and size of data sets that can be analyzed, due to the availability of technological resources. For example, *The Statistical Sleuth* (Ramsey and Schafer, 1997) and *StatLabs* (Nolan and Speed, 2000) each follow a series of case studies to demonstrate the application of intermediate and mathematical statistics tools. These examples deal with real, and often messy, genuine data sets. Students must learn to deal with the messiness inherent in real data as well as better linking their knowledge to the practice of statistics.

Current technology allows students to take advantage of, and learn from, more recent computationally intensive statistical methods. For example, Jenny Baglivo is developing laboratory materials for use with Mathematica that incorporate simulation, permutation, and bootstrap methods throughout a math/stat course. These materials are available at her Web site. Tanis (1998) has been integrating computer algebra system modules into mathematical statistics courses.

Experience using technology and the need to be able to communicate statistical knowledge are considered important competencies for students who major in statistics. This is seen by an emergence of capstone courses that require students to apply their knowledge and then use technology to produce integrated reports of their results and analysis discussion (e.g., Derr, 2000; Spurrier, 2000). Video is also used extensively by Derr to present

JOAN GARFIELD · BETH CHANCE · J. LAURIE SNELL

students with examples of good and bad consulting sessions. This is a very effective instructional tool, enabling students to "be there" and to see alternative examples of the same session. However, no one claims that such videos should completely replace personal experience.

Research on the Role of Technology in Probability and Statistics Courses

Although it is apparent to statistics educators that technology has had a huge impact on the content of current courses as well as the types of experiences students have in these courses, there is little research to document the actual impact of technology on student learning. There is also a lack of information evaluating the effectiveness of particular types of software or activities using technology. Biehler (1997) cautions that statistics educators need a system to critically evaluate existing software from the perspective of educating students, and to produce future software more adequate both for learning and doing statistics in introductory courses.

A round table conference sponsored by the International Association for Statistics Education was convened in 1996 to examine research on the role of technology in learning statistics. Although there was little empirical research to report at that time on the impact of technology on student learning, a main outcome of this conference was to identify important issues and research questions that had not yet been explored (Garfield and Burrill, 1997).

Two years later, at the Fifth International Conference on Teaching Statistics, there were 35 papers presented in seven different categories, under the topic heading "The Role of Technology in the Teaching of Statistics" (Pereira-Mendoza, 1998). Additional papers on the use of technology were in many of the other topic sessions as well. Most of these papers discussed ways technology can be used in courses, rather than offering data on learning outcomes. However, empirical studies (e.g., Finch and Cumming, 1998; Shaughnessy, 1998) provided valuable information on how technological tools can both improve student learning of particular concepts as well as raise new awareness of student misconceptions or difficulties (e.g., Batanero and Godino, 1998).

While controlled experiments are usually not possible in educational settings, qualitative studies are increasingly helpful in focusing on the development of concepts or the use of skills that technology is intended to facilitate. Biehler (1998) used videos and transcripts to explore students' thinking as they interacted with statistical software. Lee (2000) and Miller (2000) are examples of qualitative studies of how a course that integrates technological tools can support a student-centered, constructivist environment for statistics education. delMas, Garfield, and Chance (1999) provide a model of collaborative classroom research to study the impact of simulation software on students' understanding of sampling distributions.

Summary, Conclusions, Recommendations

Thisted and Velleman (1992), in their summary of technology in teaching statistics, cite four obstacles that can cause difficulties when trying to incorporate technology into college statistics courses. These include equipment (e.g., adequate and updated computer labs), software (availability and costs), projection (of computer screens in classrooms), and obsolescence (of hardware, software, and projection technologies). Eight years later, we can see increased availability of computers and access to graphing calculators, updated and more widely available software, often via CD's bundled with textbooks or on the World Wide Web, and new methods of projecting computer screens such as interactive White Boards.

The ways that these technological resources appear to have changed the teaching of probability and statistics include:

- Less of a focus on computations. This frees students to spend more time focusing on and understanding the concepts. There is also less focus on manipulating numbers, or on exercises using only small and/or artificial data sets.

- Improved visualization of statistical concepts and processes. Students are better able to "see" the statistical ideas, and teachers are better able to teach to students who are predominantly visual learners.

- Dynamic representations and analyses. Discussions or activities may focus on "what if?" questions by changing data values or manipulating graphs and instantly seeing the results.

- Increased use of simulations. Simulations provide an alternative to using theoretical probability when teaching introductory statistics, better motivate probability theory when teaching probability, and offer better ways to convey ideas of long-run patterns.

- Empowering students as users of statistics. Students are able to solve real problems and use powerful statistical tools that they may be able to use in other courses or types of work. This allows them to better understand and experience the practice of statistics.

- Facilitating discussions about more interesting problems by using technological tools to explore interesting data sets (which may be large and complicated), often accessed from the Internet.

JOAN GARFIELD · BETH CHANCE · J. LAURIE SNELL

- Allowing students to do more learning on their own, outside of class, using Web-based or multimedia materials. This frees the instructor to have fewer lectures during class and to spend more time on data analysis activities and group discussions.

- Making the course relevant and connected to everyday life. Web resources make it easy to connect course material to real world applications and problems through data sets, media resources, and videos.

Despite the capabilities that technology offers, instructors should be careful about using sophisticated software packages that may result in the students spending more time learning to use the software than they do in applying it. Even in this advanced technological society, students are not always ready for the levels of technology used in courses. It is important that videos and simulation games do not become "play time" for students and that computer visualizations do not just become a black box generating data. Rather than replace data-generating activities with computer simulations, educators may choose to use a hands-on activity with devices such as dice or M&Ms to begin an activity, and then move to the computer to simulate larger sets of data. In this way students may better understand the simulation process and what the data actually represent.

What is still lacking is knowledge on the best ways of integrating technology into statistics courses, and how to assess the impact of technology on student understanding of statistics. With an increased emphasis on statistics education at all educational levels, we hope to see more high-quality research incorporating a variety of methods and theoretical frameworks that will provide information on appropriate uses of technology.

Finally, probability and statistics are specialized subjects, and many colleges may not have a faculty member whose expertise is in these areas. The methods being developed for distance learning, which incorporate many innovative uses of technology, may allow schools to share resources and make a high quality probability or statistics class at one university available to others. However, with increased distance-learning courses, it is also unclear as to how much of a course can be taught exclusively using technology, what the appropriate role of an instructor should be, and how much emphasis should still be placed on students generating calculations and graphs by hand.

References

Batanero, C., & Godino, J. D. (1998). Understanding graphical and numerical representations of statistical association in a computer environment. In L. Pereira-Mendoza (Ed.), *Proceedings of the Fifth International Conference on Teaching Statistics* (pp. 1017–1023). Voorburg, The Netherlands: International Statistical Institute.

Ben-Zvi, D. (2000). Toward understanding the role of technological tools in statistical learning. *Mathematical Thinking and Learning, 2*, 127–155.

Biehler, R. (1997). Software for learning and doing statistics. *International Statistical Review, 65*, 167–189.

Biehler, R. (1998). Students—statistical software—statistical tasks: A study of problems at the interfaces. In L. Pereira-Mendoza (Ed.), *Proceedings of the Fifth International Conference on Teaching Statistics* (pp. 1025–1031). Voorburg, The Netherlands: International Statistical Institute.

Chance, B. (1998). Incorporating a listserve into introductory statistics courses. *1998 Proceedings of the Section on Statistical Education.* American Statistical Association.

Cobb, G. W. (1992). Teaching statistics. In L. Steen (Ed.), *Heeding the call for change: Suggestions for curricular action* (pp. 3–43). Washington, DC: Mathematical Association of America.

Cobb, G. W., & Cryer, J. (1997). *Electronic companion to statistics.* New York: Cogito Learning Media.

Cumming, G., & Thomason, N. (1998). StatPlay: Multimedia for statistical understanding. In L. Pereira-Mendoza (Ed.), *Proceedings of the Fifth International Conference on Teaching Statistics* (pp. 947–952). Voorburg, The Netherlands: International Statistical Institute.

delMas, R., Garfield, J., & Chance, B. (1999). A model of classroom research in action: Developing simulation activities to improve students' statistical reasoning. *Journal of Statistics Education, 7*(3). Retrieved from http://www.amstat.org/publications/jse/

Derr, J. (2000). *Statistical consulting: A guide to effective communication.* Pacific Grove, CA: Duxbury Press.

Finch, S., & Cumming, G. (1998). Assessing conceptual change in learning statistics. In L. Pereira-Mendoza (Ed.), *Proceedings of the Fifth International Conference on Teaching Statistics* (pp. 897–904). Voorburg, The Netherlands: International Statistical Institute.

Finzer, B., & Erickson, T. (1998). DataSpace—A computer learning environment for data anlaysis and statistics based on dynamic dragging, visualization, simulation, and networked collaboration. In L. Pereira-Mendoza (Ed.), *Proceedings of the Fifth International Conference on Teaching Statistics* (pp. 825–830). Voorburg, The Netherlands: International Statistical Institute.

Gal, I. (2000). Statistical literacy: Conceptual and instructional issues. In D. Coben, J. O'Donoghue, & G. FitzSimons, (Eds.), *Perspectives on adults learning mathematics: Research and practice* (pp. 135–150). London: Kluwer.

Garfield, J. (2000). *A snapshot of introductory statistics.* Paper presented at Beyond the Formula conference, Rochester, NY.

Garfield, J. and Burrill, G. (Eds.), (1997). Research on the role of technology in teaching and learning statistics. Voorburg, The Netherlands: International Statistical Institute.

Garfield, J., delMas, R., & Chance, B. (2001). *Tools for teaching and assessing statistical inference.* Paper presented at the Joint Mathematics Meetings, New Orleans, LA.

Grinstead, C. , & Snell, J. L. (1997). *Introduction to probability.* Washington, DC: The American Mathematical Society.

Harkness, W. (2000). *Restructuring the elementary statistics class: The Penn State model.* Paper presented at the Joint Statistical Meetings, Indianapolis, IN.

Hyde, H. , & Nicholson, J. (1998). Sharing data via email at the secondary level. In L. Pereira-Mendoza (Ed.), *Proceedings of the Fifth International Conference on Teaching Statistics* (pp. 95–102). Voorburg, The Netherlands: International Statistical Institute.

Joiner, B. L., & Ryan, B. F. (2000). *MINITAB® handbook.* Pacific Grove, CA: Brooks/Cole Publishing.

Kugashev, A. (2000). *Statistical instruction in distance learning.* Paper presented at the Joint Statistical Meetings, Indianapolis, IN.

Lee, C. (2000, August). Developing student-centered learning environments in the technology era—The case of introductory statistics. Paper presented at Joint Statistical Meetings.

Lock, R. H. (1993). A comparison of five student versions of statistics packages. *The American Statistician, 47,* 136–145.

Lock, R. H. (in press). A Sampler of WWW resources for teaching statistics. In T. Moore (Ed.), *Teaching statistics: Resources for undergraduate instructors.* Washington, DC: Mathematical Association of America.

McCullough, B. D., & Wilson, B. (1999). On the accuracy of statistical procedures in Microsoft Excel 97. *Computational Statistics and Data Analysis, 31,* 27–37.

Miller, J. (2000). The *quest for the constructivist statistics classroom: Viewing practice through constructivist theory.* Ph.D. Dissertation, Ohio State University.

Moore, D. S. (1993). The place of video in new styles of teaching and learning statistics. *The American Statistician, 47*, 172–176.

Moore, D. S. (1997). New pedagogy and new content: The case of statistics. *International Statistical Review, 635*, 123–165.

Nolan, D., & Speed, T. P. (2000). *StatLabs: Mathematical statistics through applications.* New York: Springer.

Pereira-Mendoza, L. (Eds.). (1998). *Proceedings of the Fifth International Conference on Teaching Statistics.* Voorburg, The Netherlands: International Statistical Institute.

Ramsey, F., & Schafer, D. (1997). *The statistical sleuth.* Pacific Grove, CA: Duxbury Press.

Shaughnessy, J. M. (1998). Immersion in data handling: Using the Chance-Plus software with introductory college students. In L. Pereira-Mendoza (Ed.), *Proceedings of the Fifth International Conference on Teaching Statistics* (pp. 913–920). Voorburg, The Netherlands: International Statistical Institute.

Shaughnessy, J. M., Garfield, J.B., & Greer, B. (1997). Data handling. In A. J. Bishop, K. Clements, C. Keitel, J. Kilpatrick, & C. Laborde (Eds.), *International handbook on mathematics education* (pp. 205–237). Dordrecht: Kluwer Academic Publishers.

Simon, J. L., & Bruce, P. (1991). Resampling: A tool for everyday statistical work. *Chance, 4*(1), 22–32.

Spurrier, J. D. (2000). *The practice of statistics: Putting the pieces together.* Pacific Grove, CA: Duxbury Press.

Tanis, E. (1998). Using Maple for instruction in undergraduate probability and statistics. In L. Pereira-Mendoza (Ed.), *Proceedings of the fifth international conference on teaching statistics* (pp. 199–204). Voorburg, The Netherlands: International Statistical Institute.

Thisted, R. A., & Velleman, P. F. (1992). Computers and modern statistics. In D. Hoaglin and D. Moore (Eds.), *Perspectives on contemporary statistics* (pp. 41–53). Washington, DC: Mathematical Association of America.

Velleman, P. (1998). *Learning data analysis with Data Desk.* Reading, MA: Addison-Wesley.

Velleman, P. (2000) ActivStats. Incorporating a listserve into introductory statistics courses. *1998 Proceedings of the Section on Statistical Education*, American Statistical Association.

Velleman, P., & Moore, D. S. (1996). Multimedia for teaching statistics: Promises and pitfalls. *The American Statistician, 50*, 217–225.

Utilizing Digital Video to Expand Prospective Science Teachers' Views of Science

Randy Yerrick
San Diego State University

Teacher Education: Addressing Misconceptions About Science and Science Teaching

Prospective teachers often harbor preconceptions about science teaching and these beliefs shape the way they engage children in science lessons in elementary classrooms (Abell, Bryan, & Andersen, 1998; Abell, & Bryan, 1997; Munby & Russell, 1992). As with children and their preconceptions about science (Driver, 1989; Osborne & Freyberg, 1985), it becomes essential when working with novice science teachers to confront naïve conceptions of science and assist them in recognizing children's ideas and re-examining their own personal beliefs. Research has shown that prospective teachers' personal histories learning science (both positive and negative) have a great influence on how they teach science to children (Anning, 1988; VanZee & Roberts, 2001).

Traditional approaches in teacher education do little to elicit and address the misconceptions of students, whether at the elementary or university level, and may even encourage teachers to gloss over scientific conceptual development (Lave, 1990; Solomon, 1989). In contrast, a teacher education program that guides teachers to encourage elementary students to tell stories about their ideas accomplishes several things: It gives teachers insights into what their students actually know, frees teachers to address misconceptions directly, and encourages teachers to envision alternative pedagogical options (Roth, 1994). It also guides teachers toward inquiry-based science and away from lessons that simply disseminate scientific facts (Gallas, 1995; Shapiro, 1994; Bryan & Abell, 1999).

Teacher Education Standards for Science Teachers

Field experiences that engage prospective teachers in science teaching have yielded some positive results (Abell, Bryan, & Andersen,1998). However, not all field experiences have successfully modified prospective teachers' thinking or practice (Lortie, 1975; McDiarmid, 1990). Several efforts have been made to perturb prospective teachers' beliefs through structured reflection so that alternative, more constructive models of teaching are likely

Reprinted from Exchanges: The On-line Journal of Teaching and Learning in the CSU, 2002, http://www.exchangesjournal.org/classroom/1092_Yerrick_pg1.html, by permission of the author.

to be implemented in today's classroom. Like Posner, Strike, Hewson, and Gertzog (1986), who outlined preconditions necessary for promoting accommodation and conceptual change for children, Osborne and Freyberg (1985) outlined preconditions necessary for confronting teachers' beliefs. These included the need for preservice teachers to understand children's views, to engage in self-clarification of their own views at an early stage in their training, to weigh the strengths and weaknesses of their personal views, and to consolidate evidence related to their views. Without such preconditions, many teachers find it difficult to accept beliefs and practices contrary to their own. If they believe that science is mostly factual or if they believe children are unable to think in complex ways about the world, they are likely to teach in response to those beliefs. As a result teachers may develop ways of devaluing or avoiding evidence about their students' science learning altogether.

More recent efforts to design educative field experiences have demonstrated that, when given the chance to confront their beliefs, prospective teachers develop a deeper understanding of teaching (Cochran-Smith, 1991; Hollingsworth, 1989). Teachers who have engaged in reflection are more adept at thinking critically about their own teaching as well as the teaching of others. Bryan and Abell (1999) demonstrated that teachers are able to develop a disposition of inquiry about their teaching and more closely align their teaching practices with their professed beliefs, though the researchers agreed with Munby and Russell (1992) that doing so is an arduous process.

Each of these researchers was focusing upon a definition of scientific literacy that incorporates an understanding of the nature of science, an ability to investigate the natural world, and an ability to use more traditional forms of literacy to learn about science, interpret data, and communicate scientific findings. This vision is embraced by current national reform rhetoric (AAAS, 1989, 1993; NRC, 1996). However, as teacher educators we are aware that many school districts have taken a dominant approach to developing narrow strategies based on specific skills, paying little attention to the integration of science content or cultural literacy into the prescribed curricula. It is these narrow approaches that we wish to prepare future elementary science teachers to face, for if they are unprepared in their college education and training, their efforts to implement inquiry-based science learning are likely to be drastically impeded.

Instructional Approach

With these goals in mind, I teach an elementary science methods course in which university students can observe examples of children's thinking and of alternative science-teaching strategies and can reflect upon their own science experiences as well as their efforts to teach according to current National Science Education Standards (NRC, 1996). The course in science-teaching methods is taught specifically for California elementary teachers working toward a multiple-subject credential. Prospective elementary teachers enroll in this course prior to the student teaching experience that is the culminating event for their graduation. It is a course offered in contrast to that for in-service teachers, who are actively teaching science, and it emphasizes the importance of providing preservice teachers opportunities to reflect on science teaching prior to their roles as full-time teachers. Using state-of-the-art desktop video editing software and hardware, I assist my preservice science teachers in identifying children's conceptions, I model exemplary practices for science teaching, and I facilitate their reflection on pedagogical choices. In the School of Teacher Education at San Diego State University, the faculty are committed to connecting educational theory to actual teaching practices. Hence, I teach the science-methods course in a local progressive elementary school where the preservice teachers have access to mentors and children, and practice implementing technology for the purpose of enhancing science learning. The preservice teachers are each assigned to a school in the district and they meet once per week for six hours at the site of one selected elementary school to observe, plan, develop resources, teach science lessons, and reflect together as a group.

I hope to make an impact on preservice elementary science teachers in three areas: 1) their knowledge of children's prior experiences with and understanding of scientific concepts, 2) their knowledge of a variety of pedagogical strategies for teaching science, and 3) their understanding of their own past experiences as science learners and how these experiences influence their pedagogical choices. We describe below actual strategies we have learned from research and our own experiences that have assisted us in moving multiple-subject credential teachers' thinking forward in their considerations of children's thinking and appropriate strategies for teaching science in a manner consistent with National Science Education Standards (NRC, 1996).

Strategy One: Analyzing Children's Thinking

The first strategy involves the analysis of children's thinking through the use of digital videos that record clinical interviews documenting the pre-conceptions of individual children. Preservice teachers devise interview protocols that address core scientific ideas (e.g., seasons, moon phases, heat transfer, photosynthesis, current flow) so that they can hear first-hand a child's contrary notions as well as his or her reasons and explanations. Confronting commonly held misconceptions requires teachers to guide students to a sense of dissatisfaction with their understanding of what they think they know. These interviews help preservice teachers to identify access points into the children's beliefs, which stimulates ideas for ways to use contrary evidence to perturb children's non-scientific thinking.

Sharing these videos allows my students to see a wider variety of children's thinking. Prospective teachers use these iMovies to ground their reading assignments in real-life examples. In response to these examples they can design elementary lesson plans and respond in their journals. Once my students have identified children's thinking about such questions as "Why do leaves change color?" or "Where do stars go during the day?" our task is to identify which teaching strategies might be most appropriate for addressing misconceptions. (Link to iMovie is found at http://edweb.sdsu.edu/sciencetg/ie/stars/stars.html)

Part of learning to teach well involves learning to listen carefully and weigh fully the beliefs of children as we plan, instruct, and evaluate. After analyzing the examples of children's thinking shown in the iMovies, more teachers choose open-ended questions as the basis for their planned lessons. Before I began to use the digital videos, preservice teachers rarely designed lessons focusing on central questions that require children to use scientific processes to gather evidence and construct their own interpretations. Instead, their lessons typically would focus upon transmitting factual knowledge about science topics like *the five senses* or *the food pyramid* or *volcanoes.* In contrast, during the most recent semester of the course, students developed lessons around such questions as, "How do we know there are just nine planets?" "Why is food different for plants and animals?" "How can we hear?" "Why do some things sink and some float?" "Is the life cycle for spiders the same as for butterflies?" "Where does water on the playground go on a hot day?" The lessons now reflect a greater respect for children's abilities and knowledge, and teachers further extend their own knowledge by sharing their iMovies with each other and comparing their interview results.

Strategy Two: Modeling Alternative Pedagogy

It is sometimes important to model teaching strategies that promote a deeper scientific understanding of everyday phenomena. Broadening the pedagogical repertoire of preservice elementary science teachers is a main objective of the course, and iMovies that document local progressive science classrooms can enable prospective elementary science teachers to engage vicariously in inquiry teaching.

One drawback of teacher education programs offering only one science methods course is that science is not a generic process. Learning to teach biology is different from the process of learning to teach physics but, because of the curricular constraints of the elementary schools with which we collaborate, we often must teach only one science topic. This severely limits the exposure of my preservice teachers to a variety of strategies for teaching biological, physical, and chemical sciences. This can present a challenge because inquiry-based teaching methods for biology are not equivalent to those used in physics or chemistry. For example, field experiences in which children examine organisms in their natural habitat are less applicable for the study of motion and general kinematics. However, the videos that document actual lessons and the artifacts from children (e.g., student work, drawings, small group interactions) involved in past university and elementary collaborations allow my preservice teachers to explore a wider variety of strategies for addressing the children's conceptions they have explicated in their own videos. (Link to iMovie is found at http://edweb.sdsu.edu/sciencetg/ie/elementary/pond/pond.html)

Strategy Three: Reflection on Practice

The third strategy also relies on digital video to document prospective teachers' practices and reflections. In light of McDiarmid's (1990) claim that we cannot shape young teachers' practices until we have helped novice teachers understand the limits of their own learning, methods students are required to tell their own personal autobiographies of science learning. Most of my methods students have reported experiencing poor science instruction and have had few positive science-teaching models in their personal histories. In an attempt to help pre-service elementary teachers express their widespread frustration with science and their desire to learn alternative methods, I ask students to produce autobiographical iMovies in the first week of the science methods course as they read from such provocative authors as Kohl (1984), Jackson (1986), Ayers (1990), Ball (1988) and other teacher-scholars and reflect upon their own science experiences. Preservice teachers also tape each other teaching children and then reflect on their lessons as they edit their videos with two peers. After producing their own desktop videos, prospective teachers are better able to identify the strengths and weaknesses of their own knowledge and experiences. In accord with narrative inquiry methods (Connelly & Clandinin, 1990; Cortazzi, 1993), they identify specific aspects of strong science teaching and create their own personal metaphors for science teaching that connect with assigned readings. For example, having students describe their learning about their teaching as similar to "riding a bike" or "grinding gears" helps preservice teachers to communicate their struggles and insights from literature more poignantly. They also share their personal histories with the class, which seems to establish camaraderie in collaborative, small groups.

As a culminating task for the methods course, preservice teachers edit a final five-minute video that depicts their learning process as an emerging science teacher. In these videos prospective teachers illustrate their understanding of children's thinking (strategy one), defend their pedagogical choices (strategy two), and provide evidence of their success. This third strategy serves as a way they communicate to one another how well they have addressed children's thinking in the lessons they had spent the semester planning and teaching. Rich discussions follow when the students share videos depicting themselves employing a variety of strategies, exploring children's thinking through open-ended questions, providing evidence contrary to common-sense thinking, and soliciting commentary between children about competing ideas. (Link to iMovie is found at http://edweb.sdsu.edu/sciencetg/ie/gravity/gravity.html)

As a result of these assignments, I have observed changes in actual teaching practices. Prospective teachers not only attend to the children's ideas they record in interviews, they also attempt to emulate in their lessons the teaching practices observed earlier in the semester. They incorporate in their lessons more mathematics and writing strategies than past students have done, and they report applying strategies learned in science methods to other lessons in their teaching placements (e.g.; facilitating a math or reading lesson). Students also author lessons that represent more authentic inquiry for children. In addition, students are better able to use alternative frameworks to place teaching issues within a larger context of value-laden educational settings. For example, students have always been asked in this methods course to critique available teaching resources with respect to topics of their choice. After interviewing students and conducting their analyses using iMovie, prospective science teachers are more astute at identifying weaknesses in available lesson plans.

Concluding Remarks

Engaging preservice teachers in digital video editing as described above enables us to discuss the teaching of science in much more substantive ways. Focusing on how children make sense of the world and how adults make sense of daily instruction, specifically with regard to misconceptions in science, helps me address preservice teachers' beliefs about science teaching and National Science Standards (National Research Council, 1996).

Prospective teachers learn to identify more clearly the characteristics of inquiry-based lessons in their lesson critiques, article reviews, and peer-lesson evaluations. They begin to write more articulate journal entries about teaching dilemmas and children's thinking. More teachers become able to identify the real struggles surrounding the question of how to teach less content for greater understanding, and they express these revelations in journals that address misconceptions and difficult decisions about cutting certain content.

Some of the obstacles I face in getting students hands-on experiences with iMovie include inconsistent access to laptops and digital video cameras at poorly supported schools. The teacher education program at San Diego State is committed to providing authentic teaching contexts for our students, but conducting science-methods courses in the field at sites with little technology severely hampers our abilities to teach them about science teaching or technology. In addition, some teachers at the schools affiliated with our site-based program are not open to alternative interpretations of science and want to teach only text-driven vocabulary. While the iMovies can model alternative strategies in order to offset this narrow-mindedness, the socialization of student teachers is strong and the impact of the course may be undone in subsequent weeks or months.

Like any educational technology, desktop video editing cannot respond to all of the challenges that teachers face in today's classroom. However, for my preservice teachers, the use of desktop video has encouraged individual expression, spawned creativity, revitalized content, promoted collective knowledge construction and individual reflection, and enabled them to engage in authentic learning. Digital video editing need not be confined to science teaching alone. Several practicing elementary teachers with whom we have been working have also found ways to enhance their children's writing, speaking, and research skills through such activities as coordinating school-site news teams, assigning book reports in video format, and capturing virtual field trips. Digital video editing provides a venue for children and teachers to gain a deeper and broader representation of what it means to understand content and to assess content instruction.

References

American Association for the Advancement of Science. (1989). *Project 2061: Science for all Americans.* Washington, DC: Author.

American Association for the Advancement of Science. (1993). *Benchmarks for science literacy.* New York: Oxford University Press.

Abell, S.K., Bryan L. A., & Andersen, M. A. (1998). Investigating preservice elementary science teacher reflective thinking using integrated media case-based instruction in elementary science teacher preparation. *Science Education, 82,* 491–510.

Abell, S. K., & Bryan, L. S. (1997). Reconceptualizing the elementary science methods course using a reflection orientation. *Journal of Science Teacher Education, 8,* 153–166.

Anning, A. (1988). Teachers' theories about children's learning. In J. Calderhead (Ed.), *Teachers' professional learning* (pp. 128–145). London: Falmer.

Ayers, W. (1990). *To Teach.* Columbia: Teachers College Press.

Ball, D. L. (1988). Unlearning to teach mathematics. *For the Learning of Mathematics, 8* (1), 40–48.

Bryan, L.A, & Abell, S. K. (1999). Development of professional knowledge in learning to teach elementary science. *Journal of Research in Science Teaching, 36,* 121–139

Cochran-Smith, M. (1991). Learning to teach against the grain. *Harvard Educational Review, 61,* 279–310.

Connelly, F.M. & Clandinin, D.J. (1990). Stories of experience and narrative inquiry. *Educational Researcher, 15* (5), 2–14.

Cortazzi, M. (1993). *Narrative analysis.* London: The Falmer Press.

Driver, (1989). *Children's ideas in science.* Philadelphia: Open University Press.

Gallas, K. (1995). *Talking their way into science.* New York: Teachers College Press.

Hollingsworth, S. (1989). Prior beliefs and cognitive change in learning to teach. *American Educational Research Journal, 26,* 160–189.

Hutchings. P. & Shulman, L. (1999). The scholarship of teaching: New elaborations, new developments. *Change, 31,* (5), 10–15.

Jackson, P. (1986). *The practice of teaching.* New York: Teachers College Press.

Kohl, H. (1984). *Growing minds: On becoming a teacher.* New York: Harper Collins.

Lave, J. (1990). Views of the classroom: Implications for math and science learning research. In M. Gardner, J. Greeno, F. Reif, A. Schonfeld, A. Disessa, & E. Stage (Eds.), *Toward a scientific practice of science education* (pp. 251–263). Hillsdale, NJ: Lawrence Erlbaum.

Lortie, D. (1975). *Schoolteacher: A sociological study.* Chicago: University of Chicago Press.

McDiarmid, G.W. (1990). Challenging prospective teachers' beliefs during early field experience: A quixotic undertaking? *Journal of Teacher Education, 41,* 12–20.

Munby, H., & Russell, T. (1992). Frames of reflection: An introduction. In T. Russell & H. Munby (Eds.), *Teachers and teaching: From classroom to reflection* (pp. 1–8). New York: Falmer Press.

National Research Council. (1996). *National science education standards.* Washington, DC: National Academy Press.

Osborne, R., & Freyberg, P. (1985). *Learning in science: The implications of children's science*. Portsmouth, NH: Heinemann.

Posner, G., Strike, K., Hewson, P., & Gertzog, W. (1982) Accommodation of a scientific conception: Toward a theory of conceptual change. *Science Education, 66*, 211–227.

Roth, W. -M. (1994). Experimenting in a constructivist high school physics laboratory. *Journal of Research in Science Teaching, 31*, 197–223.

Shapiro, B. (1994). *What children bring to light: A constructivist perspective on children's learning in science*. New York: Teachers College Press.

Solomon, J. (1989). The social construction of school science. In R. Millar (Ed.), *Doing science: Images of science in science education* (pp. 126–136). Philadelphia, PA: The Falmer Press.

Van Zee, E. & Roberts, D. (2001). Using pedagogical inquiries as a basis for learning to teach: Prospective teachers' reflections upon positive science learning experiences. *Science Education, 85*, 733–757.

An Innovative Approach to Teaching Software Utilizing Computer Screen Recording Technology

Paul A. Weber
William C. Epstein
California Polytechnic State University, San Luis Obispo

Abstract

Construction management, as well as most other academic disciplines, has become increasingly dependent on commercial software packages as integral tools in the educational process. With this reliance on software comes a responsibility of the professor to provide some level of instruction on how to use these software packages. The traditional methodology of illustrating software usage by conducting in-class tutorial sessions creates a situation wherein the student is watching the instructor's computer activity while trying to simultaneously take notes on the various commands being demonstrated. Supplementing these in-class sessions with text-based user manuals considerably helps; however, the learning style of today's students is much more visually based. This paper presents a case study of the lead author's use of Lotus Development's ScreenCam program as a means of teaching students how to effectively utilize various aspects of Autodesk's popular computer-aided drafting program (AutoCAD). The ScreenCam software is used to create digital movies that demonstrate some of the features of AutoCAD usage by recording both the professor's voice concurrently with his computer screen movements and activities. A collection of these movies is then made available to the students to assist them in mastering some of the more complex components of this program. Creation and dissemination of these multimedia instructional modules can meaningfully address many of the pedagogical challenges associated with teaching students how to efficiently use commercial software packages.

Introduction

Commercial software packages have become indispensable with respect to how contemporary construction educators deliver their course content. In an article about training teachers on how to best utilize technology, Cohen (1998) rightfully points out that today's college students ". . . need to become technologically literate in regard to using new software programs in the sense of how to use these tools to promote higher order thinking skills

Reprinted from the *First International Conference on Information Systems in Engineering and Construction*, ISEC 2001, by permission of the authors and the publisher.

and how these tools can help in the process of creative problem solving." The operative word in Cohen's insightful statement is the word "tools." University educators should not be in the business of training and delivering software technicians to the construction industry. Rather these professors should embrace and utilize existing and emerging technology as a "tool" for enhancing the way in which they teach the students as well as the way in which the students learn.

The traditional methodology of illustrating software usage by conducting in-class tutorial sessions creates a passive learning environment wherein the student is watching the instructor's computer activity while trying to simultaneously take notes on the commands being demonstrated. Much has been written over the years concerning students' learning styles (Kolb, 1984; Soloman, 1997), specifically with respect to how most students prefer the active approach of "learn-by-doing." As anyone who has ever attempted to master a new software program can attest, the best and most effective way to learn computer software is to jump right in and "play with it."

This article is, for the most part, a case study of the lead author's experiences derived from incorporating CAD (computer aided drafting) into the construction graphics course (CM 211- Construction Contract Documents), which is a required sophomore level class in the Construction Management Department at California Polytechnic State University (Cal Poly) in San Luis Obispo, California. Integral to this course's learning objectives is the final project wherein the student must produce a set of contract documents conforming to current building codes and standards, including a complete set of working drawings, specifications and bid documents. The computerized drafting requirements of this project call for the student to create several CAD drawings and details as part of the final submission. This CAD component has presented a number of educational issues, namely instructing the students on how to most effectively use the departmental CAD software (Autodesk's AutoCAD) in generating the necessary documents without becoming bogged down with the specific intricacies of this very powerful program. The authors' solution to these pedagogical challenges was to develop a number of multimedia instructional modules that would walk the student through many of AutoCAD's more difficult tasks step by step. These modules were created using Lotus Development's ScreenCam software, which is one of the many computer screen recording programs that are on the market today. ScreenCam is a program that can be used to compose digital movies that demonstrate software usage by recording both the professor's voice concurrently with computer screen movements and activities into an integrated file. In this case, a collection of ScreenCam movies were made available to the students to assist them in mastering some of the more complex components of the AutoCAD program. One inherent limitation of playing the ScreenCam movie is that while the student is viewing the movie, the computer screen is not available for operating the AutoCAD software and practicing the task at hand. With this in mind, there exists a supplemental course packet that contains paper-based equivalent instructions that directly support each ScreenCam movie. Armed with the course packet and having 24-hour access to the collection of ScreenCam movies, the students can now approach the task of learning to work with AutoCAD in a very active and interactive educational environment. This two-pronged strategy affords the student the opportunity of experiencing what Montgomery (1995) notes as the two main attributes of multimedia, a self-paced and individualized mode of instruction.

A Case Study

The AutoCAD software features a number of commands and icons, such as cut and paste, found in many common applications including word processors and spreadsheets. It also, however, contains many commands and icons related specifically to graphics. The software is designed generically to be used in various industries such as architecture, engineering, and manufacturing. Consequently, it is not user friendly to a specific discipline and is often confusing and has a steep learning curve; it is not very intuitive. It is not the purpose of the course for students to master the software but to comprehend its power as a tool. Due to the workload of the course in a ten-week quarter it is imperative the students learn the software as quickly as possible. The content of the lecture material is extensive, detailed, and fast-paced; too much to be able to take notes. There are no course requirements to purchase the manual for AutoCAD or other third party AutoCAD publications due to other text and supply expenses in the course. The instructions the students receive begin with a lecture in a computer lab using a computer projector while the students operate a computer, stepping through various commands and features of the software. A chapter of the "course packet" illustrates certain nuances of the software and assignment requirements by including images of the software dialog boxes in order to aid the students through the process. The students do not have access to videos of the software but are nonetheless familiar with videos as an instructional aid.

When a new file is created in AutoCAD, it is often done in what is called "model space." The assignment for drawing a site plan has the student create a drawing using the full unit size of the object. This file is saved and referred to in a new drawing created for plotting or printing. The site plan is inserted on the equivalent of a 24" x 36" sheet which has a title block. The original drawing has to be scaled down to 1/8" scale. Appendix A contains an excerpt from the "course packet" which was designed to guide the students through the process of externally referencing a scaled site plan onto a blank 24" x 36" sheet containing a title block template. From this new file, which is placed in "paper space," the drawing is being readied for plotting. The process of reading the course packet, while more germane to the student's assignment compared to a software manual, is nevertheless time consuming to comprehend. Some of the finer points, features, and thus additional images are left out in order to streamline the document.

Prior to utilizing screen capture software, students would frequently ask the instructor, oftentimes individually, to demonstrate a particular aspect of the software or assignment discussed in lecture. The need to record these lectures appeared. Videotaping a TV screen or computer monitor possesses image synchronization issues. The lead author had used ScreenCam, on occasion, in the past for instructions to individuals, but the movies were short due to limited disk capacities and slow computer and Internet connections.

Possibly due to the increasing power of computers, the nature of software, increasingly sophisticated assignments, time constraints, and learning behaviors, students are more apt to ask the instructor to "show me." There is little incentive to produce time-consuming manuals or course instructions addressing software that becomes dated. Employing ScreenCam, what Lotus calls a "show-and-tell" software, permits the instructor to record a multimedia lecture involving any software, even multiple applications including the use of the Internet. Students can review the movie at any time and from remote locations. They can replay the movie to increase retention or step through their assignment by alternately pausing the movie and executing parts of their assignment to its conclusion. The audio feature allows the instructor to stress important or difficult software eccentricities the students will have to maneuver through.

Producing your first instructional movie can occur without reading a software manual. The lead author never has. The process to record and play

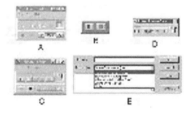

Figure 1. Miscellaneous ScreenCam dialog boxes

back the movie, and the software's appearance, is comparable to a VCR's. To create a movie the application is opened and a tool bar appears (see Figure 1A). The recording may be audio only, video only, or both. Adding text-based captions to narrate a movie for users without audio devices is possible but seems tedious. Given the cost of today's audio devices it doesn't warrant producing a silent movie. Student interest and attentiveness would consequently become an issue.

By pressing the red record button (the lower left button with the round dot), screen activity and audio is recorded (note the lower button towards the right has an icon of a video camera and a microphone). While the movie is being made, the tool bar in Figure 1A disappears and a smaller red record and red pause button, just like a VCR, appears unobtrusively (see Figure 1B). The movie can be paused and can have multiple segments. When finished recording the movie, the red stop button (rectangular button on the right in Figure 1B) is pressed and the original tool bar appears with the green play button (the button with triangle above the red record button) highlighted (see Figure 1C). Pressing the green triangular play button will play the untitled movie and a new tool bar appears (see Figure 1D). As the movie is being played, a green meter bar indicates the relative length of the movie. You may pause the movie, rewind the movie to the beginning, skip to the next segment of the movie, fast forward the movie, stop the movie, or

Figure 2. A sample ScreenCam movie

change the volume of the sound in this tool bar. If you are satisfied with the movie just recorded, you may save the movie in various formats (see Figure 1E). The movie can be saved as a ScreenCam movie (*.scm) which requires the playing computer to have the ScreenCam software, or the movie can be saved as a stand-alone movie which has an executable extension (*.exe), as a video for windows (*.avi), or as a sound only file (*.wav). Saving the file as a ScreenCam movie requires the playing computer to have the ScreenCam software. There exists a freely distributed ScreenCam player. This file type is

PAUL A. WEBER • WILLIAM C. EPSTEIN

the smallest compared to the *.exe and *.avi. The *.exe appears to add about 1 MB to a file size. A *.avi is larger yet.

A sample ScreenCam movie for plotting an externally referenced site plan drawing can be viewed by clicking Figure 2. Appendix A contains an excerpt from the CM 211 course packet emulated by the ScreenCam movie above. Students access the movies through a local area network (LAN) (see Figure 3). The movies are saved as executable files so they can be accessed by any computer; of course a sound card and speakers or headphones are required to hear the audio.

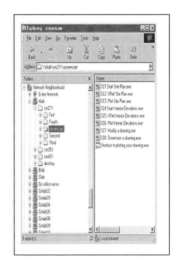

Students were informally asked to rate which instructional methods they feel work best with their learning styles in order to learn AutoCAD and to complete the assignment. The questions and their mean scores, on a 7-point Lickert scale, are reported in Table 1. The course does not use an AutoCAD manual, a

Figure 3. Movies are accessed by students via a LAN

third party "how to" manual, or video tapes for instructional purposes, but it is assumed students are aware of these implements and have an opinion of them. The course packet and the ScreenCam movies are designed specifically for the course assignments. Figure 4 illustrates student preference for multimedia and assignment-specific aids based on the mean reported in Table 1.

Anecdotally, a number of students liked the availability of the movie and the course packet concurrently. They appreciated how to maneuver through the software dialog boxes following mouse movements combined with an audio explanation of the features and pitfalls. A number reported that they learn faster with ScreenCam instead of the course packet. A few students wished the ScreenCam movies were available to use at home, possibly available on their own CD-ROM. One student appreciated the idea of having one machine to learn the assignment in a multimedia format and to do the assignment suggesting that watching a video tape utilizing a VCR then doing the assignment on the computer is less convenient compared to employing a single device. Another student thought that learning computer software "on paper" (packets, manuals) is not as effective as using the computer which forces you to apply the knowledge and learn by doing. Numerous

Table 1: Student rating of various approaches used to learn CAD software

Question No.	Question	Mean
1	Read a manual published by AutoDesk (software manual)	3.24
2	Read a "how to" manual published by someone else (ex.: AutoCAD for Dummies)	4.06
3	Read items created and printed in the "course packet"	5.89
4	View ScreenCam movies	6.17
5	Watch a video tape using a VCR and TV	4.83

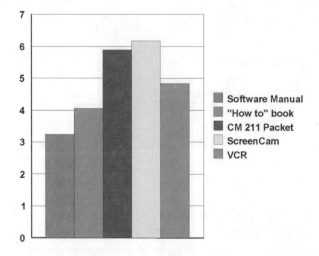

Figure 4. Student rating of various implements used to learn software

students liked the concept of possessing both the movie and the course packet. One student reported that flipping through pages in the course packet is slow, and sometimes the words in the packets, possibly technical jargon or isolated words from the activity on the computer screen, can sometimes be thorny.

Conclusions

The simplicity of screen recording software and its acceptance by students can alter the way software is typically taught. Utilizing multi-media technology can quicken the learning process, retain student interest, and improve an instructor's productivity. Reducing the amount of time to prepare and teach fundamental aspects of software frees up time for more sophisticated aspects and other applications. Instant access to multimedia tutorials improves the students' effectiveness, accommodates their schedules, and promotes self learning. Student reaction to this tool has been immediate and very positive. Out-of-class questions from students have been be sharply pared. Its simplicity creates flexibility so emerging and situational questions have been quickly addressed and the new information disseminated. Producing a screen recording movie to teach software requires little up-front costs in time and money. Since software changes rapidly, not much is lost when movies become dated because new movies can be made with little effort.

Appendix 1. Excerpt from the CM 211 course packet explaining how to import a drawing into a new drawing

Importing your drawing:

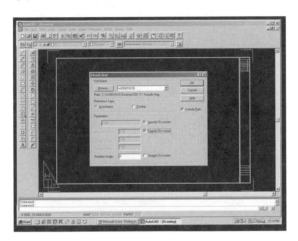

In paper space, import your site plan drawing utilizing Xreference.
Press INSERT, EXTERNAL REFERENCE, ATTACH, look in to the drive (A, C, . . .) your drawing file (?.dwg) is located.
Once you've found the file in the *Select File to Attach* dialog box
Press OPEN
Substitute the XREFl block name with a new block name (such as lastnamesiteplan)
When the Attach Xref dialog box comes on, check the lower box
Specify on-screen where the X Scale Factor, Y Scale Factor, and Z Scale Factor boxes are. They should then turn gray.
Press OK
Read the command lines at the bottom of the computer screen The computer should be asking for an insertion point of your drawing on this new sheet of paper. Place the insertion point towards the lower middle part of the drawing (see cross hair below).

You are inserting your site plan drawing at its coordinate 0,0 so your drawing will appear on the right hand side of the sheet. This will leave room for a future Interior Elevation drawing on the left hand side of the paper.

The computer will ask for the scale factor (look at the bottom of your screen). Since we want the drawing to be 1/8" scale; 8 x 12 (inches per foot) = 96. We want the drawing to be 1/96th the size of the actual building.

Enter 1/96 and press Enter

Press Enter again for a 1/96 scale in the Y direction (it's the same as X by default).

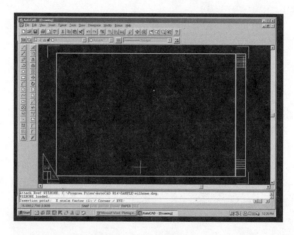

Your site drawing should appear on the sheet. Move it (it will move as one block of info) as needed.

Save the file.

References

Cohen, V. L. (1998). Multimedia cognition: Training teachers about using technology. *Proceedings of the SITE* 98. Washington, DC.

Kolb, D. A. (1984). *Experiential learning: Experience as the source of learning and development.* Englewood Cliffs, NJ: Prentice-Hall.

Montgomery, S. (1995). Addressing diverse learning styles through the use of multimedia: Material and energy balance. *Proceedings of the ASEE/IEEE Frontiers in Education 95 Conference.* Atlanta, GA.

Soloman, G. (1997). Of mind and media: How culture's symbolic forms affect learning and thinking. *Phi Delta Kappan, 78*(5), 375–380.

Using Information Technology in Community-Based Psychiatric Nursing Education: The SJSU/NT Project

Phyllis M. Connolly and Victoria L. Elfrink
San José State University

Information management is growing in importance in health care delivery. Practitioners, case managers, third-party payers, and health care policy makers are increasingly basing their health care decisions on timely and relevant clinical data. Since 1997, San José State University nursing students have been using the Nightingale Tracker, a computerized clinical communication system, to document client care, electronically transfer clinical information to their instructors, and maintain a systematic method for storing clinical data for further use in program planning, prediction of health care trends, and other research endeavors. Clearly, the potential increase in quality care makes the investment in this information technology (IT) experience worthwhile. Faculty are changing the education paradigm to a learning paradigm, preparing practitioners who can use IT in the current managed care environment to monitor costs while improving care—valuable skills to possess in this ever-evolving health care delivery system.

Background and Need

Dramatic changes in the health care system, including the advancement of information technology (IT), decreased hospital stays, and an emphasis on reducing costs, have shifted the site of care to the community. Changes in health care delivery have led to a major restructuring of clinical nursing education. Many nurse educators are shifting their clinical experiences to the community and adjusting to the challenges posed by an environment that differs from hospitals not only in the way that health care decisions are made but also in the manner that practice can be supervised.

Health care decisions once confined to hospitals under the supervision of the physician are taking place in the patient's home with the support of community-based health care professionals, including nursing students. Because students may be required to make decisions and document care without the benefit of an instructor immediately on site, there is a need for real-time communication between the student at the point of care and other supervisory health care personnel.

Phyllis M. Connolly and Victoria L. Elfrink, "Using Information Technology in Community-Based Psychiatric Nursing Education: The SJSU/NT Project." *Home Health Care Management & Practice,* 14(5), 2002: 344–52. Copyright © 2002 by Sage Publications. Reprinted by permission of Sage Publications, Inc.

As the health care delivery system advances to include a greater focus on quality of care (Martin & Martin, 1997), there is also an increased need for timely access to data that focus not only on disease management but also on health promotion and prevention with a focus on outcomes. This need is particularly challenging in the area of community-based mental health.

Quality of care issues often focus solely on treating the psychosocial needs of clients; however, study findings indicate that community-based mental health clients are also at risk for physiological and environmental problems (Chisholm et al., 1997; Haber & Billings, 1995). The need for cost-effective community-based mental health care requires relevant measurements of a holistic range of client outcomes.

Additional studies have shown that individuals burdened with serious mental illness may possess a myriad of physiological problems. Specifically, mental health clients often have limited access to necessary health care services, may suffer from chronic physical problems, may be neglectful of physiological and self-care needs, and may not obtain help for their physiological problems because their psychiatric diagnosis interferes with appropriate identification and treatment (U.S. Department of Health and Human Services, 1999). Furthermore, persons with schizophrenia may have increased risk of cardiovascular disorders, including myocardial infarction and coronary artery disease. Most important, one in five persons with a brain disorder has a medical problem that may be causing or exacerbating his or her psychiatric condition (Jeste, Akiko, Lindamer, & Lacro, 1996). In a study sponsored by the National Alliance for the Mentally Ill, 33% of the 552 consumers of psychiatric services studied reported their physical health status as fair or poor (Uttaro & Mechanic, 1994).

Other studies also support San José State University's (SJSU's) beliefs about the clients with serious mental illnesses who are served by their Nurse Managed Centers. For example, persons with brain disorders experience mortality rates that are twice that of the general population. In addition, 50% have known medical disorders, and 35% have undiagnosed medical disorders (Jeste et al., 1996).

As mental health care delivery increasingly shifts into the community, the challenge of accessing timely information to make informed decisions grows. The greater use of IT in both the delivery of care and clinical education of students offers a solution to this dilemma; however, it requires a shift in current work practices.

In response, FITNE, Inc. (formerly the Fuld Institute for Technology in Nursing Education), undertook a 3-year research and development project related to community nursing. Funded in part by the Helene Fuld Health Trust, the project named the Nightingale Tracker (NT) was field tested in 1996 and 1997 and released in the spring of 1998. The resulting computer-based electronic communication system is designed to assist in the day-to-day supervision of students in the community by (a) providing a structured and timely method for communicating clinical information and (b) maintaining a reliable, valid, and efficient mechanism for collecting, storing, retrieving, and aggregating community client-care data.

The NT project is particularly relevant to community-based mental health education because it incorporates the Omaha System, a standardized, reliable, and valid method for documenting and managing patient care. The system includes a rating scale for measuring outcomes (Elfrink & Martin, 1996; Martin & Martin, 1997) based on the client's knowledge (what the client knows), behavior (what the client does), and status (the client's physiological or psychological well-being).

The system has been used extensively and researched in a variety of settings. For example, the Omaha System is being evaluated as a tool to link standardized languages from acute care settings to home care (Bowles, 1999). The system is also being integrated into home care agencies with a required computerized documentation system, Outcome and Assessment Information Set (OASIS) (Westra & Solomon, 1999). Few data are available, however, that describe the Omaha System's use in community-based mental health settings.

This article describes the process and outcomes of an IT project geared toward helping baccalaureate nursing students practicing in the community mental health setting at San José State University maintain closer contact with their instructor and document their care in a more efficient and effective manner. The article also describes the details of the NT project implementation, informatics preparedness of the student subjects, focus of the community-based course, profile of the client base with serious mental illness, the outcomes findings for this chronic population as documented using the NT system, and the added benefits gained by students and faculty.

The NT Technology

The NT is an automated point-of-care information system that uses a client-server architecture. A handheld computer, the DataRover 840, is used to access, document, and communicate care while at the point of service. The cutting-edge technology of the NT handheld computer enables real-time voice and data communication between students and their instructor before, during, or after a student-client encounter (Elfrink & Martin, 1996). Client care data are transmitted via a telephone line to the modem attached to the server hardware. The visit information is then further processed as either a summarized report delivered via an e-mail message or as an update to the actual client's clinical record. The server acts as a data repository for the clinical record, an e-mail program for clinical messaging, and a host for local Web documents such as reference materials, procedures, and protocols.

Client data are protected from unauthorized access in a number of ways. The handheld computer maintains a procedure for entering a user access code each time the unit is turned on. Data are protected while in transit through a closed communication link to the NT Server using a separate dial-in number. In addition, client records have an identifying number or code that is known only to the student and instructor accessing the record, thereby further insuring that the information is accessed only by authorized personnel.

The NT project was timely for San José State's School of Nursing because a paper version of the Omaha System already had been integrated into the curriculum in a required process course. Moreover, the ongoing use of the paper documentation of the Omaha System within the School of Nursing's Nurse Managed Centers provided additional support of the next step to the electronic record.

The system is also compatible with the documentation needs of other disciplines and is currently being used in the SJSU's Transdisciplinary Collaboration Project with Communication Disorders faculty and students (Connolly & Novak, 2000). Training of speech pathology students in the use of the NT expanded the collaborative opportunities from the Transdisciplinary Collaboration Project among nursing and speech pathology graduate students and faculty.

NT/Mental Health Clinical Education Project

From the fall of 1998 until the fall of 2000, 45 undergraduate students and 1 graduate student participated in the SJSU NT/Mental Health Clinical Education Project. The project not only sought to gather data about student users' reactions to using IT at the point of care but also focused on the nature and quality of the documentation performed by the student users.

Setting

The setting for this project was SJSU, the oldest campus in the California state system of 22 campuses. There is a student body of 26,628: 63% are between the ages of 20 and 29, and 24% are older than 30. The ethnic profile includes the following: African Americans, 4.3%; American Indian/Alaskan, 7%; Asian, 30.2%; Filipino, 6.6%; Mexican American, 10.3%; other Hispanic, 3.7%; Pacific Islander, 0.5%; White, 31.3%; and unknown, 12.4%. The majority of students commute and come from the Bay Area.

All students have free Internet accounts; however, many do not have computers at home to take full advantage of IT, especially to e-mail faculty. Although the university resides within the well-known Silicon Valley, it has only recently begun to update its infrastructure to support the technology that is driving both teaching and learning. Many of the difficulties in instituting and maintaining the NT system are slowly resolving (Connolly, Huynh, & Gomey-Moreno, 1999). A key driving force has been the creative and forward thinking of key faculty (The Nightingale Tracker Field Test Nurse Team [NTFTNT], 1999, 2000).

The School of Nursing student population generally consists of 450 undergraduate and 100 actively enrolled graduate students from very diverse cultural and ethnic backgrounds. The undergraduate programs include a generic baccalaureate and advanced placement for licensed vocational nurses and registered nurses. The graduate programs include the clinical nurse specialist in gerontology and school nursing, the family nurse practitioner, and the educator and administrator options. Furthermore, the School of Nursing operates six Nurse Managed Centers, which were the sites for the NT project.

The school is known for its innovations in integrating a community-based curriculum. Specifically, all students have at least 7 and a half weeks in medical surgical home care and at least one obstetrical and pediatrics home care experience prior to the community health nursing semester. The Omaha System is taught as part of a process course prior to the semester in which the NT is used. Typically, 60 generic students are enrolled in the psychiatric/mental health clinical and 90 (includes the 60 generic students) are enrolled in the community health nursing clinical courses.

Participant Profile

Student user participants. The age of the students ranged from 22 to 46; most were commuters. All students had experience with e-mail, 50% had experience with electronic patient documentation (prior hospital experiences), and 55% had a formal course on computers; however, half of those students only had courses in high school.

Client participants. The clients served through the Nurse Managed Centers included ethnically diverse persons with serious mental illnesses, schizophrenia, bipolar disorder, major depression, and dual diagnoses. Their ages ranged from 18 to 65 with a higher proportion of males to females.

Procedures

Initially, the NT was used in the psychiatric/mental health clinical portion of the Transdisciplinary Collaboration Project (Connolly & Novak, 2000). Subsequently, it was integrated into one of the community health nursing clinical education experiences; all experiences were under the auspices of the SJSU Nurse Managed Centers.

Consent forms were obtained by the agency for clients receiving services as part of the project. Consent forms were also obtained for clients receiving services directly at the Nurse Managed Centers. The project proposal was also submitted to the SJSU Protection of Human Subjects prior to implementing the project. Student participants signed consent forms for participation in the project.

Student evaluation tools used included the project data instruments: NT user characteristics; NT impact questionnaire, pre- and postteaching, 6 weeks and final; weekly NT logs; training session evaluation tool; and course satisfaction tool. The data were collected and sent to FITNE for analysis. Details on the training, implementation, and student user reactions were published earlier (Connolly et al., 1999).

Client data were retrieved from the documentation of student users. Data from the records of 30 different clients who received 481 episodes of care from the fall of 1998 through the fall of 2000 were accessed and analyzed according to guidelines for documenting Omaha System problems, interventions, and outcomes.

Study Findings

The Omaha Nursing Classification System (Martin & Scheet, 1992a) is a model for clinical practice, documentation, and data management. There are 43 problems organized within four domains—environmental, psychosocial, physiological, and health-related behaviors within the system. The Omaha System includes a rating scale on three subscales: Knowledge (K), the ability of the client to remember and interpret information; Behavior (B), the observable responses, actions, or activities of the client fitting the occasion or purpose; and Status (S), the condition of the client in relation to objective and subjective defining characteristics. The rating scale ranges from 1 to 5, where a rating of 1 indicates no knowledge, behavior that is not appropriate, and extreme signs and symptoms, and a rating of 5 indicates superior knowledge, consistently appropriate behavior, and no signs and symptoms. Reliability and validity of the Omaha Classification System has been established with extensive testing (Martin & Scheet, 1992a; Martin, Scheet, & Stegman, 1993).

The intervention scheme reflects nursing actions or activities in four hierarchical levels: health teaching, guidance, and counseling; treatments and procedures; case management; and surveillance (Martin, Leak, & Aden, 1992, p. 48). Modifiers and signs and symptoms follow the domains and problems. Targets (62 are identified) are defined as objects of nursing intervention activities. Last, the system includes client-specific information that may be needed for detailed information in the client's plan. For example, the assessment for one of the clients under Domain IV, health-related behaviors, revealed a problem with personal hygiene, that is, problem number 38, in which the modifier for this problem was "deficit," and the signs and symptoms indicated inadequate laundering of clothing, inadequate bathing, body odor, inadequate shampooing and combing of hair, and inadequate mouth care. The rating for this problem was a 2 (minimal knowledge), 2 (rarely appropriate behavior), and 2 (severe signs and symptoms). A pocket guide is available for users of the system, and definitions are available that guide the application of the system (Martin & Scheet, 1992b). The care plan for this resident included interventions under health teaching, guidance, and counseling, and the specific targets were personal care and behavior modification.

Omaha System Problems and Interventions

Thirty-four of the 44 Omaha problems were identified (see Table 1). This finding reflects prior cited studies on the health care needs of persons with psychiatric disorders. Three of the most frequent Omaha problems identified under the psychosocial domain were interpersonal relationship (50%), social contact (44%), and emotional stability (24%). The most common interventions for the problems were health teaching/guidance/counseling and surveillance and, with less frequency, case management. The lower use of case management was expected because the majority of clients were under the formal case management of the mental health system.

Outcomes for Clients

Omaha System outcome data were kept for clients indicating positive changes in rating scales from the services received during the various semesters. Table 2 includes a sample of the outcomes on knowledge, behavior, and status for specific clients with specific problems. The changes are based on the interventions provided by the student; students worked with a client during the 15-week semester. These findings are consistent with the results of aggregate data collected in which an average of ratings in knowledge, behavior, and status for all contacts for a specific problem were analyzed since 1995.

Processes of Care Delivery and Communication

Using the automated point-of-care information system with the tracker facilitated the treatment of at-risk physiological health care issues such as hypertension. Timely information regarding indicators of blood pressure readings and response to the medication was communicated quickly to physicians. In addition, students who identified residents with at-risk blood pressure readings could immediately transmit that information to the nurse health care coordinator for the agency. Altering referral patterns that improve access to primary care was yet another outcome of the project.

Table 1. Identified Omaha problems

Domain	Problem
I. Environmental	01. Income
	02. Sanitation
	03. Residence
	04. Neighborhood/workplace safety
II. Psychosocial	06. Communication with community resources
	07. Social contact
	08. Role change
	09. Interpersonal relationships
	10. Spiritual distress
	11. Grief
	12. Emotional stability
	13. Human sexuality
	14. Caretaking/parenting
III. Physiological	19. Hearing
	20. Vision
	21. Speech and language
	22. Dentition
	23. Cognition
	24. Pain
	26. Integument
	27. Neuro-musculo-skeletal function
	28. Respiration
	29. Circulation
	30. Digestion-hydration
	31. Bowel function
	32. Genito-urinary function
IV. Health-related behaviors	35. Nutrition
	36. Sleep and rest patterns
	37. Physical activity
	38. Personal hygiene
	39. Substance use
	40. Family planning
	41. Health care supervision
	42. Prescribed medication regimen

We found that we could transmit patient reports quickly to case managers and other health care providers improving the outcomes of the services received. For example, on several occasions, once the student completed the documentation from a visit with a client, there was a need to arrange further care with a physician. The report of these findings was faxed immediately to the care provider. This reduced the time between identification of the problem and the visit to the appropriate health care provider.

Table 2. Initial and final Omaha ratings for sample of clients

CCF # (Client)		Problem	Initial Ratings	Final Ratings
9075		Social contact	K 1 B 2 S 2	K 3 B 3 S 3
9548		Circulation	K 2 B 3 S 1	K 3 B 4 S 5
9547		Interpersonal relationships	K 2 B 2 S 2	K 4 B 4 S 4
9012	Collaboration speech pathology	Speech	K 2 B 2 S 3	K 4 B 4 S 4
9012	Collaboration speech pathology	Personal hygiene	K 2 B 2 S 3	K 4 B 4 S 4
9523		Nutrition	K 4 B 1 S 1	K 4 B 2 S 2

Implications

The Need for Holistic Care in Community-Based Mental Health Care Delivery and Education

The findings suggested that clients had multiple physical and mental health problems requiring primary health care, supporting the importance for redesigning a primary health care system for this vulnerable population (Chisholm et al., 1997). Another related implication is the need for sustaining social support and long-term rehabilitation for persons with brain disorders (Palmer-Erbs & Anthony, 1995; U.S. Department of Health and Human Services, 1999).

Evidence-based nursing education trends based on the project indicated a need to increase the use of our Nurse Managed Centers, which provide an opportunity for continuity of care for persons with chronic health problems. In addition, there was a need to assess the curriculum for relevance in preparing students to meet the needs of primary care.

Enhancement of Patient Referrals

One continuous barrier for efficient and effective referrals and care is the lack of coordination and access to client information. In fact, a major barrier to effective care is the current funding approach that separates mental health care funds from medical care. For example, reimbursement guidelines for the county pharmacy limit prescriptions for mental health clients to psychotropic medications only. Therefore, the client must see another physician, increasing costs. This situation challenges the client to manage his or her own health care in a complex system. Because these clients are already at a disadvantage due to a psychiatric or mental health problem, this may also decrease the probability of follow-up regarding their physical condition.

The collaboration facilitated in the project enhanced and altered referrals, increasing the quality of care for the clients who were at risk for costly health care problems. The following is an example of an actual case that illustrates the importance of using information to improve referrals to preserve the quality of client care. (Some identifying information has been changed for protection of client anonymity.)

> J. R. was living in a boarding house and, already receiving mental health care, had just been diagnosed with diabetes. There was concern that impaired cognitive processes as a result of his psychiatric diagnosis (schizophrenia) might interfere with retaining all the information and instructions that he was given to perform his own testing for glucose, keep a journal of the results, and report back to the physician. The student had already been working with the client; thus, the baseline data were already entered into the NT system. The health coordinator e-mailed the faculty member requesting that when the student visited the client, she work with him to reinforce the teaching not only for testing his glucose but also for dietary changes. The student faxed the results of the glucose testing to the physician's office; the client avoided a trip to the physician's office as well as the cost of an office visit. The student was also able to review the protocol for diabetic teaching on the NT Web browser. At the end of the clinical experience, the student e-mailed the results of her visit to the faculty member for review. The faculty member reviewed the documentation and sent the student a relevant patient education Web site that she could view and bring the information to the client during the next visit. The student's plan included taking the resident to the university library to show him how to access the health education Web site for himself.

This case study illustrates how extremely important it is to have the ability to communicate referral information with the targeted at-risk population, persons with psychiatric disabilities. Because of the therapeutic relationship with the student and the nurse from the agency, the client was much more likely to allow an assessment, and that information could be conveyed to the appropriate health care provider, enhancing the appropriate interventions in a timely manner.

Other Project Outcomes

Using the NT assisted in faculty recognizing the need to shift the education paradigm to a learning paradigm (Barr & Tagg, 1995; Batson & Bass, 1996). It is essential that educators and health care providers in the next millennium possess information and communication skills in Web research, data management, and documentation that include the use of standardized vocabularies and electronic information processing (Elfrink & Martin, 1996); using the NT facilitates meeting those future workforce needs. Based on our pilot of 3 years, we have some qualitative and quantitative self-report and anecdotal data that faculty and student involvement with the point-of-care technology increases teaching effectiveness and learning outcomes (Connolly et al., 1999; NTFTNT, 1999, 2000). Specifically, the students

1. gained electronic information-processing skills,
2. increased efficiency in documentation,
3. participated in a unique experience with cutting-edge technology,
4. are better prepared for the IT-intensive job market because of increased confidence in using technology and increased use of the Internet, and
5. improved the delivery of health care to a disenfranchised population.

Additional outcomes for students included (a) increased communication with faculty; (b) participation in faculty research; (c) improved client care; (d) increased professionalism, as viewed by the clients; (e) an increased understanding of the relationship between research and practice; (f) publication and presentation opportunities; and (g) university awards and recognition. Student use of the NT system also facilitated the following course and program objectives:

- uses information technology to improve care for psychiatric-mental health clients and at-risk populations,
- uses the World Wide Web to obtain information to improve client care, and
- employs nursing informatics at the basic practice level to improve health care delivery and outcome evaluation.

Faculty Outcomes

Faculty and student involvement with the NT point-of-care technology increased teaching effectiveness and learning outcomes in this project, as cited in previous studies (Connolly et al., 1999; Elfrink & Martin, 1996; NTFTNT, 1999, 2000). Faculty reported specific improvements in evaluating students because of better access to student documentation and better supervision because of faster communication. They demonstrated scholarly activities in research, publications, presentations, grant submissions, and their own technology skills. In addition, collaboration opportunities increased outside of the university.

Project Challenges

Training of faculty and students requires additional time. A decision has to be made whether the training times come from the clinical course or through independent studies. This was a challenge in our project implementation. Initially, some release time was available for one faculty member; however, that was not sustained and has affected the ability to fully invest the time needed. In addition, training and retaining a knowledgeable technical support person was and remains a continual problem.

Other project challenges include the following:

- Maintenance of the equipment. The data in the handheld computers must be purged from the handheld computers, and new accounts must be established with each new user group. Server data should be backed up and the system constantly monitored for potential security threats.

- Phone lines in the clinical area. Because the NT requires an analog phone line, it was also necessary to install a separate outside line in the School of Nursing's Learning Center to troubleshoot tracker problems and allow students access to sending and receiving data when they were on campus. Some students lived outside the calling area; thus, having the phone access for them on campus allowed them to participate in the project.

- Involvement of more faculty. Assignments change, and trained faculty were not consistently assigned to courses in which the tracker would be used.

- Funding. Although multiple grants were submitted for both internal and external funding, none were funded.

Implications for the Future

Training of additional faculty and a technical support person is a high priority. The NT needs to be integrated into other courses and at other levels in the curriculum. Resources need to be added to the Web browser. Additional trackers will be needed, and funding resources need to be secured.

Future research for the use of the automated point-of-care information system is also a priority at SJSU. Research is being considered to investigate

- understanding more fully the variables that contribute to user frustration,

- distinguishing among factors that promote better student-faculty communication,

- describing differences in students' critical thinking between IT point-of-care users and nonusers,

- examining the effectiveness of referrals facilitated by point of service information technologies, and

- measuring the effects of increased collaboration on client outcomes.

Conclusion

It is essential that educators and health care providers in the next millennium possess information and communication skills in Web research, data management, and documentation that include the use of standardized vocabularies and electronic information processing. Using IT at the point of care helps to develop these needed skills.

The NT is used for clinical nursing education; we believe that increased use of applications such as the NT in education will promote IT use in the service area. Student users will bring new IT clinical experiences into their new positions after graduation, thereby potentially increasing the diffusion of point-of-care documentation and the electronic health care record in service. Clearly, the potential increase in quality care makes the investment in this technology experience worthwhile. We are working to prepare practitioners who can use IT in the current managed care environment to monitor costs while improving care-valuable skills to possess in this ever-evolving health care delivery system.

References

Barr, R., & Tagg, J. (1995). From teaching to learning: A new paradigm for undergraduate education. *Change, 27*(6), 13–25.

Batson, T., & Bass, R. (1996). Primacy of process: Teaching and learning in the computer age. *Change, 28*(2), 42–47.

Bowles, K. H. (1999, Winter). The Omaha System as a potential bridge between hospital and home care. *On-Line Journal of Nursing Informatics, 3*(1). Retrieved from http://cac.psu.edu/~dxm12/ojni.html

Chisholm, M., Howard, P. B., Boyd, M. A., Clement, J. A., Hendrix, M. J., & Reiss-Brennan, B. (1997). Quality indicators for primary mental health within managed care: A public health focus. *Archives of Psychiatric Nursing, 11*(4), 167–181.

Connolly, P. M., Huynh, M. T., & Gomey-Moreno, M. J. (1999, Winter). On the cutting edge or over the edge? Implementing the Nightingale Tracker. *On-Line Journal of Nursing Informatics, 3*(1). Retrieved from http://cac.psu.edu/~dxm12/ojni.html

Connolly, P. M., & Novak, J. (2000). Teaching collaboration: A demonstration project. *Journal of American Psychiatric Nurses Association, 6*(6), 1–8.

Elfrink, V., & Martin, K. (1996). Educating for nursing practice: Point of care technology. *Healthcare Information Management, 10*(2), 81–89.

Haber, J., & Billings, C. (1995). Primary mental health care: A model for psychiatric-mental health nursing. *Journal of the American Psychiatric Nurses Association, 1*(5), 154–163.

Jeste, D. V., Akiko, J. G., Lindamer, L., & Lacro, J. (1996). Medical comorbidity in schizophrenia. *Schizophrenia Bulletin, 22*, 413–430.

Martin, K., Leak, G., & Aden, C. (1992). The Omaha System: A research-based model for decision making. *Journal of Nursing Administration, 22*(11), 47–52.

Martin, K., & Martin, D. (1997). How can the quality of nursing practice be measured? In J. C. McCloskey & H. K. Grace (Ed.), *Current issues in nursing* (5th ed., pp. 315–321). St. Louis, MO: Mosby.

Martin, K., & Scheet, N. (1992a). *The Omaha System: Applications for community health nursing.* Philadelphia: Saunders.

Martin, K., & Scheet, N. (1992b). *The Omaha System: A pocket guide for community health nursing.* Philadelphia: Saunders.

Martin, K., Scheet. N., & Stegman, M. R. (1993). Home health clients: Characteristics, outcomes of care, and nursing interventions. *American Journal of Public Health, 83*(12), 1730–1734.

The Nightingale Tracker Field Test Nurse Team. (1999). Designing an information technology application for use in community-focused nursing education. *Computers in Nursing, 17*(2), 73–81,

The Nightingale Tracker Field Test Nurse Team. (2000). A comparison of teaching strategies for integrating information technology into clinical nursing education. *Nurse Educator, 25*(2), 136–144.

Palmer-Erbs, V., & Anthony, W. (1995). Incorporating psychiatric rehabilitation principles into mental health nursing: An opportunity to develop a full partnership among nurses, consumers, and families. *Journal of Psychosocial Nursing, 33*(3), 36–44.

U.S. Department of Health and Human Services. (1999). *Mental health: A report of the Surgeon General.* Rockville, MD. Author.

Uttaro, T., & Mechanic, D. (1994). The NAMI consumer survey analysis of unmet needs. *Hospital and Community Psychiatry, 45*, 372–374.

Westra, B., & Solomon, D. (1999, Winter). The Omaha System: Bridging home care and technology. *On-Line Journal of Nursing Informatics, 3*(1). Retrieved from http://cac.psu.edu/~dxm12/ojni.html

Note

The success of the Nightingale Tracker project was made possible through the award as one of the Seven Centers of Excellence by FITNE. San José State University (SJSU), the Alpha Gamma Chapter of Sigma Theta Tau International, and Dean Michael Ego provided additional resources. SJSU faculty and staff MaryJo Gomey-Moreno, Burt Favero, Dave Kessler, and DaMany Harden provided support along with the FITNE staff. A special acknowledgement is made to the students who were the pioneers in the use of this cutting-edge technology as well as residents and staff from ALLIANCE for Community Care who supported us in this unique electronic communication system.

Integrating SAP R/3 Into a College of Business Curriculum: Lessons Learned

Gail Corbitt and James Mensching
California State University, Chico

Abstract

In the fall semester of 1996, California State University Chico was the first school in the U.S. to implement the SAP ERP system into its College of Business curriculum. While the effort so far has been very successful by almost any means of measurement, many challenges still remain. This paper presents the problems encountered by the college and the approaches taken to overcome these problems.

Five major areas of concern are identified. They include:

- forming a faculty team and then getting them to agree on how the ERP system should be incorporated into the curriculum, including the order of introducing courses into the curriculum;

- acquiring adequate funding to support all of the resources needed to implement a system of this magnitude, including funding for equipment, faculty training, new teaching facilities, etc.;

- setting up a technical infrastructure and a corresponding support team to install, monitor and administrate the ERP systems;

- properly managing the recruiting activities of companies recruiting the students, and

- retaining the faculty that have SAP experience in a competitive market that offers financial rewards well in excess of academic salaries.

All of these issues must be addressed to successfully implement an ERP system. However, our experience has been overwhelmingly successful and all of the hard work has had a significant academic return on our investment.

Introduction

"This is an academic environment, not a trade school." This quote is a paraphrased synopsis of the argument that goes on in academic environments

Gail Corbitt and James Mensching, "Integrating SAP R/3 into a College of Business Curriculum: Lessons Learned." *Information Technology and Management*, 1, 2000: 344–52. Reprinted by permission of the authors and the publisher.

when "products" are introduced into the curriculum. It represents the major veil of resistance that faculty face who want to bring software products into courses, especially software products on the scale of an ERP (Enterprise Resource Planning) system.

Recently ERPs have received much attention in the trade literature. This is not surprising since AMR Research Inc. reports that over half of the software revenue for licenses and maintenance come from the ERP world market. In Europe this figure is 64%.[1] With this kind of presence, it is no wonder that some faculty in colleges and universities are looking at ways to expose students to the ERP "wave" or at least to make students aware of what these software products can do. As with any change, there is resistance. For every faculty person who wants to implement an ERP into the academic environment, there is at least one person who does not want to do this. This paper is a summary of the implementation issues that one university faced when it implemented SAP, an example of an ERP system, into its curriculum and how the university overcame the challenges.

ERP Systems in the Classroom

Historically, business school curricula have been organized around the notion of functional areas. Option, major, emphasis are words that are used to describe a student's concentration of courses in one of the functional areas. On the other hand, the AACSB (American Association of Colleges and Schools of Business) accrediting body requires a certain number of business classes in each of the various functional areas in addition to an understanding of the global issues facing today's businesses. Most Colleges of Business require the student to take individual courses in Accounting, Marketing, Finance, Information Systems, etc. While students want to gain some depth in one area for job placement purposes, the school requires students to take a common body of knowledge in a variety of functional areas. Except for a few courses that are usually capstone, the business as a whole is not addressed, and even the capstone class may emphasize a company's role in a competitive market by having the students play a business simulation game. Understanding how the business operates internally and/or how Marketing and Accounting, for example, relate to each other are lost to most undergraduate students.

This stovepipe view of business by universities is in sharp contrast with the current business environment. Businesses are concerned with teamwork, cross-functional interactions, business processes, value chains, workflow management and supply chains. All of these concepts require students to look outside a narrow discipline or a specific functional area. Instead, they must understand how that functional area relates to the rest of the business.

For example, the 1995 Baldrige criteria for Educational Quality Awards indicate that the focus of education needs to be on the learning process, not the teaching process. Curriculum needs should be derived from "requirements of the marketplace and the responsibilities of citizenship. . . A learning-centered school needs to fully understand and translate marketplace and citizenship requirements into appropriate curricula."[2] Furthermore, these schools need to keep pace with the rapid changes in the marketplace.

The stovepipe approach is also in contrast to the current AACSB standards. The AACSB standards state that the students' understanding of global issues, and technological issues for that matter, should be interwoven throughout the curriculum. At the Graduate level, the standards go even further to indicate that core areas need to be integrated and MBA programs need to include the application of cross-functional approaches to organizational issues.[3] Most colleges are struggling with how best to achieve this integration when the faculty themselves are very narrowly and functionally focused. Some schools have used team teaching across disciplines or a modular approach to curriculum development as a way to achieve integration.

In order to find an alternative way to address this need for better integration, in 1996 a group of business faculty at California State University (CSU) Chico began to look for an ERP system that could provide a more concrete type of integration. That is, it was believed that by looking at the same organization from the perspective of the data, the students could better understand how the business processes actually work. Additionally, students at CSU Chico reported that they really did not understand how a business worked at the end of their degree program, so the faculty were focused on ways to help the students better understand the big picture of how a business worked.

About the same time, this group of faculty began to look at companies in the ERP market to see if any would offer the software to the university at no or a substantially reduced cost, and SAP was formulating its University Alliance Program in the Americas. The goals of the SAP University Alliance Program are to increase the number of students graduating from colleges and universities that are "job ready" with SAP knowledge, and to gain a presence in college and university curricula. CSU Chico became the first member of the SAP Academic Alliance Program in the Americas. As of March 1999, there were nearly 100 schools in the Alliance, with 62 in the USA, 21 in Canada and 12 in South and Central America. SAP indicates that it plans to grow the Americas Alliance to about 200 schools by 2001.

In many ways there are similarities in the computing system environments in education and legacy business systems. These computing environments involve multiple diverse systems that have incompatible architectures, inadequate and costly maintenance with weak or non-existent interfaces to other systems. In business, system architectural decisions are primarily based on rational decision making that involves a limited scope of activities. This limited scope produces systems that have robust functionality within the project scope, but fail to consider factors outside of the given system, such as integration of function and common human interfaces.

A slightly different situation exists in academics. System selection is usually based on the availability of hardware and software at extremely low prices. Except in multiple section courses that are taught by more than one professor, the professor makes the software selection. In some cases, the installation and maintenance of the systems are the responsibility of the professor teaching the course. In this environment, any consideration of integrating with other existing systems or common GUI interfaces is usually beyond the scope of any one course. As in business, we believe that an ERP system can reduce maintenance costs, provide a common user interface and provide an integrated transaction-based learning environment for students in every business discipline.

Hence, the objectives of CSU Chico in joining the alliance were to:

- provide students with a better understanding of how a business works within and across functional areas;

- pursue the University's agenda to "build a state-of-the-art technological learning environment";

- provide a uniform set of tools to be used in many classes;

- establish a common human (GUI) interface for multiple classes;

- create an infrastructure to integrate the Graduate and Undergraduate curricula in order to meet AACSB standards;

- provide students with high-demand market skills;

- provide faculty with up-to-date research and development opportunities,; and

- increase CSU Chico's visibility with business/industry leaders.

Overview of SAP R/3

SAP AG produces a client/server, enterprise information system, SAP R/3, which contains an integrated set of modules, designed in theory to support all aspects of a business including sales, human resource management, accounting, finance, manufacturing, material management and logistics. With the fundamental software modules, companies are able to use a wide variety of integrated business processes. The system operates in around 50 languages, currencies, accounting procedures and tax laws encountered by today's global organization.

SAP is being used to automate and manage the complete organization by a substantial number of the Fortune 500 corporations including Hewlett Packard, Chevron, Intel, Microsoft, Lockheed Martin, Anheuser-Busch, Coca Cola, Bristol-Myers-Squibb, and IBM. Companies are counting on their SAP systems to coordinate inventories, sales, marketing, cash flows, order processing, financial management, and much more. In addition, by interfacing SAP systems between companies, organizations are partnering to create electronic commerce and extended supply chains.[4] These systems are large and complex and by their very nature require both a focused, functional perspective and a business-wide perspective at the same time.

SAP has taken the ERP systems market by storm. SAP has over 30% of the market and according to Price-Waterhouse "[SAP's] position in the market has boosted SAP R/3 to the defacto industry standard."[5] While 1999 has seen an overall market slowdown (a mere 20% annual growth), AMR Research Inc. predicts that by 2003, the market will grow at an annual compounded growth rate of 32% to $66.6 billion.[6] So while there may be changes in the software as supply chain, information/knowledge management and E-commerce applications become standard features of the software, the ERP market overall is strong and is expected to grow in coming years.

Implemenation Challenges

In order to be successful at integrating the overall business curriculum at the micro as well as at the macro level, there are several factors at play. Each of these is discussed separately in subsequent paragraphs but the critical challenges facing the implementation team in order of importance are:

- the faculty team working together toward common goals;
- the financial support of the infrastructure;
- management of the technical infrastructure;
- management of the program's success; and
- retaining and energizing qualified faculty.

First and foremost, the faculty have to agree on the direction the ERP-related curriculum needs to take and then work together to build the courses. There are two related problems: (a) an internal pedagogical "battle" between academics and skills training, and (b) having tenured independent faculty work as a real team. In summarizing the experience with this first issue, some faculty are reluctant to bow to whims or needs, for that matter, of industry. The debate about the job of a faculty member centers on educating students versus teaching job skills. With respect to the second issue, one of our professors (R. Lea, Accounting Professor) summarized the situation in the following way: "Many of today's college professors view their faculty positions as independent contractors in the sense that as long as [we] teach the concepts outlined in the course and remain professionally qualified through our independent research efforts, [we] are free, in fact, encouraged, to work alone. As business schools respond to demands for more integrated curricula, [we] are being asked to work as a team to jointly produce something."

Originally, the team at CSU Chico consisted of five people from Information Systems, Accounting and Production Management. This group of five, with the Dean as the Project Manager, avoided direct, or postponed in some cases, the pedagogy arguments surrounding the first issue. Instead they focused on overcoming the second issue, that of the independent contractor perspective. They formed a faculty team based on a common set of pedagogical, research, and industry advantages and proceeded to add ERP into the curriculum. They acquired needed hardware through the Hewlett Packard Grant program, set up the system, attended SAP training classes and offered two experimental "special topics" classes in order to get things started.

Within a year, the group expanded to include more members and began meeting for an hour once a week to discuss issues, common goals, ways to accomplish separate agendas together, etc. Topics included: (a) when in the program and in which classes to teach the underlying concepts of ERP, (b) which course(s) should be prerequisites to the program, (c) which criteria should be used to evaluate the students for the program, (d) systems administration policies, etc. Over the three years, the group has grown from 5 (10%) to about roughly 12 (25%) of the full time faculty. All business school disciplines and traditional business functional areas are currently represented.

The pedagogical arguments, while side-stepped in the beginning, were tendered with student demand and corporate interest for the courses. In other words, we let the demand by students, interest by other universities, and the interest by industry and recruiters motivate faculty to join the team. The original SAP faculty gave free one-day workshops to the rest of the faculty to show them what the product did and how it was being used in other courses so they could more accurately evaluate its use in their courses. We were also careful to separate concepts from skills building. For example, SAP Accounting Transactions and Report Writing were taught as separate labs associated with regularly taught classes such as Accounting Information Systems and Cost Accounting. The approach was to offer electives or special sections of required courses that used the SAP system. The students overwhelmingly voted with their enrollment. Subsequently, enrollment in the traditional courses dropped significantly. As recruiting by industry became more intense for students with these skills, enrollment changes became more dramatic.

Simultaneously, a second challenge presented itself to the group in that the technical infrastructure to support the instructional objectives was formidable. CSU Chico is a state-funded teaching institution and there is no endowment or state money allocated to the Alliance Program. The initial cost of about $200,000 (and this does not include the cost of a database server) to build a dedicated lab, acquire the software, and have some travel money to support faculty training needed to be raised. Fortunately, we applied for and received a sizable equipment grant from Hewlett Packard that provided the database server. But the academic proposal submitted to SAP committed us to a dedicated computer lab that still needed to be built. We formed an Industry Partner Group and asked companies that recruit our students to help support the program financially.

Thanks to the foresight of Applied Materials, Bristol-Myers-Squibb, Chevron, Foundation Health, Nortel, and IBM, we have raised enough money to build our dedicated lab and operate the program for nearly three years. In addition, the College of Business had some discretionary funds donated for special projects such as this one that were used to supplement the industry donations. A final boost to our funding was winning a $100,000 grant from SAP in 1998 to do curriculum development. We are currently in the process of securing funding for subsequent years of operating dollars. In our case, industry investments continue to be critical to our success. Even though we use students to do all of our systems administration and hold our other expenses to a minimum, we simply cannot operate our SAP program without these funds. The ongoing operating budget for our program (excluding equipment which we still plan to fund through grants) is about $250,000 per year.

A third factor is the management model of the technical support for the program. Because we are self-funded and rely on student help to keep the systems up and running, the management of the systems administrators (all students) is done by a MIS faculty member. This administration effort started out of desperation, with plans to hire full time staff to administer the program. We have never been able to afford to move away from this "stop gap" model and interestingly, it enjoys reasonable success. We have budgeted release time for the faculty member who supervises the student group, but this is the first year that we have been able to grant the 25% release. The amount of work to administer these systems is substantial. The importance of this support structure cannot be overstated.

During the first year, as recruiters started hearing about our program, a fourth challenge surfaced. From the very first class in the fall 1996 semester, our SAP program was discovered by headhunters, recruiters, potential industry partners, potential students and most recently, other universities who have flocked to our doors for advice. This attention has been very difficult to address adequately because it requires countless hours of time by the existing faculty. Short of being rude, the MIS faculty members in particular have had to learn to manage their time both inside and outside of class. At first having recruiters as guest speakers for classes looked like a great benefit. But after initiating this activity in Fall 1996 we had to discontinue this practice. We felt little or no learning was going on in class because all recruiters wanted to talk about was job opportunities at their company. We have carefully screened in-class participation and now ask for a topic outline and some commitment to our program. For example, our industry partners are the only ones invited to present to our classes. The promotional demonstrations and the job opportunity discussions have been routed to student organizations where such topics are more appropriate.

A very serious fifth challenge arose starting with the first group of students graduating with SAP skills. The undergraduate students with SAP skills are being paid more money in their first year than most of our tenure track faculty. Almost all of the graduate students are being paid more to accept a position in industry than any of the existing faculty. While all of our faculty have continued in their teaching roles, some have been offered multiples of their academic salaries to switch to industry. This is an extremely serious threat to the stability of the program.

Coupled with the faculty retention issue is the related concern of burnout. After nearly three years of conducting classes using SAP software in a variety of disciplines, some of the original faculty team are at or near burnout. The commitment to learn this system, to integrate it with a heavy hands-on component into classes, and to stay abreast of the frequent updates and changes has been exhausting. All faculty who have integrated SAP into their classes have significant preparation each semester along with the ongoing demands to publish and teach other mainstream classes. The issue is how to keep the current faculty going under stressful workloads. One thing that has helped is rotating leaves whereby everyone gets time off but not all at the same time. In addition, summer faculty internships in industry are strongly encouraged. The internships have proven to be energizing as they provide ongoing training on the SAP system, a break from teaching and some added dollars to address the salary gap issue.

Results

The real question remains: Is all of this effort worth it? Have we met our original objectives in joining the alliance? Certainly the SAP Program at CSU Chico has contributed to the overall University objective of "building a state of the art technological learning environment." We have SAP running on a variety of presentation platforms, a dedicated lab where even Accelerated SAP tools are available for student use, and are currently bringing up a Java-Sun e-commerce lab that will hook into the SAP system. In

Table 1. Overview of courses (as of September 1999). (Dates indicate when course was introduced into the curriculum.)

Accounting and finance areas:

ACCT 110:	Cost accounting (Fall 1997)
ACCT 111:	Accounting information systems (Spring 1997)
ACCT 115:	Intermediate accounting (Fall 1998)
ACCT 230:	Financial planning, control and performance evaluation (Spring 1998)
FIN 155:	Financial management (Fall 1998)
POMG 145:	Cost accounting for POM majors (Fall 1997)

Production management area:

POMG 244:	Procurement systems (Spring 1997)
POMG 246:	Quality management (Spring 1999)
POMG 247:	Production planning and inventory control (Fall 1996)
POMG 248:	Production planning and control systems (Spring 1997)

Management information systems:

MINS 110:	Introduction to management information systems (Fall 1999)
MINS 208:	Systems analysis (Fall 1997)
MINS 218	Data warehousing (Fall 1999)
MINS 220:	ERP configuration and use (Spring 1998)
MINS 222:	ERP systems administration (Fall 1996)*
MINS 224:	ABAP programming (Spring 1997)
MINS 298C:	E-Commerce and SAP applications (Fall 1999)
MINS 320:	Graduate: Strategic information systems (Spring 1999)

Other planned courses:

Management:	Business processes and change course added to CORE (Spring 2000)
Marketing:	Sales logistics (Spring 2000)
	Project management (uses SAP PS module) (Spring 2000)
	Sales management (Fall 2000)
POMG:	Production management information systems (Spring 2000)

* This course started as configuration and systems administration combined—about 70% of the original course is now in MINS 222.

addition, we have four HP J series and three HP A-series servers so we can run a three-tiered landscape, and we have seven other smaller servers that we dedicate to web server, print spooling, and application server functions.

With respect to the objective to meet AACSB standards for integration, the re-accreditation report from the visiting team highlighted the SAP initiative as a strength of our Business program. Table 1 displays the courses that currently incorporate SAP into the class as an example of an integrated business case.

We have also met the objective of adding market value to our graduates. As a result of data received from our placement office for May 1996 through December 1998 graduates, we find that there is about a $10,000 difference between SAP-trained and non-SAP-trained graduates. In addition, while non-SAP students stay in California, about a third of the SAP students leave the state, confirming our feeling that for SAP skills, companies are coming from outside of California to recruit our students. The data from the placement office are incomplete because once a company hires a few of our students the former students recruit their friends and only about 50% of the students actually register with and use the placement office. But from what we can tell, the data, while incomplete, are representative of the whole. The data in Table 2 summarize the results of the placement data.

Interpretation of the data in Table 2 is not as straightforward as it appears. One factor that inflates SAP offers is the fact that admittance to some of the SAP classes is by invitation only. Hence, only the best students (those that have potential for better job offers) are admitted into the classes. A factor that greatly under-reports SAP salaries is that most of the very best students are recruited directly by companies and hence do not report any offers to placement. For each of the tabulated semesters, the authors know students that accepted offers even exceeding those reported in Table 2. In this light, the difference in offers between SAP and non-SAP students is significant.

The university has traditionally had a regional mission. However, the College of Business' success with SAP has catapulted us into a position of national prominence. The use of SAP in our curriculum has placed CSU Chico on the national map for recruiters, industry leaders and with academic professional associations. Over 100 companies currently recruit the College of Business students and this number has more than doubled from the number recruiting here in 1996. Our status with industry leaders who recruited here before we implemented SAP has also been elevated in the last two years. Examples include (a) receiving an upgrade in recruitment priority by IBM to be in the same group as Stanford University, (b) becoming one of four schools with which Cisco Systems (who doesn't even use SAP) has developed partnerships, and (c) taking two special bus trips from

Chico to Palo Alto to meet with managers from SAP Labs in the past two years. In addition, within the last year, our SAP faculty has been invited to present papers at five international conferences and visit campuses in Europe and Australia.

Table 2. Salary comparison SAP and Non-SAP graduates in MIS*.

Total	SAP	Non-SAP	Difference
Spring 1996			
Max – $52,000	N/A	N/A	N/A
Min – $24,000			
Mean – $38,916			
Spring 1997			
Max – $70,000	Max – $70,000	Max – $56,000	Max – $14,000
Min – $32,400	Min – $45,000	Min – $32,400	Min – $12,600
Mean – $44,357	Mean – $54,357	Mean – $41,023	Mean – $13,334
Fall 1997			
Max – $65,000	Max – $65,000	Max – $56,000	Max – $9,000
Min – $40,000	Min – $40,000	Min – $40,000	Min – $0
Mean – $49,200	Mean – $52,270	Mean – $44,454	Mean – $7,816
Spring 1998			
Max – $63,000	Max – $63,000	Max – $55,000	Max – $8,000
Min – $32,000	Min – $40,200	Min – $32,000	Min – $7,800
Mean – $47,641	Mean – $53,350	Mean – $43,611	Mean – $9,739
Fall 1998			
Max – $75,000	Max – $75,000	Max – $52,500	Max – $22,500
Min – $34,000	Min – $42,000	Min – $34,000	Min – $8,000
Mean – $49,754	Mean – $53,746	Mean – $44,922	Mean – $8,824

* Note: These results are from a dataset from the placement office that includes about 50% of the graduates in MIS.

The remaining objective, to provide students with a better understanding of how a business works, still has not been measured. However, an unexpected consequence of introducing an ERP package into the curriculum has been observed. Unlike typical software packages that are primarily used to reinforce the theoretical material presented in lectures, ERP systems demand that the breadth of the course subject matter be increased. These systems are so comprehensive and so highly integrated that much additional learning takes place by doing the class assignments. In many cases, this alters the presentation of the class material. Instead of the initial presentation of theory followed by the introduction of the software package, the presentation of material and the use of the ERP system must be integrated together. So not only do you achieve integration of the topical business disciplines, the use of the technology and the theoretical subject matter are also interwoven.

A brief survey that was sent to our SAP faculty confirms this interwoven nature of business disciplines. Every faculty member who responded (7 out of 12) said that positive changes in teaching included more exposure "to functional dependencies," "a more holistic view of the organization," or better understanding of business processes as evidenced by improving test score grades when compared to test scores prior to using R/3. Negative changes in teaching all centered around the increased time commitment to learn R/3 and develop relevant material. While the use of SAP has not necessarily increased the opportunity to do more research for every member of the team, the negative responses indicate that the opportunity was there but the individual declined to take advantage of it. Table 3 summarizes the results.

Similarly, survey data from students completing the ERP Configuration classes indicate that students have a sense that they understand the integrated nature of the disciplines better. (An informal open-ended survey is administered to exiting students the last day of class. Students return the forms anonymously and about 85% of the class responds.) A rank ordering of group-defined benefits included the following three items in the top five choices two semesters in a row. The three are (a) understanding how business processes are translated into a functional system, (b) integration of modules and understanding how the modules fit together, and (c) understanding my own functional area and its interdependencies. We are in the process of developing a "test" that we can give to all students that compares SAP trained and non-SAP trained students with respect to their understanding of how a business works. (At this point we only have anecdotal evidence through this informal survey of the configuration students and focus group discussions held at the end of the semester for the Systems Administration students.)

Table 3. Survey results of SAP faculty spring 1999, CSU Chico

Question	# of responses	Positive	Negative	Unknown
1. Does SAP improve student understanding of business?	6	5		1
2. Has teaching SAP increased research related opportunity?	7	4	2	1
3. Has teaching SAP increased the visibility of CSU Chico with industry?	7	7		

GAIL CORBITT · JAMES MENSCHING

Summary

In short, the SAP Alliance initiative at CSU Chico has been successful because we have carefully managed both the infrastructure and the interaction with the external environment in positive ways. We have built partnerships with SAP, Hewlett Packard, as well as key users of SAP such as Applied Materials, Bristol-Myers-Squibb, Chevron, Foundation Health, Nortel, and IBM. At the same time, we have carefully managed the interest of recruiters that have flocked to our campus to gain access to our students.

The amount of interest in courses dealing with SAP R/3 has been overwhelming. The student demand in the MIS courses is so intense that only the very best students can be selected to participate. POMG is also experiencing rapid growth in both recruiting activities and student enrollment. This is contrary to the trend of decreasing POMG enrollments in many other universities. As the other disciplines expand their offerings, they may also begin to feel the impact as well. Industry response has been impressive. Almost all of the companies that recruit business students at CSU Chico have been extremely supportive. Interestingly, even companies that are not presently using SAP and have no plans of adopting SAP, see value in this integrative approach to educating business students. For example, Baan sponsors our help desk because they like to hire our ERP students.

Finally, it is clear that students who have taken it upon themselves to gain a greater understanding of the SAP R/3 software have also seen their value in the job market greatly increase. The students leave the program with the highest salaries of any discipline on campus and have a deeper understanding of how a business works. Our objective of increasing the student's understanding of how a business works in a state-of-the-art technological environment has clearly been met.

Notes

1. AMR Research Inc., *Electronic Buyer's News* (July 8, 1998).

2. Malcolm Baldrige National Quality Award, *Education Pilot Criteria* (1995).

3. AACSB, Achieving quality and continuous improvement through self-evaluation and peer review, in *Standards for Accreditation Business Administration Handbook.*

4. S. Aluise and L. F. Cooper, IBM teams with ISVs to extend ERP reach, *Enterprise Systems Journal* (January 1999).

5. Price Waterhouse, *Technology Forecast*, 1997, version 7.

6. AMR Research Inc., http://www.amrresearch.com/press/990519.htm (May 18, 1999).

3

USING TECHNOLOGY IN THE DESIGN OR REDESIGN OF COURSES

Introduction

Suellen Cox
California State University, Fullerton

Today designing an academic course means a great deal more than identifying course goals, preparing a syllabus, and choosing a textbook. For faculty who intend to use technology, course planning has become more complex, sophisticated, and rewarding. Designing a technology-enriched course includes reconfiguring classroom or laboratory space, creating assignments and projects that incorporate technology, discovering new instructional methods, developing or identifying relevant Web sites, and, in general, rethinking what it means to teach and to learn.

Since the late 1980s, the use of academic technology has been promoted and supported at the system and campus levels to augment and enhance quality teaching and learning. System-focused and campus-focused initiatives have greatly facilitated expansion of academic technology within the CSU. Research support and faculty development in the use of technology and the shared development of digital learning materials have dramatically increased. As more faculty develop and implement technology-based courses and materials, students are moving from passive learners to active, engaged participants.

In *Engines of Inquiry: Approaches to Teaching, Learning, and Technology in American Culture Studies* (www.georgetown.edu/crossroads/engines; 2003), Randy Bass asks the question "How can information technologies play a role in the engines of inquiry that drive learning?" The five articles in this chapter present overviews of courses that have been successfully designed or redesigned to use technology as a tool to enhance teaching and learning. Moreover, the articles provide concrete examples of and useful recommendations for the roles that technology can play in extending access to and encouraging learning among an increasingly diverse student population. Above all, the articles effectively highlight the very "student-centered" nature of these courses, illustrating how students are reading, understanding, practicing, exploring, sharing, and creating with academic technology.

In "Preparing Tomorrow's Science Teachers to Use Technology: An Example from the Field," Laura Henriques describes how she models the appropriate and effective use of technology in an entry-level science education course. Rather than teach prospective science teachers about technology, Henriques uses overhead projectors, VCRs, televisions, computers, the Internet, CD-ROMs, and other equipment in her Introduction to Science Teaching course. "Students see technology seamlessly incorporated into lessons," she writes, "and we discuss the advantages that technology offers in specific situations. This point needs to be specific." This and other courses in the science credential program thereby incorporate the new science technology standards throughout the teacher preparation curriculum.

Christina A. Bailey, Kevin Kingsbury, Kristen Kulinowski, Jeffrey Paradis, and Rod Schoonover explain how they have revised a general chemistry course sequence—not just the curriculum, but also the facilities themselves—to create an "integrated learning environment." They describe the redesigned facility in detail, from computer hardware to electrical connections to cabinetry, and discuss scheduling modifications, faculty training needs, technical support, and student responses. The new layout of the facility is comprised of computer learning clusters that facilitate easy access, and collaborative interactive online exercises. "With the pedagogical opportunities that this facility gives us," they conclude, "we are able to establish an experimental teaching environment where we can study the effectiveness of various modes of instruction."

In "Cyber-Teaching in the Oral History Classroom," Rina Benmayor tells of redesigning her undergraduate oral history course. Having participated in workshops in new media sponsored by the American Social History Project—Center for Media and Learning (CUNY) and the American Crossroads Project (Georgetown University), Benmayor was inspired to "rethink and restructure" her pedagogical approach. Previously designed much like a graduate seminar, her undergraduate course on oral history became a collaborative project structured around the theme of first-generation college students and how campuses can help them succeed. "The digital world provides exciting new possibilities for representing, interpreting, archiving, and teaching ethnographic and field-based research," she writes. "But the key words are 'enable, help, enhance, facilitate, promote,' emphasizing the role of technology as a tool." Her narrative describes the redesigned course, the tools she and the students used, and the course outcomes, including public presentations, a feature in the campus newspaper, and a complex Web page.

A truly inspiring group of short papers describing how new digital technologies are transforming the learning space is included in "New Media Technologies and Pedagogies," featuring Rina Benmayor and Cecilia O'Leary from the CSU, as well as their collaborators Tracey M. Weis and Bret Eynon. Benmayor asks students in her "Latina Life Stories" course to create "digital stories," or brief multimedia movies that use images, music, and the author's narration to create and theorize autobiographies. O'Leary helps students become "citizen historians," using software and other tools to research and create "digital histories." Tracey M. Weis explains how students in an African American history course work as "novice historians," examining interpretations of race and slavery by public historians and by academic historians, evaluating Web sites on historic places, conducting online research, then formulating and documenting their own reactions in narrated PowerPoint presentations. Eynon provides details on his capstone liberal arts course, "Going Places! Immigration, Education and Change in New York City 1999-2002." In this course, students examine the immigrant experience through films, novels, Web sites, discussion boards, and online scholarly databases and in the process develop electronic portfolios. The students' final projects—life history interviews—become part of a digital archive.

Offering a somewhat different perspective, Suellen Cox and Elizabeth Housewright provide insight from outside the formal classroom, but from inside the emblematic heart of a learning-centered campus—the library. They discuss the process of collaboratively designing and implementing a required information technology course for first-year students in their article, "Teaching from the Web: Constructing a Library Learning Environment Where Connections Can Be Made." In addition, they describe how ongoing assessment and advances in technology facilitated not only changes within the required course, but the evolution of the library's entire instruction program as well.

The authors of these five articles express similar experiences in developing, implementing, and utilizing technology. They stress that ongoing faculty development is critical as technology continues to advance, and that adequate technical staff support is essential to curricular enhancement—and is very much appreciated. Above all, these authors embrace and celebrate how good pedagogical practice enhanced with technology and new media can transform the classroom into a more interactive, creative, collaborative, and student-centered learning environment.

Preparing Tomorrow's Science Teachers to Use Technology: An Example from the Field

Laura Henriques
California State University, Long Beach

Overview of Course and Technology Requirements

The examples presented in this article are from an entry level science education class, Introduction to Teaching Science (EDSS300C), at a large state university. Students enrolled in this class will apply to the university's credential program at the end of the semester. Most have bachelor's degrees in science and want to teach at the secondary level. With the current teacher shortages in California, several students in the class are already teaching. Course enrollment is limited to 30 and the class is offered both fall and spring semesters. There are 45 contact hours, and students must participate in 45 hours of fieldwork in local middle and high schools. The class serves as an introduction to science teaching and the credentialing process, while helping students determine if K-12 science teaching is a personally appropriate career goal. An ability to use technology as a teacher tool and as a teaching tool are among the goals of the science education credentialing program (this course and subsequent classes). To find out more about the class see the course homepage (http://www.csulb.edu/~lhenriqu/300.htm).

The California Commission on Teacher Credential (CTC) recently adopted new technology standards (http://www.ctc.ca.gov/codcor.doc/ 999916/999916.html). A new Senate Bill requires California to re-evaluate teacher preparation. Their draft technology standards (standard 9, page 22; see http://www.ctc.ca.gov/profserv/draft_stds/doc2.pdf) are less strenuous than those initially proposed by the CTC for earning an initial credential. As of July 1, 2002 students applying for an initial, nonrenewable teaching credential must demonstrate technology competence at Level 1 standards, and teachers applying for a permanent, renewable credential must satisfy Level 2 technology competency. These standards were developed with the *National Educational Technology Standard* (International Society for Technology in Education [ISTE], 2002) in mind. We address the Level 1 standards in the credential program. They include proficiency in use of software and hardware, electronic communication, evaluation of programs and techno-

Laura Henriques, "Preparing Tomorrow's Science Teachers to Use Technology: An Example From the Field." *Contemporary Issues in Technology and Teacher Education*, 2(1), 2002. Reprinted by permission of the author and the publisher. http://www.citejournal.org/vol2/ iss1/science/article1.cfm

logical resources, knowledge of and use of electronic databases and research tools, and an understanding of best practices related to technology.

Students can meet these requirements in three major ways. They can take an educational technology class, the technology standards can be infused throughout their teacher preparation program, or students can test out. With pressure to get teachers into the field faster, the idea of requiring an additional class was not appealing. We also believe that students will better implement the technology if it is meaningfully infused into their classes and assignments, as opposed to offering a stand alone course, which might teach students how to use the technology devoid of content. As a result, the science credential program opted to incorporate the various technology standards into existing courses.

In addition to the ISTE standards, we are guided by *National Science Education Standards* (National Research Council, 1996), Project 2061 (American Association for the Advancement of Science, 1993) and the *California Standards for the Teaching Profession* (California State Board of Education [CSTP], 1997). Students must use technology to facilitate learning, not simply to use technology. Their suggestions are consistent with Flick and Bell (2000). As a result, teachers need to know how to create a physical environment that engages all students. In so doing, they must "manage student and teacher access to materials, technology, and resources to promote learning" (CSTP, 1997).

Some of these basic skills are met by having students submit assignments by way of e-mail and having certain course information only available through the website. The latter poses some problems in terms of access as not all students have easy access to the Internet. Students get free accounts on campus, and there are many computer labs available for student use, but not all students have Internet access at home (although the number of college students without web access decreases every year). Other skills must be explicitly taught and practiced by the students in the course of their credential program.

Guidelines for Preparing Tomorrow's Science Teachers

Flick and Bell (2000) proposed a list of technology guidelines to use when working with science teachers.

1. Technology should be introduced in the context of science content.

2. Technology should address worthwhile science with appropriate pedagogy.

3. Technology instruction in science should take advantage of the unique features of technology.

4. Technology should make scientific views more accessible.

5. Technology instruction should develop students' understanding of the relationship between technology and science.

Their suggestions are aimed at science teaching. The guidelines show how technology should significantly strengthen science instruction. Technology is used as an aid in science instruction, but it is not the endpoint. The course I teach is an introductory education class. The content of my class is pedagogy, not science. As a result, the examples I give employ technology as a means of teaching pedagogical knowledge and pedagogical content knowledge, but the class does not deal explicitly with science content knowledge.

This article provides examples of how technology and teaching with technology are infused in the science credential program. Before beginning, however, it is important to point out my biases.

I do not believe that technology is the silver bullet for education's woes. Throughout history there have been many innovations touted to be the solution for all our problems. Remember the advent of the television and VCR for classroom use? The motion picture (and later the TV/VCR incarnation) was supposed to be a revolutionary device that would improve all classroom teaching, making teachers more efficient (King, 1999). While many teachers were able to successfully incorporate the innovation, it did not prove to be the quick fix hoped for.

Technology can help teachers and students—when used properly. Technology *can* help teachers to teach and students to learn. Studies show that students who used technology in conjunction with hands-on instruction had increases in knowledge and attitudes about science (Gardner, Simmons, & Simpson, 1992). The key is that it must be used properly. The technology should enhance the learning. Often educators get so caught up in the technology that we lose sight of the content we are trying to teach.

Technology means more than computers. To many, technology is synonymous with computers. For science classrooms in particular, technology encompasses so much more. While computers and their related paraphernalia are part of technology (probeware, electronic databases, CD-ROMS, the Internet, and multimedia presentations) so too is the overhead, the television, the VCR, videodiscs, and traditional science equipment. Science teachers need to know how to effectively use all of it.

Technology Should Be Introduced in the Context of [Science] Content

The idea that technology has a legitimate role to play in instruction, as opposed to being the point of instruction, is key. If learning is to be meaningful, the technology should be infused in a way that strengthens the lesson without taking away from it. Students must learn to use and infuse technology to improve their teaching, not because technology is the wave of the future.

A wide array of technology is used in EDSS300C. I model effective use of the overhead, VCR, and multimedia when I teach, and I give explicit instruction on their use. Students see technology seamlessly incorporated into lessons, and we discuss the advantages that technology offers in specific situations. This point needs to be explicit. Students in this course are just starting their professional education program. Until this point in their careers, they have focused on the content of lessons. They need help looking at instructional aspects of the lesson. A major goal for the class is that they begin to analyze effective (and ineffective) teaching strategies.

Classroom examples:

- My students learn how to use low-budget technology such as the overhead, VCR, and chalkboard. Until this class, they have not thought about the best way to use these tools. When using the overhead, for example, most students quickly realize that they need to write legibly and large. They also know that having a preprinted transparency can help with readability. However, they forget that their students cannot copy down material as fast as they can read it, or that students will "read ahead" if all the class notes are on the screen. They also need to learn that K-12 students cannot simultaneously listen, read, and write. Future teachers need to learn how to pace a lesson that is based on transparencies, make the type legible (24 point or larger, sans serif works best), cover up material not being used (a sheet of white paper underneath the transparency allows the teacher to read what comes next), and they need to practice standing/writing at the overhead so that students' views are unblocked.

- I use presentation software during lecture segments of class. Photographs, graphs, and images can be incorporated into the lecture in ways that cannot be done with chalkboards and overheads. Introducing a laboratory activity through presentation software allows photographs of the setup along with directions. This reduces the need to explain and demonstrate multiple times (see Appendix A). This is a helpful strategy for use with second language learners. Our students will have many English language learners in their classrooms.

- We use the VCR to watch video clips. I often stop the video during viewing to ask questions or cue them to an important upcoming event. We rewind and watch the same tape looking for different things. A taped lesson can be viewed for multiple purposes. We can watch it as many times as needed to exhaust all possibilities.

- I use the overhead for lessons but also to help with doing demonstrations. It can magnify things on the screen and in some cases its use as a light box makes the demo easier to see. For example, the demonstration of soap breaking surface tension done with a petri dish of water and pepper is much easier to see when the petri dish is on the overhead. Students look at the screen to see the motion of the pepper instead of gathering around a demonstration table.

- Students microteach several times during the semester. They incorporate technology into their lessons. The point of including technology is not to have technology there, but to improve the overall quality of the lesson for increased student understanding. The hope is that they will begin to see how technology can support their instruction.

Technology Should Address Worthwhile Science with Appropriate Pedagogy

Science teachers often use demonstrations and models to illustrate scientific phenomena. Not only do preservice teachers need to learn where to find these, they need practice performing and critiquing them. Some activities are better done without the use of technology while others are greatly enhanced by its use. Students need to see the difference so they can make informed decisions. When the technology gets in the way of the science and the learning, my students must reevaluate. These questions can be asked at that point. Is there a better way to teach this? Is the technology more interesting than the content? Are students meaningfully involved? Does the inclusion of technology increase active student involvement? Does inclusion of technology make the content more understandable?

Classroom examples:

- Students evaluate science CD-ROMS as a teaching aid. Sometimes the investigations that can be done on a computer program allow for more creativity and increased numbers of investigations. Students can "grow" a plant under hundreds of different conditions on the computer. This in no way should replace actually growing plants under different conditions, but it can supplement the investigation and provide students with a greater understanding. It is feasible for each student to grow hundreds of virtual plants with a computer simulation and virtually impossible to do that in the classroom.

- Students use spreadsheets and graphing programs. I would argue that students still need to know how to create a graph and how to make sense of the data, but once that skill is mastered, computer generated graphs are nice. Students can easily display their data in multiple formats and incorporate them into lab reports.

- I use the VCR and recorder to show scientific phenomena in slow motion. This is a useful technique, because the event can be shown repeatedly, which increases the likelihood that all students will see the phenomena we are trying to demonstrate. It also allows us to stop at any time—something we cannot do in the real world. Phenomena that are very time consuming to set up lend themselves nicely to this mode of presentation, as they need to be done only once. Similarly, events that take a while can be filmed ahead of time and shown at a faster speed. Constructive and destructive interference of waves on a slinky and mechanics demonstrations are examples I use in class.

Technology Instruction in Science Should Take Advantage of the Unique Features of Technology

There are things that we can do and show with technology that are better than what we can do without it. Certain skills and knowledge can be taught in ways that are more realistic; the abstract can be made concrete. For example, probeware, data collection devices attached to a computer, let students gather data in ways different from traditional science equipment.

Classroom examples:

- Students can take equipment outside and gather data, which can be later loaded onto the computer. Students in my class have the opportunity to observe and assist in an exemplary middle school with a science teacher who uses technology in all his labs. His middle school students collect real time water quality data in the nearby lagoon and waterway. The monthly excursion requires additional adult supervision so my students spend some of their 45 hours of fieldwork in his classroom. They are able to see how this teacher incorporates technology for a purpose—data collection with more precise tools. Students then use that data to come up with explanations and answers to their questions.

- Probeware can collect data over extended periods of time. For example, a temperature probe can be set to record temperature every 30 minutes for 2 days. In this way students can monitor the temperature of their experiment, classroom, and so forth, over long periods of time when no one is around to collect the data. The computer stores the data, which students can later access.

- Flexible cameras connected to the television allow for better viewing and more realistic situations. Learning to read a meniscus is easier to do with a "flex cam" and television (or projector) than with a drawing on the board. The teacher is able to show students the real thing, enabling students to better learn it (see Appendix B).

- Microscope cameras, or flexible cameras attached to a microscope, allow the entire class to look at a specimen together. At that point the teacher can instruct students in what they should be looking for. Likewise, they can point out air bubbles, or other extraneous sites, eliminating the intricate yet useless drawings rendered by many K-12 students (see Appendix C).

Technology Should Make Scientific Views More Accessible

Technology has made educational research, teaching activities and labs, and scientific information available to anyone with an Internet connection. Students can now find teaching resources online, read the latest research (scientific and educational), and share their ideas with others. The electronic databases and educational websites have made teaching information much more accessible.

Students are introduced to science education research in this course. As they progress through the program they will develop their own research supported educational philosophy. The process of developing this statement begins in EDSS300C. Students modify and revisit the paper in their secondary methods course (http://www.csulb.edu/~acolburn/EDSS450C/methods.htm) and during their student teaching experience (http://www.csulb.edu/~lhenriqu/StT.htm). We want our teachers to leave the program knowing about and utilizing the research base to inform their practice. They need to know where to go to find summaries of research, how to find articles about specific topics (i.e., ERIC searches) and how to find appropriate content and activities for inclusion in their classes. Much of this can be done online if you know where to look.

Classroom examples:

- Students access the ERIC-Digest database (http://www.ed.gov/databases/ERIC_Digests/index.html) and the National Association of Researchers in Science *Teaching Research Matters to the Science Teacher* (http://www.educ.sfu.ca/narstsite/research/research.htm) database during the course. Each student selects an entry to read and summarize for the class. Their summaries are done with presentation software. This assignment requires them to learn how to create a presentation, figure out how to print multiple slides onto a single page (as they must provide a single-page handout to their peers), and do a presentation using the computer and projector. I require that students include at least one appropriate graphic in their short summaries. Student presentations are videotaped for self-analysis. (See more information about this assignment at http://www.csulb.edu/~lhenriqu/techday.htm)

Students learn many things from this assignment beyond the content they summarize. They quickly learn that many of the bells and whistles found in presentation software get in the way of the lesson. They figure out that 200 words on a single slide is too many, that font size must be readable, and that slides need not be a script. They receive instruction on how best to create presentations, but they tend to be more receptive to the ideas when they are revisited after doing their own presentations. For example, presentations should have a light or white colored background with dark color fonts if there is any glare from lighting or sunlight, while the opposite is true if there is not glare (Allen, 2001). This advice is taken to heart when students see multiple presentations in class. Multimedia presentations require a different mindset. We can use hundreds of slides, each containing just a small amount of information. While this is not practical when using transparencies, it makes sense when using a computer. This requires a different way of thinking about how we present information (Allen, 2001).

Technology Instruction Should Develop Students' Understanding of the Relationship Between Technology and Science and Science Teaching

Pre-service students need to be critical consumers of technology. Just because information is on a published CD, in game format, or on a glitzy website does not imply that it is educationally worthwhile. Nor does it mean that it will be a good fit with their instructional goals. Students need to determine how technology can fit into their lessons.

Classroom examples:

- Students evaluate science CD-ROM and web-based science activities/sites. They must first ascertain what the product teaches. They then decide how well that fits into the curriculum. (At this point in their careers they do not have intimate knowledge with the curriculum associated with any grade level, so this goal is met by matching the content reviewed to state and national science standards.) They list prerequisite skills or knowledge that students need to succeed and give an overall assessment of the product. Their reviews are shared electronically on the course website.

- Students begin to evaluate the value of web-based materials. Anyone can publish online. Most websites have not been peer reviewed, so students and teachers need to be critical consumers of what they read. There is no substitute for thorough research and multiple sources. Far too many students think, "If it's on the Internet, it must be true." We need to help them learn that this is not always the case (November, 2000). For teachers, just because a lesson is on the Web does not mean it will work or fit their instructional goals. My students must try out any lesson before they are allowed to include it in an assignment.

As Flick and Bell (2000) noted, the increase in digital technology has changed the way we interact, find resources, and teach. We must pass on the skills we learned to our preservice teachers so they are able to effectively integrate technology into their science lessons.

Perhaps the largest change we are noticing is in the area of communications. Students and faculty regularly send e-mail. List-servs allow students in the program to contact each other and allow the instructor to send announcements and program information to all with great ease. Information is posted on web pages, which students can access at all hours. As future teachers they will be able to contact many parents through e-mail and websites. While this mode of communication works very well, it does not replace the need for telephone and face-to-face interactions. The chasm between those who have ready access to technology and those who do not continues to grow. Inequities in our school systems are not new (Kozol, 1991), and the digital divide is very real and continues to grow (U.S. Department of Commerce, National Telecommunication and Information Administration, 2000). As might be expected, household income correlates to access. However, just as science courses become a filter or gate-keeper for higher education, competence with technology is likely to be a gate-keeper for jobs and economic prosperity (U.S. Department of Education, Office of Educational Research and Improvement, 1999), making it incumbent upon our teachers to use and teach it to their students.

Conclusions

Students are beginning to understand the role of technology as an aid to instruction. The use of probe-ware in laboratory settings will be dependent upon schools having the resources for multiple computers and equipment. The use of multimedia presentations in K-12 classrooms is more common, and the use of a computer by the teacher for managing classes (record keeping, grades, word processing, and Internet searches) is almost universal.

When future teachers become comfortable with the seamless infusion of the technology to enhance instruction, we will see more of it used in K-12 classrooms. Currently, this is not universally done in the K-12 arena, so it is incumbent upon preservice teacher educators to teach our students successful technology infusion.

References

Alien, T. H. (2001). *Tips for enhancing student learning with powerful presentations*. Presentation at Teaching with Technology Showcase, California State University, Long Beach.

American Association for the Advancement of Science. (1993). *Benchmarks for science literacy*. New York: Oxford University Press. [Online]. Available: http://www.project2061.org/tools/benchol/bolframe.html

California State Board of Education. (1997). *California standards for the teaching profession: A description of professional practice for California teachers*. Sacramento, CA: Author. [Online]. Available: http://www.sfsu.edu/~seconded/castandardsl .html

Flick, L., & Bell, R. (2000). Preparing tomorrow's science teachers to use technology: Guidelines for science educators. *Contemporary Issues in Technology and Teacher Education* [Online serial], *1*(1). Available: http://www.citejournal.org/vol1/iss1/currentissues/science/article1.htm

Gardner, C. M., Simmons, P. E., & Simpson, R. E. (1992). The effects of CAI and hands-on activities on elementary students' attitude and weather knowledge. *School Science and Mathematics, 92*(6), 334–336.

King, K. P. (1999). The motion picture in science education: "One hundred percent efficiency." *Journal of Science Education and Technology, 8*(3), 211–226.

Kozol, J. (1991). *Savage inequalities: Children in America's schools*. New York: Crown.

International Society for Technology in Education. (2002). *National educational technology standards for teachers: Preparing teachers to use technology*. Eugene, OR: Author

National Research Council. (1996). *National science education standards*. Washington, DC: National Academy Press. [Online]. Available: http://bob.nap.edu/readingroom/books/nses

November, A. (2000). Validating information on the Internet. *Education Update, 42* (4).

U.S. Department of Commerce, National Telecommunication and Information Administration. (2000). *Falling through the net: Toward digital inclusion* [Online]. Available: http://www.ntia.doc.gov/ntiahome/fttn00/contents00.html

U.S. Department of Education, Office of Educational Research and Improvement. (1999). *Bringing education to after-school programs* [Online]. Available: http://www.ed.gov/pubs/After_School_Programs/

Note

This article builds on the suggestions of Flick & Bell (http://www.citejournal.org/vol1/iss1/currentissues/science/article1.htm). They make recommendations for teaching science with technology. I make recommendations and provide examples for teaching preservice science teachers how to infuse and use technology.

Several of the images in this article have been updated from the originals. (Ed.)

Appendix A: Comparison of Lab Directions

Partial directions for lab—no pictures

Materials:

funnel	2 beakers
filter paper	mixture of sand, salt, and iron filings
ring stand	water

Setup:

Attach the round ring clamp to the ring stand.

Put the funnel inside the clamp.

Place an empty beaker underneath the funnel.

Fold the filter paper in quarters and place inside of the funnel. You will separate the filter paper so that three pieces are on one side and one is alone. Wet the filter paper with distilled water so that it will stay in place.

***

Partial directions for lab—with drawings

Materials:

funnel	2 beakers
filter paper	mixture of sand, salt, and iron filings
ring stand	water

Setup:

Attach the round ring clamp to the ring stand.

Put the funnel inside the clamp.

Place an empty beaker underneath the funnel.

Fold the filter paper in quarters and place inside of the funnel.

You will separate the filter paper so that three pieces are on one side and one is alone. Wet the filter paper with distilled water so that it will stay in place.

***

Partial directions for lab—with photographs

Materials:

funnel	2 beakers
filter paper	mixture of sand, salt, and iron filings
ring stand	water

Setup:

Attach the round ring clamp to the ring stand.

Put the funnel inside the clamp.

Place an empty beaker underneath the funnel.

Fold the filter paper in quarters and place inside of the funnel. You will separate the filter paper so that three pieces are on one side and one is alone. Wet the filter paper with distilled water so that it will stay in place.

A picture's worth a thousand words!

Especially if you are trying to learn the words at the same time you are trying to learn the science. This can be displayed with a projector and computer.

Appendix B: Example Setup with a Flex Cam
We have to exaggerate with drawings.

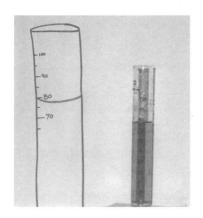

Showing a real meniscus is more helpful. You can zoom in and focus on key areas with the camera.

The image can be projected on the class television or through a projector.

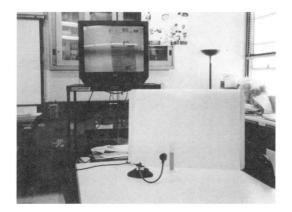

Appendix C: Using the Flexible Camera With a Microscope

This example of crystals under the scope can be easily seen and discussed. The flexible camera simply attaches to a sleeve which fits over the eyepiece of a microscope.

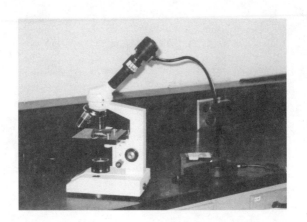

An Integrated Lecture-Laboratory Environment for General Chemistry

Christina A. Bailey, Kevin Kingsbury, Kristen Kulinowski,
Jeffrey Paradis, and Rod Schoonover
California Polytechnic State University, San Luis Obispo

This paper describes the physical attributes and uses of an integrated learning environment for a large-enrollment general chemistry course sequence. The room was opened in Spring Quarter 1997 and 2000 students have passed through its doors since then. The facility is one in which experimentation, collaborative student involvement, lecture, technology, and individual attention can be maximized for more effective learning.[1] With it we hope to foster a healthy spirit of pedagogical experimentation in a modern technological environment—education for a new millennium. See our Web site at *http://chemweb.calpoly.edu/chem* for links to laboratory experiments, current instructors' pages, and other course materials.

History of Course and Facility Development

Chemistry 124/5 is one of four general chemistry course sequences taught at California Polytechnic State University, San Luis Obispo (Cal Poly) in the Department of Chemistry & Biochemistry. The student clientele comes from the College of Engineering (Computer Science, Mechanical, Materials, Industrial, Environmental & Civil, Electronic) as well as from Architectural and Agricultural Engineering. About 1000 students are enrolled in these courses every academic year.

Cal Poly is on the quarter system, that is, terms with 10 weeks of instruction and an added week for final exams. It is an undergraduate teaching institution, with lecture and laboratory sections taught by faculty, lecturers, and part-time instructors. We currently do not have a graduate program and therefore have no graduate teaching assistants.

From Fall 1994 to the present, we have been revising the content of both the lecture and lab in Chem 124/5. The revised approach stresses materials science and the solid state,[2, 3] the use of computers in laboratory for data acquisition, molecular modeling, tutorials, and simulations, and an increase in the expectations for student entrants to the sequence.

Even though the department scheduler had attempted to link lecture and laboratory sections with the same instructors, we still experienced a

Used with permission from the *Journal of Chemical Education*, Vol. 77, No. 2, 2000, pp. 195–199; copyright © 2000, Division of Chemical Education, Inc.

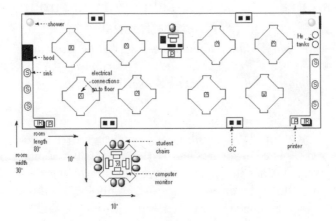

Figure 1. Diagram of studio classroom showing detail of a cluster

discontinuity of time, place, and instruction in the traditional lecture-lab format. Although our lab sections held a maximum of 24 students, the lecture sections contained 100–144 students. When funding became available, existing space was redesigned to accommodate an integrated environment in the mode of workshop physics studio classrooms developed at Rensselaer Polytechnic Institute.[4]

The Room

Existing space was redesigned for two integrated classrooms: chemistry and physics. Two prep rooms, one for each discipline, were included in the construction. As diagrammed in Figure 1, the chemistry facility has floor

Figure 2. Close-up of the table in one of the clusters (see detail of Fig. 1)

Figure 3. View from one end of the studio classroom

space measuring 30 x 80 feet. There are 32 student stations arranged in 8 clusters of 4 stations, 2 students per station, for a total capacity of 64 students per class section. A cluster is about 10 feet square. This means there are 64 students in one room for both lecture and laboratory. An instructor's desk and computer station are positioned in the middle of the room with complete access both visually and physically to all parts of the room.

Figure 2 shows a standard cluster and Figure 3 is a view from one end of the room. Each computer station is also equipped with a Vernier interface box with standard probes for measurement.

We schedule the room for 6–7 course sections each quarter. Each section meets for 6 hours in the room. Classes run from 7:30 a.m. to 7 p.m. Monday through Thursday and 7:30 a.m. to 5 p.m. on Friday. Monday through Thursday evenings, the facility is staffed by teaching assistants for open hours, that is, for class-related computer work and tutoring.

We have experimented with several variations on the length of time per class meeting as well as the sequence of days of instruction. This is facilitated by the fact that the room is dedicated to this course sequence. The current time configuration for most sections consists of three meetings per week: two are 2.5 hours in length and one is 1 hour. This allows us sufficient time for experiments, activities, and discussion and provides a convenient period for testing.

As the faculty and staff become familiar with the possibilities inherent in such a facility, other courses have been scheduled in the studio, such as an upper-division biochemistry class on protein folding and modeling and individual meetings of physical chemistry. The room is also used for department workshops on computer training.

The Environment

There are two computer servers for the courses: a file server for class management and a Web server. A Macintosh Workgroup Server 8550/200 Power PC (64 M RAM, 2 x 2 GB HD, Tape Backup) and a Macintosh Workgroup Server 9650/233 Power PC (64 M RAM, 4 GB HD) fill these roles, respectively. Both servers are on an APC Smart UPS 1400. The Web server (*http://chemweb.calpoly.edu*) is also used for the physics studio classroom.

The side counters and cabinets are used to store and supply common equipment. These areas also house six sinks with deionized water and eyewash fountains. There are two safety showers, one over each door, and all equipment and desks are accessible to the disabled.

Electrical connections are placed beneath the raised floor, which consists of carpeted, removable tiles. Deionized water and helium gas lines pass above the dropped ceiling. The fluorescent lighting is recessed; it is usually unnecessary to darken the room because information from the instructor's computer is delivered simultaneously to every student monitor via a Robotel Ml60 System for feeding simultaneous images to all classroom monitors.

This is a "wet" laboratory environment. We use 1 M and 6 M HCl, small amounts of organics and water solutions. Since we introduced computers into the traditional laboratory four years ago, we have not lost a single machine to chemical spills. This includes the monitor, keyboard, CPU, and mouse. Instructors and TAs are very safety conscious and the students are constantly reminded of the proper procedures to prevent and remediate spills.

Instruction

Each section is facilitated by a faculty member with the help of two undergraduate teaching assistants. Most of the teaching assistants are engineering students who have successfully completed the course sequence. Some are chemistry and biochemistry majors. Therefore students within a course section experience consistency of instruction and a number of human resources. The layout of the clusters allows easy access to every student and individual contacts are maximized.

All course information, syllabi, and lab manuals reside on the instructors' Web pages. Traditional "lecture" topics are integrated with experimentation, collaborative exercises, and the utilization of Web resources.

Most lab reports are in the form of Excel documents designed by the instructors. Students fill in the required data, generate graphs and statistics, and compose conclusions in the same document. They then use the "Hand In" function of the At Ease (Apple Network Administrator's Toolkit) File menu to submit their reports. Since the server for the room is self-contained and secured, the students can email Excel documents to their own university or personal Internet accounts in order to work at home. Quizzes, exams, and other learning exercises are hand written. Collaborative Web assignments are also part of the instruction. Assessments before, during, and after the course are taken manually and through Web instruments. The assessments are currently being collated, evaluated, and further developed.

Technical Support

The chemistry studio classroom is one of five such facilities within the College of Science and Mathematics at Cal Poly. In addition there are two rooms for math, one for statistics, and one for physics. The statistics lab is located in a building separate from the other four labs. Two technicians manage all these environments with the help of student assistants. One of the technicians has the major responsibility for the chemistry studio. The prep room for chemistry has space for several technicians and teaching assistants to work at the same time and houses the servers for the room.

It is important to note that adequate technical support is *essential* to the

Table 1. First-quarter traditional General Chemistry course

Lecture Topic	Laboratory
Review of equations, mole concept, stoichimotry	Physical properities: boiling point, refractive index, gas chromatography (2 weeks)
Thermochemistry	Emission spectra
Atomic theory	Titration (2 weeks)
Bonding	Compounds of copper
Introduction to organic chemistry	Reactions of organic compounds

effective function of an integrated lecture-lab environment. We are fortunate to have excellent electronic, computer, and chemical technicians who function not only to support the curriculum, but who also help in the development of course and lab materials.

Curriculum—Past and Present

Tables 1 and 2 give an overview of the more traditional curriculum for Chemistry 124 (the first-quarter course) taught prior to 1994 and the course as it is presented today. The curricular changes in the lecture and laboratory were developed during the period from the 1994–95 academic year to the opening of the studio facility in spring 1997. It is important to realize that the integrated pedagogy seemed to be a logical evolution of the curriculum revision.

Table 2. Integrated First-Quarter General Chemistry

Topic	"Laboratory"
Diagonistic quiz	Excel graphing exercises
Thermochemistry	Heat of sublimation
	Heat of combustion
Nature of the atom	Emission spectra
Bonding: metallic, covalent, ionic	Solid-state modeling: cubic cells, ionic solids, and stoichiometry
Properties of metallic and covalent substances	Conductors, semiconductors, and superconductors
Nature of organic compounds	Organic structure and nomenclature
	Building organic models
Polymers	Organic analysis: Unknown compounds and mixtures--
IR spectroscopy	*Pure organic liquid: refractive index, density, and infrared spectra*
	Gas chromatography: qualitativeand quantitative analyses
	IR: spectra of common packaging materials

Instructional Examples

The first topic covered in the first-quarter course is thermochemistry. The box compares the traditional and integrated approaches. It is important to note that students would most likely encounter two instructors in the traditional mode, whereas only one instructor is involved in the integrated pedagogy. Breaking up the laboratory with discussion and problem-solving sessions reinforces the empirical nature of chemistry, allowing for a discussion of sources of error and experimental limitations before proceeding to a more intensive part of the lab. Quick feedback on the statistical validity of the class submissions on sublimation encourages the students to work collaboratively on Hess's law, for which each pair of students (one computer station) is responsible for a metal and the cluster of 8 students must produce the data for all the metals.

Lab reports are submitted individually. Although the data, calculations, and results will be common, the other sections of the report—purpose, format, conclusion (discussion of three sources of error, three things learned during the lab, and at least two questions which still remain)—are a student's individual responsibility. The conclusions are some of the most insightful student feedback we have seen.

The Web explorations are occasions for collaborative work in ever-expanding groups. We have used an initial Web assignment to acquaint students with the course. This exercise can be found in our Web site at *http:// chemweb.calpoly.edu/chem/bailey/studiochem.html.*

The exploration using metals combines descriptive material with a practical introduction to the use of Web search engines. A table cluster is assigned a metal such as Al, Cu, Mn, or Cr. Then each pair of students at a computer station is assigned a particular search engine (Alta Vista, Excite, Infoseek, Yahoo). Students have to write out the answers to several questions. At the end of the designated search time, each cluster discusses the results and makes a recommendation with supporting statements about the best and the worst of the search engines. In addition, each cluster comes up with the most interesting and unexpected fact they could find about their metal. Brief oral presentations follow. (See *http://chemweb.calpoly.edu/chem/bailey/studiochem.html*).

A Comparison of Pedagogical Approaches

Traditional Approach	
Lecture (ca. 3, 1-hour)	Demonstrations
	Assigned readings and problems
Laboratory (3 hours)	Heat of sublimation
	Hess's law--Heat of neutralization

Integrated Approach
Demonstrations
Work sheets and discussion
First lab: Heat of sublimation; Electronic submission of data
Discussion and problem-solving
Second lab: Hess's law--Heat of Combusion for Mg, Al, Zn
Web explorations: Nature and properties of metals

The idea of an ever-expanding collaborative exercise can be used in the development of bonding concepts for ionic salts, that is, learning the workings of the Born-Haber cycle. A pair of students is given an envelope containing strips of paper with equations. The goal is to put together the equations, Hess's-law fashion, to find a "target"—the lattice energy of a particular salt. Each of the four groups in a cluster has a different salt comprising monovalent and divalent ions. From pooling their information the cluster should be able to hypothesize a periodic relationship of lattice energies and draw up some general rules. The class enjoys this activity and seems to be able to grasp the concepts involved, especially in comparing ionic compounds with metallic and covalent elements and compounds. Incentives involve extra credit for being the first correct group of theoreticians.

In the second quarter kinetics is introduced through some clock reaction demonstrations. This is followed by data collection using computer-interfaced pH probes (Vernier) to follow the hydrolysis of tertiary butyl chloride.

Clusters work at assigned temperatures and results are exchanged between clusters in order to produce the Arrhenius relationship.

We are developing an environmental analysis theme for the second-quarter course because most of our experiments involve spectrophotometric analyses. For example, in conjunction with a discussion of solution concentration terms, we combined analyses of nitrite and sulfate measured in ppm with Web explorations on EPA air and water standards and the health effects of certain contaminants.

Overall, we find that the release from the constrictions of time and place found in traditional lab-lecture formats have stimulated creative approaches to collaborative work and the integration of Internet resources with the curriculum.

Student Response

Although our assessment program is still in its formative stages, we have gathered enough data from evaluations of the facility and curriculum to see that this approach is extremely well received by the students.

A very small sample of student comments:

"I think that the course work really challenged me to work harder and so made me really want to learn."

"The computers made the class go faster. I have never been in a class where computers played such a vital role."

"I like the studio chemistry setup and would like to take more classes in this type of classroom. It is more like what I expect to encounter in the future."

The students have also offered some valuable criticism on presentation and conditions in the room.

"The room was always very hot." (The room has been air-conditioned.)

"Only one problem: the instructor's microphone needs some adjustment so that it will not get disconnected all the time." (We have converted to a wireless system.)

"I liked having the syllabus on the Web, I would have liked to have had a running total of the points I received in my folder so I could compare and see what grade I was getting." (We are pilot-testing the use of course management software during the 1999–2000 year.)

CHRISTINA A. BAILEY, ET AL.

Overall, there seems to be a sense of community engendered by the entire environment. We look forward to the results of longitudinal studies to confirm whether this approach has strengthened technological and laboratory skills, improved content retention, and increased appreciation for the role of chemistry in the core curriculum of the engineering disciplines.

A Word to the Wise

Instructors new to this integrated form of teaching tend to fall back on traditional lecturing. This has not worked at all in this environment. Lecturing should be limited to perhaps 30 minutes at most. It is advantageous to have the students physically move around during every long class period. This keeps their attention and involvement.

A break is a necessity during the 2.5-hour class periods. Sometimes students will stay to work at their computers, but they are aware that they had the opportunity for a break.

Something to note: we have had many visitors and observers at the facility since its opening; most are unannounced to the students (the faculty member teaching at the time is usually given notice). To a person, all have remarked that the students are "to task," whether in an experiment, individual work, or group work. The students are eager to show the visitor what they are doing and learning. There is a sense of involvement that we have not experienced in the traditional mode of instruction.

Future Development

With the pedagogical opportunities that this facility gives us, we are able to establish an experimental teaching environment where we can study the effectiveness of various modes of instruction. We are trying different types of collaborative learning experiences, working on multimedia presentations, incorporating assessment instruments into Web-based formats, and working on the correlation of instructional goals with valid assessment tools. [4–7]

Conclusion

This integrated facility is a unique prototype for general chemistry instruction, especially for large-enrollment courses. It is technologically current, versatile in accommodating discovery-type classes, and conducive to collaborative exercises, and most importantly, it promotes a cohesive mode of instruction that allows experimentation to be interfaced with concept development. Not only are students working together more effectively, but faculty and staff also work in concert to promote a curriculum that can attune itself to the individual as well as the masses.

Acknowledgments

This entire project and its future depend upon a foundation of intellectual, professional, and financial support. The reconstruction of facilities and purchase of computers and equipment were financed by the Chancellor's Office of the California State University System; the President, Warren J. Baker; the administration of California Polytechnic State University; and the Dean of Science and Mathematics, Philip S. Bailey.

A modern university runs through the expertise and collaboration of students, faculty and staff. Our highly competent technical colleagues are John Teclaw, Jim McLaughlin, and Jack Collins. And to all of our undergraduate TAs—thank you for your enthusiasm and dedication.

Notes

1. Committee on Undergraduate Science Education, National Academy of Sciences. *Science Teaching Reconsidered*. National Academy Press: Washington, DC, 1997.

2. Ellis, A. B., Geselbracht, M. J., Johnson, B. J., Lisensky, G. C., Robinson, W. R. *Teaching general chemistry: A materials science companion*. ACS Books. American Chemical Society: Washington, DC, 1993.

3. Gulden, T. D., Norton, K. P., Strecert, H. H., Woolf, L. D. *J. Chem. Educ.* 1997, *74*, 785–786.

4. Wilson, J. M. *Phys. Teach.* 1994, *32*, 518–523.

5. Bailey, C. A., Kulinowski, K., Paradis, J. Studio chemistry: A feasible environment for large general chemistry courses? Presented at the symposium Developing Instructional Technologies—Where Is the Cutting Edge? 215th National Meeting of the American Chemical Society, Dallas, TX, March–April 1998. Paper 091.

6. Bailey, C. A., Kingsbury, K., Kulinowski, K., Schoonover, R. General chemistry in a studio format. Presented at the Cancun International Congress, Mexico—Fifth Chemical Congress of North America, Cancun, Mexico, November 1997.

7. Bailey, C. A., Baker, B., Paradis, J., Scholefield, M. New environments for old lectures. Presented at the 217th National Meeting of the American Chemical Society, Anaheim, CA, March 1999. Paper 831.

8. Bailey, C. A., Kulinowski, K., Paradis, J. Studio vhemistry: A feasible environment for large general chemistry courses? Presented at the symposium Taming the Whale: Innovations for Large Chemistry Courses; 215th National Meeting of the American Chemical Society, Dallas, TX, March–April 1998. Paper 634.

CHRISTINA A. BAILEY, ET AL.

Cyber-Teaching in the Oral History Classroom

Rina Benmayor
California State University, Monterey Bay

Abstract

This essay[1] details how digital communication tools and strategies facilitated teaching oral history differently, enabling students to build a collaborative oral history project from beginning to end in the course of one semester. Students designed, conducted, analyzed, interpreted, archived and disseminated the results of their work in print, web-based, and public formats. The use of new media changed the pedagogy of the classroom, turning it into a highly interactive and collaborative workshop environment. Students experienced working together as a team, using oral history to engage in real research, advocating for change on their own college campus. The essay suggests that new media technologies provide more than ease of communication. They lead to better teaching and learning.

Until recently my undergraduate oral history course was structured much like a graduate seminar. After fifteen weeks, students completed an oral history project from beginning to end, from design and implementation, to analysis and dissemination, including some form of public "return" of the research to the relevant communities and the interviewees. My approach stresses oral history as a form of action research, in which memory and the investigation of the past is connected to community efforts for social change. Each student chose a topic of personal interest, defined a research question, found and used relevant secondary sources, learned interview techniques, constructed an interview guide, identified interviewees, conducted field interviews, logged or transcribed the interviews, synthesized their primary and secondary findings, produced a final research paper, gave an oral presentation to the class, and archived their interviews and research. In sum, a very tall order, favoring the self-motivated, highly organized, outgoing student with sharp research and critical thinking skills.

Aside from being ambitious, my model also contained problematic assumptions. While my course provided a comprehensive oral history research experience, it assumed, for one, that students could accomplish all these tasks in one semester. In addition, I would be expected to have content expertise in topics about which I might know nothing. More importantly, although I believe that students learn best when following their individual

Rina Benmayor, "Cyber-Teaching in the Oral History Classroom." *Oral History,* Spring 2000: 83–91. Reprinted by permission of the author and the Oral History Society, www.ohs.org.uk

interests and passions, working individually also turns them into lone researchers who experience the process as isolating and intimidating. Ironically, my own experience as an oral historian has been within a collaborative framework, and as part of an interdisciplinary team.[2] And yet, I was asking my students to do otherwise.

My encounter with "new media" led me to rethink and restructure my approach to teaching oral history. For the last two years, I have participated in a number of New Media Classroom workshops, sponsored by the American Social History Project-Center for Media and Learning (CUNY), and the American Crossroads Project (Georgetown). These workshops introduced me to ways in which new media can help convert the "architecture" and "ecology" of the classroom into a more interactive, collaborative and student-constructed learning space, in which students engage in oral history practice as active, dialogic agents, critical thinkers, and collaborators in their own learning.[3] New media pedagogy suggested ways to revamp my oral history class and its objectives.

Technology played an important role in this process, but it was not the focus of my endeavor. I used information technologies to *facilitate* organization, communication, and collaborative production, and to *enhance* the classroom learning experience. I underscore "facilitate" and "enhance" to emphasize that technology was harnessed to pedagogical concerns, to a desire to engage students in all the phases of oral history research, and to teach oral history in a more interactive, participatory, and collaborative way.

This class was an experiment in applying information technologies to transform oral history teaching into a more interactive and collaborative learning experience. The end result of fifteen weeks of collaboration was a study—in three different forms—of the impact of higher education on students who are, or will be, first in their families to go to college. The study appeared first as a special four-page feature insert in our campus newspaper. This was followed by a public presentation by all eighteen students to the University community and interviewees. Finally, we put up a more comprehensive webpage (http://classes.monterey.edu/HCOM/HCOM314SL-0l/world/index.html), with scholarly references and notations, visuals, voice, and video. And we built an archive of interviews. This paper describes and assesses how we were able to reach these goals as a group, using information technologies to support the collaborative process. As one student said at the end, "We really bonded in this class and it feels really good to do something to better our University."

The Context and the Topic

I teach at California State University Monterey Bay (CSUMB), a new campus in a large state university system. CSUMB was established to serve the working-class, ethnically diverse, and immigrant populations of California and particularly of the tri-county region, communities which have been traditionally under-represented and under-served in higher education.[4] Ours is a largely working-class student body, thirty percent of which is of Mexican heritage—self-identified as either Chicana/o, Mexican American, or Mexicana/o. Many are the children of migrant farm workers who settled in the surrounding Salinas Valley and Watsonville. Most of our 1800 plus students combine school with full- or part-time work. Many are raising families, and many are re-entry students. Sixty per cent of our students are transfers from community colleges in the region, and six of every ten students are female.

As one might expect of a new university, many of the student support structures are yet to be established.[5] Mandated to be a multicultural, pedagogically innovative campus "for the 21st century," institutional programs need to ensure access, retention, graduation, and quality opportunity for working class and under-served students. What are the effects of these programs, or lack of them, on the lives of students—particularly those for whom the public university is a new experience?[6] Here was an opportunity for oral history to play an action-research and community service role.

When I began designing the course, I decided to structure the entire class around a theme that I hoped students would find personally engaging and rewarding. The central question became: What is the experience of first-generation college students on our campus, and what does the campus need to do to ensure their success? Students would conduct life histories of other students (on and off campus), and through their research, provide University administrators with culturally-specific insights into the needs of our first-generation students. These insights could have direct impact on the design, structure, philosophy, and quality of services to support their retention, success, and graduation.

I hoped that the students would be able to approach this topic with passion and personal investment. Although they did not take part in defining this topic, they felt connected to it from the start. Some in the class were first-generation, some were Chicana/o, Mexican American or Mexicana/o, some were from migrant farm-worker families, some were re-entry women students, most were working class, and all had friends and classmates who fit the category. Moreover, all the students had an acute understanding of the need for more and better student support services on campus.

It was a happy choice. By the end of the course, students demonstrated a passion not only for the topic but for the collaborative learning process as well.

Integrating Technology

From the outset, let me say that while I am exploring the use of new media for teaching oral history, I remain critical about where and when new technologies should be used and about what value they can add to the learning process. I continue to believe that the real (versus virtual) classroom is the primary and best space for interactive learning. However, new media (multimedia, CD-ROMs, web-based archives, hypertext authoring, email, electronic discussion lists and chat rooms) have interesting implications for pedagogy in the broad sense, and for the teaching of oral history in particular. The digital world provides exciting new possibilities for representing, interpreting, archiving, and teaching ethnographic and field-based research. But the key verbs are "enable, help, enhance, facilitate, promote," emphasizing the role of technology as a tool. Even in the most utilitarian sense, electronic media can make a difference in the architecture of the classroom. Rather than a space to "deliver" information, technology can help to turn the oral history classroom into a project-based, collaboration workshop.

In *Engines of Inquiry*, a pathbreaking "cyberbook," Randy Bass argues that:

> There are three things that drive the learning of experts: the *questions* that we want to ask, the *cultural record* and materials that we have to work with, and the *methods* and theories that govern our practice. . . . The question confronting us as teachers . . . is how can information technologies play a role in the engines of inquiry that drive learning?[7]

Bass offers a useful synthesis of how "information technologies can serve to enhance six kinds of quality learning"—distributive learning, authentic tasks and complex inquiry, dialogic learning, constructive learning, public accountability, and reflective and critical thinking.[8] I refer to many of these categories throughout this essay, to suggest ways in which my experiment with oral history and new digital media embodied many of these quality learning goals. I found that even very simple electronic applications facilitated the learning process, enhancing communication, building teamwork and collaborative construction, facilitating reflection and interpretation, and enabling socially responsible research and almost instant archive-building. Some of these moments of good learning are worth capturing here.

Initial Strategies

One of the advantages of beginning an oral history class with a pre-selected topic is that students do not have to begin secondary research from scratch. Having a bibliographic point of departure (secondary readings already on reserve) students were able to advance swiftly to discussing issues and theoretical approaches and preparation for fieldwork.

Identifying subjects for interview creates tension and takes time. My pre-planning included establishing connections with college-bound programs at local middle, high school, and on our own campus.[9] In addition, students were able to draw upon their own friends and peers on campus for some interviews. The eighteen students in the class conducted a total of thirty-six interviews, on and off campus, with Chicana/o, Mexicana/o, African American, Asian American, and European American students. Interviews were conducted in the traditional one-on-one fashion, and each student was asked to transcribe and critically annotate their best interview. Other than this, all other stages of the process involved group work, culminating in a collaboratively constructed newspaper feature, a webpage, a public presentation, and a new section of the Oral History Archive (all detailed further ahead). The availability of electronic communication and centralization was a critical ingredient to our ability to work collaboratively.

Digital Tools

Before moving into the more substantive discussion of teaching and learning, let me diverge briefly to detail some of the technological strategies that facilitated the learning process — the design of digital tools, email communication, electronic assessment, and archiving. First, I set up a class folder on email, where course materials, assignments, original documents (transcripts),

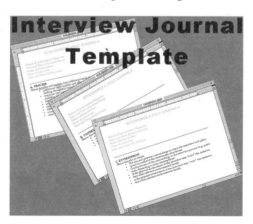

and student work could be easily accessed and exchanged. This became our "class central." Then I designed templates to facilitate field journaling and interview transcription. And finally I developed a comfortable process of electronic commentary, assessment, and an instant electronic archive.

1. Interview Journal Template

Students were asked to write field journals for each interview, attending to three main areas: the interview process, interview content and new knowledge gained, and interview environment. Journals became field records for consultation during the analytical process. In order to habituate students to keeping journals, I designed a three-page Interview Journal Template.[10]

The template specified the questions and issues to be addressed in the student's reflection. The template was posted to the Class Folder so that students could download it to their desktops and enter their field notes and comments. Having the questions and form readily available helped students complete this assignment within hours after the interview. Once completed, students posted their journals to the Class Folder for me to retrieve, read, insert comments, assess, and return via email. The entire process was electronic.

2. Transcription Template

One of the most difficult and time-consuming steps in the oral history process is transcription. Therefore, I asked the head of our technology support office to design a template to make transcription easier on the students. He

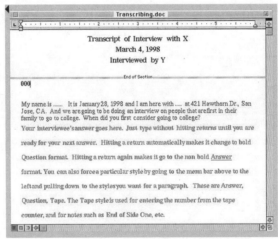

used the "Style" function in MS Word to construct a template whereby students could focus on typing what they were hearing, rather than worrying about format. Striking the "Enter" key automatically switched the format from Question to Answer, and back to Question (from Non-Bold to Bold and back). Students could then transcribe tapes without stopping to format manually each voice shift. Once transcribed, they went back to revise spelling, punctuation, and format errors. Format revisions encouraged re-listening to the tape for accuracy of content transcription.

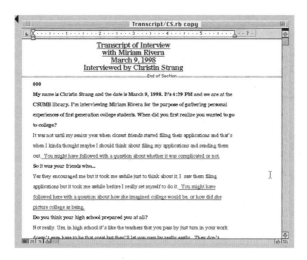

3. Email Communication

Our campus email network —*First Class*—provided a centralized communication space, a Class Folder. I used the Class Folder to facilitate information exchange, teamwork, assessment, and archival development. The Class Folder provided a virtual "workshop" space that complemented and supported in-class group work. It also provided an automatic electronic file for document exchange of field journals, transcripts, logs, critical annotations, and other student work.

The Class Folder provided twenty-four-hour access, enabling students to access class materials and templates, retrieve and post assignments and exchange interview excerpts and drafts of their critical commentaries. I posted all the digitized tools, such as the Journal Templates, Transcription Template, Release Forms, the Interview Guide, and Guidelines for Sound Recording. Students downloaded the materials when they needed to. They returned completed assignments and documents by email to the Class Folder, where I or other students could retrieve them. One of the advantages of electronic centralizing is that students are more able to access and learn from each other's work. I set strict deadlines for submissions, and deducted points for late postings, so that stragglers would not have the advantage of reading others' work before submitting their own. Although the danger of plagiarism exists, I found the pedagogical advantages more compelling. Most students agree that learning improves dramatically when, in retrospect, they can see how others approached the assignment or when an advanced model is provided.

4. Assessment, Class Management and Grading

One of the more significant impacts of these experiments with technology is that it changed the way I organized and managed record keeping. I kept electronic folders for each student in which originals and graded versions of their work were archived. Electronic exchange also changed my assessment practices. Email and MS Word enabled me to download, assess, grade, and return assignments to students with surprising ease. While student work was posted on the open Class Folder, I returned graded work to each student individually, protecting the confidentiality of grades. Using the "Revision" or "Track Changes" function (under Tools), I entered comments directly in the students' electronic documents. Revisions appear in another color and underlined, and can be inserted anywhere in a text. I would insert my comments as I read the text, and then review and often revise them for clarity and precision. I found that the screen focused my attention. This strategy is less useful, perhaps, in assessing very long papers, as it is more difficult to retain a sense of the whole when working on the screen. However, I found electronic commentary very useful in helping students acquire better oral history field research and archival skills. Because commentaries and revisions appear in another color, attention can be drawn to detail. For example, I could signal exact sites of format errors in transcripts or subject indexes, and of course, call attention to spelling errors or incomplete citations. More importantly, I could signal sites of effective or ineffective interview techniques, of good or poor listening, thus attending to the dynamics of the oral process.

I did not find any significant time difference between electronic and hand grading. In fact, I found that for journals and transcripts, the screen helped me focus my attention on the dynamics of interview process and the detail of good transcription and archival techniques. And the comments were always neat and legible. Nonetheless, I also asked students to maintain course portfolios with the hard copy of every assignment handed in, and a printout of the graded version they received back.

5. Electronic Archive Development

Electronic delivery of documents automatically created a virtual archive of all transcripts, subject indices (tape logs), and other materials (field journals) pertinent to a particular interview.

Distributive and Constructive Learning

As Bass points out, new technologies give "direct access to the growing distribution of cultural knowledge across diverse resources."[11] It also provides

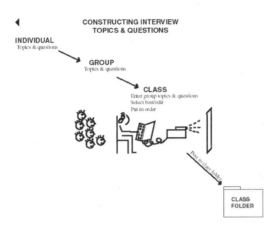

the means to "distribute the responsibility for making knowledge . . . and to construct and share their ideas . . . in a whole range of public learning contexts." The experience of our oral history classroom confirmed that, indeed, technology enabled and enhanced sharing particular cultural knowledge gained by each student in the field. It also facilitated students' ability to share responsibility for building a collective analysis that took multiple public forms.

Building an Interview Guide

Technology significantly facilitated collective construction of a framework for fieldwork and interpretation. The computer enabled us to turn the classroom into a hands-on workshop, and to expose everyone to a critical design and selection process. Based on team assessments of secondary research, students determined which issues needed to be explored through oral history. Then we came together in our "smart classroom," and with professor at the keyboard, digitally built an Interview Guide. The various topics for exploration (transition from high school to college, expectations of college, financial support, cultural support, campus support, culture/race/gender issues, and future goals), formed categories for interview questions. Subsequently, these same categories provided a framework for analysis, interpretation, and writing.

Each student was asked to bring to class ten questions they thought important to ask his/her interviewees, In class, students met in small groups to put forward five best questions from the group. Each group entered their selections into the computer. We projected all the entries on the large screen, and while I sat at the keyboard, students guided the revision process. They determined the categories, clustered the questions by category, and analyzed the efficacy of each question (identifying whether it was an open- or closed-ended, leading or non-leading, double barreled, loaded question, and so on). They made collective choices - to keep, revise, or dump a question. They identified repetitions, natural clusters, sequences, and closed gaps. All eyes were focussed on the screen and voices freely called out, "That's a loaded question," "That's a good one," "That goes together with . . .," "That's a good follow-up."

By the end of the session, students not only had a comprehensive interview guide, but they also understood how to construct open-ended questions, follow up questions, questions asking for feelings as well as facts, questions that would elicit longer or shorter narratives, and so on. Their guide had been constructed collaboratively, reflecting critical thinking, collective deliberation, and a new understanding of interview methods and strategies. Coupling digital technology with group work enabled the class to address the dialogic nature of oral history, understand how teamwork can produce best thinking, and practice shared responsibility. And, although blackboards can serve the same didactic function of recording group thought, digital technology in the classroom enabled us to produce a needed document on the spot (we did the same for our Release Forms), that could be emailed immediately to everyone for use in the field.

Cross Talk: Weaving a Collaborative Analysis

To construct their analysis and build a collectively-authored article, students worked in groups. They broke into small teams of two or three. Each team had the responsibility to develop and write that section of the analysis

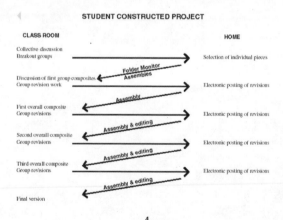

(for example, the transition from high school to college, financial aid, family supports and mentoring, institutional support structures, culture, race, and gender issues). This way, the topical categories of the Interview Guide structured the outline of the article and the division of labor in the classroom. Based on extensive classroom discussions of interview findings, each team outlined the points it wanted to make, drew on transcripts and secondary readings to develop its critical analysis, negotiated a point of view and conclusions, integrated specific life history excerpts, and wrote drafts of each section. Drafts were then circulated, reviewed and revised by the entire class until we had a polished and integrated piece.

How did technology support this process? Email facilitated a sustained dialogic environment outside the classroom. It enabled immediate access to and circulation of primary documents (transcripts, excerpts) and drafts for collaborative review. The digital medium enabled students to "pull out" the texts they wanted to use, assemble drafts, and print them out for review the next day in class. The classroom then became a workshop space, where teams brainstormed, outlined arguments, identified materials, discussed perspectives, built collaborative interpretations, defined next steps, assigned homework tasks, edited texts, arranged for the next stages of document sharing, revised and polished drafts. Technology enabled a "weaving" process, where electronic exchange from home facilitated group process in class and built each successive stage of production.[12] Electronic communication helped build the momentum of the project and significantly streamlined production of various collectively-authored pieces (newspaper feature, oral presentation, and webpage).

In the end, technology stimulated a student constructed process and product. Technology also enhanced the decentralization of the learning. Students worked autonomously within their teams, and I became a resource and facilitator rather than a singular authority in the classroom.

Complex Inquiry and Critical Thinking

There are several ways in which new media helped model the complexity of interpretation. To begin with, we produced a digital working archive of primary interview documents. I asked each student to transcribe their best interview. Once the transcripts existed in digital form, the entire corpus or select pieces were immediately accessible to other members of the class. In essence, we created our own primary database which the student teams could retrieve, examine, and use with great ease. They could now place pieces of transcript side by side, compare texts, compare perspectives, and construct interpretations. The interpretation process, however, was guided.

In order to engage students in collaborative analysis, I devised inquiry assignments. The objectives were to engage students in analysis from more than one perspective, to stimulate "cross talk," and to help weave different pieces of narrative into a collaborative interpretation.

Multiple Perspectives

At the beginning of this class I had hoped to find a way to merge the multiple interpretations of a single piece of text into one document. This way, many students could comment on the same piece of text, and examine each other's interpretations. Such an exercise might help train students to consider varying interpretations and to engage in more complex analysis. However, I was not aware of any program that would allow me to do this easily. I wanted to keep my use of technology simple, requiring a minimal learning curve for all.

Instead, in order to illustrate multiple levels and perspectives in critical interpretation and the dialogic interaction between the text and the interviewer's analysis, each student developed a multilayered *explication de texte*. Each successively annotated the same piece of interview transcript, as described below.[13] Each student selected a substantial segment of transcript addressing one of the interview topics. Criteria for selection include:

- Does the segment give insight into the topic?
- Does it reinforce/contradict secondary readings and research?
- Does the emotion and tone influence meaning?
- Does it convey something about memory?

Each segment of transcript was annotated four different times, each time attending to a different dimension of analysis:

1. Subject content: What issues related to first-generation students stand out in this excerpt and why? Does your material reinforce/contradict secondary research or present new insights into our subject?

2. Oral v. Written: How does the meaning you derive from reading the written transcript stack up against your impression from listening to the oral delivery on tape? How do tone and emotion add meaning to the topic?

3. Memory: What can you say about the strategic role of memory in this excerpt? Is memory here nostalgia? Is it breaking or reinforcing silences? Is it playing a role of historical affirmation?

4. Self-reflection: What is your own personal experience with regard to the issues and experiences narrated by your interviewees?

Annotations were posted to the Class Folder, so students would be able to read each other's interpretations prior to class discussions and group work.

Although we were not able to merge and juxtapose the various annotations into one document, students learned how to build analysis in stages, using different criteria and different perspectives. From a pedagogical standpoint, the ability to easily confront texts in their original and edited versions, in their visual, spoken, and written representations, provides a richer palette for illustrating the constructed nature of interpretation itself. Clustering also has the potential to promote a more dialogic critical practice. The single authoritative control of a body of material and its interpretation can be reshaped into a more polysemic, dialogic model, where multiple and competing interpretations of, and debates around, a single text are linked.

Real Research and Public Accountability

Oral history involves producing primary research materials. At teaching institutions, where funds for research are often limited, deficits can be turned into opportunities for what Bass terms "authentic inquiry."[14] Our Oral History and Community Memory Archive is being built through student coursework and independent projects. The interviews, transcripts, logs, and research papers are accessible to other students, faculty, and the public. In this way, students are engaged in real research that exists beyond the life of a class. Oral history is not a make-believe exercise. The policy outcome of this particular class project also made the work all the more purposeful.

When I designed the class, I expected that students would present the results of their research in a public forum. The tapes and transcripts would also comprise a new section of the oral history archive. It was the students' idea to publish a special insert in the school newspaper and to make a webpage. Understanding that they were engaged in real research, they pointed out that newspaper and web publication would extend the life of the project beyond the class experience and provide lobbying tools for planning student services. The products emerged in succession, each building on the one before it: Newspaper Article > Public Presentation > Webpage.

Newspaper Article

In an extensive four-page feature article, titled "First In My Family To Go To College," students synthesized their research and presented their findings to the campus community. The article was read widely by students and administrators, and students felt a strong sense of individual and collective accomplishment - that despite the labor-intensive nature of oral history research, the end result made an impact. The newspaper article provided the narrative framework for the more extensive webpage.

Public Presentation

Once the newspaper article had been assembled, students then had to grapple with how to best take this material to the "stage," and adapt it for public presentation. Not surprisingly, the face-to-face human context in which eighteen students spoke directly to an audience composed of the people they had interviewed, other students, and campus administrators and planners, was moving. It was a bonding experience that concluded three months of teamwork. Students were challenged to produce a synthesis that was didactic, critical, dramatic, and attentive to ethical oral history practice. Again in teams, they scripted out a presentation that combined dramatic readings of selected oral histories, paraphrasing of narratives, and analytical interpretations.[15] Many students also wove in their own personal stories, as many were first generation college students themselves.

The process of developing the script followed a similar working pattern to that of the newspaper article. Students used the classroom to work in teams to script and rehearse the presentation. They used email exchange at home to produce drafts. The entire event (ninety minutes) was videotaped, and a clip of this material, along with audiotape, was integrated into the webpage.

Class Webpage

The web provided an important forum for presentation of our research, one that increased the afterlife and purposefulness of the project far beyond a grade. The class webpage (http://classes.monterey.edu /HCOM/ HCOM314SL-0l/world/index.html) now forms part of the permanent electronic archive of the University. It stands as an example of the relationship of oral history research to the life of the students and the campus itself.

Structurally, the webpage permitted us to link a kaleidoscopic set of materials for multiple (different) readings by multiple (distinct) audiences. These materials include:

- primary texts - narrative excerpts
- research tools and templates
- interpretive analysis
- critical commentaries and references
- multimedia integration of audio and video
- still photographs and graphics
- links to the Archive
- links to related documents - the class syllabus, the Interview Guide
- an email box inviting commentaries and questions from website visitors.

The website also serves as a permanent archive for all the class materials and assignments. In time, I hope to be able to add readings and make the webpage the digital reserve reading site as well. Since the subject of first generation college students lends itself to longitudinal study, I will teach the class in Spring 2000, focusing on the same topic. Students will be able to re-interview many of those who participated as interviewees in Spring 98. In this case, the webpage provides an already structured resource for comparative study.

Archive

As with all my other oral history classes, the interviews and final work are archived in our campus Oral History and Community Memory Archive. From the beginning, students were aware that they were producing primary documents to be archived for future research. Thus, the importance of care, accuracy, appropriate transcription and formatting. Students also felt that their work had a lasting value and tried to produce the best primary documents they could.

Currently, the interview tapes, transcripts, and subject logs are physically archived with appropriate releases. Except for the tapes and releases, all other materials also exist in electronic form. Building a fully functional *virtual* archive will be a long and complex process, involving the establishment of ethical protocols of permissions, access, and so on. Even the process of digitizing audio and video documents involves complicated technical questions for experts. In the meantime, students in other classes may access the materials by coming to the physical archive.

Digital technology enables the construction of rich virtual archival sites that cluster primary documents, original and translated texts, complete and edited versions, secondary resources, visuals, sound, competing critical analyses, and lengthy bibliographies.

Next Steps

Since Spring 1998, the work of the oral history class has been presented to various planning committees concerned with student success and retention. The research has been recognized as a model of how our own curriculum can effectively tie student learning to institution building. I look forward to the follow-up longitudinal study. In terms of technology, I will be enhancing the webpage to include an electronic reserve reading room, more voice and video, student field journals, and I will continue to design and refine exercises for critical inquiry. In these ways, my course will become "web-based" but it will remain a course delivered in the real classroom. I am anxious to find appropriate software tools for modelling the polysemic and dialogic nature of oral history process and interpretation. We will also be experimenting with mounting a virtual archive, with streamed audio and video.

The comfort which successive generations of students will have with information technologies suggests that creative adaptation of oral history teaching methods must include electronic strategies. If there is one image in my mind that represents this class, it is the day we built our interview guide, when I was able to completely step out of my role as professor, to become the "inputter," the person at the keyboard who merely executed instructions. The screen had everyone's rapt attention, and students became the directors, empowered through new media to become constructors of their own learning.

Notes

I would like to acknowledge the invaluable help I received from Troy Challenger, Faculty Technology Consultant, Academic Technology and Media Services at CSUMB, in conceptualizing the use of technology in this class and in designing the electronic tools. I am also very grateful to Yael Maayani, a former CSUMB student, for the creative digitial illustrations throughout this text.

1. A shorter version of this article was published in *Works and Days* 31/32, vol 16, nos 1 and 2, 1998, pp. 177–192.

2. The oral history project I helped develop and conduct at the Center for Puerto Rican Studies, Hunter College, always involved a team of researchers and community activists.

3. Randy Bass, *Engines of Inquiry; A Practical Guide for Using Technology to Teach American Culture*, Georgetown: American Studies Crossroads Project, 2nd ed, 1997, pp. 1–14.

4. California State University at Monterey Bay opened in Fall 1995 with very little advanced planning. Consequently, the infrastructure, the curriculum, the student support services and policies are still being designed and planned with the University in full swing.

5. Students who are first in their families to go to college are a growing college population. Campuses recognize their responsibility in providing targeted, culturally informed support to ensure college success. This often involves programs and support mechanisms that are sensitive to the combined emotional, practical, academic, financial, social and cultural pressures felt by students who do not have this experience in their family memory and history. Support services include advising, academic and emotional counselling, career counselling, mentoring, tutoring, and the provision of social spaces, cultural clubs and organizations.

6. Our student body reflects larger state demographics: increased immigration, and a general explosion in numbers of college-age youth. It also feels the effects of right-wing California politics: increased xenophobia reflected in the passing of Propositions 187 (denying social services to undocumented immigrants), 209 (rolling back Affirmative Action, which has had dramatic immediate effects in the public university systems), and 227 (abolishing bilingual education). In this right-wing political climate, increased pressure is placed on the public university to remove what conservatives call "special interest" programs and courses of study—those that serve the interests of women, immigrants, and students of color in general.

7. Bass, 1997, pp. 1–14.

8. Bass, 1997, pp.1–14.

9. A group of Chicano/Mexicano freshmen agreed to participate in the research. They were recruited to our campus by Educational Talent Search, a programme that works with middle schools and high schools to bring first generation students to college. We also worked with local middle and high school programmes that give skills training and support to students who will be first in their families to go to college.

10. To design the Interview Journal templates, I used the Header and Footer function in Word.

11. Bass, 1977, pp. 1–14.

12. Most students have personal computers at home. The emphasis given to technology on our campus encourages students to acquire home computers. Low-income students are often able to acquire economic assistance for purchase of a personal computer, and email, word-processing, and internet software is provided to all at no cost. In addition, the campus has computer laboratories accessible throughout the day and evening for students to complete assignments on campus.

13. For a discussion of text annotations in oral history, see Ronald J Grele, "Personal Narratives: What and How," *Acomo, Rivista Internazionale di Studi Nordamericani*, vol 10, Spring 1997, pp. 4–6. The entire volume serves as an excellent model of this process, as each essay is built around extensive annotations.

14. Bass, 1997, pp. 1–14.

15. The webpage integrates an audio clip of an interview, and video clips of the public presentation.

New Media Technologies

Rina Benmayor and Cecilia O'Leary
California State University, Monterey Bay
Tracey M. Weis
Millersville University
Bret Eynon
La Guardia Community College, City University of New York

New digital technologies and multimedia are transforming how we teach and learn. They are transforming our classrooms from spaces of delivery to spaces of active inquiry and authorship. New digital media are empowering students to become researchers, storytellers, historians, oral historians, and cultural theorists in their own right. Whether constructing their own life stories or interpreting the life stories of others, the digital format transforms students' capacity to synthesize, interpret, theorize, and create new cultural and historical knowledge. In this way, digital formats potentially democratize learning and produce critical subjects and authors.

The four short papers that follow are snapshots of experiments with new media in our respective classrooms. They were presented at the Annual Meeting of the Oral History Association, in San Diego, California (October, 2002), to a standing-room-only audience.

- Rina Benmayor, CSU Monterey Bay, incorporates Digital Storytelling in her Latina Life Stories class. Students, the majority of whom are Latina/o, author their own life stories, digitally combining voice, music, and images. Then, they theorize their digital stories, much the way Latina writers have done, exploring how to create new knowledge and theory.

- Cecilia O'Leary, CSU Monterey Bay, has students construct Digital Histories, many of which are family oral histories. The digital storytelling form authorizes them to lay claim to their own histories, their own voices, and to use primary sources in authoritative ways. Digital history-telling enables students to see themselves as citizen-historians.

- Tracey Weis' African American History students conduct archival research in Web-based historic sites and repositories, and construct collaborative interpretations in PowerPoint. Through their digital presentations, students become more conscious and reflective about the power and responsibilities of historical synthesis and interpretation.

Reprinted from *Social Justice, 29*(4), 2002: 344–352, by permission of the authors and the publisher.

- Bret Eynon works with a predominantly immigrant student body of color. His students conduct oral histories with their peers and develop electronic portfolios, in which hypertext facilitates multi-faceted self-representation.

The four of us are principal researchers in the Visible Knowledge Project (VKP). Headquartered at Georgetown University (http://crossroads.Georgetown.edu/vkp), VKP is a five-year, multi-million dollar project involving seventy faculty and twenty-one college and university campuses nationwide. It is one of the most significant projects in technology and learning, and the largest in the humanities, social sciences, and interdisciplinary culture fields. Through its focus on both student learning and faculty development in technology-enhanced environments, faculty investigators are exploring effective pedagogies that incorporate new media technologies. Research projects focus on creating and researching models of teaching and learning that promote distributive learning, authentic tasks, complex inquiry, dialogic learning, constructive learning, public accountability, reflection, and critical thinking. Within VKP, the four of us comprise a Digital Storytelling Affinity Group. Through videoconferencing, we share our work with each other and with other faculty across the country, discuss pedagogical strategies and tools, give workshops and conference presentations, and co-author articles such as this one.

Digital Stories

Rina Benmayor
California State University Monterey Bay

In 1997, I saw my first Digital Story. Three years later, I took a Digital Storytelling workshop and produced my own story.[1] Since then, digital storytelling has become a main feature of my "Latina Life Stories" class. Along with reading and analyzing the autobiographical writings of U.S. Latinas (Chicanas, Puerto Ricans, Cubanas, Dominicanas, and mixed heritage Latinas), my students, who are predominantly of Mexican heritage, write their own autobiographies and they produce their own digital stories. They become authors in their own right, inscribing their own identities and life experiences through this compelling digital format. At the end of the course, each student receives a CD of all the class digital stories to keep.

"What's a Digital Story?" you are asking. Essentially, it's a three- to four-minute digital multimedia "movie" that combines an original story or script with images, music, and above all, a narration in the author's own voice. We are using this format to tell identity stories and to "theorize" them. We start by turning a personal narrative into a short script (about a page and a half, double-spaced). The author then records her/his script, selects and scans visuals (photographs, video, and creative drawings or clip art), and chooses a music track to run underneath. While there are many multimedia-authoring softwares available, my students use Power Point, as it is a program with which they are somewhat familiar. Once completed, the stories are converted into Quick Time movies and burned on a CD-ROM so that they can be played on any platform.

My purpose, however, is not to elaborate the technological "How-Tos." I am more intrigued by Digital Storytelling as a medium of empowerment, a system of representation, and a pedagogical tool.

What are these digital stories about? They are transformational stories that engage histories of resistance, struggle, and survival and affirm new consciousness in the making. For example, Jacinto's story is a tribute to his grandfather, to the many life lessons his grandfather taught him, above all, how to sing with all his heart and all his soul. Using the conventions of Chicano humor, Viana tells about "The Day I Became a Chicana," about awakening one morning to suddenly find herself transformed, with an entirely new consciousness. Dawn reclaims her Bolivian identity and heritage, and denounces ways in which she is stereotyped and homogenized by mainstream society. Leon tells about his journey to recenter himself in his indigenous heritage. Carlos reflects on his migration trajectory from rural Mexico to picking strawberries in California, to ESL classes, to community college, and finally, to the university.

Emily, whose half-sister and brother are mixed race, challenges identity based on color rather than on consciousness. Mary resists being forced to only check one identity box and claims her multiple identities and positionalities. Gabriela and Rocio name the cultural oppressions inscribed upon their bodies.

These stories are not born out of the blue. They are inspired by the auto-biographical writings of Latinas and by the cultural theories these writings embody—the concepts of borderlands and new mestiza consciousness (Anzaldua, 1986), hybrid identities that go beyond ethnic heritage (Morales and Levins Morales, 1986); border feminism (Saldivar-Hull, 1998), and feminist latinidades (Latina Feminist Group, 2001). The readings trigger memories and emotions. Students, female and male, begin to voice their own stories in class—remembrances of painful, difficult, or joyful moments in their lives. For many, this is the first time they have thought about their lives as embodying larger social forces, theories, and identities. Others who have find that the class unleashes long-held feelings. The class provides them a context not just for telling their stories but also for drawing upon new theoretical thinking regarding identity, ethnicity, and culture. Students frequently find that they are now telling the story differently, putting it through historical and theoretical lenses they did not have before. Personal experience becomes theorized, situated.

In the class, students also see the digital stories produced by previous classes. Suddenly, they feel authorized to inscribe their voices and create their own digital texts. They begin to envision their own digital contributions to the testimonial literature on cultural identity. Many students find that in constructing this digital story, they are re-constructing a self, re-situating their subjectivity within broader social frameworks. The stories link their tellers to real and imagined communities of meaning and belonging. The digital medium also enables students to produce and "publish" their stories for multiple audiences of viewers and listeners. Digital stories navigate through the Internet, through CD-ROMs, through public presentations, in family viewings, and become part of the broader corpus of Latina/life story collections. The medium becomes a tool for constructing a self, but also for contributing new generational perspectives on identity, community, belonging, and selfhood. There is no gatekeeper here, no editorial competition, only encouragement to author life stories. In terms of production, the digital story is a more democratic form that enables new voices to emerge through an immediate and self-determined process. Creating the digital story has proved to be an empowering and transformative process.

Two years ago, our campus was invited to become part of the national Visible Knowledge Project (VKP). As one of the VKP principal investigators, I chose Latina Life Stories and the digital storytelling process as my research laboratory. I am currently exploring how digital storytelling can help students understand in a more conscious and visible way, the process of building theory from personal experience. I am wondering whether and how digital authoring may demystify theory and empower students to become theorizers of their own historical and cultural experiences.

I believe that students find it easier to deconstruct and interpret a multimedia text theoretically and conceptually than they do a written text. As generations born and raised in visual cultures, students feel free to use the multiple idioms that new digital technologies afford, the multiple languages of representation—oral, written, aural, visual, and technological. The digital story situates the authors as tellers, writers, performers, producers, and interpreters of their own stories. In recording their narratives, students intentionally tell the story to an imagined audience. The personal voice constructs the "subject," while the nuances of tone, mood, and emotional intent provide clues for interpretation. The visual text also constructs the subject, whether literally, through photographs or video or by means of symbolic imagery (abstract images, clip art, or drawings). The visual text provides a second "voice," a second signifying track, which in the best stories does more than simply illustrate the spoken word. For example, one story is told in a fotonovela style, playing on the Mexican cultural tradition of the romance comic book. Musical tracks constitute a third signifier, dialoguing with the script, through lyrics and mood. A story about linking back across generations of ancestry places particular song lyrics in dialogue with the narrative, giving the story two interconnected tellers.

We used to end the class with a Digital Testimonio festival, where we viewed all the stories for the first time. Now, I have moved up the production date earlier in the semester, in order to leave three weeks at the end for analysis and theorizing. We are just beginning this process. Through structured reflections, discussions, and group work, students will begin deconstructing their own and each others' stories, articulating connections with the readings and theories, analyzing their visual and aural texts, and hopefully making claims for new understandings and, yes, theories, from their own generational, geographical, gendered, and culturally situated perspectives. It is my hope that they will become cultural theorists in a more conscious, engaged, and personally invested way. Stay tuned.

Note

1. I came to learn about digital stories through the work of the Digital Storytelling Center in Berkeley, California, (www.digitalstorycenter.com). Subsequently, we invited them to give a weekend workshop on our campus. In creating my own story, "Where Do You Come From?" <http://media.csumb.edu/mediadetail.asp?FormatID=1&MedialD=84>, I was able to see how to integrate this medium into my course. Thanks to the unfailing pedagogical commitment and technological wizardry of Troy Challenger, our head of Faculty Development, and his assistant John Bettencourt, my students receive sustained technological instruction and support to produce their digital stories.

Works Cited

Alvarez, J. (1992). *How the Garcia girls lost their accents*. NY: Plume.

Anzaldua, G. (1999). *Borderlands/La frontera: The new mestiza* (2nd ed.). San Francisco: Aunt Lute.

Cantti, N. E. (1995). *Canicula: Snapshots of a girlhood en la frontera*. Albuquerque: University of New Mexico Press.

Cisneros, S. (1984). *The house on Mango street*. New York: Random House.

Cisneros, S. (1991). *Woman hollering creek*. New York: Random House.

Digital Story Center. www.digitalstorycenter.com

Latina Feminist Group. (2001). *Telling to live: Latina feminist testimonios*. Durham: Duke University Press.

Levins Morales, A., & Morales, R. (1986). *Getting home alive.* Ithaca, NY: Firebrand Books.

Moraga, C. , & Anzaldua, G. (1983). *This bridge called my back: Writings by radical women of color.* New York: Kitchen Table/Women of Color Press.

Obejas, A. *We came all the way from Cuba so you could dress like this?*

Ortiz Cofer, J. (1990). *Silent dancing: A partial remembrance of a Puerto Rican childhood.* Houston, TX: Arte Publico Press.

Multicultural History in the New Media Classroom

Cecilia Elizabeth O'Leary
California State University, Monterey Bay

How can we design undergraduate history courses that make history come alive? How can we facilitate students being able to both learn history and make history? Inspired by the work in digital stories, I am now teaching digital histories. I have adapted this powerful new medium to engage students in history making. For two semesters now, students in my course, "Multicultural History in the New Media Classroom," have created digital histories. In this process, I have witnessed their ability to *see* connections between their own lives and history that their written essays, while important, just do not impart. Students first begin to see themselves as citizen historians as they search for a topic that really matters to them. For example, one student wanted to write about the struggle for farmworker rights and remembered that her grandfather had marched with César Chávez. She spent hours at the public library in Salinas searching through old newspapers and suddenly came across a photograph of her grandfather, her younger sister in his arms, marching under the United Farm Workers flag.

"Multicultural History in the New Media Classroom," is framed by the belief that students not only need to learn history, but also to be trained to become citizen historians. While students may not go on to become professional historians, they all will need to know how to bring a historical perspective to contemporary issues as they become our future leaders and teachers. History, with a capital "H"—that is the History written by professional historians—does not account for the many different ways that all of us contribute to the social construction of the past. Just as history does not exist in the singular, knowledge and responsibility for communicating information about the past is not limited to the written word or professional historians.

As citizen historians, students grapple with forming a historical interpretation of complex research data and struggle with linking personal histories with larger national and global developments. For example, a student researching her dual identities as a Latina and a child of immigrants, had to learn about the political history of U.S.-backed repression in Latin America when she discovered that part of her family had been rounded up in an anti-leftist sweep of peasants in Guatemala. In her digital history, she presented pictures of repression alongside pictures from her family's scrapbook.

Students' sense of themselves as citizen historians deepens as they uncover new, and at times surprising or disturbing, historical evidence. The weight of being accountable to the people who have lived and died in the past is heightened for students as they take responsibility for who and what will be included or excluded from the public digital histories they are about to create. For example, one student found two photographs of her grandmother along with other family members dressed in KKK robes. She struggled with whether to tell this part of her history and in the end decided that as an anti-racist she would. As students view the digital histories of fellow students, the experience of being taught history by one of their peers is electric.

Digital histories represent a dramatic way that new media computer technologies can facilitate students directly contributing to the on-going project of uncovering and disseminating information about the diversity of our past(s). First, digital histories provide students with tools to creatively narrate their family or community's history in ways that resonate with today's visual culture. Second, the use of popular software, such as PowerPoint, allows students to incorporate different kinds of primary evidence—from photo albums, newspapers and artifacts to songs, oral histories and film clips. And third, students can easily take a CD copy of their digital history out of the classroom and share it with family, friends and community.

Students combine primary evidence with their own taped voices narrating what they have researched in a four-minute visual presentation. They draw upon their diverse backgrounds and experiences to produce new pieces of history that would otherwise have remained invisible. The project of creating a digital history from their research findings, in addition to writing a scholarly paper, allows students to move their own family and community from the in-between spaces of history into the center. In the process, they gain the power of voice—their own-recorded voices narrating, interpreting, and teaching the history they have researched.

As a member of the CSUMB Visible Knowledge Project (VKP) research group, I have focused my research on how Digital Histories affect students becoming citizen historians. Over the two semesters that I have taught "Multicultural History in the New Media Classroom" I have been able to for-

RINA BENMAYOR, ET AL.

mulate my research questions, identify the evidence of student learning I plan to collect, and pre-test the use of computer instruction in a reading and writing intensive class. The course meets twice a week, two hours in seminar and two hours in a computer lab. Students learn to analyze primary and secondary sources from research archives on the Web and from assigned books. After writing a substantial historical essay that locates their family or community history in a broader context, students then must figure out what part of their analysis and narrative they want to present visually.

There are numerous parts to making a digital history including scanning images, digitizing sound, and editing film clips. Similar to an outline, students organize their presentation by creating a storyboard that they divide into columns. Scene by scene, students track their own narration, as well as the music and images they intend to incorporate. They are required to scan and digitize primary materials they have collected. Hands-on instruction and "How-Tos" on every aspect of the technical and conceptual process are made available to the class each step of the way. Staff who are new media experts assist in the computer lab, and I also invite colleagues to guest lecture.[2] For example, a colleague from Visual and Public Art introduces students to theories of visual communication. Later, a colleague from Teledramatic Arts helps them make a critique of the dramatic qualities of an early version of their digital history.

At the end of the semester, students present their digital histories to fellow classmates, other students, and community members they have invited. The digital histories are then burned onto a CD-ROM that students can take with them. The CD is also archived in the Oral History and Community Memory Institute at CSUMB. With the student's signed permission, their digital histories can be used by professors for evidence of student learning, in the classroom to teach other students about historical topics, at conferences for scholarly presentations, and by fellow students who want to learn more about a certain topic. Eventually, Rina Benmayor and I, as co-directors of the Oral History and Community Memory Institute, envision establishing an ever-growing archive of student-produced digital histories and digital stories on the Web that people from around the world will be able to access and learn from.

Note

1. I both create "How-Tos" for the class and have students use the "recipes" provided by the Digital Storytelling Center in Berkeley, California, <www.digitalstorycenter.com>. At this point, my course would not be possible without the support of my chair, Renee Curry, and the technological instruction provided by Troy Challenger, head of Faculty Development, and his student assistants John Bettencourt and Thomas Freeburg. Thank you.

Gaining a Claim on the Past: Novice Historians Tell Stories About Race and Slavery at Our Nation's Historic Sites

Tracey M. Weis
Millersville University

For the past five years I have been incorporating new media resources and technologies into my courses. The immediate catalyst for this venture was my participation in the New Media Classroom summer institute, held in July 1997 and sponsored by the American Social History Project. However, this relatively recent innovation in my teaching, I can see now in retrospect, had its origins in my experiences as a community organizer in the central Appalachian coalfields twenty years ago. Living in communities compromised by large-scale absentee ownership, environmental degradation, and increasing levels of poverty, coalfield residents imaginatively used images of various kinds (posters, photographs, slide shows) to tell stories of their lives and communities that contradicted "official" versions of events. Accessible and relatively inexpensive media permitted residents in strip-mining areas (and in gentrifying urban cores) to exchange sets of slides that documented both the challenges they faced and the strategies and forms of resistance they employed. Similarly, deploying new media in college classrooms enables students to tell stories of their own lives and communities in ways that allow them to gain an authoritative claim on the past.[1]

I teach African American History, a course that in its most recent iteration tacks back and forth between the national narrative of Africans in the United States and the local history of African Americans in Lancaster County, Pennsylvania. A comparative focus on historic places, as "tangible forms of our legacy from preceding generations . . . [that] embody and reflect the traditions, experiences, ideas, and controversies of our past," connects these ostensibly local and national investigations (Patrick, 1993, p. 8). In this course, we consider nationally known historic sites as essentially local sites that are deeply embedded in community and regional economic, political, social, and cultural contexts. Students conduct a virtual field study at the beginning of the semester to identify and evaluate the practical and theoretical advantages of using historic sites (or places) as "laboratories" for learning history. Working in teams, they combine their observations as virtual visitors to selected historic sites with additional research to produce and present PowerPoint presentations, complete with narration.[2] The implicit objective of this exercise is to encourage students to compare and contrast the content and the tone of interpretations presented by public historians in historical sites and academic historians in scholarly journals. This inquiry, then, invites students to situate themselves as participants in the ongoing debate about the significance of race and slavery in America history and culture.

I am especially interested in understanding how novice historians develop and refine narrative authority and historical sensibility. I hoped that the multimedia format and presentation (the juxtaposition of text, image, and recorded voice) would prompt students to be more attentive to the components of "good stories." I suspected that the act of preparing a script and recording their own voices would encourage them to develop a point of view about historical events and processes. More specifically, I wondered if the digital format would encourage them to present the essential elements of effective and engaging historical interpretations in sharper relief than conventional historical essays. In other words, I wanted to test my hypothesis that the act of producing a multimedia project would allow them to "see" and to represent the relationships between evidence and argument with more sophistication and subtlety.

The exercise began with paired online exploration of four historic sites that interpret the colonial and early national periods: Monticello, Mount Vernon, Colonial Williamsburg, and the National Park Service.[3] To complicate the reading of the original Web sites (and to forestall conventional responses such as "No one questioned slavery in this time period," "Everyone accepted it," "The Founding Fathers had no choice"), each group was asked to examine a second Web site that presented an alternative or contradictory narrative of race and slavery.

For example, the Mount Vernon group examined an online biography of Ona Judge Staines, a bondswoman who escaped from George and Martha Washington in June 1796 while the Washingtons were in residence in Philadelphia.[4] Consulting *America: History and Life*, an online periodical index, these students found pertinent information that they could use to support both George Washington's defense and Ona Judge Staines' accusations for their presentation, "Mt. Vernon: A Slave's Haven? Or Hell?" George Washington defended himself against charges of harsh and cruel treatment by pointing out that enslaved men and women on other plantations endured worse living and working conditions.[5] Ona Judge's allegations were bolstered by observations made by visitors to Mt. Vernon, among them Henrietta Liston, wife of the British ambassador.[6] "Everyone knows George Washington," the students acknowledged at the beginning of their presentation, "but what about Ona [Judge Staines]?" Ona Judge Staines' courage in fleeing slavery and her refusal, despite repeated entreaties from the Washingtons, to return to Mount Vernon, raised vexing questions about "good" masters and encouraged students to re-think benevolent paternalism.

Using digital tools shapes how novice historians approach the fundamental challenge of establishing temporal order, how to assemble what frequently seem to them like discrete and unrelated fragments into coherent narratives. For example, something inspired or enabled one team of students telling the story of Colonial Williamsburg to situate the story of that specific community in the broader context of the evolution of slavery in Virginia and in colonial America. The imperative of a multimedia format forces a greater rigor in deciding what to show and what to tell. The redundancy, for example, of merely reading the slide is obvious—if not to the storytellers in the preparation stage then to both the storytellers and to the audience in the actual presentation. In their efforts to avoid this boring repetition, students are challenged to elaborate a point of view and to develop a perspective about what they are showing. While students can struggle to fill a slide in the same way that they agonize to fill a page, it seems that novice historians can more easily "see" the difference between presenting evidence of various kinds (showing) and explaining the significance of the evidence (telling).

Are these digital stories telling or revealing in ways that conventional historical essays are not? Less likely to simply report as they are wont to do in their papers, these novices working with multimedia are both more confident and more tentative. They are more convinced that their research has complicated rather than resolved the vexing questions posed by the Web sites of the various historic places. The effect has been to arouse rather than dampen intellectual curiosity and to make them more comfortable with assuming a more critical (even if at times a more provisional) stance.

They are more inclined to admit uncertainty and lack of resolution; more inclined to come up with questions rather than definitive answers. In short, researching and retelling these stories about race and slavery has persuaded most of these young historians that "reading historical sources directly allows [them] to make their own decisions about the meaning of the past and the intentions of historical characters" (Horton, 2002, p. 4). In searching the Web sites of various historic sites for the agency and presence of African Americans, the novice historians discovered their own narrative authority and historical sensibility. As they pondered how the Web site authors constructed their relations with their audiences and how the authors constituted themselves as authoritative interpreters of the past, they began to ask themselves fundamental questions about the purpose of history and memory making:

- What constitutes history?

- How is historical memory cultivated, perpetuated, deflected and overturned?

- What do we need to know about the past and who is entitled to reconstruct it?

- How does the past help us make sense of the present?
- Who has the authority to answer these questions?

Approaching these historic sites as visitors and students of history, students in African American History moved from "outside the circle of cultural arbiters" to the inside circle of historic interpreters.[7] They gained their own claims on the past by interrogating the controversies that these "tangible legacies" embodied and by telling more complicated stories of race and slavery than those presented at the sites.

Notes

1. For an intriguing exploration of the complex process of memory making in what is arguably one of the nation's most historic places, see Nash, 2002.

2. They used the online index *America: History and Life* to locate recently published scholarship related to the sites they investigated.

3. Monticello, The Home of Thomas Jefferson, http://www.monticello.org/; George Washington's Mount Vernon Estate and Gardens, http://www.mountvernon.org/; Colonial Williamsburg, http://www.history.org/; Cane River Creole (Louisiana), http://www.nps.gov/cari/; Fort Mose Site (Florida), http://www.cr.nps.gov/nr/travel/underrground/fl2.htm; British Fort (Florida), http://www.cr.nps.gov/nr/travel/underground/fl1.htm; Robert Stafford Plantation (Georgia), http://www.cr.nps.gov/seac/arch79.htm

4. Evelyn Gerson, "Ona Judge Staines: Escape from Washington" on the Black History section of the SeacoastNH.com website, http://ww.seacoastnh.com/arts/ona.html November 3, 2002

5. Stratford Hall Plantation, the Birthplace of Robert E. Lee, http://www.stratfordhall.org November 3, 2002.

6. Peter R. Henriques, "George Washington and Slavery," History 615: The Age of George Washington, George Mason University. http://chnm.pmu.edu/courses/henriques/hist615/gwslav.htm November 3, 2002.

7. In the introduction to *First City,* Nash acknowledged that his involvement with the exhibition *Vision and Revisions: Finding Philadelphia's Past* "obliged me to confront ... the ongoing process of rediscovering and redefining American history" and argued that in Philadelphia (as in every other site of human habitation) the process of constructing memory is "continuously under negotiation," as his questions above suggest. Nash, 10.

Works Cited

Horton, J. O. (2000). On-site learning: The power of place. *CRM Online,* 23(8), 4. Retrieved November 3,2002 from http://crm.cr.nps.gov/issue.cfm?volume=23&number=08

Nash, G. B. (2002). *First city: Philadelphia and the forging of historical memory.* Philadelphia: University of Pennsylvania Press.

Patrick, J. J. (1993). Prominent places for historic places: K–12 social studies curriculum. *CRM Online,* 16(2), 8. Retrieved November 3,2002 from http://crm.cr.nps.gov/issue.cfm?volume=16&number=02

New York Stories:
Student Oral Histories and Electronic Portfolios

Bret Eynon
LaGuardia Community College, City University of New York

With the exception of the United Nations, LaGuardia Community College may be one of the most international institutions in New York City. Set in a working class area of Queens, the borough that has emerged as today's immigrant portal, the Lower East Side of the 21st century, LaGuardia serves the city's new immigrant working class, more complex and diverse than ever before. More than two-thirds of LaGuardia's students are immigrants—and many of the native born are either African American or Puerto Rican in background. Reflecting the new patterns of global migration, LaGuardia's immigrant students come from 152 different countries, speaking 108 different native languages.

These statistics are striking. Walking the halls of the college makes the impact even more visual and immediate. One is immediately immersed in a riot of cultures, colors, and languages, a swirl that mixes traditional heritage with the beat of contemporary music and style. Let's meet some of these students:

Mamadou Mdoup is 26 years old, from Senegal, and a liberal arts major. He works as a taxi driver to support himself, pay his tuition, and send money back to his family in Africa. A member of the college's Muslim Club, Mamadou recently took advantage of LaGuardia's "Exploring Transfer" program to spend a summer studying at Vassar College. The hardest part about college for him is balancing his time. "Learning is more than books and tests," he says. "I have made sure I have time for social events, because I learn by interacting with people." When he graduates, he hopes to return to Senegal and work towards social change and a united Africa.

Sarita is 41 years old, and came to New York in the late 1980s from Peru, after a short stay in Mexico. "I decided to change my life, to look for opportunities," she explains. When she first arrived in New York, she worked as a house cleaner, 12 hours a day. Then she found work in a travel agency serving a largely Latino community. Studying accounting at LaGuardia, she found that the college's language and literacy tutorial programs made a big difference in helping her learn English and overcome what she saw as the biggest obstacle she faced. The college was also the first place where she really got to know people from outside her own community. "I particularly enjoyed the multicultural parties," she explains. "I had never done anything like that."

Ei Sander Khine came from Myanmar with her family, refugees from the repressive Burmese government. When she was eight years old, the government squashed a wave of student demonstrations and strikes, and her memories from that time are filled with "gun shots and blood in the night." Now she lives in Sunnyside, Queens, with her extended family, in a household of 18 people. Studying at home is difficult for her, due to noise and crowding, so she often stays in the LaGuardia library till it closes. Her father, who had been a teacher, now works in a restaurant, but she is studying statistics and hopes to go on to a four-year college and become a mathematics teacher herself one day.

Esra is 23 and came to New York from Bangladesh four years ago, against the wishes of her family. Small, slight, and shy about speaking in public, she seems to possess an inner strength. Growing up, she was determined to find education and more independence than she felt most women got in Bangladesh. "Just give me a chance," she told her parents. At times, her life still seems poised between two worlds. She lives with her husband in an arranged marriage; meanwhile, she studies computer science and designs course Web pages for LaGuardia faculty. Since her marriage, Esra has worn a headscarf, covering her hair in obedience to religious guidelines; more recently, however, the scarf is often draped around her shoulders, with her dark hair flowing over it.

These stories, which are by no means exceptional, were gathered by LaGuardia students themselves, as part of a course that helps students see the college—and their own lives—as a part of major historical changes. "Going Places! Immigration, Education & Change in New York City, 1900-2002" is my version of a Liberal Arts capstone course. In this course, students examine the immigrant experience, past and present, using scholarly articles, films, novels and Web sites. Their final project is an extended life history interview with another LaGuardia student, plus a 10-page paper that examines the links between that student's life and the themes and patterns studied in the course.

What different experiences do immigrant students have at LaGuardia? How do we as individuals experience and shape the individual, social, cultural, and political changes now framing the 21st century? What do students bring to the college from their families, their work, and their worlds? And how does the process of going to college affect their families and their communities— their own identities? These questions guide the project.

The project helps students examine their own experiences and place them in a larger social and historical context. It is a challenging research assignment, requiring students to conduct primary research and integrate their findings with insights from a range of sources. And in the process, the students create a rich archive of first-person testimony, documenting and preserving a process of historical transformation.

LaGuardia is in one sense the equivalent of the Henry Street Settlement House, one of the famous institutions of 100 years ago, a border zone between the immigrant world and the dominant culture, a place where differences were negotiated and new cultures created. Historians would be delighted to find a cache of interviews documenting immigrant views of life in the settlement houses. The students of *Going Places!* are helping to document the complex life of a comparable contemporary institution, the experiences of its members and, through them, the changes taking place in surrounding communities. What is particularly significant is that the students, the immigrants, are the ones asking the questions and writing the interpretations.

Certain themes come up repeatedly in the student papers—and in the reflections of the student interviewers as well. Over and over again, students talk about how important education is to them, a route away from the dead-end jobs in restaurants and sweatshops that loom as alternatives. The mix of hope and desperation articulated by both interviewers and interviewees is striking. Another common theme of the conversation is the powerful transformation of gender roles taking place in immigrant families and communities, a process fed by cultural and economic factors as well as educational processes; the excitement and uncertainty associated with this process is a recurring topic for both female and male students. A third common theme is the way that immigrant students struggle with their identity as Americans. Attracted by America and much that it stands for, LaGuardia's immigrant students are nonetheless ambivalent.

"After doing this interview, I sometimes wonder, what is the point of all the pain of being separated from loved ones, of culture shock, of discrimination," writes Gabriella Guerrero, in the conclusion to her paper. "Yes, we may make more money. . . . But I believe that we shouldn't be blinded by what the consumerist world offers." Others disagree. "This is where I plan to stay," notes Gurvinder Virk, from Pakistan by way of London. "I'm an American citizen now. In my head, in my conscience, I'm still Punjabi. But now, I'm pretty much American. I don't feel like an outsider anymore."

Digital technology plays a significant but not fundamental role in the "Going Places!" classroom. Students examine Web sites to learn more about immigration, historical and contemporary. They extensively use the discussion board on the course Web site, sharing questions, problems, and ideas. The discussion board also facilitates the exchange of draft papers for peer editing processes, which students rate as one of the most valuable elements of the course. And the site also provides a place where students deposit their final projects, creating a digital archive where the student papers are available to scholars and other students.

In the future, digital tools will play an even larger role in this process. By 2004, students' "Going Places!" projects will become a part of their electronic portfolios, as LaGuardia advances with a project now in its pilot phase. The electronic student portfolio, or ePortfolio, is a Web-based presentation of student work, created by the student. The ePortfolio can include research papers and essays, as well as projects that incorporate images, audio, and video. It asks students to analyze the meaning of their work, to reflect on it as a demonstration of their learning. And it offers the opportunity for students to supplement course work with sections on personal interests, family, culture and career hopes and dreams.

Linking pedagogy, technology, and assessment, the ePortfolio initiative is an ambitious one for LaGuardia. A small but growing number of colleges nationwide have begun to explore the use of ePortfolios. Most of the schools experimenting in this area, however, are small liberal arts colleges serving more traditional students. LaGuardia may be the first large urban community college to institute a significant ePortfolio project.

Coordinated by the LaGuardia Center for Teaching and Learning, which I direct, LaGuardia's ePortfolio project has already attracted major funding. In fall 2001, the US Department of Education awarded the College two multi-year grants allowing the college to plan and launch the project. Having completed a planning year, the College has begun its pilot year, with twenty faculty and 400 students from across the college taking part in a yearlong process of classroom testing of ePortfolio processes.

Building on classes and projects such as Going Places!, the ePortfolio may also provide a unique way for scholars and observers to better understand the changes taking place in 21st century America. At the same time, the ePortfolio project offers LaGuardia students a chance to build their technology and communication skills, and learn new ways to tell their own stories. In concert with Digital Storytelling and other such projects, it offers students an opportunity to become the authors of the Web, to bridge the Digital Divide, and to make visible the stories that have been too invisible for too long.

Teaching From The Web: Constructing a Library Learning Environment Where Connections Can Be Made

Suellen Cox and Elizabeth Housewright
California State University, Fullerton

Abstract

Faculty librarians at California State University, Fullerton, collaborated with Management Science and Information Systems and Computer Science faculty to develop a new course, "Introduction to Information Technology and Presentation." This course has been taught to 125-150 freshmen each Fall for the last three years as part of the pioneering Fullerton First Year program. Several elements inherent in the process of designing and teaching this course have contributed to changes in the library's large formal instruction program. These include collaboration and feedback from team teaching, formal assessment and student evaluations and, above all, the increasing use of Web-based resources and state-of-the-art technology. This article will focus on the evolving nature of the instruction program, which is informed by the elements listed above as well as by ongoing experimentation with innovative, student-centered, active learning methods.

Introduction

California has a three-tiered system of public education, including the University of California system, the community college system, and the California State University system, which occupies the middle tier. The twenty-three California State schools enroll students from the top one-third of high school graduating classes and offer baccalaureate and master's degrees in both traditional liberal arts and applied fields.

California State University, Fullerton (CSUF), is a large, diverse commuter campus located in Orange County in southern California. The campus currently has an enrollment of 27,000 students. Over the next few years this enrollment will increase due to a tidal wave of more than 700,000 additional students expected to enter California public college and university campuses by 2010. According to the *Los Angeles Times* (1999), the new incoming students will be more ethnically diverse than in the past, with an increasing percentage comprised of Latinos. In addition to being an ethnically diverse campus, CSUF has a broad range of ages represented in the student body. Many students transfer in at the junior level from community colleges and many are more mature re-entry students. In fact, each year less than 10 percent of the entire student body is traditional 18-year-old first year students. CSUF is a commuter campus, with the inherent challenges of building a sense of community and maximizing retention rates, in contrast to the built-in campus connections more easily achieved in a traditional educational environment.

To give further coherence to the educational process, the university is currently in the process of defining "Marks of a Cal State Fullerton Graduate" (California State University, 1999). These marks attempt to succinctly describe the distinctive characteristics of a CSUF education. These characteristics include graduates who are experienced contributors on teams and in collaborative settings and who are skilled in using technology for research, analysis, and presentation. As a step toward actualizing these goals, the university president has made technology a priority for our campus. In 1997, an ambitious initiative was launched to fully network the campus. All faculty and staff received state-of-the-art computers with a common suite of programs and applications.

Overview of the Library Instruction Program

In July 1996, the Pollak Library opened a new library wing. The new building added 130,000 square feet, almost doubling the size of the facility. Seating space increased from 650 to more than 3,000. In keeping with the president's technology initiative, the building was outfitted with new computer workstations, docking stations, fiber-optic cabling, and four fully equipped library instruction rooms. The library is often a campus leader in the rollout of new equipment and programs and has the support of a large and responsive library computer systems section. These elements contributed to a growth and expansion of the library instruction program. Since 1996, the section has been on what Dupuis (1999) refers to as "a fast track of change that has challenged instruction librarians to continually develop new services and methods for teaching" (p. 288).

The Pollak Library has a very vigorous proactive instruction program that has been designated the number one priority for the library. The opening of the new building, with its state-of-the-art instruction rooms, provided enhanced opportunities for innovation in library instruction and in what Gresham (1999) has termed "dynamic learning environments" (p. 28). Instead of one room with one portable projector, there are now four rooms with varied technological capabilities. Two rooms have student computer workstations that will accommodate twenty students, or forty students working in pairs. These rooms have ceiling-mounted projection units, and fully equipped instructor stations, with a computer console, an ELMO overhead projector, video capability, and a v-net control system that allows for alternative teaching techniques. The instructor can control all workstations, permit the students to have local control of their computers, or project any device to the overhead screen. Two additional rooms can accommodate larger classes. Each has a fully equipped instructor station, with the exception of the v-net system. One room has lecture seating for over 150 students. The other room has seventy-five tablet armchairs facing the screen and ten independent computer workstations around the perimeter. The room can be used in a lecture configuration or with up to five students, working in teams, at each station. The flexibility of this room offers instructors multiple choices in instruction techniques.

Building on the campus technology initiative and the enhanced facilities available because of the library expansion, the library instruction program has increased dramatically since 1995. Prior to the expansion, ten instruction librarians were teaching 125 faculty-requested sessions per semester. In Fall 1999, thirteen instruction librarians taught over 300 sessions in most disciplines and at all levels from remedial to master's level. In addition to these sessions, other learning opportunities include one-on-one research consultations, workshops, and the Fullerton First Year library component described below. The experience gained over the last three years has given instruction librarians at CSUF expertise in innovative student-centered, technology-based teaching.

Within the CSU system there has been a strong initiative to incorporate information competence into the curriculum. This is considered by librarians to be a critical skill for all students. Our current instruction program has evolved with this initiative in mind.

Fullerton First-Year Program

Due to the CSUF campus demographics, there is an ongoing need for programs that will foster a stronger sense of community, improve the first year experience, give students the tools necessary for academic success, and increase student retention. The Fullerton First Year (FFY) program was designed to address these needs. With support from the university president, the program was planned as an academically integrated year-long experience with a service learning component that was open to all incoming first year students by application. In reading the applications, the selection committee looked for interest, motivation, and commitment and selected a diverse cross-section of students. The initial cohort of 125 students was extensively profiled during this first year, 1997/98. According to Walker-

Guyer (1999), results showed that these students would indeed benefit from such an integrated community-rich program. Most were 18 years old, over 65 percent were non-Caucasian, 75 percent were female, many commuted to campus, and 27 percent worked over 21 hours per week during the academic year.

The integrated nature of this program ties courses together with a central theme—"Education, Social Responsibility, and Community"—and encourages collaboration across disciplines. An initial call went out for campus faculty and student affairs professionals who would be interested in working collaboratively to shape this program. The FFY program was clearly addressing several of the "hot initiatives" mentioned by Ianuzzi (1998)— i.e., student retention, learning communities, and technology in the classroom (p. 99). Due to the library's strong commitment to information competency, the existing and very successful library instruction program, and the technological tools available, the library was in a good position to help this initiative succeed. Because of the collaborative nature of the project, a team of six librarians applied to the program. The FFY steering committee had not previously thought of including the library in the program, but realized the potential value of having a library component. The library's ongoing participation in the program, including the week-long FFY summer planning retreats, has built alliances with discipline faculty and student affairs professionals across campus and has increased library visibility.

The library team was paired with one faculty member from Computer Science (CPSC) and one faculty member from Management Science and Information Systems (MSIS). This group worked together to design a course that would include elements from each discipline—i.e., information competence, computer competence, and presentation skills. The new course, "Introduction to Information Technology and Presentation (IITP)" was designed as a two-unit class to be taught in one two-hour session each week during the fall semester. There were six sections of the course with approximately twenty-five students in each section. This course joined the roster of several other required courses planned for the FFY program and has been taught each Fall for the last three years.

MSIS and CPSC faculty taught computer competency, including computer basics such as Windows, e-mail, and Internet searching, and presentation skills including PowerPoint and Web page creation. This component was taught in computer-equipped classrooms for eleven weeks. Library faculty team-taught electronic library resources, the distinction between popular and scholarly sources, interpreting and citing electronic resources, evaluating information on the Web, and electronically requesting books and articles. The six sections of this component were taught by one or·two librarians each for a four-week period in the library's state-of-the-art computer classrooms. The library team has worked collaboratively to create and modify the syllabus, in-class exercises, group activities, homework assignments, final exams, and Web materials. Student performance in the FFY library component was assessed using graded assignments and a final examination. These counted for 20 percent of the total IITP grade.

FFY and Library Instruction Evolution

The design and implementation of the FFY library component initially reflected experiences gained in the existing library instruction program. Both have changed dramatically during the past three years. In working collaboratively through issues of assessment, class structure and content, exercises, and assignments for the FFY library component, a more student-centered approach to instruction has evolved. Ideas generated and techniques used during each Fall's FFY library component were tested and refined during the following Spring's/general library instruction sessions. The reciprocal lessons learned and changes made have greatly strengthened each. The most significant change has been the increased use by students and instructors of Web technology in all facets of the instruction program. Librarians have created both general and subject specific Web guides that augment general

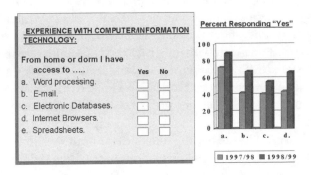

Figure 1. Profile of entering FFY freshman in 1997/98 and 1998/99

instruction. FFY library component course materials, including the syllabus, in-class exercises, assignments, and ultimately the final exam, were modified in the third year and posted on the Web using Blackboard CourseInfo software.

Assessment

The concept of assessment is central to the overall instruction program. A variety of assessment techniques are used to measure student learning and program effectiveness in order to determine what changes are desirable and to ascertain the effectiveness of changes. These techniques include both objective and subjective measurements such as class profiling, grading, and student and program evaluation. Increasingly, Web technology is being considered as the medium to assess student learning and acquisition of information competency.

In order to build a profile of FFY students, an assessment instrument was used to collect information on students' experience and confidence with technology and their attitudes toward technology. Data collected and shown

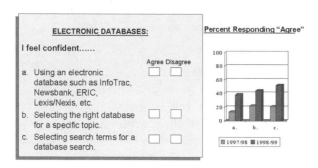

Figure 2. Profile of entering FFY freshman in 1997/98 and 1998/99

in Figure 1 indicate that FFY students entering CSUF in 1998 were far more familiar with computer and Internet use than students entering in 1997. Although they are increasingly confident in their ability to effectively use these tools prior to taking the class (see Figure 2), performance on assignments and tests that measure student learning indicate that instruction in the area of information competency is still needed.

Content, Structure, and Delivery of Instruction Sessions

The decision to include the FFY library component within the IITP course influenced the choice of library component course content and the method of delivery. While the component was designed to provide students with a working knowledge of the library, whenever possible, students were introduced to Web-based, instead of more traditional paper-based, resources. A specialized Web guide was developed to create a well-defined and manageable set of introductory resources and explanatory materials. Experience teaching from this Web guide led to the modification of existing discipline-specific instruction Web guides, the creation of additional instruction Webs, and a more student-centered approach to teaching.

The FFY students came to the library in the tenth week of classes, after the computer component, with a good foundation in computer basics and general

Internet use. The library component syllabus articulated specific learning goals for the four-week course module. Students would learn to identify principal library services and major collections as well as learn to access and use relevant library electronic resources. These included the library home page, the online public access catalog (OPAC), basic full-text background resources, full-text article and newspaper resources, and a discipline-specific citation database. Students would also be able to use and evaluate relevant World Wide Web sites, distinguish between popular and scholarly periodicals, interpret electronic bibliographic citations, and cite electronic materials. These learning goals have changed relatively little during the three-year period. The methods used to achieve them, however, have been modified significantly.

Library Home Page and OPAC. The library home page was used as a launch point to introduce students to library services, materials, and policies. Students were briefly shown how to locate floor maps, library navigation aids such as location codes, and general information such as library hours. This virtual tour was followed by a brief exploration of the OPAC. Students were then given a homework assignment designed to provide them with practice searching the OPAC and familiarity with one of five key areas of the library: reference, periodicals, audiovisual materials, curriculum materials center, and two floors of circulating books.

In this assignment, each student was asked to go to one of the five designated areas, explore the physical environment, and identify any existing service points such as help desks or reshelving areas. While in the area, they were required to pull an item randomly off the shelf, find the record in the OPAC, and print it. This gave them a better idea of the connection between the OPAC record, with its fields and controlled vocabulary, and the physical item and its location in the library. To ensure that they could read and interpret the bibliographic record, they were also asked to use the citation to find additional materials in the OPAC under the same subject heading. This engaged students in a more active way than a traditional library walking tour. The following week this homework assignment was followed by an in-class exercise in which students were grouped according to which of the five areas they had visited. Students were given time to discuss their findings and observations and answer several preselected prompts. Each group's recorder then reported to the class as a whole, giving everyone, including librarians, a more three-dimensional picture than is possible using the online maps.

Both the homework assignment and the group exercise provided a student-based perspective of the library and the OPAC and highlighted unexpected challenges. Students were often unable to select required information from the formal bibliographic record and provide full information on titles and/or subject headings. Although much of the information needed for the assignment was available on the Web, such as location codes and floor maps, students often relied on more immediately accessible (and low tech) materials such as people at help desks and signs posted in elevators.

An assessment of the experience with Fullerton First Year students, and taking a cue from Dupuis' (1998) maxim "Call it what they'll understand and put it where they'll find it" has led to an evolution of the home page (p. 16). Twelve major links have been reduced to eight, providing more streamlined navigation. The language has been changed to reduce the amount of library jargon, making the page more easily understood by students. For example, "Indexes/ Abstracts/Full Text" changed initially to "Electronic Information Resources" and now reads "Find Articles and More." The "Introduction to Library Research" Web guide, originally created for FFY, has been modified and expanded, renamed, and given a prominent place on the home page.

An overview of the library given in most general library instruction sessions has also changed based on the Fullerton First Year experiences. Most sessions requested by faculty do not offer the luxury of eight hours of intensive library instruction. Introductory walking tours, as a result, have become briefer and are sometimes eliminated altogether unless they add significantly to the ability to complete a specific assignment. Instead, in-class hands-on exploration of the home page is used to address typical questions. Students who have previously experienced the sometimes frustrating process of finding library materials are often excited about and appreciate the ability to access floor maps and location codes.

Web Evaluation. During the first year of FFY, students were relatively inexperienced in general with using the Web to find information. A lecture/ demonstration of useful sites was included to show them the potential of the Web for research purposes. During the second FFY year, a change was made. Due to the explosion of information on the Internet and its increased availability, and in response to some faculty concerns about the growing student use of inappropriate Web sites for assignments and papers, librarians sensitized students to the need for appraisal and together explored ways to evaluate sites on the Web. Many excellent Web evaluation resources exist. The library team surveyed these resources and chose the criteria established by Jim Kapoun in his "Seven Criteria for Evaluating Web Sites" (1998). These criteria were modified with the author's permission, retitled "Six Criteria for Evaluating Web Sites," used in a demonstration, applied by students in an assignment, and discussed during a group exercise.

The demonstration modeled for the students indicated how a team librarian evaluated and rated two contrasting Web sites on the use of alcohol among teenagers using the seven criteria: authority, objectivity, accuracy, currency, content, relevancy, and aesthetics. For each of the criteria, evidence was provided from the sites to substantiate the evaluation. This was a preview for their homework assignment. For the homework, students received one of three versions of the assignment; each version listed a different URL for an informative site dealing with the issue of smoking. Students evaluated and rated the site using the seven criteria. The previous group exercise on the OPAC had been so successful that library team members created a similar exercise for this assignment, allowing students to interact informally, discuss their evaluations, and present the group's consensus rating of their site. Discussion was lively as students used different evidence to defend their rankings. As concluded by Sholz-Crane (1998), students need more than a simple checklist of criteria for evaluating Web sites, and the modeling of the assignment and subsequent group discussion provided this.

A review of final exam results by the library team showed that students had at least gained an awareness of the necessity to evaluate Web sites. In fact, the exam also indicated a strong student preference for library subscription databases that had been evaluated and selected for them. The "Six Criteria for Evaluating Web Sites" is accessible from the home page and now serves as the basis for most instruction involving Web evaluation. It has proven very popular with discipline faculty, who often request this learning module as part of the general library instruction session.

Online Full-Text Background Sources. The core classes that Fullerton First Year students take during the first year experience have varied over the three-year period. In addition to the IITP and University 100 courses, other required core courses have included basic English, political science, speech communication, ethnic studies, math, and science. In order to help students with assignments for written and oral presentations given in these courses, the library team decided to include instruction on two basic online full-text background resources: *Britannica Online* and *CQ Researcher*. Many students are familiar with encyclopedias and weekly publications and understand the structure and the concepts associated with them, such as authority and currency. In addition, both resources include citing examples, which makes it easy to introduce one of the IITP course learning objectives—the correct use of citations and style manuals. Students appreciated the ease of use and comprehensiveness of these resources, and immediately grasped the utility of both *Britannica Online* and *CQ Researcher* for completing assignments in their other introductory classes.

During the first year, both resources were demonstrated during a class session, and students were given homework assignments for each. There was no hands-on practice time allotted. Previous assumptions about student learning via lecture-style presentations were challenged. Students were not able to apply immediately what had been demonstrated, and they found the lecture-demonstration boring and excessively long. Because they often did not begin to work on the homework assignment until almost a week after the demonstration, they had trouble navigating to and within both resources. They also had difficulty interpreting the assignments' sometimes ambiguous wording. In grading the homework, which had been considered relatively straightforward assignments, team librarians discovered these problems, but were unable to correct misconceptions in a timely manner.

To address some of these challenges, this learning module was modified to include more active learning. Demonstrations were kept to brief segments, followed by frequent practice searching and in-class exercises that modeled the upcoming homework assignment. The exercises were structured, with step-by-step instructions for navigating to the database, performing specific searches, and locating relevant information that would answer the exercise questions. This guided exploration activity, which highlighted the mechanical process rather than more conceptual thinking, assured the library team that students could follow instructions and effectively use the resources. Students were actively engaged, serious, and focused as they worked through the exercise. Librarians were able to observe navigating problems first hand, give useful browser tips like how to find words in a page, and immediately clarify any misconceptions. Difficulties in navigating and interpreting on-screen information can be discussed and resolved to the benefit of the entire class.

As is the case when utilizing Web technology, additional challenges were encountered. License agreements sometimes precluded extensive hands-on use because of limits to the number of simultaneous users. Moreover, too many users could sometimes slow the loading of information to the screen. To address these issues, several techniques were used: for example, having students work in groups of two or three, or having students volunteer or be selected to keyboard and project their work to the class. Additionally, due to the fluid nature of the Web, resources often changed without much advance notice. This necessitates designing or reviewing exercises and assignments as close to class time as possible.

Due to these experiences in FFY, our general library instruction sessions have changed dramatically. Most library instruction now includes hands-on practice, student keyboarding, formal in-class exercises, and group work, which reinforce course material and help students develop and apply information competence skills. This often means covering less in any one session but assures librarians that students learn what was explored more effectively, and that they enjoy the sessions more. Our experience corroborates the conclusion of Bren, Hilleman, and Topp (1998) that using a guided hands-on method increases student retention of information.

Full-Text Broad Periodical and Newspaper Indexes. To meet several other learning goals, students were next introduced to electronic full-text article and newspaper resources, including *Expanded Academic ASAP, Lexis/Nexis,* and *Proquest Direct.* These resources were used to illustrate concepts such as the distinction between popular and scholarly materials, the effective use of subject headings and journal indexes to conduct library research, and the interpretation and use of citations. Active learning techniques were expanded on a constructivist model.

These three resources were chosen because they are user friendly, have significant full-text content and broad subject coverage, and can be used to gather information for other FFY course assignments. In addition, *Expanded Academic* usually defaults to a subject search with the capability of narrowing by subdivision. Students conversant with using Internet subject directories such as Yahoo find the hierarchical approach of this database familiar, and librarians appreciate the ability to reinforce the utility of controlled vocabulary subject headings. *Expanded Academic* includes several publication types, and there is a limit function to restrict results to refereed publications. This provides an opportunity to discuss the distinction between popular and scholarly sources.

Students learned *Expanded Academic* quickly and appreciated the ability to focus their searches and e-mail complete articles. In grading assignments from the first two years, library team members noticed that students were still having difficulty distinguishing between popular and scholarly sources. They were unable to utilize elements in the citation and abstract to determine whether or not the item was likely to be from a scholarly source. Due to the electronic nature of the article, students saw it out of context and many of the clues normally utilized in this evaluative process, such as extensive advertising or author submission requirements, were missing.

To meet this challenge for the second year, a handout was modified and placed on the Web, which detailed the scholarly, versus popular, distinction. This was, however, too passive, and the students still had difficulty with the concept. Librarians endeavored to shift their role toward King's (1993) vision of "a facilitator who orchestrates the context, provides resources, and poses questions to stimulate students to think up their own answers" (p. 30). For the third year, a group exercise was created that would afford students the opportunity to physically handle and discuss different publication types. These included a newspaper, a popular weekly, a trade journal, and a scholarly journal. Each group was given a sample issue and asked to discuss what constituted the defining elements of the publication and report their findings to the class. They were asked the following questions:

- Who publishes or owns the periodical?
- Does the publication have ads? If so, what kind?
- What types of articles are published?
- Can you tell how the articles are selected?
- Do the articles have authors? If so, is any background information included?
- Are the articles long or short?
- What kind of illustrations or graphics do the articles have?
- Is there a bibliography at the end of any articles? If so, is it long or short?

In their group discussions, students came to understand and appreciate the different processes that go into creating these publications and the different audiences that they target. They gained skills that they could use to better interpret online citations and full-text material. As electronic journals evolve and proliferate, however, students new to the research process may have increasing difficulty evaluating the relevance of these online materials for their academic needs. As new models of publication are created, new techniques will need to be developed to ensure that students have the necessary tools to place these materials in an academic context.

In using *Expanded Academic*, students are also exposed for the first time to periodical citations without accompanying full text. They need to correctly read and interpret the article citation to find successfully a copy of the article in the CSUF library. Predictably, this proved to be difficult. Although the students had used the OPAC for other purposes in a previous session, few of them thought to utilize it for this task. Moreover, it was problematic for them to know which term from the article citation to use for their OPAC search. Actually, they needed to start with the journal title. In addition, once the journal record was located in the OPAC, they had difficulty interpreting it to find the necessary issue availability and location information. Graded assignments revealed that, despite repeated in-class discussions on this, students often had problems.

During the past three years, teaching techniques for this critical series of steps have been altered for FFY sessions. To negotiate these steps, students are now taught to open two browser windows and switch between the OPAC and the article citation to obtain the information they need more efficiently. This also makes the distinction between the two resources more visually apparent. Brief and frequent hands-on modules are used to ensure that all students are more successful with the process. Finally, the library team has decided that the OPAC fits more naturally at this periodical citation stage of the process rather than in the customary first session. Students are naturally excited by full-text databases and, at this stage, more readily grasp the utility of the OPAC to augment and find additional materials.

Lexis/Nexis Academic Universe and *Proquest Direct* were selected as examples of online full-text newspaper resources. Students could use these to find information on current topical issues for many assignments in their other FFY courses. Also, because of the prior group activity in which they explored various publication types, students were familiar with the defining elements of a newspaper format. The varied ways to search these full-text resources provided both a challenge and an opportunity. Keyword searching of full-text information often results in too many hits and may also miss relevant articles. Library team members and students briefly utilized techniques to search within specific fields like headline and lead paragraph to make results more focused and precise. Brainstorming was used to find appropriate synonyms to broaden their results.

Many of these techniques have also been adapted for general library instruction, from fifty-minute introductory level to three-hour graduate level sessions. Abbreviated group discussions based on the popular/scholarly distinction exercise provide students with concrete representations of this sometimes abstract concept. A two-minute critical thinking exercise can often clarify the task of interpreting periodical citations and locating library materials. Discipline faculty attending the sessions are often surprised at the difficulty students at all levels have with this process. As more citation databases integrate library holdings and links to full-text journal articles, this difficulty will most likely be eliminated. Some library team members are introducing students to the OPAC at a more relevant stage—at the point when cited material must be found in the library.

Discipline-Specific Resources. To reflect the IITP course content, *Microcomputer Abstracts* (now called *Internet and Personal Computing Abstracts*) was selected by librarians as an example of a more typical discipline-specific periodical database. Due to their prior exposure to the citation and abstract format in *Expanded Academic*, students quickly grasped how to use this resource to locate technology-related articles and product reviews. This provided another opportunity to reinforce the use of the OPAC to locate materials in the CSUF library. In fact, in the third year, at the beginning of the final class session, students were given an exercise and asked to explore this resource independently without a brief introductory demonstration. The in-class discussion that followed the independent hands-on exercise focused on techniques that could be used to approach any new or recently changed electronic resource. For example, reading the introductory material that explains the scope and content of the database may be useful for determining its utility for a specific assignment. Also, all online resources have help screens that can explain various functions or search tips that can make searching more efficient and precise. Finally, use of limit functions or searching within specific fields can lead to more relevant results.

Librarians are experimenting with this in-class group exploration and subsequent student demonstration of databases that have not previously been discussed in class. Although the Web is a very dynamic medium, lecture demonstrations and step-by-step in-class exercises are typically controlled and linear. These student explorations have the advantage of presenting a variety of unscripted scenarios that may mirror far more realistic student information-seeking behavior. This unscripted exploration can provide a bridge for students to move from terms and techniques chosen by librarians to conducting their own research in unfamiliar databases. It also gives librarians insight into how students search and how well user interfaces work.

The Evolution of the Library Component Web and Other Library Research Webs

In the third year, library component materials, such as the syllabus, in-class exercises, homework assignments, component grades, and the final examination, were made available via a Blackboard CourseInfo Web site. From this site, students could also link to the "Introduction to Library Research" Web page, which had been created for the second year. This introductory Web included links to resources used in the class and explanatory materials such as the criteria for Web site evaluation and guidelines for distinguishing between popular and scholarly materials and citing sources.

This CourseInfo Web site provided several advantages to both students and librarians. The syllabus, with course objectives, course requirements, schedule, and contact information, was always available. Students could access the site twenty-four hours a day and, if absent, were required to retrieve necessary class materials. They could also check the status of their grades. Students could review concepts presented in class and refer to examples given. Library team members found it an advantage no longer to have to bring copies of the previous week's handouts, exercises, and assignments to class. They also felt that this site provided a more manageable library universe for these beginning students.

Because so much of the FFY library component is Web based, it was deemed a natural progression to experiment with migrating assessment instruments, such as the final exam, to the Web. In the third year, the library component final exam was given electronically. This had several benefits. Students were able to utilize and reinforce skills, such as interpretation of on-screen information, that had been practiced over the four weeks. In addition, students were given instant feedback on their exam results. Benefits to librarians included automatic grading and recording of exam results and the ability to analyze answers from individual questions in order to discover ambiguities or areas needing further explication. From this experience, additional Web-based instruments are being developed to assess student learning during general library instruction sessions as well as electronic workshops.

Although students and library team members responded very favorably to the course component Web site, several potential disadvantages must be noted. The elimination of paper handouts and twenty-four hour reliance on electronic access and delivery makes the course vulnerable because server or online access problems can make information unavailable. The protected CourseInfo software requires students to register with user name and password, and although students were cautioned to remember or record this information, many did not. The necessity of posting library documents in both HTML and Word formats, to ensure wide access while preserving efficient formatting and printing, created additional work for the library team. With each new release of the software, considerable time and effort by the library team will be required to take advantage of new features. The site was successful in providing easy and convenient connections to all course-related resources and explanatory materials. However, the library team is concerned that small, extremely focused Webs, such as this one based on librarians' assumptions about student research needs, may be too restrictive and could inhibit student exploration of a wider array of useful resources. Also, multiple paths to a resource sometimes confuse students.

Despite these drawbacks, the library team and other instruction librarians continue to create and expand on Web-based library research guides for specific majors, specific classes, and special topics. The guides for majors contain pages that provide information on finding relevant books, articles, journal holdings, recommended and related Web sites, and annotated reference sources. Although each guide is organized in a standard format, information is tailored to the major, and the guide may include other relevant links and explanatory material. These guides are useful in several ways. Library instruction sessions often begin with an introduction to a specific major's guide, which provides an overview of discipline-appropriate resources. After the library session, students can refer to these guides when they are working on course-related assignments. The guides can be quickly modified and updated as resources change or new ones become available. The guides are prepared by a subject bibliographer and are useful to non-subject specialists who may do library instruction or provide reference assistance.

In working with students during FFY and library instruction sessions, librarians gain firsthand knowledge of how students navigate and use these Webs. From these observations, Webs have changed to become more student centered. For example, the Communications Web provides scanned images of the cover and sample pages from selected communications reference sources. This facilitates student recognition and use of these resources. Library jargon has been replaced with vocabulary that students more readily understand. This will also make the sites more useful to any student doing research remotely. Faculty preparing Web sites for distance education courses would be well advised to field test their course Web to avoid constructing artificial roadblocks for their targeted users.

FFY Component and Library Instruction Evaluation

In order to monitor, evaluate, and improve the library component, feedback was sought from library team members and FFY students. During informal wrap-up discussions immediately following the second and third years of FFY, library team members reviewed the course objectives, individual sessions, and course materials.

Concerns were raised on the issue of standardization, including presentation of materials, attendance, and other classroom management policies, and grading of assignments and exams. Moving course materials, including the final exam, to the Web, has facilitated the standardization process. Team members found this "structured brainstorming" approach, as used by Keyser and Lucio (1998), to be very beneficial (p. 225).

Librarians also developed and administered an instrument in order to obtain direct student feedback on the library component. Evaluations were generally positive, although many students commented that they would have liked even less lecture and more hands-on practice with the Web. This reinforced the observation from graded assignments that students learned better when more actively engaged.

Lessons learned from FFY library component evaluations have also informed the general library instruction program. Prior to the session, library and discipline faculty often discuss and agree on common objectives. At the beginning of the class, these objectives are communicated to the students. The sessions often begin with some type of short informal assessment to determine such things as student expectations, experience with computers, and prior library use. With this knowledge, the librarian can modify the session to better meet the needs of the student.

An information competence pilot project was developed, and a Web-based instrument was created to assess student learning during selected library instruction sessions. Classes represented a cross-section of disciplines and grade levels. Data from this pilot program will be analyzed to determine if the library instruction program is meeting information competence objectives. The instrument will be modified for use in future library instruction sessions.

Workshops are offered throughout the semester to introduce students to the library and several basic electronic resources. Every participant now completes a short Web-based evaluation of the workshop. Feedback will be used to revise the workshop program to meet student needs more effectively. A more objective instrument to measure student learning is being developed for use in workshops and general library instruction sessions.

Recommendations

Librarians need to remain committed to the primary goal of academic library instruction—i.e., providing students with the tools necessary to use the library in order to succeed in college and beyond. But students are changing, technology continues to evolve, higher education is adapting to these changes, and librarians need to anticipate the effects of these changes and continually re-create library instruction:

- Because of the constantly changing Web environment, which requires continuous learning, librarians need to remain strong advocates for information competence.

- Whenever possible, librarians and faculty requesting library instruction sessions should synthesize library instruction, course goals, and objectives for the session. This approach ensures that librarians can help provide the tools necessary for students to complete research assignments that meet discipline-specific learning goals.

- Although students will have differing levels of experience with technology, increasingly students will arrive in college equipped with basic computer skills. This allows librarians to spend more time on the research process, including evaluation and interpretation.

- As more campus labs are equipped with computers, and as Web-based library resources proliferate, librarians should consider providing instruction through these labs. The library can remain central to the educational experience while becoming more fully integrated with subject-based learning.

- Because students do not all have access to state-of-the-art equipment, care should be taken when creating interactive materials so that as many students as possible can take advantage of them.

- Because many students learn best by doing, online exercises should be structured to provide guidance, practice, and feedback. This also makes the learning experience available to distance students.

- Librarians should encourage students to make connections between resources and techniques learned during a specific library session and ways these can be applied to other assignments or other courses.

- Chat rooms or group Web sites can be added to class Web sites to substitute for, or augment, group activities.

- Assessment is fundamental in order to determine if goals are realistic and if they are being met by the instruction session. Distance education faculty should take advantage of Web-based instruments to profile their class and should also utilize synchronous or asynchronous methods to elicit student feedback.

- Assessment instruments should be administered online for ease of data collection.

- Librarians should lobby publishers to provide basic reference sources online to facilitate ease of access any time, anywhere.

- Librarians should provide feedback on student perceptions and use and should lobby database publishers for changes that would promote standardization, such as truncation symbols and ease of use.

Conclusions

The library instruction program has benefited in several ways from participation in FFY. Many connections have been made with discipline faculty and student affairs professionals that have provided opportunities to understand campus needs and to communicate that library faculty have the skills, knowledge, experience, and vision to help address these needs. Library faculty have worked collaboratively to design and implement effective library instruction techniques for FFY and have learned from each other, and been supported by each other, when proposing new ideas that can lead to enhanced student learning during these sessions. The responsibility of constructing goals and objectives and grading students in FFY has led to a growing appreciation of the role that assessment can play in determining the effect of all library instruction. Librarians who have participated in FFY over the last three years have worked with students increasingly familiar with the Web. To accommodate this familiarity and student information needs, most library instruction materials have been moved to the Web. The library component of FFY continues to function as a laboratory for new materials, better instruction techniques, and increased sharing of ideas among discipline and library faculty.

The convergence of a newly built library wing, campus administrators who had a vision of a technology enhanced environment, and faculty committed to connecting students to the campus and building community, have enhanced the experience for first year students. Library faculty, using technology and active learning, are creating an environment where students are encouraged to think for themselves and to construct a meaningful understanding of how the library and its resources can contribute to the success of their academic experience.

References

Bren, B.; Hilleman, B.; & Topp, V. (1998). Effectiveness of hands-on instruction of electronic resources. *Research Strategies, 16*(1), 41–51.

California State University, Fullerton. University Planning Committee. (1999). The marks of a Cal State Fullerton graduate. *Bulletin University Planning Committee, 16.*

Dupuis, E. A. (1998). The times they are a'changin': Students, technology, and instructional services. *Reference Services Review, 26*(3-4), 11–16, 32.

Dupuis, E. A. (1999). The creative evolution of library instruction. *Reference Services Review, 27*(3), 287–290.

Gresham, K. (1999). Experiential learning theory, library instruction, and the electronic classroom. *Colorado Libraries, 25*(1), 29–31.

Iannuzzi, P. (1998). Faculty development and information literacy: Establishing campus partnerships. *Reference Services Review, 26*(3-4), 97–102, 116.

Kapoun, J. (1998). Teaching undergrads WEB evaluation: A guide for library instruction. *College & Research Libraries News, 59*(7), 522–523.

Keyser, M. W.; & Lucio, L. R. (1998). Adding a library instruction unit to an established course (at Texas A&M University, Kingsville). *Research Strategies, 16*(3), 221–229.

King, A. (1993). From sage on the stage to guide on the side. *College Teaching, 41*(1), 30–35.

Sholz-Crane, A. (1998). Evaluating the future: A preliminary study of the process of how undergraduate students evaluate Web sources. *Reference Services Review, 26*(3-4), 53–60.

Walker-Guyer, L. A. (1999). Making connections for students and educators in higher education through a systemic learning community model (collaborative teaching, curriculum development) (Doctoral dissertation, Claremont Graduate University, 1990). *Dissertation Abstracts International, 60*(2), ADG9917989.

Weiss, K. R. (1999). College crowd finding campuses jammed. *Los Angeles Times*, September 20, p. A3.

4

CHOOSING VIDEO, ONLINE, AND/OR FACE-TO-FACE INSTRUCTION: THE HOWS AND WHYS

Introduction

William C. Epstein
California Polytechnic State University, San Luis Obspo

With the wave of technology that has swept through universities in the past decade, it is no longer mandatory that students and professors meet face-to-face in classrooms at designated times. Distance education has long been available in the form of correspondence courses, but technology now offers a variety of options: courses offered via cable TV or videos, through point-to-point live broadcasts, over the Internet, or with some combination of all these mixed in with some face-to-face instruction. Faculty have chosen to teach in different modes and media for a host of reasons, many of them illustrated in the following articles. In some cases, students live too far from campus to commute easily, they have jobs that prevent them from taking classes during regular hours, or they like the opportunity to pursue lessons at their own pace. In other cases, technology provides access to highly specialized, low-enrollment courses that are too expensive for many universities to offer.

The five articles in this chapter highlight how various educators from five CSU campuses have chosen to use technology in their instructional delivery systems. The academic fields of study represented by these publications and their authors cut a wide swath across the CSU. The first offering contained in this collection is a paper that focuses on teaching animation, while the next two articles are from the technical disciplines of construction management and electrical engineering. The fourth paper describes the design and pedagogical theories associated with producing successful multimedia teaching and learning tools, and this chapter's final article looks at marketing strategies as they relate to the business of distance learning.

Courney Granner, in "Interactive Distance-Learning Animation," describes a systemwide project that allows industry professionals from Warner Brothers Feature Animations (WBFA) to teach students from a variety of locations, including several CSU campuses; a local occupational program;

and a high school, a community college, and a university in Alabama. Initiated in response to the industry perception that recent graduates lacked adequate animation skills, the ACME Virtual Training Network (AVTN) "was established [by Warner Brothers] to bring industry knowledge directly to students through instruction that is relevant, current, and taught by the best of the industry's insiders." Granner recounts the development, implementation, and improvement of the project, emphasizing the significant technical support required. During the first year, for example, "Distortion, signal break up, equipment incompatibility, and human error made the transmission seem like an impossibility one moment and a miracle the next." She also describes the "cooperative learning sessions" that she and her colleagues have implemented, during which the CSU students lead all other participants (except the AVTN instructors) in peer review of the student work. Granner offers this advice to other educators who may want to experiment with this form of delivery system: "Be prepared. Be flexible, have backup plans, and by all means, maintain your sense of humor."

The second article of this chapter, "Videoconferencing: The Virtual Guest Lecturer" by William C. Epstein, continues the theme of interactive videoconferencing. Epstein describes the importance of introducing his students to current construction-related issues by inviting local industry practitioners into his classroom as guest lecturers. Because his institution is located hundreds of miles from any significant urban center, it is removed from easy access to substantial construction activity and associated personnel. To provide his students with this essential exposure to industry professionals, Epstein organized a series of interactive videoconferences between his students in the classroom and qualified construction personnel in the field. Epstein's article is a case study of how he was able to utilize the California State University and Community College Network (4CNet) to offer, free of charge to his department, point-to-point videoconferencing in his construction project management class. Epstein offers not only technical details about the videoconference delivery, but also a number of teaching tips, including warnings about scheduling too many videoconferencing sessions and sessions that are too long.

The third article in this chapter also details the course-specific use of computer technology, but with a notable reservation. In "Applications of Computer Technology in Tandem with the Traditional Classroom," Jean-Pierre R. Bayard states that "The present work stipulates that the traditional classroom is an effective and surprisingly efficient learning environment." Acknowledging an "increasingly adversarial" debate between administrators and faculty regarding instructional technology and particularly distance education, Bayard describes how he uses particular technologies (e.g., the

Internet, cable television, Web-based course management software) to enhance student performance and facilitate course and program assessment. As he says, he "promotes the technology portion of the teaching as complementary to the classroom environment, not as an equivalent self-paced learning option."

In "The Web as a Delivery Medium to Enhance Instruction," Bijan Gillani describes the development and subsequent use of his Web site for a graduate class entitled "Learning Theories and Multimedia Design." Gillani explains that the course focuses on the effective educational use of multimedia and the Web, and he illustrates how the course Web site supports the course learning objectives. He provides a number of recommendations, suggesting for example that an instructor proceed through four stages when designing a course Web site: analyze, organize, develop, and evaluate and revise.

Unlike the other articles in this chapter, "Applying E-Marketing Strategies to Online Distance Learning" by Neil Granitz and C. Scott Greene does not focus on the course-specific use of technology. Instead, this article is an exercise in using business-marketing strategies to theorize about improved implementation of distance education. "By recognizing online distance learning as e-commerce," they argue, "new e-marketing theory and knowledge developed by academics and business practitioners can be applied to meet many of the challenges of distance learning." Addressing the business themes of "personalization and customization, community, disintermediation, reintermediation, consumer tracking, enhanced customer service, and mixing bricks and clicks," Granitz and Greene offer a unique perspective on the challenges faced today in distance education.

The articles in this chapter come from varying academic perspectives, and together they represent a broad spectrum of instructors' approaches to the use of technology in higher education. Most of these articles discuss course-specific uses of academic technology, while one uses business strategies to consider models of distance education. Some of the authors are reserved in their embrace of technology, while others are more enthusiastic, but all would seem to agree both that technology has a solid role in enhancing student learning and that the incorporation of technology is no simple task. In closing this introduction, a last thought from one of the authors seems appropriate. At the end of her article, Courtney Granner counsels educators to "expect extra time, energy, and resources to be required for any interactive distance-learning program, especially in the start-up stages." She goes on to remind the reader that these resources "represent investment, and that this kind of experience constitutes professional development for faculty, technicians, and students."

WILLIAM C. EPSTEIN

Interactive Distance-Learning Animation

Courtney Granner
San José State University

The shortest distance between two interactive distance-learning points is seldom a straight line. Technological problems as well as the vagaries of human participation ensure that the anticipated straight line is unattainable. Now entering into the third year of a fully interactive distance-learning animation project, my colleague, Professor Alice Carter, and I discovered it to be a far more complex model than we had ever envisioned.

Every Tuesday from October to May, forty San José State University (SJSU) animation students cross campus to crowd into a small SJSU Television Education Network (TEN) studio for a two-hour distance-learning class with Warner Brothers Feature Animation (WBFA). Six other educational sites participate in the program: California State University (CSU) Fullerton, CSU Northridge, and Rowland Heights Regional Occupational Program in Los Angeles, as well as Phillips High School (an arts magnet institution), Jefferson State Community College, and Lawson State College, all in Birmingham, Alabama. Thirty-two two-hour sessions are scheduled each academic year, with the students voluntarily attending the transmissions during the traditional winter and spring breaks.

Termed the ACME Virtual Training Network (AVTN), it is the first CSU systemwide project linking the system's campuses to a specific industry and simultaneously to non-CSU institutions. SJSU is the coordinating center of this collaboration sponsored by WBFA and Next Wave Learning (NWL), an innovative teaching and learning institute within the CSU system. AVTN was initiated by Dave Master, Manager of Artist Training and Development at WBFA, after he reviewed work from top animation schools by students who often did not meet industry standards for entry-level positions. Master found that most new hires had to be instructed in fundamental principles at a time when the demand to fill new positions was at an all-time high. WBFA was concerned that animation programs across the country were weak at the foundation level and that most graduates, though talented, demonstrated inadequate animation skills. AVTN was established to bring industry knowledge directly to students through instruction that is relevant, current, and taught by the best of the industry's insiders.

There was no animation component in the nationally recognized Illustration Program at San José State University when WBFA visited in the spring of 1996. However, after multiple meetings and after reviewing student work, WBFA selected SJSU as the host site to inaugurate this pioneering teaching and learning program. Professor Carter and I had minimal experience in animation. Our careers are based in the traditional print media associated with illustration. The instructors at the other participating sites faced similar challenges.

The SJSU interactive classroom is equipped with two video cameras, one at the front of the class and one at the rear, and with microphones positioned between every two seats. Students can speak directly to the WBFA artists or to participants at the other sites. Classroom video cameras are voice activated. When a student begins speaking, the camera tracks to the microphone in use, and video and audio of that student is transmitted to all the sites. The technology grants video priority to the last site using the audio, and protocols have been established to eliminate signal overlap. WBFA's video and audio always have priority. Two 55-inch monitors are placed at the front of the room; one displays the incoming video signal, while the other displays the outgoing signal. Additional smaller monitors are located throughout the classroom. Students can see themselves on the outgoing monitors at all times regardless of whether the signal is being transmitted to the other sites. A videotaped copy of each transmission is made available to the faculty and students for review of the material covered each week.

The fully interactive classes are taught by the leading artists at WBFA. Instruction and assignments repeatedly test students' ability to demonstrate a thorough knowledge and practice of animation principles. Additional WBFA lectures address layout, background, story, character development, acting, improvisation, figure drawing, and special effects. Each Tuesday the WBFA artists provide a new lecture, a demonstration, and an assignment. Transmission time is allocated for the WBFA artists to review and critique student work from the previous week's assignment.

The SJSU curriculum includes intensive drawing in addition to the assignments by WBFA. The rigorous drawing component incorporates working from the model, animal studies from life, perspective problems for layout and background work, and master classes with visiting artists. Los Angeles-based animator, drawing instructor, and former AVTN artist Sheldon Borenstein flies to SJSU every Friday to teach a figure-drawing class for animators. Included in Mr. Borenstein's curriculum at SJSU are an industry prep class for graduating seniors and a film class currently working on a public-service announcement.

Thursday classes, non-WBFA, are used for traditional lectures, instructor contact, personal instruction, studio time, and Learning Community Sessions (LCS). The Lcss take place in the TEN studios and are student-led cooperative-learning sessions that include all participating sites except WBFA. Our goals with the cooperative learning sessions are for students to enhance their skill set through articulation of thoughts and ideas, to review and critique the work of peers beyond the boundaries of the traditional classroom, and to provide the sites with guest lectures by industry professionals outside the sphere of WBFA. The students return to the traditional classroom after each transmission, where instruction and studio time resume for one more hour. Interactive sessions start 30 minutes earlier than scheduled to accommodate the sites located in the central time zone, bringing the total time for class on transmission days to 3 hours and 30 minutes.

Students record their animation assignments on VHS tapes, which are then played on a standard VCR unit for the WBFA and LCS critiques. The video signal is transmitted over telephone lines using CODEC equipment at 768 kilobytes per second (KPS). The nuances and subtleties of animation require distortion-free images, and as it is, 768 KPS challenges the slowest acceptable speed.

This innovative project has required an enormous technical support commitment from each site. SJSU requires two technicians during transmissions. One technician, a CSU full-time employee, monitors all video, audio, and related equipment. The second technician is a student intern who assists by controlling camera angles and managing peripheral equipment. Additionally, CSU system technicians at SWRL in southern California play a critical role in the success of each transmission. SWRL is the CSU switching point for the compressed video signal sent and received from all sites. System preparation and testing begins one hour before each transmission.

Costs to participate in the AVTN are in constant flux. The third year is proving to be the most formidable. Initially, NWL founded a consortium of several major phone companies willing to donate phone lines for the project. Grants and seed money surfaced to help with equipment, tech support, instructor-release time, training, and travel. In a few cases, equipment was loaned or discounted to ensure a site's participation. Currently, each individual site is totally responsible for its own operating budget and funding. No hard money is available from WBFA, which has agreed instead to coordinate the curriculum, provide professional instruction, and internally fund its own tech support.

The first year pioneered this new teaching and learning model. No paradigm previously existed under comparable circumstances, though distance learning was fast becoming popular. We began the pilot program in the fall of 1996 with three interactive and two auditing sites. The auditing sites received all video and audio but were unable to transmit. All the sites became fully interactive the second year. According to assessment results, the sites changing from auditing to interactive status saw dramatic increases in the levels of material assimilation, problem solving, communication skills, commitment, and enthusiasm.

Technical problems abounded the first year. Distortion, signal break up, equipment incompatibility, and human error made the transmissions seem like an impossibility one moment and a miracle the next. The system would freeze up momentarily, crash entirely for the two hours, or leave two or three sites to carry on without WBFA or other participants. At the completion of the second year, technical problems were almost nonexistent, and tolerance for such problems was low. Time spent in advance of the weekly transmissions resolving technical problems facilitated closer integration of technical personnel and curriculum. This preparation does not, however, account for the avoidable human errors that frustrate students and instructors alike. Contemporary television delivers a seamless product, and students expect no less. They quickly become bored if the technology does not deliver as promised and unless instructors intervene, tend to be passive during AVTN instruction. As sites are added interactively or as the personnel changes, the learning curve appears destined to repeat itself at the expense of veteran participants.

Faculty- and student-assessment results from the Learning Community Sessions varied from site to site. Though the sessions were meant to foster reflective learning practices and to provide non-WBFA guest lectures, the students responded by saying that except for the guest speakers which they felt were helpful, they would have preferred to use the time working on their animation. As so often happens, students are apt to grasp short-range goals rather than the intangible long-range intentions of instructors. At SJSU we believe that the Learning Community Sessions have avenues deserving more experimentation, but as a changed model. Though still scheduled this year, the LCSs are to be reduced in frequency and the WBFA instruction is to increase. The students did respond favorably to breaching the nonexistent walls of the virtual classroom, noting that all AVTN-site participants have become peers.

The WBFA instruction is the foremost component of the distance-learning class. Lectures and assignments from professionals sustaining industry standards have substantially changed our classroom methodology. Particularly impressive is the rapid rate of student improvement. The variety of WBFA instructors provides accessible experiences for students of diverse backgrounds and learning styles. Though workloads increased substantially, students enthusiastically met the challenge of completing assignments from the professional community. Students demonstrated enhanced critical thinking skills and gained confidence in their ability to express themselves cogently on camera. They also benefited from their role as mentors to the high school and community college classes and as colleagues to the other university students.

The Acme Virtual Training Network is not a WBFA farm system, although WBFA does have the opportunity to see promising students develop and is quick to encourage top candidates to apply for openings when such become available. AVTN graduates are not assured jobs but are given the same opportunity to apply as students from other programs. Nevertheless, recent graduates who were enrolled in AVTN classes secured very competitive jobs at WBFA. Former ATVN students have also been hired at Walt Disney Company, Dreamworks SKG, Industrial Light and Magic, Nickelodeon, Film Roman, and traditional illustration venues such as Hallmark Cards.

As with any pilot program, there are increased responsibilities for faculty. AVTN magnifies the usual instructional tasks, and even with two professors in the classroom, the workload at times is overwhelming. Challenges continue to arise daily and include efforts to expand the project; to secure continued funding for support staff; to purchase, update, and maintain equipment; and to pay transmission costs. The length of the transmission limits our time in the classroom, and the hour left for critiques after WBFA signs off is not an adequate amount of time in which to address all questions and concerns. Students who are accustomed to individualized attention by their site instructors continue to want that attention even though they are receiving intensive instruction during WBFA transmissions.

With the help of AVTN, at San José State University we have developed a viable, competitive animation program from the ground up in two years — but not without considerable struggle. For educators planning to establish similar programs we offer the following suggestions. Expect extra time, energy, and resources to be required for any interactive distance-learning program, especially in the start-up stages. Remember that resources spent on initial efforts represent investment, and that this kind of experience constitutes professional development for faculty, technicians, and students. Let students know what to expect and how to function in this kind of social situation. Be prepared. Be flexible, have backup plans, and by all means, maintain your sense of humor.

Videoconferencing: The Virtual Guest Lecturer

William C. Epstein
California Polytechnic State University, San Luis Obispo

Abstract

Effective construction education often requires intimate connectivity to the field in order to meaningfully present the requisite information. One tried and true method of developing this connectivity and bringing current field issues to the classroom is by inviting local constructors to the class as guest lecturers. This works well in urban settings where access to qualified construction personnel is plentiful. However, what happens when the university is located hundreds of miles away from any significant urban center and therefore removed from easy access to substantial construction activity and associated personnel? One solution is to bring the field to the classroom electronically. This article is a case study of the author's experiences derived from teaching a project management course at just such a remotely located university. Due to the fact that organizing traditional face-to-face guest lecturing sessions was difficult, it was decided that a series of point-to-point videoconferences would be conducted, electronically linking the students in the classroom to qualified construction personnel in the field.

Introduction

Construction education is a very experience-laden academic pursuit. This fact can be evidenced by the premium that construction management programs place on actual field experience when advertising for and selecting their faculty (Epstein and Herbsman, 1993). However, when a person leaves industry to pursue a full-time academic career, they give up much of their personal contact with the day-to-day operations associated with the construction process. Although unfortunate, this situation is inevitable given the current level of demands placed on today's full-time tenured and tenure-track university professors.

Certain courses within a standard construction management curriculum demand more interaction with the field than others. Some classes are theoretical in nature, and, as such, actual relevance to day-to-day construction operations is less critical. Other classes however, require intimate connectivity to the field in order to meaningfully present the requisite information to the student. One type of class that dictates this kind of close relationship with field operations is the category of construction management coursework associated with the concepts of project level management and administration. When the professor is able to bring to the classroom people from outside the university setting who are presently working in the construction industry, this can only serve to enhance the students' overall academic experience. There is no substitution for currency when the goal is to effectively educate the student about real-life project management issues faced by today's construction industry.

One tried-and-true method of bringing current field issues to the classroom is by inviting local constructors to the class as guest lecturers to speak on some relevant topic. This works well in highly urban locations where access to qualified construction personnel is plentiful, and the impact on their busy schedules is minimal due to their close proximity to the university. However, what happens in the cases where the main campus is located hundreds of miles away from any significant urban center and therefore removed from easy access to substantial construction activity and associated personnel (a situation, by the way, which is very commonplace among many of the larger state universities in this country)? As Krammer, Sankar and Hingorani (1995) suggest, one solution is to bring the "project managers to the classroom electronically."

This article is for the most part a case study of this author's experiences derived from teaching two cycles of the required junior-level project management course (CM 364) at California Polytechnic State University (Cal Poly) in San Luis Obispo. Cal Poly certainly falls into the category of a large state university located in a nonurban setting. San Luis Obispo is located on the coast of California mid-way between Los Angeles to the south and San Francisco to the north. This location places the campus 250 to 300 miles away from any significant level of construction activity. As one might expect, it is very difficult to organize traditional face-to-face guest lecturing sessions due to Cal Poly's relatively remote location. It was decided that a series of point-to-point videoconferences would be conducted, electronically linking the students in the classroom to qualified construction personnel in the field. Presentation of this case study will begin by outlining the course, CM 364, and examining the method of incorporation of the videoconferences into the framework of this class. Next, the article will take a layman's approach in reviewing the telecommunications network and the equipment at Cal Poly which provided the opportunity to experiment with this mode of distance learning. Finally, this paper will conclude with a discussion of some of the lessons learned while attempting to integrate a rather significant videoconferencing component into a traditional in-residence academic offering.

The Course (CM 364—Project Administration)

The course that is the subject of this article is one which addresses the general procedures, methods, and documentation associated with project level management of the construction process. At Cal Poly, this course is a junior-level class titled CM 364—Project Administration. The syllabus contains the following class description:

> Procedures, methods and documentation associated with management of the construction process. Integral to the course is an ongoing simulated construction project designed to allow the student to "role play," and thus examine the relationships among the various members of the project team, namely the general contractor, subcontractors, the architect/engineer, and the owner.

The learning objectives of CM 364 are stated as follows:

- Familiarize the student with the concepts of project/contract administration through the use of construction drawings and specifications, contracts and subcontracts, and a variety of other project documents.

- Develop an understanding of the roles, responsibilities, and problems faced by each of the disciplines (constructor, architect/engineer, and owner) associated with a typical construction project.

- Develop a sense of how best to communicate project problems and their solutions to all members of the project team.

- Afford the student the opportunity of learning and working with some of the latest project management computer software.

Integrating Videoconferencing into the Course

Once the decision had been made to experiment with this technology, the next pedagogical step was to organize a series of videoconferences which would complement the course objectives and enhance the educational experience of the students. Barney and Pirkl (1990) recall the old real estate adage in describing what makes an effective videoconference. They say "In real estate there are three things to look for when making a purchase—location, location, and location; in a successful videoconference there are also three things—content, content, and content." They go on to note that "A strong presenter with depth and mastery of the topic is the first and foremost criterion for a good videoconference." With this in mind, an initial group of guest lecturers and associated topics were compiled. Based on numerous conversations with these potential presenters, as well as their availability and willingness to participate, a final list was generated and incorporated into the class schedule. Table 1 contains the schedules for both cycles of the class as taught by the author wherein videoconferencing was utilized. This table is presented so as to demonstrate the integration of the videoconferences into the basic framework of the course. Additionally, Table 1 serves to illustrate various changes made to the schedule between the first offering of this class (Fall Quarter 1997) and the second (Summer Quarter 1998).

Table 1. CM 364—Class Schedules for Fall 1997 and Summer 1998

Class No	Topics of Class Discussion Cycle 1— Fall Quarter 1997	Topics of Class Discussion Cycle 2— Summer Quarter 1998
1	Course Introduction	Course Introduction
2	The Project Team	The Project Team
3	Jobsite Construction Documents	Jobsite Construction Documents
4	Subcontract Agreements & Expedition	Introduction to Class Project and VC # 1
5	VC # 1—Subcontractor Relations	VC # 1—Subcontractor Relations
6	Procurement, Documenting, & Expedition	Subcontract Agreements & Expedition
7	Jobsite Scheduling and P3	Procurement, Documenting & Expedition
8	VC # 2— Submittals, RFI's & Logs	Jobsite Scheduling and P3
9	The Preconstruction Meeting	The Preconstruction Meeting
10	Class Project Preconstruction Meeting	Class Project Preconstruction Meeting
11	VC # 3— Meetings & Negotiations	Jobsite Layout and Control
12	Jobsite Layout and Control	Class Project Progress Meeting
13	Jobsite Labor Relations	Expedition and P3 Workshop
14	VC # 4—Jobsite Productivity	TEST No. 1
15	Class Project Progress Meeting	Class Project Progress Meeting
16	TEST No. 1	Measurement, Payments & VC # 2 Intro
17	VC # 5—The Permitting Process	VC # 2—Jobsite Productivity
18	Class Project Progress Meeting	Class Project Progress Meeting
19	Measurement & Payments	Jobsite Labor Relations and VC # 3 Intro
20	VC # 6—Changes and Extra Work	VC # 3—Safety Management
21	Class Project Progress Meeting	Class Project Meeting
22	Changes and Claims	Personnel and Safety Management
23	VC # 7—Safety Management	Changes and Claims
24	Class Project Progress Meeting	Class Project Progress Meeting
25	Personnel and Safety Management	Quality Management and VC # 4 Intro
26	VC # 8—Project Closeout	VC # 4—Project Closeout
27	Class Project Progress Meeting	Project Closeout
28	Quality Management	Class Project Progress Meeting
29	Class Project Progress Meeting	Class Project Closeout Meeting
30	Class Project Closeout Meeting	TEST No. 2
31	TEST No. 2	

For the first cycle of the class, given the fact that the course, the concept and technology associated with videoconferencing, as well as the presenters themselves were all new and unfamiliar, it was decided to basically give the participating experts relative "free rein" in developing their presentations. One of the identified limitations of the videoconferencing projection technology within the classroom was that if the presenter was referring to a particular document during his or her videoconference, unless the documents displayed had extraordinarily large fonts they were unreadable via the in-class monitors. Given this fact, the remote participants were asked to provide a package that contained any documents that they would be referencing during their presentations. They were also given a copy of the relevant sections of the class text that pertained to their upcoming videoconference as an aid for assisting them in developing an outline for their presentation. These outlines and associated document packages were then distributed to each student for their reference during the videoconference.

For the second cycle of the class, modifications were made to the videoconferencing component based on the lessons learned from the first cycle. As can be seen from Table 1, only four of the original eight sessions were repeated. This was done because it was realized that trying to conduct eight videoconferences in a ten-week quarter with all the other happenings associated with conducting class was simply too much. Additionally, on the second time around, the author became much more involved in generating the outlines and suggesting which documents should be included in the distributed packages and which documents were unnecessary. The presenters from the first cycle had a tendency of inundating the students with many extra pages of company documents which were not necessarily germane to their videoconference topic or consistent with the learning objectives of the class. Another lesson learned was to distribute the document packages to the students prior to the scheduled videoconference, so that the students could review the packages, relate these documents to the relevant sections in their class text, and become more familiar with the topics that were going to be addressed by the guest lecturer.

The Telecommunications Network

Cal Poly is part of a telecommunications network throughout California known as The California State University and Community College Network (4CNet). This network's legislatively mandated, stated mission is to "... provide telecommunications service and connectivity to support the educational mission of the California State Universities, and the California Community Colleges." Actually, from its inception in 1984 up until the 1996–97 fiscal year, this system was known as the "CSUnet," so named because it only linked together the California State University (CSU) system, which currently numbers 23 campuses. However, with the 1996–97 Fiscal Year Authorized Auxiliary Funding Measure, the California Community College (CCC) system was added to the network, expanding the connectivity by another 125 locations throughout the state (4CNet, 1999). What this means for the participating institutions is that, given that time is available (reservations are required), any member of the 4CNet can set up a point-to-point videoconference with any other 4CNet member free of charge. This can be a significant savings. With respect to this case study, the 4CNet afforded the Construction Management (CM) Department the luxury of avoiding a potential expenditure that could have easily exceeded $3,000.00 in line charges alone. That cost is calculated assuming a typical line charge of $100.00 per hour at 2-1/2 hours per videoconference (2-hour conference plus 1/2-hour pretesting) for a total of 12 sessions and equals $3,000.00. The scheduling for the videoconferences was therefore controlled by the availability and locations of the various 4CNet sites. The presenters were given a list of the CSU or CCC campus in their area, and they then indicated which ones would be most convenient for them. The particular sites were contacted, hardware compatibility verified, air time reserved, and the schedules finalized, all at no cost to either the presenter or the CM Department.

The Videoconferencing System at Cal Poly

Cal Poly is one of the more sophisticated sites on the 4CNet system. Figure 1 is a connectivity diagram of the university's videoconferencing system. Moving from right to left on the diagram, the digital transmission can be accomplished either via the 4CNet lines (free of charge) or the 3xBRI (Basic Rate ISDN) lines for a cost of $100.00 per hour. The 4CNet lines to Cal Poly are T1 connections. A TI line, or more formally called a T1 digital carrier, can carry up to 24 DS0 channels. Each DS0 (Digital Signal Level) has a bit rate of 64 Kbps (kilobits per second). Therefore the total bandwidth for a T1 line is 1536 Kbps (24 channels @ 64 Kbps per channel). Today's standard in videoconferencing is 30 frames per second. This can be accomplished at a transmission rate of 384 Kbps, which equates to 1/4 of a T1 line (1536 / 4 = 384). This same rate can be achieved utilizing the 3xBRI lines. A typical ISDN (Integrated Service Digital Network) line has a rate of 128 Kbps (Duran and Sauer, 1997). Bundling three of these lines together gives the same 384 Kbps capacity (3 x 128 = 384) as was possible with the 1/4 T1 connection. Either way, Cal Poly is able to transmit videoconferencing at the industry standard of 30 frames per second. The basic generic difference between ISDN and T1 is the fact that T1 lines are always on, as opposed to ISDN which are activated on demand (dialed up).

Whether using a 3xBRI connection or a 1/4 T1 line, bandwidth availability is still a very limited resource. This fact has been driving technological advancements towards ways in which to minimize the size of the transmitted data stream. In videoconferencing, this is accomplished by compressing the video signal, transmitting the signal in this compressed mode, and then decompressing it on the receiving end. The device used for compressing

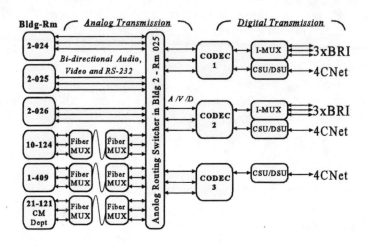

Figure 1. Videoconference room routing at Cal Poly (Woodworth, 1999)

and decompressing the video signal is called a CODEC (COmpression/ DECompression). Referring again to Figure 1, it can be seen that currently Cal Poly has three CODECs in service. Without these devices, videoconferencing would be impractical due to the extraordinarily large amount of data required to digitally describe uncompressed video images. Continuing to move right to left through Figure 1, the digital signal moves from the CODEC in a decompressed mode and is converted to an analog signal. This analog signal is then transmitted to the various rooms across campus that have been configured for videoconferencing. The CM Department's videoconferencing room is shown on the bottom left corner of Figure 1 as Bldg 21-Rm 121.

The CM Department's videoconferencing room consisted of a class camera mounted near the ceiling in the front of the room which transmitted Cal Poly's video signal outbound to the remote location. This camera had the capability of panning left or right, tilting up or down, and zooming in or out. Directly under the class camera was a 35-inch television monitor projecting the incoming video signal from the remote location. A second

35-inch television monitor was positioned in the front of the classroom and displayed the class camera's transmitted images. Two desktop multidirectional microphones were provided to pick up and transmit the outgoing audio signal, while an amplifier and associated speakers were used to distribute the incoming audio signal from the remote location. On the remote side, at most there were only two presenters, and they would therefore typically be assigned to a conference room type setup. This configuration generically would provide the presenters one monitor for receiving Cal Poly's signal from the class camera. The remote location also had a second monitor enabling the presenters to view the video signal that they were transmitting. Also at their desk was a document camera and a manual controller which would allow the presenter to switch back and forth from the conference room camera to the document camera, creating more of a sense of interaction, rather than simply an image of a "talking head."

Lessons Learned

The lessons learned from this particular experience fell within three general categories: technical, operational, and pedagogical. Looking at the first category, technical, two things stand out above the rest. First and foremost is the criticality of high audio quality. A few of the videoconferences suffered from substandard audio, and this severely detracted from the overall effectiveness of these sessions. As many of the experts have written (Storck & Sproull, 1995; McLeod & McLeod, 1994), high quality audio is far more important than the quality of the video signal in conducting a successful videoconference. Another important point to remember is that as Holland (1996) notes, "Given the fact that the failure of technological devices is predictably unpredictable, technological redundancy is imperative." Unfortunately, this lesson was learned the hard way during Videoconference # 8 in the Fall Quarter of 1997 (see Cycle 1—Table 1). On this day, the technicians were never really able to establish a viable connection, and the session had to be canceled and rescheduled, a considerable imposition for both the presenter and the instructor. For the second cycle of the class, in anticipation of similar connectivity problems, a speaker telephone setup was installed in the CM Department's room, the thought being that if the videoconference signal could not be established, the presenter could at least place a telephone call to the CM Department's room, and a simple audio teleconference could be conducted. Fortunately this backup system never had to be utilized.

On the operational front, one of the more valuable lessons learned had to do with the placement of the second television monitor which displayed the class camera's transmitted images. Positioning this monitor in the front of the room made the entire class very aware of the images being transmitted to the presenter. This had the beneficial effect of motivating the students to better focus on the presentation and not mentally wander, given the fact that they could clearly see themselves throughout the entire videoconference session. Another setup issue was the placement of the first television monitor, displaying the incoming video signal, directly beneath the class camera. To the remote location, this configuration makes it appear that the students are looking directly at the presenter, encouraging a more natural type of interactive experience. Along those same lines, the controllability of the class camera proved to be a very useful tool. By tilting, panning and zooming, the transmitted image could be varied at will, giving the presenter the sense that he or she was actually in front of a live class, rather than simply having them stare at an unchanging fixed image. An additional advantage of the controllability of the class camera was when a student wanted to ask a question or make a comment. By zooming in on that particular student, the presenter and the student were then given the opportunity to interact with each other more or less "face-to-face." Another issue that appeared to enhance the interactivity of the videoconferences was to have multiple presenters at the remote location. Of the twelve videoconferences in this study, nine had single presenters, and three were conducted using two presenters at the remote site. The three sessions using the two-person setup seemed to develop into much more of a panel type discussion rather than a lecturing "talking head." This format clearly engaged the students more thoroughly and proved to generate the more interactive videoconferencing sessions.

Pedagogically speaking, one of the issues that was previously noted was the reduction in the number of videoconferencing sessions from eight in the first cycle to four in the second cycle (see Table 1). It seemed that in the first cycle, the students became somewhat overwhelmed by the sheer number of videoconferences, and therefore the effectiveness of some of the later sessions clearly suffered. In the second cycle, the class on the whole appeared to be much more engaged for each videoconference, which made the overall experience for the students more rewarding the second time around. Another change instituted from the first cycle to the second cycle was a shortening of presentation time. In the first cycle, the presenter was given the whole two-hour class period in which to lecture. For the second cycle, the formal remotely based presentation was limited to 75 minutes, and the remaining 45 minutes were used for a more informal class discussion period. The remote presenters were encouraged to stay and participate in this locally based review and comment session, known in videoconferencing circles as a wraparound (Brown, 1998; Pirkl, 1990). Another change, alluded to earlier, in moving from the first cycle to the second cycle was the increased participation of the author in developing the presenters' outlines and associated document packages. This collaborative effort was greatly appreciated by the guest lecturers because it obviously reduced their time required in preparing for their videoconference sessions. It also benefitted the class in a number of ways, one of which was to assure that the videoconference would be more focused and compatible with the stated course objectives. The fact that the class instructor had significant involvement in shaping the proposed presentation enabled him to give an informative introduction to each upcoming videoconference during the class period just prior to the scheduled guest lecture (see Cycle 2—Table 1). This involvement also allowed for more control in the production of the class documents, ensuring that the packages would be completed and ready for distribution to the students at least one class period prior to the scheduled videoconference session.

Conclusion

Free access to California's 4CNet telecommunications network certainly encouraged and facilitated the use of videoconferencing as presented in this article. However, even if these sessions were conducted over commercial networks, their educational value would have far outweighed any nominal line charges incurred. The underlying motivation behind these videoconferences was to overcome the inherent constraints of a nonurban campus and bring professional constructors and their expertise to the classroom. The importance of this case study comes from recognizing the shortcomings experienced in the first cycle of this course, and then applying those lessons learned to the second offering of this class. Many of these lessons were rather generic and therefore could be implemented in other future academic endeavors attempting to incorporate a similar type of videoconferencing component. Today most, if not all, major universities in the United States have in place the capability of conducting a point-to-point videoconference. For those construction management programs which find it difficult to provide for in-class guest lecturers due to their remote locations, the use of this type of videoconferencing technology can be a very viable and exciting alternative mode of instruction.

References

4CNet History. (1999, June 16). [WWW document]. http://www.4c.net/documents/4cnet-history.htm

Barney, D., & Pirkl, R. (1990). Video teleconferencing: Tapping an emerging reserve and producing a new service. *Community, Technical and*

Junior College Journal, 61(4), 24, 26–28.

Brown, C. E. (1988). The live video teleconference in distance learning. *Lifelong Learning: An Omnibus of Practice and Research, 11*(5), 8–10, 24.

Duran, J., & Sauer, C. (1997). *Mainstream videoconferencing: A developer's guide to distance multimedia.* Reading, MA: Addison-Wesley.

Epstein, W. C., & Herbsman, Z. (1995). Dual careers in construction education: A solution for the educational crisis of the 21st century. *Proceedings of the Association of European Civil Engineering Faculties Symposium 1995,* Prague, Czech Republic, 53–58.

Holland, M. P. (1996). Collaborative technologies in inter-university instruction. *Journal of the American Society for Information Science, 47*(11), 857–862.

Krammer, S. W., Sankar, C. S., & Hingorani, K. (1995). Teaching project management issues through live cases from construction sites. *Journal of Professional Issues in Engineering Education and Practice, ASCE, 121*(4), 250–255.

McLeod, J., & McLeod, S. (1994). A doubly useful and important infra-structure: Progress, problems, and evaluation of technologies involved. *Simulation, 63*(5), 346–350.

Storck, J., & Sproull, L. (1995). Through a glass darkly: What do people learn in videoconferences? *Human Communication Research, 22*(2), 197–219.

Woodworth, P. (1999, February 17). *Videoconferencing @ Cal Poly.* [WWW document]. http://www.fmdc.calpoly.edu/comsrv/conf.html

Applications of Computer Technology in Tandem with the Traditional Classroom

Jean-Pierre R. Bayard
California State University, Sacramento

Abstract

Electronic teaching methods are used to stimulate the teaching and learning of basic electrical circuits at California State University, Sacramento (CSUS). Television and the World Wide Web are combined with traditional classroom teaching to address the issues of attendance, or lack thereof, poor performance, and timely assessment at a comprehensive urban university. While the circuits course is taught in the regular classroom, it is simultaneously broadcast through cable television in the larger Sacramento area. The course is also entirely available through the World Wide Web including audio-video segments captured from the classroom, as well as testing/assessment modules. The significance of this experiment lies in that the instructor promotes the technology portion of the teaching as *complementary* to the classroom environment, not as an *equivalent* self-paced learning option. This paper will describe the process in details, including how Web-based materials are used to assess students' performance, provide dynamic feedback to the instructor, and give students an opportunity for timely remedial action.

Introduction

Over the past few years there has been a strong nationwide initiative to incorporate technology in the delivery of instruction. Not surprisingly, across campuses this technology initiative has taken the form of electronic courses being delivered through distance education programs. In these times of shrinking instructional budget and expected increase in student population, the focus is very much on the potential economic benefits of this mode of delivery, rather than on its real educational value. Here at CSUS, a debate on the merits of distance education is just beginning, a lateness which can be explained by the following positions: 1) Administrators see distance education as the magic solution to our budget ailments, and believe that if they fund it, students will come, and 2) the majority of faculty experience a great deal of anxiety and insecurity being asked to learn a technology they did not grow up with, and one they think will replace them in the future. These positions are increasingly adversarial, and the majority of faculty members are more likely to take sides on the technology issue without having critically evaluated its pedagogical merits.

While distance education is becoming widely used across campuses, there is strong evidence that engineering students, if given a choice, benefit from learning in the traditional classroom settings. Indeed while the traditional classroom environment may appear somewhat old-fashioned, it offers invaluable learning enhancement features, which can hardly be duplicated in other forms of instructional delivery. This work attempts to enhance the learning of and student performance in a basic electrical circuits course taught in the traditional classroom through the use of technology. This technology supplement is accomplished in several ways: (a) while students are strongly urged to attend all classes, the material is made available on the World Wide Web and on local cable television; (b) communication and discussion of content continues outside the classroom using a course list; (c) using the streaming capabilities of our servers, key examples are narrated by the instructor providing a constant reminder of the important concepts and techniques learned in the classroom; and (d) using Web-based course management software, test problems covering all important segments of the course are administered electronically. Each category is described in detail with an emphasis on its relationship to the classroom. Examples are also provided for items (a) and (b) to demonstrate their effectiveness.

Classroom Enhancement with Technology

The present work stipulates that the traditional classroom is an effective and surprisingly efficient learning environment. The technology enhancements proposed here are warranted in order to stimulate the teaching, learning and advising of an increasingly diverse student population, as well as for the sake of convenience. For years, the introductory course on circuit analysis (ENGR 17) has been offered through the CSUS distance education program.[1] While the lectures are broadcast live on Sacramento cable, they are also taught in the traditional classroom using PowerPoint slides, toolbook learning modules and a writing pad with a permanent overhead camera. The traditional teaching is accomplished here not by using blackboard and chalk, but by taking advantage of the instructor-student eye contact, the instructor's ability to adapt his teaching style to the moment and to his students, and his ability to encourage his students to become independent learners. Because of these electronic tools and the fact that students do not have to take notes, the course content can be covered with some modest timesaving. As a result, problems or exercise sessions can be scheduled during class meetings. While students work on an assigned exercise, the instructor works the classroom providing one-on-one help and discussing strategies for solving the circuit. That setting is ideal for identifying the areas of weakness in students' ability to carry out a circuit analysis procedure.

One day after the live lecture, the tape is made available in the multimedia section of the CSUS library where students can check it out or view it in one of the VCR-TV combo booths. The library option is an important one for students who are unable to attend a live lecture, yet wish to remain current in the coverage when they rejoin the class.

The traditional classroom is complemented by a complete course Web site at http://gaia.ecs.csus.edu/~bayardj/engr17/index.html. The first time students go to this address, they are asked to fill out a questionnaire, which focuses on their preparation, courseload, and workload. The results are plotted dynamically and used by the instructor for advising purposes. Other interesting features of the site are an electronic subject index and access to all homework, quizzes, and exam scores and solutions online.

Email Forum

CSUS is a comprehensive urban university with a commuting student population. The traditional campus life model wherein between classes students head to the library study rooms, or visit instructors during office hours is less and less applicable. In the College of Engineering & Computer Science (ECS), most students work 15 or more hours per week while maintaining a full course load. The challenge for us engineering educators is to try to rekindle the kind of socialization that was once a valuable part of our campus life. Every student enrolled in the technology section of ENGR 17 is asked to join a course list and commit to accessing his or her email account at least once a day. Using the list, the instructor communicates with students and encourages them to share their thoughts and suggestions about the course content. The objectives and the key topics of ENGR 17 (described later) are emphasized as they are covered in the classroom. Comments on and inquiries about the use of technology in the course are common occurrences. Typically for a class of 32 students, there are 4 to 6 email messages sent to the list daily.

Streaming Content

In a lower-division course on circuit analysis, the method for teaching content is one based on exercise-solving skills. As explained earlier, in a problem session, the instructor acts like a coach, providing insights and strategies for solving circuits. This approach, if it is to be successful, must be followed in the not-so-distant-future by study hours in which students will practice on their own using these strategies learned in the classroom. The reality is one where most students do not refine their problem-solving skills right after learning the method in class, but procrastinate until a scheduled quiz or exam. The World Wide Web provides a time-invariant platform for making available to students the kind of discussion which reproduces the classroom environment during these exercise sessions. Using Real Presenter, a PowerPoint plug-in from Real Player, exercise slides are narrated, and modules are created for every important segment of the course. These modules are compressed and streamed from our servers. The end result is that an example describing (voice and graphics for 9 min 39s – 209K) how to *do* a nodal analysis procedure for a given circuit can be seen and heard with virtually no wait with a 28.8K modem access.

Electronic Assessment

With the coming of the ABET Engineering 2000 criteria, the assessment topic seems to dominate every discussion among faculty at engineering colleges. Here at CSUS, given our inexperience in assessing educational programs, we thought it would be far more productive to begin this process by focussing on course-based assessment, something that most faculty members are familiar with. The first step in developing an assessment plan for a course is the establishment of clear goals and objectives as well as expectations for enrolled students.[2] The following topics constitute the central focus of our basic circuits course (ENGR 17), and students will be expected to perform in those areas at levels that will later be determined:

- Nodal & Mesh Analyses
- Thevenin's & Norton's Circuits
- First- & Second-order Circuits
- Phasor method in sinusoidal circuits
- Sinusoidal power

The present work describes a small portion of the assessment plan being considered for the course, in particular how the Web can be used in course-based assessment with potential to improve students' performance in the classroom. Using the software Toolbook Instructor, over 50 test problems covering the above topics are created with the following characteristics:

1. Each test problem has a time limit enforceable on the Web. While there is ample time allocated for each test problem, we also want students to perform in a setting that is somewhat comparable to the classroom environment for which they are being trained.

JEAN-PIERRE R. BAYARD

2. Each test problem can be taken twice; however, for each attempt, the circuit values are generated randomly, giving rise to a different solution. For example, there are 20 test problems available in the nodal analysis section potentially resulting in 40 attempts. Figures 1 and 2 show one of these nodal test examples. In Figure 2, a button allows a student to access a matrix calculator (see Figure 3) to solve the system of equations.

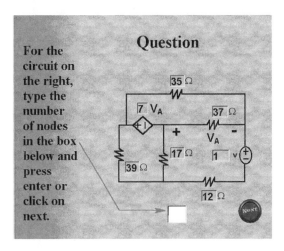

Figure 1. Nodal example—First question

The test problems are administered over the World Wide Web using the course management software *Librarian*. Students are assigned individual

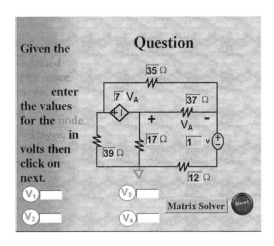

Figure 2. Nodal example—Second question

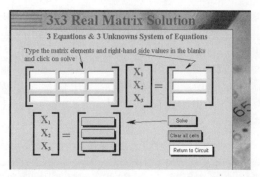

Figure 3. A matrix calculator

accounts and, if they own a personal computer (PC), they can access the test interface from home. Those who do not own a PC (~30%) take the tests in two open computer laboratories equipped with 400 MHz Pentium. With *Librarian*, a student can assess his/her knowledge level in a particular topic and take appropriate action if his/her performance in that topic is deemed poor.

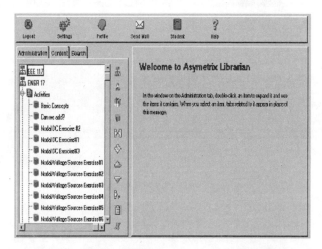

Figure 4. The *Librarian* instructor interface showing the nodal problems

Such remedial action may range from reviewing the lecture material on the Web or using the television tapes available in the library to attending our faculty-staffed workshop focussing on circuit problem solving. Figure 4 shows the *Librarian* instructor interface with the problems on nodal analysis. The instructor uses the student's record to dynamically evaluate the effectiveness of his lectures on that topic. Depending on the scores, additional supervised exercise sessions may be scheduled, and in some cases an advising meeting with a student may be necessary.

JEAN-PIERRE R. BAYARD

The Web-based tests count for 5–10% of the course grade, an amount small enough to discourage cheating but decent enough to encourage participation. In addition, the instructor clearly articulates the benefits of such practice, particularly the potential improvement of students' scores on the in-class tests, which make up at least 90% of their grades.

The implementation of Web-based tests in ENGR 17 is not without challenges. In order for PC owners to take the tests, they must spend time downloading and installing Java class files, browser plug-ins and a specific version of Netscape or Internet Explorer. Even with a detailed step-by-step user procedure, there are typically a few students who are not able to set up their machines correctly. For those who take the tests in the open labs, occasionally a student will try to use a machine that has been previously corrupted. In both cases, a struggling student is likely to express some degree of frustration and blame the technology for all of his/her problems in the course. In general, the minor technology-related snags are quickly dealt with, given that students have the ability to communicate constantly with the instructor.

Results and Concluding Remarks

In this age of assessment and accountability, it is reasonable—indeed expected—that the reader would ask if this approach has led to measurable performance improvement for the students enrolled in ENGR 17. From an enrollment standpoint, the addition of computer technology to ENGR 17

Table 1 Grade Distribution for E & EE 177—Fall 1998

Section	A	B	C	D	F	# of students repeating
TECH	0	4	5	0	3	2
TRAD	6	4	5	0	3	8
XFER	3	9	6	1	2	2

has certainly made the section more popular because of the convenience the technology offers. For the past several years, the technology-enhanced section has been offered at or near full capacity. In regard to the quality of the content and its effects on performance, it is difficult to provide convincing data that could demonstrate the success or lack thereof of mixing technology with classroom teaching. There are too many factors besides the use of technology that can affect class performance. The teaching ability of the instructor and the preparation and commitment of the students who venture in a technology section are just a few examples. Having said that, we consider the performance of students enrolled (Fall 1998) in Network Analysis, E&EE 117, an upper-division electrical engineering course with ENGR 17 as its foundation. Of the 63 students who complete E&EE 117, 12 were repeating the course. For the remaining 51 students, the grades are tabulated for 3 categories: 1) students who earned a passing grade in the technology section of ENGR 17 (TECH); 2) students who earned a passing grade in a traditional section of ENGR 17 (TRAD); and 3) students who transferred to CSUS with their ENGR 17 requirement completed (XFER). The reader should note that ENGR 17 is a course required of all engineering majors in the college. Thus only a small fraction of the ENGR 17 students end up taking E&EE 117. Also the effects of the electronic assessment and the streaming content having been implemented during the fall 1998 semester are not included in the sample. Considering the grade distributions for the 3 groups and the rate at which students repeat E&EE 117, one can infer that students who took the technology section of ENGR 17 perform in E&EE 117 at levels comparable to those from students taught in he traditional classrooms at CSUS or at transfer institutions. In the future, we hope that the Web-based tools will become a more integral part of the teaching and learning culture, and in turn lead to higher student performance in the electrical engineering program at CSUS.

References

1. Bayard, J-P. R., & deHaas, S. "Multimedia Teaching Tools for An Introductory Circuit Analysis Course," presented at the 1996 Frontiers in Education Conference, November 6–9, 1996.

2. Olds, B. M., & Miller, R. L. "An Assessment Matrix for Evaluating Engineering Programs," *Journal of Engineering Education*, Vol. 87, No. 2, April 1998, pp. 173–178.

JEAN-PIERRE R. BAYARD

The Web as a Delivery Medium to Enhance Instruction

Bijan Gillani
California State University, Hayward

Abstract

Educational Web design has been evolving since its inception. During its early stages, educators needed only basic knowledge of HTML (Hypertext Markup Language) to develop Web sites. As experience with Web sites grew, educators went further and added graphics and animation to their sites. Such a focus on tools gave rise to the concept of "cool" sites. As the evolution of Web design advances, we now need to find ways to make educational sites more effective, rather than just cool. To be effective, educators need to go beyond cool and apply a process that would allow them to integrate various components of the Web into their Web-based instruction. This article addresses the need by first describing an existing online course and then by explaining the design process which made the site an effective learning and teaching tool.

Course Description

"Learning Theories and Multimedia Design" is a course in the Educational Technology Graduate Program at California State University, Hayward. The purpose of this course is to examine learning theories and cognitive science research that have direct implications for creating effective educational materials for the Web and multimedia. The design process presented is interdisciplinary, involving three major fields. We explore

- trends in behavioral, cognitive, social, psychological and humanistic theories as they relate to content development. The course also focuses on how research from the fields of cognitive science and human information processing contribute to the design of effective user interfaces;

- technological tools in general and in particular Internet services used to develop effective Web sites; and

- principles of instructional design that relate to multimedia and Web development.

Bijan Gillani, "The Web as a Delivery Medium to Enhance Instruction." *Educational Media International* 35.1 (1998): 197-202. Reprinted by permission of the author and the publisher, Taylor & Francis, Ltd., www.tandf.co.uk/journals

Students in this course are school technology specialists. For two years I taught the course on the main campus with long-distance facilities simultaneously broadcasting video to a branch campus. The course evaluations from the remote students revealed that they were concerned about the advantages students on the main campus had in terms of accessing the course resources and the professor.

During the summer of 1997, I planned an online version of the course first to support the needs of the students at the branch campus and second to add some collaborative components of the Web that enhance instruction for both groups of students. I then designed and developed a course Web site (http://etleads.csuhayward.edu/6200.html) and placed it on a UNIX server that I had configured for the Educational Technology Graduate Program (http://etleads. csuhayward.edu).

Figure 1 *Main page for the course* (A black and white copy of a color screen).

Figure 1 shows the main page for the course. The seven buttons on the main page show how the site is organized and constitute the navigational system. These buttons function in two ways. The four larger buttons (Technology, Learner, Design, Overview) represent the lectures, related multimedia units, and links to other resources on the Web. The three smaller buttons (Resources, Students, Discourse) represent various interactive Web components that students can use to discuss, publish, collaborate and develop their final projects. The page serves as a central point unifying several technologies used in the course.

Another purpose of the site was to show students what they could do with multimedia on a Web site. The site was intentionally designed to use cutting edge technology (Shockwave for Director, Flash, JavaScript, frames, forms, imagemaps, Quicktime, Quicktime VR, and RealAudio, Chat, Forums, FTP capability). This design modeled for students how the Web can integrate teaching components into one site. The following briefly describes the function of each of these buttons.

Overview

The overview introduces the course and emphasizes that three major phenomena have rocked the very foundations of education. The first is the enormous advances in technology with hypertext, multimedia, the Internet, and the Web. The second is the contributions of learning theories to curriculum planning for multimedia and the Web. The third phenomenon is the emergence of instructional design as the guiding force for software, multimedia, and Web development.

Learning

The learner button leads to pages that present learning theories. The main focus of this section is to show that instruction should have a student-centered design. The only way to achieve this is by implementing the findings from learning theories and cognitive science. The learning theories in this section focus on behavior, cognitive, social, and humanistic theories that relate to developing student-centered course design. Some sections include multimedia units developed using Director. Other sections representing different scholars (e.g. Piaget, Vygotsky, Erikson) provide appropriate links to enable the students to obtain further information about specific theories.

Technology

The technology button leads the students to pages where an extensive tutorial and literature are provided. These Web tutorials and references include basic knowledge of the Internet, HTML images, frames, imagemaps, forms, embedding, multimedia (e.g., Flash), and JavaScript. I am still working on these pages to allow some online exercises that are corrected by the server.

Design

The design button leads to information dealing with the three phases of instructional design: needs analysis, design steps, and development. In addition to practical steps, links are provided to other resources on the Web where students can gather more information.

Discourse

The discourse button leads to another page with a Chat and a Forum area. These interactive components of the Web proved to be the most productive and interesting to the students. The Chat and Forum areas were used for informal discussions and for a formal publishing of thoughts, respectively.

The assignments for the course included a series of informal discussions, two midterm projects, and a final group project. Students were required to do some research or pondering upon the lectures as they were delivered in the class and represented on the Web. They were then scheduled to attend a series of informal discussions related to the specific topic in the lecture. Here is how the informal chat sessions were conducted:

- Students were divided into two groups.

- Each group was required to participate in the Chat area for a group discussion every other week.

- Specific topics related to the topics being discussed during the lecture were assigned for the Chat area.

- Informal discussions on predetermined topics were moderated by the faculty.

The Chat area proved to be the most popular of all the Web components implemented in this course. In addition to the scheduled sessions, students created their own special interest groups for the course and had nightly discussions. Furthermore, the Chat area, to be discussed shortly, became an excellent tool for students' discussions for their final projects. The Forum had a more formal design. Students were required to post their comments about their mid-term and final projects in the Forum according to specified dates. All students were required to read comments by other students and provide constructive criticism. Here's a description of their assignments:

- Project 1: Find and discuss a CD-ROM or an educational Web site in terms of its content organization, interface design, site architecture, and interactivity. Document your findings in the Forum.

- Project 2: Create one small instructional unit on the Web that uses one or more of the technologies that are discussed in the lectures (e.g. multimedia, frames, imagemaps, or JavaScript). Justification of your design must be documented on the Web in the class Forum.

- Final Group Project: Join a group in the class and plan to create an educational Web site based on one or more of the learning theories presented in lectures. You may choose any discipline such as science, math, or a thematic unit. Justification of teaching model(s) for the project must be documented on the Web in the class Forum. The final project was also posted on the students, homepages on the class server. This allowed students to see and comment on each other's work.

Students

Students worked as groups to design their final assignments. Each group was responsible for collaborating as a team to complete their final assignment. Upon completion each group placed their final assignment on the server and used it to make a final presentation in the class. To facilitate the collaboration process, I created two types of folders for each student: an individual folder and group folder. Students used the group folders to share their collaborative efforts on-line. The individual folders were used by students to create personal Web sites with links to their final project.

The Chat area also played a role for the final project. In fact, students requested a group Chat area where they could discuss their projects. A great majority of the work for their final project was done online, either in the chat area or in their group folders.

At the beginning of the course, some students were not familiar with Unix machines and the FTP process or even the Chat areas. During the course, not only did they master these functions, but they also used them to create online projects. Furthermore, they learned that creating these collaborative Web features is not that difficult. Some students are planning to use these components on their own Web pages at their respective schools.

Resources

Initially, the resources used in the class included a printed course syllabus and some books placed in the reserved library on the main campus. The Web site allowed me to expand the resources to include search engines, compressed audio, video, Chat area, Forum, related sites, and book references. Numerous search engines were included on the site. In addition to Yahoo and Excite, students could Telnet to the University library and search for available books. This proved to be useful for the students at the branch campus who did not have easy access to the main library. Arrangements were made to deliver books overnight to remote students.

The menu for the Resources area was slightly modified during the course because the audio component was not practical to deliver via the Web. Audio reference was designed to include lectures of each class. However, the Audio section was eliminated for two reasons: The process was time consuming; and it was not practical because videos of all lectures were available upon request. Instead I created a video button that would bring up a form requesting the video of a lecture. The video was then delivered to the other campus overnight. Other resources included links to related Web sites and book references.

The students really enjoyed the class (comments from both campuses are available on the site under Resources). There are comments such as "extraordinary," "fantastic" class. Apparently, both groups of students considered the course and its design to be effective, innovative and original. Readers are encouraged to read the students' comments.

Recommendations

Designing and developing an effective Web site to enhance instruction is a time-consuming process. In the following pages, I describe the systematic process I followed to develop the course's Web site. This process will save valuable time and yield a more effective result.

The Design Process

The design process included four phases: analyze, organize, develop, and evaluate and revise.

Phase I: Analyze

The tasks during the analysis phase include:

- Defining the problem for the Web site to solve. (This was to enhance instruction and provide resources to both groups of students.)

- Reviewing related existing Web sites. (Using educational starting points I searched and found similar online courses.)

- Identifying the team members for the project. (Unfortunately, I did not have the resources to assemble an effective team.)

- Identifying the needs of the targeted students, their characteristics, and their learning styles. (Analysis revealed that students in this course were mature, and comfortable with the Web. Their learning styles were appropriate for a teaching model that followed modelling, researching, discussing and finalizing a project).

Student analysis is critical to designing an effective Web site. With the students' needs and characteristics established, you can thoughtfully structure the site to reflect their needs. Such an analysis also provides essential information for the next phase of the development.

Phase 2: Organize

The tasks during Phase II include content organization, site architecture, and interface design.

Content organization. This is the effective presentation of the educational goal that is determined during Phase 1. Content organization includes both the structure of the information and how it will be presented, the treatment. The content structure should adhere to the educational needs of the students. These educational needs are best supported by using learning models derived from appropriate learning theories. Deciding which type of teaching model to use for a Web site is best done through the results of the student analysis (done during Phase 1). For example, the teaching models I used to develop the Web site are based on Vygotsky's sociocogntive theory (1978), Gillani (1994) and Gillani and Relan (1997).

Very briefly, this model emphasizes that learning occurs as the result of interactions between the learner and the environment and is mediated by tools. Vygotsky insisted on the primacy of language as a psychological tool that mediates between the learner and the environment in the process of development of higher mental functions. However, tools can be anything including the Web. Learners progress through roughly three sequential steps: modelling, interaction and internalization.

In step 1, the learners are passively active as they rely on the modelling and presentation of the mentor on concepts. During the second step, the students become active in construction of their own knowledge base by using tools to interact with the environment. In the third step, students internalize the new concept by using generating cognitive strategies to transfer and use the new concept to solve problems.

This teaching model for the course's Web site allowed the students to experience these steps:

1. *Modelling* (The four larger buttons on the main page of the site, Technology, Learner, Design and Overview, served as modelling of how you can structure the lectures and related multimedia as new concepts to be presented.)

2. *Interaction* (The two smaller buttons on the main page, Resources, and Discourse, represent various interactive components of the Web that students used to gather information, discuss, publish and collaborate about the concepts that were presented to them.)

3. *Internalizing* (The other small button on the main page, Students, represents various interactive Web components that students used to collaborate and develop a project to solve an educational problem. Such generative strategy is essential in internalization of the concepts that are modelled.)

Content treatment. This is concerned with making sure the presentation of the Web site is effective. For example, how can text, images or animation support the needs of the student? Or, how can videoconferencing, interactivities or Chat areas enhance the educational goal(s) of the site? Or, is JavaScript necessary to make the site more interactive? You need to think about the balance among all the elements and media types. Do they enhance the effectiveness of your Web site?

Site architecture. This governs how the pages are linked to one another. This relationship should be based on the teaching model that supports the site. Depending on the students' needs, or the function of the Web site, the architecture of the site may be structured in a variety of forms (tree structure, jumping structure, or looping structure). I had adopted a combination of tree and jumping site architecture for the site because they supported my teaching model.

Interface design. This includes the screen design, navigational tools, and the interactivity of the Web site. The styles of graphic presentations and other elements of interface design (menu system and the navigational elements of the site) play an essential role in the design of effective sites. For example, you need to carefully design what navigational tools are available and how far the students can stray from the main site. These decisions should be based upon the needs of the students and the goals of the site.

Phase 3: Develop
The tasks in Phase 3 include development, testing and publication.

Developing. Web sites require that you have some knowledge of new technologies, specifically Internet tools, server, HTML and multimedia. Many Web projects miss the fact that Web development is a collaborative effort. A team of specialists is generally required: interface designer, content provider, and producer. Most Web projects that ignore the building of effective team members are likely to fail. With a team in place the next step can begin. The development of the Web site includes construction of prototype sites using HTML, multimedia, and other Internet technologies. The development process usually includes the following steps:

- Outline the content showing objectives.
- Develop flowcharts based on the outline.
- Review the flowchart as a team.
- Determine the media types to be used.
- Storyboard (A sketch of each screen).

- Determine the programming required.
- Produce first module.
- Review with peers and revise the first module.
- Produce the remaining modules.
- Perform formative evaluation.
- Revise at all levels.
- Test on students.
- Perform summative evaluation.
- Revise.
- Test on more students.

Testing. Testing is essential. It is wise to construct only one module and test your design before investing much time. The testing should include all team members and the pilot student(s). If the prototype module is effective, then the other modules can be developed. Testing at this level should be done with a variety of browsers and platforms to ensure that your document works regardless of who is using it.

Publication. The publication of the Web site includes placing the final Web product on a server, testing everything, announcing it to the targeted students, and maintaining and updating the content and its design. During publication, you are concerned with the quality and distribution of the final product. Do not be surprised if the evaluation and revision continues during both production as well as post-production.

Phase 4: Evaluate and Revise
The evaluation process determines the extent to which you have achieved the expected educational outcomes. Evaluation is a continuous process. It starts from Phase 1 and continues even after the site has been developed and published. The evaluation of the Web site and its effectiveness can be done by applying standard techniques from the formative and summative types of evaluation. The formative type of evaluation provides data for revising and improving the site as it is being implemented. The summative evaluation is done after the first version of the Web site is completed.

References
Gillani, B. B. (1994). *Application of Vygotsky's social cognitive theory to the design of instructional* materials. Unpublished dissertation, University of Southern California.

Gillani, B. B. and Relan, A. (1997). Incorporating interactivity and multimedia into Web based instruction. In B. Khan (Ed.), *Web-based instruction.* Englewood Cliffs, NJ: Educational Technology Publications.

Vygotsky, I. S. (1978). *Mind in society: The development of higher psychological processes.* (M. Cole, V. John-Steiner, S. Scribner, & Soubermann, Eds. and Trans.). Cambridge, MA: MIT Press.

Note

I appreciate the comments and suggestions from all the wonderful graduate students who participated in this class. Special thanks goes to Ms. Tamara Nicoloff for reading the first draft of this article and making suggestions.

Applying E-Marketing Strategies to Online Distance Learning

Neil Granitz and C. Scott Greene
California State University, Fullerton

Abstract

This article uniquely identifies distance learning over the Internet as a form of e-commerce and applies e-marketing strategies to the implementation of online distance learning. Challenges posed by faculty and students of distance learning, as well as those resulting from incompatibilities between media and course content are outlined. The e-marketing strategic themes of personalization and customization, community, disintermediation, reintermediation, consumer tracking, enhanced customer service, and mixing bricks and clicks are then applied to the challenges for the purpose of providing guidance towards the most appropriate deployment of the Internet for distance education.

Introduction

Distance learning is defined as "the acquisition of knowledge and skills through mediated information and instruction" (United States Distance Learning Association, 2001). At the heart of it, distance learning corresponds to education that takes place when time or space separates student and educator. Expected to grow from 710,000 students in 1998 to 2.3 million students in 2002 (Lichtenberg, 2001), fast-changing professional knowledge and a growing segment of adult working students continues to fuel the growth of higher education distance learning (Tucker, 2001).

With the rapid growth of the Internet, online distance learning has become a viable form of education. In their seminal article, Ives and Jarvenpaa (1996) stated that

> the knowledge revolution, though propelled by the twin engines of computer technology and communication technology is a revolution of minds and ideas rather than of mass and energy. . . the World Wide Web lets anyone, at a moderate cost, publish information accessible to others anywhere in the world.
> (pp. 33–34)

Currently 375 million people worldwide use the Internet (Cyberatlas, 2001), with expectations of that number increasing to over 765 million by 2005 (CommerceNet, 2001). Forecasts call for the number of higher education institutions offering online distance learning to double from 1,500 in 1999 to 3,300 in 2004 (Burger, Boggs, & Webber, 2000).

Changing the communication medium from face-to-face to distance learning creates challenges for faculty and students, as well as compatibility issues with the course content. Thus, numerous articles and books discuss these distance learning challenges and issues. Some focus on how to implement distance learning over the Net (Cartwright, 1994; Eastman & Swift, 2001; Kaynama &Keesling, 2000; Lloyd, 1997; Porter 1997), personal experience with distance learning (Canzer, 1997; Flaschner, 1999; Kendrick 1998), policy and organizational issues (Rahm & Reed, 1997), impact on teaching evaluations (Clow, 1999), and comparisons of Internet classes versus conventional classes (Mehlenbacher et al., 2000; Ponzurick, Russo-France, & Logar, 2000; Smith, 2001). However, none actually identifies distance learning

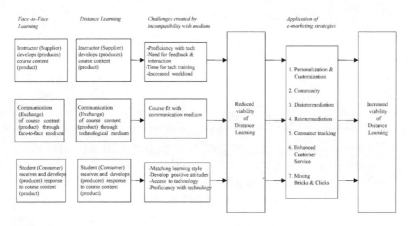

Figure 1. Applying e-marketing strategies to the challenges of distance learning

over the Internet as a form of e-commerce. By recognizing online distance learning as e-commerce, new e-marketing theory and knowledge developed by academics and business practitioners can be applied to meet many of the challenges of distance learning.

In the context of e-commerce, this article applies a basic business exchange model (Bagozzi, 1974) by outlining challenges engendering unmet needs of students as consumers of course content; educators as suppliers of course content; and challenges arising from incompatibilities with course content itself, when the communication medium changes from face-to-face to distance learning media (Figure 1). In response to the decreased viability

NEIL GRANITZ · C. SCOTT GREENE

of distance learning created by these unmet needs, the e-marketing strategic themes of personalization and customization (Kahn, 1998; Kasanoff, 1998), community (Armstrong and Hagel 1996), disintermediation (Magretta, 1998), reintermediation (Hanson, 2000), consumer tracking (Koprowski, 1998), enhanced customer service (Seybold, 1998), and mixing bricks and clicks (Gulati & Garino, 2000) developed for e-commerce, are applied for the purpose of providing guidance toward the most appropriate employment of the Internet for distance education in marketing, and other higher education courses. Thus, this article offers solutions based on established e-marketing strategies to the challenges arising from online distance learning. The article concludes with practical implementation guidelines, or tactics, for educators wishing to utilize these strategies.

Business Models and Education

Numerous researchers have viewed education as a business, and applied business models or strategies to the educational process, most notably in the areas of Market Strategy and Total Quality Management (TQM) (Allen, 2000; Lutz & Field, 1998; Malouf & Sims, 1996; Rudzki, 1995; Schwartzman, 1997; Tsichritzis, 1999; Waits, & Agnew, 2001; Zappia, 1999). While opponents fear it moves decision power away from faculty to managers concerned with the bottom line and mass-production techniques (Jorgensen 1992; Scrabec, 2000), proponents embrace it as a way to understand the viability of education (Bridges, 1999; Motwani, 1995; Shank, Walker, & Hayes, 1995; Simmons, 1999).

Especially for online distance learning, the mass-production paradigm appeals to university administrators who see it as an opportunity to increase the instructor-to-student ratio, free from the confines of physical space. In reality, accounting for the added resources and time required to develop and implement a course, online distance learning is better suited for smaller classes (Eastman & Swift, 2001). Therefore, the value of a business paradigm applied to online distance learning is not rooted in its power to employ mass-production techniques, but in its ability as a tool to analyze and enhance the viability of online distance learning. A business paradigm allows us to recognize that education constitutes a marketplace comprised of constituents having particular needs. Moreover, business (e-marketing) concepts can be applied to meet constituents' needs, being challenged by a change in communication medium. From a business perspective, instructors with particular needs are suppliers of e-commerce content, students with particular needs are consumers of e-commerce content, the actual content of the course constitutes the product, while the communication medium provides the distribution channel, which facilitates exchange. Applications of e-marketing strategies help meet the needs and increase the viability of the online distance learning communication medium. The next section focuses on needs of the constituents and their challenges.

Distance Learning: Challenges Created by a Change in Communication Media

Distance education alters the traditional message channel. This affects the student as sender and receiver, as well as the educator as sender and receiver, creating challenges due to unmet needs. Additionally, course content may be incompatible with the message channel. If educators do not respond to these challenges, reduction in the viability of distance learning will result (Figure 1). The following sections outline the challenges.

Faculty Challenges

As suppliers of distance learning content, faculty become responsible for producing and distributing content through a technological interface. As a result, instructors face four challenges to their needs. First, many instructors dislike or fear technology and therefore do not embrace distance learning (Romiszowski 1988). Second, some faculty more strongly require feedback and interaction (Besser 1996; Comeaux 1995). In a face-to-face classroom, an instructor receives feedback in the form of questions, body language, facial expressions and eye contact. Knowing whether students are paying attention and even if they are still connected to the host site persist as problems with many forms of distance education. Third, technology training takes extra time, yet most faculty are not provided with relief from their teaching and research responsibilities. Finally, distance learning requires instructors to give greater attention to "advanced preparation, student interaction, visual materials, activities for independent study, and follow-up activities" (Kendrick, 1998; Pool, 1996; Young, 2001; U.S. Congress, 1989) for which instructors have shown little enthusiasm (Pearce, 1999). This is particularly true of faculty who employ active learning techniques (Daly, 2001; Gremler et al., 2000; Johnson & Johnson, 1993; Lamont & Friedman, 1997; Petkus, 2000; Warren, 1997; Wheeler, 1998; Wright et al., 1994).

Course Content Challenges

From a business paradigm perspective, course content now constitutes a product being transmitted via telecommunications technology. Thus, course content challenges focus on the compatibility of course content with the communication medium. Massy and Zemsky (1996) suggest that subject areas most suited for distance learning are those with large volumes of students, standardized curricula, content over which faculty are less possessive

Table 1. Felder-Silverman Student Learning Styles

Learning Type	Description
Sensing learners	Focused on practical and oriented towards facts and procedures
Intuitive learners	Oriented towards theory and meaning and do not like complexity
Visual learners	Learn from visual presentation of materials such as pictures and diagrams
Verbal learners	Learn from verbal materials such as written and spoken word
Active learners	Learn well in groups and interacting with others
Reflective learners	Concentrate on thinking things through
Inductive learners	Prefer to see cases first and then work out principles by inference
Deductive learners	Prefer to see theory first and then cases
Sequential learners	Learn in a linear fashion by absorbing small connected chunks
Global learners	Achieve understanding by connecting fragmented pieces to arrive at a whole.

and outcomes which can be easily delineated. Viewing this recommendation from the perspective of Eastman and Swift (2001) (who recommend small classes), subject areas with large volumes of students means total volume coming from many smaller classes, not just one large section. Other researchers suggest that distance delivery is best suited for teaching a fixed and narrow set of skills and knowledge, to students with a strong desire to learn (Besser & Bonn, 1996; Rahm & Reed, 1997).

Student Challenges

As consumers of distance learning content, students must receive and respond to course content through a technological interface. Consequently, four challenges emerge. First, student learning style is less likely to match the presentation of the information. Students have different learning styles: characteristic strengths and preferences in the ways they take in and process information. Table 1 illustrates the Felder-Silverman Learning Style Model (Felder, 1993; 1996), which incorporates dimensions from several models (Herrman, 1990; Kolb, 1984; Lawrence, 1994). While face-to-face instruction may allow instructors to adjust their presentations based on questions, body language, and facial expressions to suit different styles, the time and space separation occurring in distance learning hinders this process. Incompatibility between presentation and learning style leads to lower student satisfaction (Stanton & Baber, 1991) and a higher drop out rate (Terrell & Dringus, 1999/2000). Therefore, higher education institutions offering online programs must address learning style issues.

Second, compared to students taking a face-to-face class, students in a distance learning class demonstrated significantly less positive attitudes and lower motivation attributed to ill-prepared and unresponsive faculty and administration (Armstrong-Stassen, Landstrom, & Lumpkin, 1998), and lack of interactive course-related activities (Ponzurick, Russo-France, & Logar, 2000). Third, students may not have access to the latest technological resources, including hardware, software and broadband access. This may be more prevalent in countries with lower technology penetration. Fourth, while Young (2001) found that students are using computer and telecommunications technology effectively, strong variation in computer proficiency still exists. Some students are techno-savvy, yet others remain techno-phobic (McCorkle, Alexander, & Reardon, 2001). Thus, there must also be responses to these four student needs. The next section relates these challenges to e-marketing strategies and practical tactics. It explains criteria for including each strategy and demonstrates how educators can meet the challenges to make online distance learning a more viable medium.

E-Marketing Strategies and Online Distance Learning

Criteria for Choice of E-Marketing Strategies

All distance-learning challenges discussed above emerge in the product development and exchange stages of a business. Thus, e-marketing strategic themes that focus on product development and exchange are relevant and applied below. Technical themes (i.e. Web design, security, etc.) and themes related to selling (i.e. viral marketing, cost transparency, etc.) were not included.

In assembling the list of e-marketing strategic themes, the authors perused e-marketing textbooks, articles focused on e-commerce in major marketing journals from the last 5 years, and 25 different e-marketing syllabi, randomly collected from the Web. Additionally, as one of the authors sits on a practitioner-based e-commerce advisory board, e-marketing managers were consulted to ensure relevancy of the themes. Because of the interrelated nature of e-marketing themes to many individual challenges, their specific application to online distance learning appears after all relevant themes are explained.

Personalization and Customization

Personalization refers to a site's ability to tailor information for each unique user. Customization refers to the ability of a user to tailor the site information (Nunes and Kambil, 2001; Rayport & Jaworski, 2000). They both occur when users tell the provider or the provider deduces their preferences. For example, the Web site of the *New York Times* queries its readers on what topics they want to see on the opening page, and then uses specialized software to deliver it.

Community

Community arises when a particular site becomes a place of interest, where participants interact extensively and repeatedly with one another on specific topics (Armstrong & Hagel, 1996). A community can evolve through chat or bulletin boards. For example, WebMD has varying communities dealing with different medical conditions (pregnancy, aging, cancer, etc.). Community becomes a key benefit when it continually brings members to the sponsor site, and thereby involves them more deeply with the product or service.

Disintermediation

Disintermediation refers to the elimination of a channel intermediary (Magretta 1998). However, when a channel member is eliminated, its functions are not gone and must be assumed by another (Stern & El Ansary, 1992). For example, Dell excluded wholesalers and retailers, selling computer hardware directly to consumers. In the information world, disintermediation refers to the direct sharing of information between and across any members of a value chain, rather than flowing sequentially through the members. Benefits of this direct model include better customization due to direct contact with customers, better customer service, and overall reduced costs.

Reintermediation

Reintermediation refers to adding channel intermediaries that collect and distribute information (Hanson, 2000). For example, Autobytel.com has been successful in aggregating and presenting impartial information on the auto industry to consumers. Consumers benefit by receiving more information and greater control over the information (Hagel & Singer, 1999). Suppliers benefit because infomediaries create the infrastructure to present their products (or services) online.

Consumer Tracking

The Internet constitutes the most accountable media ever. Web-site log software and real-time profiling track the number of users who view each page, location of previously visited pages, date of view, time of view, duration of viewing, links followed, etc. These metrics are used to analyze Web site effectiveness, and to track and respond to consumer behavior (Koprowski, 1998). For example, while perusing the Nissan site, if a consumer spends time on a page, a pop-up box offers him more information on the page topic.

Enhanced Customer Service

Customer service takes on new meaning in an e-commerce world due to the ability to create a direct link with the customer. In her book,

Customers.com, Patricia Seybold (1998) addresses several key principles. First, target the right customer, in terms of both current customers and potential customers. Second, own the customers' experience. Once they buy something from you, keep them updated and in the communication network during and after the product/service delivery. Third, from a customer viewpoint, streamline business processes for easy customer transactions, and provide strong and relevant opportunities for customer self-service.

Mixing Bricks and Clicks

Mixing bricks with clicks focuses on how traditional brick and mortar organizations can go online (Gulati & Garino, 2000). Should they go alone, form a partnership or joint venture with a knowledgeable partner? Should the e-commerce and brick and mortar businesses be pure extensions of one another, or should each target different segments with different products and services? Several key considerations pertain. First, if consumers want to shop through multiple channels (i.e., buy something online and return it to the brick and mortar store), then the organization should be ready to serve customers through multiple channels. Second, if consumers differ between the channels, the company should meet the differing needs of each segment. Third, if the organization lacks the expertise or resources to implement an e-commerce solution, then the organization should consider a form of partnership or joint venture.

E-marketing Strategies Applied to Distance Learning Challenges

Educators and educational administrators can utilize the seven e-marketing strategic themes to meet challenges posed by distance learning. How to apply these strategies and concrete examples of their implementation follow.

Meeting Faculty Challenges

All faculty challenges arise from changing the job requirements. First, proficiency with technology requires that educators learn new technology skills. Second, faculty must adjust to different and usually less feedback from students. Third, technology training takes extra time, which is not accounted for. Fourth, increased workload leads to negative attitudes. Based on their responses to these challenges, faculty can be grouped into three categories: those who already embrace online learning, those who are ambivalent towards online distance learning, and those who are averse to participating in online distance learning. While educators in the first category are not challenged, research suggests that the majority of faculty fall into the latter two categories (Pearce, 1999). For educators who are ambivalent or uninterested in extending their teaching into this frontier, education, experience, training, as well as university-wide distance learning initiatives may help

Table 2. E-marketing strategies and tactics to meet distance learning faculty Challenges

Challenges	Strategies	Tactics
Proficiency with technology Increased workload Time for technology training	Disintermediation and customization	Schools form alliances with other universities interested in a disintermediation strategy. Committee of instructors from the universities choose a publisher /service provider with expertise in converting class materials into a Web-friendly format. Committee then meets with publisher/service provider to convert lecture, exercises, quizzes, cases and exams into online course template, leaving opportunities for individual professor customization. Publisher completely administers course to students.
Proficiency with technology Increased workload Need for feedback/ interaction Time for technology training	Reintermediation, customization, and community	Schools form alliances with other universities interested in a reintermediation strategy. Committee of instructors from the universities choose a publisher /service provider with expertise in converting class materials into a Web-friendly format. Committee then meets with publisher/service provider to convert lecture, exercises, quizzes, cases and exams into an online course template, leaving opportunities for individual professor customization. Suppliers develop an easy Internet communication interface and train faculty on this software (WebCT, Blackboard, eCollege). Faculty then administer course with technological support from supplier. Faculty participate in community.
Proficiency with technology Increased workload Need for feedback/ interaction	Bricks and clicks	Universities or departments form partnerships with expert online distance learning schools. The two schools form a joint committee of professors to oversee and administer courses. Instructors interested in distance learning teach distance learning courses and/or distance learning portions of hybrid courses. Instructors preferring face-to-face teach face-to-face courses and/or the face-to-face portion of hybrid courses.
Proficiency with technology	Consumer tracking	1. Technological intermediaries or instructors generate click stream reports to diagnose student patterns in viewing the material. Lecture/class activities can be re-structured to better emulate student click stream. 2. Technological intermediaries or instructors generate student diagnostic reports tracking each student's quantity of participation, assignments handed in with date and grade of assignment, as well as dates lectures were accessed by student. Instructor offers suggestions for improvement.

overcome these challenges (Irani, 2001; LeBlanc, 1997; McCorkle, Alexander, & Reardon, 2001). If willing and motivated educators in a department cannot meet the demand for online distance learning, universities can focus upon the e-marketing strategies of disintermediation, reintermediation, customization, bricks and clicks, and/or consumer tracking. Table 2 summarizes how these e-marketing themes can be implemented to meet the faculty challenges. With several e-marketing strategies meeting distinctive needs, educational institutions must select the solution that best fits their organization.

In one view of education, the textbook can be considered the repository of knowledge about a subject, the student can be seen as the final consumer, while the instructor can be regarded as the middleman delivering the knowledge. A disintermediation strategy (i.e. direct model) eliminates the instructor as principle communicator of the material. The publisher communicates directly with the student. As they have in the past, educators work with publishers to develop the product, course content. However, the publisher's responsibility consists of converting the lecture, exercises, quizzes, cases and exams into an interactive online course, administering it to students and communicating with them. Since the publisher or service provider would be a paid supplier to the university, yet also work with instructors, this constitutes true disintermediation from a student viewpoint.

In an example of supplier capabilities, Thomson Learning announced an agreement with Universitas 21, a consortium of 18 universities in 10 countries, to develop distance learning higher education courses to be delivered online (Hilts, 2000). Thomson Learning will be responsible for course design, delivery, testing, assessment and student database management. Universitas 21 will award degrees to students who complete the course requirements. In another example, Harcourt General (education publisher) offered college level courses over the Internet and was prepared to grant bachelor degrees (Kirkpatrick, 2000). One year later, Reed Elsevier acquired Harcourt and the program was abruptly closed due to incongruency with the business strategy of the new parent company (Emery, 2001). The low total enrollment of 20-30 students was likely due to the fact that Harcourt has no reputation for administering education. As Emery (2001) notes, most successful online programs are those offered by established brick and mortar schools. Since Harcourt was acting on its own and not as a supplier of the information, this example is meant to illustrate publishers' potential of facilitating disintermediation.

Another option uses an e-learning application service provider, such as Vcampus, who develops, manages and hosts turnkey web-based learning solutions. Vcampus currently develops content for George Mason University (Anonymous, 2002).

Since publishers or service providers cannot create separate courses and technologically interface with every professor or university, to achieve economic viability, universities can form alliances with other schools interested in this strategy. A committee of professors could then work with a chosen supplier to develop the course and its implementation.

Completely moving the implementation of distance learning to the publisher or service provider overcomes faculty challenges in several ways. First, it eliminates instructors' need for proficiency with the technology. Second, it decreases the need for technology training by moving the labor-intensive production of course materials to the publisher. Third, with the possibility of removing the instructor from the actual teaching, meeting instructors' need for feedback is mitigated. Finally, in removing the professor from the implementation, the need for technology training is eliminated.

A strategy of disintermediation lacks the important social role of an instructor in online education (Buchanan, 1999; Palloff & Pratt, 1999). That role entails mentoring students, ensuring class discussions stay on track and reasonably correct, plus providing discipline-specific scholarly feedback to students.

Introducing a reintermediation strategy overcomes this obstacle. In a reintermediation strategy, the publisher, or another service provider, would become the instructional technology designer (intermediary), while the instructor would actually deliver the course. Several examples of technological intermediaries are emerging. By incorporating textbook chapters, quizzes, and examinations into online vehicles such as Blackboard, publishers like Prentice Hall are already moving in this direction. McEwan (2001) recounts successfully employing publisher-generated technology using the online resources of his textbook, including PowerPoint slides, tutorials, and links to countrywide newspapers into his class. Additionally, the intermediaries discussed above (Thomson Learning, Vcampus) would fulfill only the technological role for this reintermediation strategy.

For reintermediation, a cross-university committee might work with a publisher or service provider to develop content and environment (i.e., chat rooms, bulletin boards, etc.). However, given the responsibility of the instructor to administer the course, the software/hardware tools must be easy to use. Tidd (2001) recommends user-friendly packages such as WebCT and Blackboard. From a faculty perspective, this represents true reintermediation - all communication is mediated through the systems of the supplier.

A reintermediation model where a publisher or service provider assumes responsibility for the technical delivery of materials, while a professor assumes the social role (face-to-face or online) should be considered. This recommendation resolves increased workload and minimizes training and proficiency with technology issues, while also providing the crucial social role of an instructor. Monitoring and participating in community, and increasing interactivity through chat and bulletin boards can satisfy the need for feedback. It should be noted that in either a disintermediation or reintermediation strategy, faculty are needed to work with the supplier to develop the course. Thus administration will need to compensate faculty through release time or financial incentives.

In the context of disintermediation or reintermediation, the theme of customization can be applied. From an instructor perspective, customization refers to on-demand publishing of course content (i.e., custom published texts). At Cornell University, some 21% of classes now use custom course packets (Anonymous, 2001 a). Each course packet contains a collection of materials assembled by the professor that can include published articles, selected chapters from several textbooks and essays from various sources. While the Cornell example refers predominantly to face-to-face classes, in preparing material for disintermediation (for the supplier to administer) or reintermediation (for the instructor to administer), custom course packets would contribute to a more positive attitude for professors. While a committee of cross-university instructors would work with a technology supplier to develop the course materials, whether the instructor is personally delivering the course (reintermediation) or the technology supplier is delivering the course (disintermediation), various materials could be configured differently by each instructor. For example, one professor could choose to incorporate ethics examples throughout a marketing course, while another could treat it as a separate section.

Another e-marketing theme accommodating challenges to faculty focuses on a bricks and clicks strategy. Recall that mixing bricks and clicks refers to the mix between online portions and brick and mortar portions of a business. For universities, a bricks and clicks strategy can be implemented at the macro and micro levels. At the macro level, traditional universities desiring to increase distance learning may need to do so with partners experienced in distance education. The macro level, while similar to disintermediation and reintermediation, differs because the relationship is one of partnership versus supplier. While traditional universities bring much-needed reputation and knowledge (Weinstein, 2000), the partner schools bring expertise through motivated lecturers experienced in teaching distance-learning courses. For example, Unext.com, a virtual university, has agreements with Colombia University, the University of Chicago, the London School of Economics and Stanford University to receive course materials from them. In another example, Arthur R. Miller, a Harvard Law Professor, provides video courses for the Concord University School of Law (Ellin, 2000). While both cases focus primarily on the technology partner, with the brick and mortar university lending knowledge and reputation to the cyber-university, the relationship can be reciprocal, where the cyber-university lends technological expertise to the brick and mortar university.

Table 3. E-marketing strategies and tactics to meet distance-learning course content challenges

Challenges	Strategy	Tactics
Course fit with communication medium	Disintermediation	Apply to subject areas with large volumes of students with a strong desire to learn, standard ized curricula, content with a fixed and narrow set of skills over which faculty are less posses sive and common across universities.
	Reintermediation	Apply to classes with large volumes of students with a strong desire to learn, standardized curricula, content with a fixed and narrow set of skills over which faculty are less possessive and common across universities.
	Bricks and clicks	1. Respective instructors determine the portion that they believe is best suited for online delivery. 2. Determine what is best by adopting a hybrid strategy and letting students decide which they would like to attend.
	Community	Portions of the course suited for interactivity occur online.

At the micro level, bricks and clicks can refer to a single course with two portions (hybrid): a distance learning component and a face-to-face component. Faculty who do not wish to instruct in distance learning can teach the traditional component, while other faculty can teach the distance-learning component of the course. Removing reluctant professors from the distance learning portions of teaching can solve the challenges. It should be noted that all of these alternatives are subject to meeting students' needs for distance learning versus face-to-face instruction.

For those professors engaged in online distance learning, the theme of consumer tracking (Koprowski, 1998) can be implemented several ways to appease instructors' need for feedback. First, instructors can optimize their Web page designs by studying consumer click streams. For example, if an instructor determines that students continually refer back to a particular page, more links from other pages to that page can be inserted. Additionally, by studying which pages were viewed and the sequence in which they were viewed, pages and links can be re-ordered. Finally, consumer tracking can be a diagnostic tool for student participation and performance. Smith (2001) points out that instructors can grade participation more accurately in online courses by monitoring and rereading student comments in electronic discussion forums. In the context of performance, if students score low on an exam, an instructor can diagnose the situation by tracking students' participation, dates assignments were submitted, course content they accessed and when they accessed it. When students study from printed copies of the online lectures (Karuppan & Karuppan, 1999), the latter diagnostic may be limited. That limitation notwithstanding, by reviewing available information, the professor can offer suggestions for improvement.

Meeting Course Content Challenges

Please recall that distance learning best suits subject areas with large volumes of students, smaller class sizes, standardized curricula, content over which instructors are less possessive, outcomes that can be easily delineated (Eastman & Swift, 2001; Massy & Zemsky, 1996) and/or classes teaching a fixed and narrow set of skills to students with a strong desire to learn those skills (Besser & Bonn, 1996; Rahm & Reed, 1997). Several of the e-marketing strategies apply to course content challenges (see Table 3).

Since disintermediation and reintermediation (as discussed above) require several brick and mortar schools to form alliances to develop common courses with the supplier, logic dictates that common core classes (e.g., Marketing Principles) be considered first. This strategy is compatible with Massy and Zemsky's recommendations for subject areas with many students, but subject to the restriction of students with a strong desire to learn the skills and small class sizes. If the recommendation for a "fixed and narrow set of skills" is followed, electives present across many campuses can be developed for distance learning through disintermediation and reintermediation.

In a bricks and clicks strategy, instructors who enjoy distance learning teach the distance learning portion of the course, while other instructors teach the face-to-face portion. For these hybrid courses, the respective professors, based on their experience and criteria discussed above, could decide content amenable to online distance learning.

Applying a bricks and clicks strategy involves asking students, and possibly experimenting with courses, to determine which modules are best suited for which delivery medium. The Berkeley Digital Chemistry course offers the same classes simultaneously online or face-to-face. Students can choose to participate in either format (Murphy, 2001). By experimenting, most

Table 4. E-marketing strategies and tactics to meet distance learning student challenges

Challenges	Strategies	Tactics
Matching learning style	Personalization and customization	Instructors develop several configurations of the course that differ in the media (audio, video, etc.) used, in the sequence of the content presentation, and in focus for various business concentrations. Students fill out Myers-Briggs or other learning style classification scale, as well as information on their concentration. The course configuration matching student's learning style and concentration is presented when the student signs in.
Developing positive attitudes	Customer service and customization	1. Instructor and Student Services query current and potential students on their needs. 2. Customer service from Student Services: Create a communication coordinator position for online distance learning (housed in student services). Students receive e-mails before, during, and after the course on registration, status towards degree, accounts, library, etc. Student services responds quickly to any e-mails received. Build simple, university-wide portal where students can access information on programs, courses, careers, accounts, status towards degree, etc. 3. Customer service from faculty: Instructor sends e-mails to students before, during, and after the course regarding the syllabus, grades, status, course materials, reminders of assignments, chat times, etc. Instructor responds quickly to any e-mail. Instructor creates simple Web site with course content, tutorials, bulletin board, chat, and links to e-mail, site to purchase class materials, grades, status reports, etc. 4. All developed portals and Web sites should allow for students to customize. 5. All technological interfaces must be user-friendly.
	Customization	Create quizzes that test students to determine whether they are ready to move onto the next module. If they fail the quiz, program automatically feeds them the information they got wrong—including examples.
	Community	1. Create homepages with biosketches. 2. Schedule structured chat around cases and simulations. 3. Build bulletin boards for questions about class content/assignments. 4. Encourage e-mail/ net conferencing among students by creating introductory and participative exercises online. 5. Schedule guest speakers online to participate in a topic discussion using chat.
Access to technology	Disintermediation	Suppliers provide technology to students
	Reintermediation	Course configured for broadband access or dial-up modem. Internet speed boosters supplied to students.
Proficiency with technology	Bricks and clicks	1. Live training with technology or online tutorials with tech supplier. 2. Integrate online portions into regular classes as optional. 3. Have first class in degree structured so that it is a hybrid course—or implement obligatory tech training with exam/quiz.

course content could be offered both online and face-to-face. Analysis of students' preferred delivery method for each type of content (lectures, tutorials, exams, etc.) will indicate which portions of courses could be offered online.

Course content fitting with a community strategy would also be appropriate for online distance learning. For example, Kalkstein-Fragiadakis (Anonymous, 2001b) has students learn English as a second language through discussions with one another in chat rooms. Discussions of marketing cases could occur in community.

Meeting Students' Challenges

The following section applies various e-marketing strategic themes to each of the students' challenges. Table 4 summarizes the recommended strategies and tactics.

Table 5. Applying personalization and customization to student learning styles

Learning style	How they learn	How to personalize or customize
Sensing, inductive, and global	Take in relevant information to arrive at a theory	Present examples of theory followed by theory itself. Example: Show how Gap Inc. segments its three stores by price (Gap, Banana Republic, and Old Navy) followed by definition of segmentation.
Intuitive, deductive, and sequential	Learn best when material follows a logical progression	Present theory followed by examples. Example: Begin with a discussion of segmentation followed by examples of how Gap Inc. segments by price.
Visual	Learn best through visual presentation of material	Present material using pictures. Example: In any sequence, show print ads for each Gap Inc. price segment. Illustrate definition of segmentation through a multidimensional scaling map.
Verbal	Learn best through verbal presentation of material	Present material through written or spoken word. Example: In any sequence, on an audio-clip, explain how Gap Inc. segments by price and what is segmentation.
Active	Learn best through interaction	Allow students to construct understanding. *Example*: Show advertisements for Gap Inc. and ask students to describe the main target. Via chat, have students construct a definition of segmentation to compare to actual definition.
Reflective	Learn best by taking time to think things through	Present content in asynchronous (nonconcurrent) mode. Example: In any sequence, present ad illustrating how Gap Inc. segments by price; later offer a definition of segmentation.

Matching Student Learning Styles

As previously discussed, different students prefer different learning styles. Karakaya, Ainscough and Chopoorian (2001) used text, graphics, animation, digitized sound and video clips to produce one face-to-face multimedia presentation that accommodated all student learning types. Sonwalker (2001) suggests that asynchronous online distance learning (nonconcurrent communication) allows for the creation of individualized presentations to match each learning style. However, an educator need not personalize all course material. Felder (1996) states that an objective of education should be to help students build their skills in their preferred and less preferred styles of learning.

Applying the e-marketing themes of personalization and customization allows professors to adapt portions of course content to different learning styles. The online channel seems most conducive for this approach because, as examples below demonstrate, some of the adaptation simply requires rearranging the material, which may be easily accomplished through personalization or customization software. At the start of a course, students could complete scales (e.g., Myers-Briggs scales) to identify their dominant learning styles. Students would then choose (customization), or the software would automatically provide (personalization), portions of the course content or review materials tailored to their particular dominant learning style. For example, visual learners learn best through presentation of material using pictures. Thus, their configuration of the lecture online could illustrate segmentation by showing print ads of how Gap Inc. segments its three stores by price (Gap, Banana Republic and Old Navy), or by having students construct a multidimensional scaling map of the Gap and its competitors. Further illustrations of this concept for each of the learning styles appear in Table 5.

In another student application of personalization/customization, the presentation of the material could be adjusted to suit the students' chosen concentration. For example, at the New Market Vocational Skills Center, students take applied math, science, and English courses to suit their chosen line of work (Anonymous, 2000). Although the personalization occurs at the curricular level, in a marketing class this could be implemented within a course. That is, in discussing competitive analysis with accounting students, examples could focus on the competitive behavior of accounting firms; for information system students, examples could demonstrate the competitive behavior of technology providers.

Developing Students' Positive Attitudes

Recall that Ponzurick, Russo-France and Logar (2000) found more negative attitudes toward distance education resulted from students who felt that distance education allowed less participation and other desirable course-related activities. And Armstrong-Stassen, Landstrom and Lumpkin (1998) determined that, in the eyes of distance learners, distance education administrators and instructors proved unresponsive and ill prepared. Personalization and customization, as just applied to learning styles and areas of concentration, certainly will meet students' need for greater interactivity and better customer service, fostering more positive student attitudes toward distance education. The strategic themes of reintermediation and bricks and clicks, as applied previously for challenges to faculty, will improve the responsiveness and preparedness of faculty. In addition to those previously discussed strategies, customization (applied differently than above), and community will meet the needs and enhance those attitudes through greater service responsiveness and interactivity.

Excellent service has been strongly linked to positive consumer attitudes (Berry & Parasuraman, 1991; Bitner, Booms, & Tetreault, 1990; Keaveney, 1995; Smith, Bolton, & Wagner 1999). Through adequate preparation and attentiveness to student needs, educators can offer excellent service and thereby foster positive attitudes toward distance education. Based on Seybold's (1998) recommendations, educators may take several initiatives:

1. *Target the right customer*: Target customer service toward potential as well as current distance learning students. That is, some core on-campus students might also benefit from the time/space flexibility of an online distance learning delivery mode. Stewart (1991) conducted a survey querying students on their needs from higher education, and called on educators to respond to those needs. Similarly, faculty and administration should conduct research on current and potential students of distance learning to understand their needs in terms of product, price, distribution and promotion.

2. *Own the experience*: This refers to creating an experience for the customer, then communicating and controlling it throughout the relationship. For distance learning students, two levels of communication must be present for the university to "own the experience". First, students must receive communication from university Student Services. Second, students should receive communication from the professor regarding the specific course. This communication should take a proactive form, such as e-mail (Seybold, 1998). To optimize the content and amount of correspondence, a communication coordinator position appears warranted.

Once students sign up for a distance-learning course, student services should follow them and correspond with them throughout the experience. Usually before the course begins, students should receive a first e-mail focusing on registration, semester course schedule, final exam schedule, accounts, status towards degree, information for online technology help, online text vendors, extracurricular activities, as well as information on university services such as library resources (hours, status of loans, etc.), advising, financial aid (aid available, deadlines, status), student clubs, student life, and career planning. During the course, students should continue to receive relevant information on extracurricular activities, accounts, future registration, and tech help. Upon completion of the course, e-mail to students should contain information about their accounts, next term schedule, registration procedures, academic record (grades and GPA), progress towards their degree and their next prerequisites or electives.

The instructor should be in continuous correspondence with distance learning students. At Nova Southeastern University, instructors give students a weekly participation grade based on the quality and quantity of their postings to a class bulletin board (Gibson, Tesone, & Blackwell, 2001). Before the course begins, students should receive correspondence from the professor introducing him/herself, information on the format and technology of the course, plus a copy of the course syllabus which would include class procedures, class schedules, instructor office hours, books required, and links to book vendors and grading scales. During the course, students should receive updates on course materials and content, reminders when lessons and tutorials are available and when assignments are due, attendance and participation in chat rooms, exam dates, and a status chart of their grade performance. Finally, the instructor and student services must give students quick turnaround on their questions and work. Gibson, Tesone and Blackwell (2001) have achieved a 24-hour turnaround with queries from online distance learning students.

3. *Self-service*: The same information required to "own the experience" should be accessible to students on a self- service platform. To address self-service from Student Services, many higher education institutions have built university-wide portals (sites with a large number of links to other sites) to offer Web access of all university services to its constituents: students, parents, alumni and prospective students. For example, the University of Minnesota has created an integrated student service portal with information on courses, programs, exams, financial and career planning, and book sales (Kravik & Handberg, 2000). The site also contains tools to assess academic progress towards the degree and desired grade point average. Universities can create portals that provide access to all services associated with "owning the experience," including registration, status towards degree, online technology help, programs and courses, exam schedules, academic record, text vendors, appointment scheduling, career planning, advising, and library resources (Buchanan, 2001). Departments also can implement

self-service portals. Benbunan-Fich et al. (2001) recommend information on programs, courses, careers, and assignments.

To address self-service from faculty, students should have the ability to e-mail the professor, view the course syllabus, buy required materials, receive course material (lectures, exercises, etc.), access tutorials, post comments on a bulletin board, view grades and current standing in the course, and take exams wherever and (possibly) whenever they want. To minimize the risk of students falling behind and dropping out, a time frame should be placed on the course duration, assignment due dates, and exams (Gibson, Tesone, & Blackwell, 2001).

Since no two persons have the same interests, portals or Web sites can be customized. For example, through a MyUCLA portal, students can organize the content that they would like to see on a regular basis when they sign on (Looney & Lyman, 2000).

While setting up a technological system that allows the university and faculty members to "own the experience" and to provide "self-service" to students may seem daunting, the faculty member or department can implement either a solution of disintermediation, reintermediation, or bricks and clicks, as discussed in the Faculty Challenges section.

4. *Streamline services*: This connotes facility with using the services. The Web site must be simple, easy to navigate, use a standard format (sidebar on left, banner across top, etc.), and download quickly (Flanders & Willis, 2002; Koprowski, 1998).

Please recall that in addition to ill-prepared and unresponsive faculty and administration, negative student attitudes also resulted from a lack of interactive activities. McAlpine (2000) found that high levels of interactive involvement through online discussion forums resulted in a more positive evaluation by students. Two recommendations have already been discussed that will increase interactivity, and thereby, attitudes. First, when students customize to their learning style and area of concentration, they will initially fill out a questionnaire, identifying their learning style and their area of concentration. Second, strategies discussed to implement self-service and "own the experience" will also increase interactivity. Additionally, the following applications to online distance education further enhance interactivity and improve student attitudes.

Incorporating personalization and customization, students can customize the amount of information they want on a topic or let a quiz help them decide whether they understand a concept. For example, the first time they study the concept of segmentation in a Marketing Principles class, students might not understand it or might fail a quiz. They can then click on a link that explains it differently or gives an application.

The second method increases interactivity by fostering community. Please recall that community occurs when a particular site becomes a place of interest where participants interact extensively and repeatedly (Armstrong & Hagel, 1996). In a strong example of community, through the use of chat, bulletin boards, e-mail and net meeting conferencing, Bryant College has created community between professors, practitioners and students at Bryant and at Belarus, in the former U.S.S.R. (Ilacqua, Langlois, & Barrett-Litoff, 2001). Technology-facilitated interactions between the students of different cultures led to heated debates, as students shared experiences and negotiated their diverse perspectives.

There are several actions that instructors can take to foster community.

1. *Create homepages*: Online distance learning students at Nova Southeastern University are required to create a homepage biosketch, which includes the information one would find on a C.V., as well as information on families, hobbies and pets. Students comment on each other's biosketches, which forges friendships (Gibson, Tesone, & Blackwell, 2001). Thus homepage biosketches can aid in establishing community.

2. *Schedule chat*: The professor can designate several times during a semester requiring students to meet in a chat room. Atwong and Hugstad (1997) advocate presenting guest speakers via Internet conferencing. Canzer (1997) implemented a chat cafe where students could go to socialize. To instigate chat, the professor should administer a weekly participation grade.

3. *Encourage use of bulletin board*: Students can use a bulletin board to post questions to each other about homework. Eastman and Swift (2001) recommend requiring all questions about the class be posted to allow other students to answer the questions. However, Palloff and Pratt (1999) urge limitations on length and number of posts per week to preclude students from dominating class discussion. While the above discussion implies using homepages, chat and bulletin boards within a class, the Bryant-Belarus project shows their use between classes to foster cross-functional or global community.

4. *Use e-mail*: The use of e-mail should be encouraged between students and instructors, as well as students and other students on campus or across campuses to foster community (Benbunan-Fich et al., 2001).

By implementing these recommendations, educators and administrators can create responsive and interactive, service-oriented sites. Students will use them to complete administrative requirements, obtain knowledge, talk, exchange ideas and collaborate leading to more positive attitudes.

Access to Technology

A disintermediation or reintermediation strategy (as discussed above) where, on a rent or buy basis, the technology supplier also provides the students with the necessary technology and broadband access, may alleviate this problem. In dealing with the low-speed telecommunication linkages, there are two actions that can be taken. First, the actual content may be configured to offer students an option that would minimize download speeds (less graphics, pages, etc.). Second, programs that enhance the speed of dial-up modems, such as Ascentive's webROCKET and Propel's Accelerator may be utilized.

Proficiency with Technology

In addition to proper technological training (Irani, 2001; McEwen, 2001), implementation of a bricks and clicks strategy can aid in developing students' computer proficiency. In this case, bricks and clicks can refer to giving students options to choose their method of exchange (online or face-to-face). Students that are techno-phobic can opt for a hybrid structure where they have a choice of viewing virtual lectures or attending lectures in lecture halls, similar to Berkeley's Digital Chemistry course (Murphy, 2001). Comparing the results of hybrid classes to traditional face-to-face, researchers found students enrolled in hybrid classes showed higher performance (Brown, 2001). A hybrid structure allows students to get acquainted with the technology while maintaining some human contact as support. For students requiring entire courses through distance learning, the first course in their distance-learning program could be structured this way to allow students to become proficient with the technology.

Conclusions and Future Research

Distance education requires changing the traditional face-to-face message channel to a different communication medium. This decreases the viability of distance learning by creating new challenges posed by faculty and students, as well as those resulting from incompatibilities with the course content. Conceptually viewing online distance education as a business paradigm allows for identification of the challenges as needs, and the application of e-marketing themes to meet these needs, thereby increasing the viability of online distance learning. An e-commerce perspective is not meant to reinforce the position of mass-production-oriented university administrators striving to increase class sizes, because numerous studies support the opposite—distance learning better suits smaller classes.

As applicable to any business plan, once strategy is implemented, it should be evaluated to determine whether objectives have been met. Scales developed for marketing can measure the effectiveness of strategy. For example, variations of attitude scales (Fishbein & Ajzen, 1975; Parasuraman, Zeithaml, & Berry, 1988) could be applied to measure student and faculty attitude changes resulting from implementing e-marketing strategies. Researchers should also develop valid assessment measures of learning. That is, distance-learning students might exhibit positive attitudes, yet have not learned the right material or the extent of information possible through the traditional education medium. Additionally, further research measuring the impact of online distance learning on learning styles would be beneficial.

The question remains whether students and faculty are best served through the application of these strategies to entire courses delivered by distance learning, or to a hybrid model. Given the importance of personal relationships (Lowman, 1984) to effective teaching, it seems reasonable to conclude that for most courses, a hybrid delivery channel made up of face-to-face instruction plus selected modules of distance learning incorporating e-marketing themes, offers the best learning environment. Preliminary evidence appears to support the superiority of the hybrid approach (Brown, 2001). This is reinforced by Ferrell(1995) and Smart, Kelley, and Conant (1999) who suggest that educators must employ technology to improve their teaching due to our increasingly competitive educational marketplace. Additionally, Benbunan-Fich et al. (2001) offer a useful guide to integrating information technology into the marketing curriculum for developing valuable marketing skills, business core competencies, and proficiency with technology. Using valid assessment tools to examine the extent of learning and student satisfaction, future research should test the effectiveness of the e-marketing strategies across varying mixes of face-to-face and Internet instruction.

References

Allen, R. C. (2000). Why can't universities be more like businesses? *The Chronicle of Higher Education, 46*(6), B4–B5.

Anonymous. (2002, January 10). George Mason University and Vcampus teach trainers to deliver Web-based learning through new online course. *Business Wire,* Sic 611310.

Anonymous. (2001a). Cornell university employs new digital technology. *T.H.E. Journal, 28*(8), 60–62.

Anonymous. (2001b). ESL meets DSL. *Syllabus Magazine,14*(11), 39.

Anonymous, (2000). Electronic tests enhance individualized instruction for vocational students. *T.H.E. Journal, 28*(5): 58–59.

Armstrong, A., & Hagel, J. (1996). The real value of on-line communities. *Harvard Business Review, 74(3),* 134–141.

Armstrong-Stassen, M., Landstrom, M., & Lumpkin, R. (1998). Students'

reaction to the introduction of videoconferencing. *Information Society,*
14, 153–164.

Atwong, C. T., & Hugstad, P. S. (1997). Internet technology and the future
of marketing education. *Journal of Marketing Education, 19*(2), 44–55.

Bagozzi, R. P. (1974). Marketing as an organizational behavior system of
exchange. *Journal of Marketing, 38*(4), 77–81.

Benbunan-Fich, R., Lozada, H. R., Pirog, S., Priluck, R., & Wisenblit, J.
(2001). Integrating information technology into the marketing curriculum: A pragmatic paradigm. *Journal of Marketing Education, 23*(1),
5–15.

Berry, L., & Parasuraman, A. (1991). *Marketing services: Competing*
through quality. New York: The Free Press.

Besser, H. (1996). Issues and challenges for the distance independent
environment. *Journal of the American Society for Information Science,*
47, 817–820.

Besser, H., & Bonn, M. (1996). Impact of distance independent education.
Journal of the American Society for Information Science, 47, 880–883.

Bitner, M. J., Booms, B. H., & Tetreault, M. S. (1990). The service encounter: Diagnosing favorable and unfavorable incidents. *Journal of*
Marketing, 54(1), 71–84.

Bridges, E. (1999). Experiential learning and customer needs in the
undergraduate marketing research course. *Journal of Marketing Educa-*
tion, 21(1), 51–59.

Brown, D. G. (2001). Hybrid courses are best. *Syllabus Magazine, 15*(1), 22.

Buchanan, E. A. (1999). Assessment measures: Pre-tests for successful
distance teaching and learning? *Online Journal of Distance Learning*
Administration, 2(3). Retrieved 10 January 2002 from http://
www.westga.edu/~distance/buchanan24.html

Buchanan, E. A. (2001). Ready or not, they're here: Library portals.
Syllabus Magazine, 13(11). Retrieved 23 January 2002 from http://
www.syllabus.com/syllabusmagazine/article.asp?id=4138

Burger, J., Boggs, R., & Webber, S. (2000). *Distance learning in higher*
education: Market forecast and analysis, 1999–2004. Framingham, MA:
IDC Corporation. Retrieved 8 June 2001 from http://www.idc.com/
getdoc.jhtml?containerId=23539.

Canzer, B. (1997). Marketing education on the Internet: A World Wide
Web-based introductory marketing course design for the Virtual-U
Project in distance education at Simon Fraser University. *Journal* of
Marketing Education, 19(1), 56–65.

Cartwright, G. P. (1994, July-August). Distance learning: A different time,
and a different place. *Change, 26,* 30–33.

Clow, K. (1999). Interactive distance learning: Impact on student course evaluations. *Journal of Marketing Education, 21*(2), 97–105.

Comeaux, P. (1995). The impact of an interactive distance learning network on classroom communication. *Communication Education, 44,* 353–361.

Cyberatlas. (2003). *Online population.* Jupetermedia Corporation. Retrieved 1 February 2003 from http://cvberatlas.internet.com/big_picture/geographics/article/0,1323,5911_151151,00.html

Daly, S. P. (2001). Student-operated Internet businesses: True experiential learning in entrepreneurship and retail management. *Journal of Marketing Education, 23*(3), 204–215.

Eastman, J. K., & Owens Swift, C. (2001). New horizons in distance education: The online learner-centered marketing class. *Journal of Marketing Education, 23*(1), 25–34.

Ellin, A. (2000, 6 August). The battle in cyberspace. *New York Times,* 4A.

Emery, T. (2001, 30 July). Virtual college closes its doors one year after it opens. *The Associated Press State and Local Wire.*

Felder, R. (1993). Reaching the second tier: Learning and teaching styles in college science education. *Journal of College Science Teaching, 23*(5), 286–290.

Felder, R. (1997). Matters of style. *ASEE Prism, 6,* 18–23.

Ferrell, O. C. (1995). Improving marketing education in the 1990s: A faculty retrospective and perspective view. *Marketing Education Review, 5*(1), 69–79.

Fishbein, M., & Ajzen, I. (1975). *Belief, attitude, intention, and behavior: An introduction to theory and research.* Reading, MA: Addison-Wesley.

Flanders, V., & Willis, M. (2002). *Web pages that suck: Learn good design by looking at bad design.* San Francisco: Sybex.

Flaschner, A. (1999). Response to distance learning—An oxymoron. ELMARAMA (elmar@columbia.edu) Digest #622 (December).

Gibson, J. W., Tesone, D. V., & Blackwell, C. W. (2001). The journey into cyberspace: Reflection from three online business professors. *S.A.M. Advanced Management Journal, 6* (1), 30–34.

Gremler, D. D., Hoffman, K. D., Keaveney, S. M., & Wright, L. K. (2000). Experiential learning exercises in services marketing courses. *Journal of Marketing Education, 22*(1), 35–44.

Gulati, R., & Garino, J. (2000). Get the right mix of bricks and clicks. *Harvard Business Review, 78*(3), 107–114.

Hagel, J., & Singer, M. (1999). *Net worth: Shaping markets when customers make the rules.* Boston: Harvard Business School Press.

Hanson, W. (2000). *Principles of Internet marketing.* Cincinnati: South-Western College Publishing.

Herrman, N. (1990). *The creative brain.* Lake Lure, NC: Brain Books.

Hilts, P. (2000). Thomson to develop global e-university courses. *Publishers Weekly, 247*(49), 16.

Ilacqua, J. A., Langlois, G. A., & Litoff, J. B. (2001). Reaching across boundaries: The Bryant College-Belarus connection. *Syllabus, 15*(3). Retrieved 10 February 2002 from http://www.svllabus.com/svllabusmag;azine/article.asp?id=5O88

Irani, I. (2001). Going the distance: Developing a model distance education faculty training program. *Syllabus Magazine, 15*(1). Retrieved 7 February 2002 from www.syllabus.com/syllabusmagazine/article.asp?id=4575.

Ives, B., & Jarvenpaa, S. L. (1997). Will the Internet revolutionize business education and research? *Sloan Management Review, 37*(3), 33–41.

Johnson, D. W., & Johnson, R. T. (1993). What we know about cooperative learning at the college level. *Cooperative Learning, 13*(3)17–18.

Jorgensen, S. (1992, June). Business is one model schools don't need. *Executive Educator, 14,* 48.

Kahn, B. (1998). Dynamic relationships with customers: High variety strategies. *Journal of the Academy of Marketing Science, 26*(1), 45–53.

Karakaya, F., Ainscough, T. L., & Chopoorian, J. (2001). The effects of class size and learning style on student performance in a multimedia-based marketing course. *Journal of Marketing Education, 23*(2), 84–90.

Karuppan, C. M., & Karuppan, M. (1999). Empirically based guidelines for developing teaching materials on the Web. *Business Communications Quarterly, 62* (3), 37–45.

Kasanoff, B. (1998, May). Are you ready for mass-customization? *Training, 3,* 70–78.

Kaynama, S., & Keesling, G. (2000, August). Development of a web-based Internet marketing course. *Journal of Marketing Education, 22,* 84–89.

Keaveney, S. M. (1995). Customer switching behavior in service industries: An exploratory study. *Journal of Marketing, 59*(2), 71–82.

Kendrick, J. (1998). Increasing access through multimedia instruction to timely marketing information and techniques. *American Journal of Agricultural Economics, 80*(5), 984–989.

Kirkpatrick, D. (2000, 19 August). Harcourt seeking approval to operate an online college. *New York Times,* C2.

Kolb, D. A. (1984). *Experiential learning: Experience as a source of learning and development.* Englewood Cliffs, NJ: Prentice Hall.

Koprowski, G. (1998, 7 December). The (new) hidden persuaders: What marketers have learned about how customers buy on the Web. *Wall Street Journal,* R10.

Kravik, R. B., & Handberg, M. N. (2000). Transforming student services. *Educause Quarterly, 23*(2), 30–37.

Lamont, L. M., & Friedman, K. (1997). Meeting the challenges to undergraduate marketing education. *Journal of Marketing Education, 19*(3), 16–29.

Lawrence, G. (1994). *People types and tiger stripes* (3rd edition). Gainesville, FL: Center for Application of Psychological Type.

LeBlanc, P. J. (1997). Master of the Internet. *Connection, 12,* 41–44.

Lichtenberg, J (2001). Going the distance. *Publishers Weekly, 248*(26), 37–40.

Lloyd, L. (1997). *Technology and teaching.* Medford, NJ: Information Today Inc.

Looney, M., & Lyman, P. (2000). Portals in higher education: What and what is their potential. *Educause Review, 35*(3), 28–36.

Lowman, J. (1984). *Mastering the techniques of teaching.* San Francisco: Jossey-Bass.

Lutz, F. W., & Field, R. W. (1998). Business valuing in academia: The American university as a center for profit or inquiry. *Higher Education, 36*(4), 383–419.

Magretta, J. (1998). The power of virtual integration: An interview with Dell Computer's Michael Dell. *Harvard Business Review, 76*(2), 72–84.

Malouf, J M., & Sims, R. L. (1997). Applying an employee-motivation model to prevent student plagiarism. *Journal of Education for Business, 72,* 58–61.

Massy, W. F., & Zemsky, R. (1997). Information technology and academic productivity. *Educom Review, 31*(1), 12–14.

McAlpine, L. (2000). Collaborative learning online. *Distance Education, 21*(1), 66–80.

McCorkle, D. E., Alexander, J. F., & Reardon, J. (2001). Integrating business technology and marketing education: Enhancing the diffusion process through technology champions. *Journal of Marketing Education, 23* (1), 16–24.

McEwan, B. C. (2001). Web-assisted online learning. *Business Communication Quarterly, 64*(2), 98–103.

Mehlenbacher, B., Miller, C. R., Covington, D., & Larsen, J. S. (2000). Active learning and interactive learning online: A comparison of web-based and conventional writing classes. *IEEE Transactions of Professional Communications, 43*(2), 166–183.

Motwani, J. (1995). Implementing TQM in education: Current efforts and future research direction, *Journal of Education for Business, 71*(2), 60–63.

Murphy, C. (2001). Taking chemistry online with digital video. *Syllabus Magazine, 36*(1), 28–29.

Nunes, P. F., & Kambil, A. (2001). Personalization? No thanks. *Harvard Business Review, 79*(4), 32–34.

Palloff, R. M., & Pratt, K. (1999). *Building learning communities in cyberspace.* San Francisco: Jossey-Bass.

Parasuraman, A., Zeithaml, V. A., & and Berry, L. L. (1988). SERVQUAL: A multiple-item scale for measuring consumer perceptions of service quality. *Journal of Retailing, 64*(1), 12–40.

Pearce, J. A., II. (1999). Faculty survey on business education reform. *The Academy of Management Executive, 13*(2), 105–109.

Petkus, E., Jr. (2000). A theoretical and practical framework for service learning in marketing: Kolb's experiential learning cycle. *Journal of Marketing Education, 22*(1), 64–70.

Ponzurick, T. G., Russo France, K., & Logar, C. M. (2000). Delivering marketing graduate education: An analysis of face-to-face versus distance education. *Journal of Marketing Education, 22*(3), 180–187.

Pool, P. (1997). Teaching via interactive television: An examination of teaching effectiveness and student satisfaction. *Journal of Education for Business, 72*(2), 78–81.

Porter, L. R. (1997). Creating the virtual classroom: *Distance learning with the Internet.* New York: John Wiley and Sons Inc.

Rahm, D., & Reed, B. J. (1997). Going Remote: The use of distance learning, the World Wide Web and the Internet in graduate programs of public affairs and administration. *Public Productivity and Management Review, 20*(4), 459–474.

Rayport, J. F., & Jaworski, Bernard J. (2000). *E-Commerce.* Boston: McGraw- Hill/Irwin Market Space U.

Romiszowski, A. J. (1988). *The selection and use of instructional media.* New York: Nichols Publishing.

Rudzki, R. (1995). The application of a strategic management model to the internationalization of higher education institutions. *Higher Education 29,* 421–441.

Schwartzman, R. (1997). Gaming serves as a model for improving learning. *Education, 118*(1), 9–17.

Scrabec, Q., Jr., (2000). A quality education is not customer driven. *Journal of Education for Business, 75*(5), 298–300.

Seybold, P. (1998). *Customers.com.* New York: Random House.

Shank, M. D., Walker, M., & Hayes, T. (1995). Understanding professional service expectations: Do we know what our students expect in a quality education? *Journal of Professional Services Marketing, 13*(1), 71–76.

Simmons, J. (1999). Customer service: It's elementary. *Journal of Quality and Participation, 22*(2), 50–54.

Smart, D. T., Kelley, C. A., & Conant, J. (1999). Marketing education in the year 2000: Changes observed and challenges anticipated. *Journal of Marketing Education, 21*(3), 206–16.

Smith, A. K., Bolton, R. N., & Wagner, J. (1999). A model of customer satisfaction with service encounters involving failure and recovery. *Journal of Marketing Research, 36*(3), 356–372.

Smith, L. J. (2001). Content and delivery: A comparison and contrast of electronic and traditional MBA marketing planning courses. *Journal of Marketing Education, 23*(1), 35–44.

Sonwalker, N. (2001). The sharper edge of the cube: Pedagogically driven instructional design for online education. *Syllabus Magazine,15*(5). Retrieved 1 February 2002 from www.syllabus.com/syllabusmagazine/article.asp?id=5858

Stanton, N., & Baber, C. (1991). An integration of styles and strategies in self-directed learning. *Journal of Educational Multimedia and Hypermedia, 1*(2), 147–167.

Stern, L., & El Ansary, A. I. 1992. *Marketing channels* (4th edition). Englewood Cliffs, NJ: Prentice Hall School Publishing.

Stewart, K. L. (1991). Applying a marketing orientation to a higher education setting. *Journal of Professional Services Marketing, 7*(2), 117–124.

Terrell, S. R. , & Dringus, L. (1999/2000). An investigation of the effect of learning style on student success in an online learning environment. *Journal of Educational Technology Systems, 28*(3), 231–238.

Tidd, R. R. (2001). Creating your learning community: online sources, *Journal of the American Taxation Association, 23*(2), 74–76.

Tsichritzis, D. (1999). Reengineering the university. *Communications of the ACM, 42*(6), 93–100.

Tucker, R. (2001, 26 January). *Sea changes and market forces in higher education.* CSUF Faculty Day, CSUF, Fullerton, CA.

U.S. Congress, Office of Technology Assessment. (1989). *Linking for learning: A new course for education.* Washington, DC: Government Printing Office.

United States Distance Learning Association. (2001). *Research information and Statistics.* Needham, MA: United States Distance Learning Association. Retrieved from http://www.usdla.org/04_research_info.htm.

Waits, T., & Agnew, D. M. (2001). A business and industry model with application in agricultural mechanics. *The Agricultural Education Magazine, 73*(6), 22.

Warren, R. G. (1997). Engaging students in active learning. *About campus,* *2*(1), 16–20.

Weinstein, B. (2000, 26 November). Online college degree programs draw mixed reviews: More enrolling despite misgivings of some colleges and employers. *Boston Globe,* J8.

Wheeler, B. C. (1998). The state of business education: Preparation for the past? *Selections, 14*(2), 19–21.

Wright, L. K., Bitner, M. J., & Ziethaml, V. (1994). Paradigm shifts in business education: Using active learning to deliver services marketing content. *Journal of Marketing Education, 16*(2), 5–19.

Young, M. R. (2001). Windowed, wired, and webbed—now what? *Journal of Marketing Education, 23*(1), 45–54.

Zappia, C. A. (1999). Academic professionalism and the business model in education: Reflections of a community college historian. *The History Teacher, 33*(1), 55–65.

5

ASSESSING THE IMPACT OF ACADEMIC TECHNOLOGY

Introduction

Rowena S. Santiago
California State University, San Bernardino

So what's the difference? What difference does it make to use technology to enhance instruction? Is instruction really *enhanced*? Is it revolutionized, or even altered? How do we know?

During the past decade, the CSU system has actively encouraged its faculty to integrate academic technologies into the teaching and learning environment. The CSU Integrated Technology Strategy initiated in 1996[1] has facilitated the development of innovative teaching and a variety of nontraditional learning environments, particularly hybrid and fully online courses. According to a November 2002 report, "In academic year 2001/2002, 2.32 percent of full-time equivalent student instruction occurred outside of state-support spaces. Of these 8,069 FTES, 2,106 resulted from online teaching and learning."[2]

As the number of hybrid and online courses increases, much is being asked about their impact on teaching and learning. Both users and nonusers of online instruction debate the benefits and best uses of the Internet for distance or distributed learning in the CSU. Many CSU faculty have been asking what difference technology makes in terms of effectiveness, efficiency, and appeal. To understand how the use of technology affects learning, then, three questions might be asked:

- *Effectiveness:* Was student learning enhanced, and were higher-order learning objectives accomplished through the use of technology?

- *Efficiency:* Did the use of technology lead to increased access, time flexibility, self-pacing, reusability?

- *Appeal:* Did learners' motivation and satisfaction remain high, and was the experience perceived to be favorable to learning?

In this chapter, faculty from six CSU campuses take a closer look at the issues of effectiveness, efficiency, and appeal that affect students in online environments. These issues include student characteristics, perceptions, and satisfaction; student roles in an online environment; and student use of and access to online courses. There is great benefit in investigating the impact of technology on teaching and learning, whether the method used for the inquiry is narrative/anecdotal or research-based. Both methods give the opportunity to be reflective and critical of how technology and the factors that affect learning and teaching interact.

In "Online Learning as an Improvement? The Case of Economic Principles," Chiara Gratton-Lavoie and Denise Stanley look into student performance in online courses as compared to students in traditional courses. They analyze student characteristics for patterns that could affect performance in an online course, and they report interesting results that support differences between online and traditional learners and gender-performance relationships in an introductory economics course.

In the second article, "Assessing Differences in Instructional Methods: Uncovering How Students Learn Best," Nancy Ostiguy and Ann Haffer compare learning outcomes between online, classroom, and cable TV modes of instruction for an introductory Environmental Science course. In addition to results on learning outcomes, the authors address student perception of asynchronous learning environments, particularly student satisfaction (or dissatisfaction) with the level of online interaction.

Maria Roberts-DeGennaro, in "Constructing and Implementing a Web-Based Graduate Social Policy Course: A Pilot Test in Cyberspace," reports on the construction and implementation of a course that was taught using the course-management software, Blackboard. She discusses student satisfaction and student perceptions of the effectiveness of the online activities (discussion rooms, assignments), as well as student feedback on the video and PowerPoint presentations.

Students with learning disabilities are the important focus of "Utility of Course Web Resources for Students with Learning Disabilities" by Charles M. Slem and Steven T. Kane. They investigated how a web-based course for general students benefited students with learning disabilities in mastering course concepts and in terms of access to and use of technology. The article contributes to additional understanding of students with learning disabilities and their use of web resources for learning.

Dawn Poole, in "Student Participation in a Discussion-Oriented Online Course: A Case Study," discusses her investigation of the nature of student participation as moderators in an online course and how their online posts contributed towards a learning community. The author applies rubrics analyzing verbal interaction and message content, and she analyzes quantitative data involving online communities.

The final article in this chapter is James M. Monaghan and Rowena Santiago's "Critical Examination of the Use of Online Technologies in Diverse

Courses at a Large Comprehensive University." They explore three classes that implemented online teaching as part of the campus' faculty development program. Student learning, student use of technology, and student satisfaction are among the factors that were surveyed. Faculty syllabi, grant proposals, and final grant reports were also analyzed. A proposed model and implications for campuswide implementation of online teaching-learning technologies are included in the report.

While this chapter reviews many factors that impact students and learning in hybrid and fully online courses, the issues investigated and reported herein do not exhaust all the possible factors that affect learning and learners. It is the expectation that the articles in this chapter will lead to further inquiry and reflection on students, learning, and online teaching.

Notes:

1. Master Plan Goal for the CSU Integrated Technology Strategy, 1996. See http://its.calstate.edu/systemwide_it_resources/BOT_Status_Report_031996.doc

2. MOS IV Report, November 2002. See http://its.calstate.edu/documents/Data_Collection/I_Reports_MOS/mos4_2002/MOS4_index.html or http://its.calstate.edu/documents/Data_Collection/I_Reports_MOS/mos4_2002/MOS_IV_ExecutiveSummary_11302002.doc

Online Learning as an Improvement?
The Case of Economic Principles

Chiara Gratton-Lavoie and Denise Stanley
California State University, Fullerton

Abstract

How do students enrolled in online courses perform, when compared to students who choose a more traditional classroom environment? And are there any student characteristics that can help to explain differences in student academic achievement in the two modes of instruction? This study addresses these important questions in relation to the teaching of introductory economics courses. We find that students in the 'live' section of the course perform significantly better than students enrolled in the virtual class, according to standard performance measures.

Introduction

Online Learning in the 21st Century

Online learning has been described as a solution to many of the educational challenges emerging in the 21st Century. As the children of the Baby Boomers enter college, both public and private universities face greater student enrollments and reduced budgets. This surge in enrollment figures, which was predicted in the 1980s and named Tidal Wave II, has posed financial strains on many colleges across the nation. At Cal State Fullerton, for example, reported total enrollment for fall 2001 was 20,701 full-time-equivalent students (FTES), and the number jumped to 21,003 FTES in spring 2002 (Cal State Fullerton, 2001). One full-time-equivalent corresponds to 15 units of course work, and it is the measure used by the State of California to allocate financial resources across campuses. Because one FTES can be the sum of units taken by part-time students, the actual students' headcount is always higher than the reported FTES.

As institutions of higher education become more crowded and financially strained, students reside at greater distances from universities, and they face increasing work and family demands on their time (Bonca, 1998). Because of these changes in student population's characteristics and in general economic conditions, colleges and universities have implemented

Chiara Gratton-Lavoie and Denise Stanley, "Online Learning as an Improvement? The Case of Economic Principles" in *Best Practices in Online Learning*, Boston: US Distance Learning Association and Information Age Publishing, Inc. 2003. Reprinted by permission of the authors and the publisher.

numerous innovations to the traditional classroom-based experience, ranging from classes incorporating the Web-based delivery of material to completely online instruction.

Online education could provide a cost-effective solution to these challenges. It is often argued that online students can master concepts as well, or better, than those in a traditional setting, and that the information technology can help to reduce the costs of education. The delivery costs per student and per-concept taught could be lowered, with online delivery mode at least as effective as the classroom-based delivery (see Twigg, 2001, for in-depth analysis of the issue of cost in distance learning environments).

A widespread debate has begun to emerge among academics undertaking online activities. In a survey of instructors teaching economics online, Navarro (2000) found that the majority of respondents believed students would do as well or better in an online class, and that most pedagogical aspects of learning could be met in the online environment.

On the positive side, an online class provides faster information access, it can be structured to accommodate different learning styles and student types (i.e., more motivated, self-directed and independent students, or older students with families), and it encourages students to take a more responsible, constructive role in the learning process, fostering independence of thought and critical thinking, rather than passive learning (Zhang, 1998; see also Brewer & Erickson, 1997; McCollum, 1997). And, of course, student time is used more efficiently when long travel times to a distant campus are eliminated. In one study, it was clear that more time-constrained students (not just long-distance commuters) are attracted to online classes (Vachris, 1999). Students can gain computer skills useful for future career paths (Agarwal & Day, 1998). Finally, student-professor interaction may be enhanced by online instruction. On the one hand, some students might prefer the relative anonymity of online communication to a face-to-face discussion. On the other hand, the distance learning format allows the instructor to rely on asynchronous communication for content delivery, while dedicating the time spent (synchronously) online with the students to class discussion and student-instructor interaction (Navarro & Shoemaker, 2000b).

However, critics say that students taking classes online do not learn as well as they do in a traditional setting, since class, student-to-student interaction is missing. Furthermore, if the instructor structures the online course as a replica of the traditional course, simply transferring existing course material online, then the potential advantages of online learning (individualized instruction to accommodate different learning styles, interactive, hands-on learning material, etc.) would not be realized, and students might tend to stress memorization more than they would in the traditional setting (Twigg, 2001). Technical problems related to Web infrastructure and incompatible systems are common, and higher withdrawal rates occur in online teaching (Navarro, 2000). Finally, as Navarro (2000) points out, poorer students with limited computer access may be excluded, and small colleges with tighter budgets will lag behind.

There are few studies to document the performance of students in online classes. Most studies discuss perceptions of the benefits of the online mode, rather than assessing in a rigorous manner, student performance. Even fewer studies attempt to explore and compare the factors underlying student performance in traditional versus online delivery systems. This study investigates the variables impacting performance of students in the online setting, and compares outcomes between two different modes of instruction, for the case of teaching economics principles.

Some Lessons from the Social Sciences and Previous Studies of Economics Online

Online learning methods have been implemented across nearly all academic disciplines. A noted expert in the field, Thomas Russell of North Carolina State University, has synthesized the findings of many studies comparing online and traditional courses. Nearly half of the studies cited find that learning outcomes are comparable in the two teaching modes (Cahill & Catanzaro, 1997 and Ridley, 1997, cited in Vachris, 1999). The "no significant difference" outcome occurred in English, Accounting, Economics, Philosophy, and Nursing classes (Green & Gentemann, 2001; Gagne & Shepherd, 2001; Navarro & Shoemaker, 1999; Virginia Tech, 1998; and Blackley & Curran-Smith, 1998). Another group of studies suggests that student performance in Engineering, Psychology, English, Management, and Accounting did improve in the online setting (Kashy, et al. 2001; Maki, et al. 2000; Stinson & Claus, 2000; Morrissey, 1998; and Vasarhelyi & Graham, 1997). These studies represent only those incorporating Web-based materials in the online teaching mode, with the exclusion of studies concerning the use of video learning techniques.

Regarding Economics, to date over 50 institutions offer at least 100 online economics courses (Navarro, 2000). The online component varies from simple use of email after lectures, to full online delivery, testing, and teleconferencing, to provide content and evaluate students. Most offerings and related analyses focus on introductory economics. But, as Navarro and Shoemaker (2000b) emphasize, this body of literature consists typically of case studies rather than rigorous, controlled comparison of outcomes between live lecture-based economics and economics online. A common trend is to integrate Web-based news or active games (e.g., the Iowa Electronic Markets) into class work (Simkins, 1999), but the effectiveness of these techniques has not been fully assessed. Gregor and Cuskelly (1994, cited in Agarwal & Day, 1998) just note greater student participation through bulletin boards, rather than focusing on student performance evaluation.

Agarwal and Day (1998) offer one of the first attempts to measure the value-added of a "partial" online learning experience that used supplemental Internet email, Web exercises, and class discussion lists. They focused on both student learning and retention of concepts, as well as on students' perception of instructor effectiveness, and possible changes in students' attitude toward economics. They examined both undergraduate principles classes and graduate courses across two semesters, with each course mode taught by both instructors across periods. They found that the "partially online" students performed significantly better on economic concept questions added to the final exam. The Internet students also received higher final grades in the course, after controlling for a variety of students' background characteristics. Interestingly, they suggested that the Internet enhancements worked better for students with higher initial GPAs.

Navarro and Shoemaker (2000) found that online learners perform better than traditional students in a macroeconomics principles class. In their case, a more costly innovation, multimedia CD-ROMs containing video, audio and text lectures, was the principal online delivery mode. Their study examined the results on a final exam of a short-essay nature, graded by a single person. The statistical significance of the difference in performance was consistent across various subgroups of students.

A contradictory result was reported by Brown and Liedholm (2002). Their study compared performance across three teaching modes: traditional lecture, online video lecture, and a hybrid course consisting of traditional lectures supplemented with online assignments. While online students had higher GPAs and ACT scores, they scored significantly lower on a common set of multiple-choice questions. However, women students did perform a bit better in the online setting, suggesting that the traditional gender gap in economics learning might be reduced by the use of information technology.

One should note that not all educational institutions have sufficient financial means to obtain, maintain, and support the technology required by the online video lectures referenced in these studies. The simple posting online of lecture notes, and the use of email, discussion board, chat rooms and Web-based interactive exercises, may be more suitable for some colleges and universities than others.

For our experiment at California State University, Fullerton (CSUF), we chose to adopt easy-to-use and relatively simple Internet tools, rather than more expensive and sophisticated multimedia technologies.

A New Experiment at CSUF

In this study we analyzed academic performance of students enrolled in two sections of Principles of Microeconomics at California State University, Fullerton in Fall 2001.

Specifically, we attempted to address some of the questions raised, among others, by Navarro and Shoemaker (2000a, b), and by Brown and Liedholm (Spring 2002), on whether students in Introductory Economics perform better online, and whether student background characteristics have an impact on performance, as well as on the choice of the mode of learning.

The Research Design

We taught two sections of Introductory Microeconomics using two alternative modes of instruction, hereafter referred to as the online mode and the hybrid mode.

As detailed below, while the instructional methods used for the control and the test groups had many features in common, they differed by design in *the degree* to which they used the online technology.

The two groups were similar in size (22 and 29 students respectively); we adopted the same textbook (Case & Fair, 2001), and the same exam format and exam content for both groups. Additionally, the same online support and instructional technology (Blackboard CourseInfo 4.0) were used to create course Web sites for communication through posting of class information and material, class announcements, and email.

The main differences between the two courses were: 1) the instructor teaching the course, and 2) the extent to which the classes relied on online instructional technology for student-to-instructor and student-to-student interactions. The online class was taught by Gratton-Lavoie, and it met in person only three times, for scheduled in-class examinations. Stanley taught the hybrid format of the course, and her class met face-to-face for two and a half hours per week.

Two potential sources of bias had to be addressed by our research design: the instructor bias, and the student self-selection bias. To minimize instructor bias, we controlled for factors affecting teaching methodology and course information content. We selected the same textbook, and we jointly prepared syllabi, reading and homework assignments, exams, lecture notes, and any other material used in the course. Additionally, during the semester of instruction we carefully coordinated the sequence in which topics were covered, as well as the timing of exams, assignments, etc.

We administered a confidential entry survey to all students in the first week of instruction. We used the survey to collect data on students' personal characteristics as well as information on their academic background and computer knowledge at the beginning of the experiment. These data, together with additional information from official university records, allowed us to control for selection bias, and to isolate the effect of the instructional technology on students' performance.

Table 1. Summary statistics of student personal characteristics

Variable		Online Group N=22		Hybrid Group N=29		Test Statistics
Age*		23 (5.78)		21.62 (3.19)		t test=1.07 df=47, p=0.29
Gender						Chi square =2.48 df=1, p=0.12
	Male	8	36.36%	17	58.62%	
	Female	14	63.64%	12	41.38%	
Ethnicity						Chi square=2.01 df=4, p=0.73
	Caucasian	3	13.64%	7	24.14%	
	Hispanic	4	18.18%	6	20.69%	
	African Am.	1	4.55%	1	3.45%	
	Asian	9	40.90%	13	44.83%	
	Other	5	22.73%	2	6.89%	
Primary Language						Chi square=0.88 df=2, p=0.64
	English	16	72.73%	21	72.41%	
	English + Other	4	18.18%	7	24.14%	
	Other	2	9.09%	1	3.45%	
Marital Status						Chi square=1.70 df=1, p=0.19
	Single	18	81.82%	27	93.10%	
	Married	4	18.18%	2	6.90%	
Children						Chi square=4.48 df=1, p=0.03
	Yes	5	22.73%	1	3.45%	
	No	17	77.27%	28	96.55%	
Distance to Campus						Chi square=5.64 df=4, p=0.23
	On campus	0	0.0%	1	3.45%	
	Very Close	2	9.09%	1	3.45%	
	2-5 Miles	0	0.0%	4	13.79%	
	6-10 Miles	6	27.27%	4	13.79%	
	10+ Miles	14	63.64%	19	65.52%	

* Mean, with standard deviation in parentheses.

Table 2. Summary statistics of student academic and computer background characteristics

Variable	Online Group N=22		Hybrid Group N=29		Test Statistics
Major					Chi square=0.00
Bus/Fin/Econ	15	68.18%	20	68.97%	df=1, p=0.95
Other	7	31.82%	9	31.03%	
College Algebra					Chi square=0.12
Yes	19	86.36%	24	82.76%	df=1, p=0.73
No	3	13.64%	5	17.24%	
College Calculus					Chi square=0.20
Yes	10	45.45%	15	51.72%	df=1, p=0.66
No	12	54.55%	14	48.28%	
Previous Econ Class					Chi square=0.83
Yes	17	77.27%	19	65.52%	df=1, p=0.36
No	5	22.73%	10	34.48%	
Previous Online Class					Chi square=1.45
Yes	5	22.73%	3	10.35%	df=1, p=0.23
No	17	77.27%	26	89.65%	
Student Status					Chi square=1.65
Full Time	19	86.36%	24	82.76%	df=2, p=0.44
Part Time	0	0.0%	2	6.90%	
Evening Only	3	13.64%	3	10.34%	
Hours/wk. Work*	19.80	(13.54)	24.19	(13.50)	t test= 1.15, df=49, p=0.26
Hours/wk. Study*	13.43	(7.93)	14.87	(14.05)	t test= 0.42, df=45, p=0.68
Access to PC					Chi square=2.42
Yes	22	100.0%	26	89.66%	df=1, p=0.12
No	0	0.0%	3	10.34%	
Access to Internet					Chi square=2.42
Yes	22	100.0%	26	89.66%	df=1, p=0.12
No	0	0.0%	3	10.34%	
Computer Skills* (1= Poor to 5=Expert)	3.36	(0.95)	3.28	(0.75)	t test=0.37, df=49, p=0.71
Email Skills* (1=Poor to 5=Expert)	4.41	(0.80)	4.59	(0.78)	t test=0.80, df=49, p=0.43
Web Skills* (1=Poor to 5=Expert)	4.23	(0.92)	4.48	(0.83)	t test=1.04, df=49,p=0.30
Computer Knowledge (Score: 0-4)*	3.77	(0.43)	3.76	(0.51)	t test=0.10, df=49, p=0.92
Math Knowledge* (Score: 0-5)	2.45	(1.06)	2.4	(1.21)	t test=0.13, df=49, p=0.90
Cumulative GPA*	2.17	(1.16)	2.53	(0.89)	t test=1.26, df=48, p=0.21
CSUF GPA*	1.96	(1.22)	1.69	(1.33)	t test=0.70, df=46, p=0.48
SAT Scores*					t test=0.12, p=0.90 df=22
Verbal	482.5	(93.16)	475.63	(81.89)	t test=0.19, p=0.85
Math	520	(77.83)	529.38	(69.71)	t test=0.02, p=0.98
Enrollment Date* (w/r to 1st day of class)	-7.86	(22.19)	-19.39	(17.99)	t test=2.03, df=48, p=0.048
Credits Enrolled*	11.38	(3.94)	12.28	(3.43)	t test=0.85, df=48, p=0.40
Credits Earned*	10.58	(3.47)	11.25	(3.71)	t test=0.62, df=45, p=0.54

* Means, with standard deviations in parentheses.

Class Composition, Course Design and Evaluation Instruments

Table 1 and Table 2 present the statistics regarding students' personal characteristics (Table 1), and their academic background and computer knowledge (Table 2) at the beginning of the experiment, for both the online class and the hybrid class.

The raw data show that the online students were on average older than the students in the hybrid group, and they lived farther from campus. The online group had more female students, had stronger mathematics background and economics class experience, and admitted studying fewer hours.

Table 3. Course designs

Online Course (N=22)	Hybrid Course (N=29)
Standard Textbook	Standard Textbook
Instructor's Lecture Supplements Online	
Textbook Companion Website with Online Study Guide	Textbook Companion Website with Online Study Guide
Instructor Website for Announcements, Posting of Relevant Material, Grades, etc.	Instructor Website for Announcements, Posting of Relevant Material, Grades, etc.
Weekly Online Chats, Synchronous Discussion Board, Asynchronous Email	Face to Face Lectures
	Email
Mandatory Online Participation/Online Attendance	**Weekly Computer Lab Assignments**
Electronic Testing: Online quizzes	In-class quizzes
In-class Midterm Examinations and Final Exam	In-class Midterm Examinations and Final Exam

They also reported working fewer hours per week than the hybrid group. Students were asked to rate their computer, email and Internet skills using a scale from 1 = poor to 5 = expert. Levels of expertise were very similar across groups. Wary of the reliability of self-reported data, particularly with respect to computer skills, we decided to include in the survey a set of multiple-choice questions, testing the students on their Internet and computer knowledge, as well as on their math background. Table 2 reports the average scores on the two sets of questions, as Computer Knowledge and Math Knowledge respectively. With regard to the technology-related questions, the two groups scored virtually the same.

To test for the statistical significance of differences in background characteristics, we performed Chi-squared tests of independence for the categorical, non-numerical variables, and we computed t-test statistics to capture possible differences between mean values of non-categorical, numerical variables. Our tests indicate that statistically significant differences did not exist between the online students and the more traditional group,

Table 4. Performance evaluation instruments

Common Instruments

Three Quizzes (online for Online Students Only)
    Common Multiple Choice Questions
    Open Books/Notes
Two In-Person Exams
    Common Format and Content
    Multiple Choice, True/False, and Essay Questions
In-Person Final Examination
    Common Format and Content
    Multiple Choice, True/False, and Essay Questions

Online Course Only

Weekly Online Chat/Online Participation

Hybrid Course Only

Weekly Computer Lab Assignments
(Students had to attend class to be allowed to work on the lab assignments)

with two notable exceptions. The online students had more children, and official records indicate that they enrolled in the class much later than the students in the hybrid course did. In fact, virtual learners enrolled only slightly more than a week before the beginning of the term, while the average student in the hybrid group enrolled almost 20 days in advance. For both variables, the differences are statistically significant at the 5% level.

Overall, we can conclude that the two groups were rather homogeneous in their entering characteristics, with the exception of number of children and date of enrollment. The higher number of children, coupled with the fact that the online class had more women enrolled than the traditional course, suggests the possibility that convenience and schedule flexibility were both important factors affecting students' enrollment decision. Particularly for women who work outside the house and have family responsibilities, a distance learning class might fit a tight and busy schedule when other options might not.

On the other hand, the fact that students enrolled in the virtual course quite late indicates the possibility of another source of selection bias in the sample. It raises the question of whether many students who chose the virtual environment were actually forced to do so by lack of viable alternatives, due to a combination of personal constraints on their schedule, and closed enrollment in other sections of Introductory Microeconomics.

In short, the background data suggest the possibility that students selected the online option because it was the most convenient and flexible alternative, and/or because they did not have an alternative at all.

Table 5. Summary statistics of assessment outcomes

Variable	Online Group* N=22		Hybrid Group* N=29		Test Statistics t-test (p value) df=49
Quiz 1	16.36	(4.61)	17.84	(4.32)	1.18 (0.24)
Quiz 2	17.73	(5.40)	17.59	(6.66)	0.08 (0.94)
Quiz 3	17.84	(4.10)	14.40	(7.55)	1.93 (0.06)
Midterm 1	68.34	(23.95)	78.97	(10.99)	2.12 (0.04)
Midterm 2	52.68	(28.52)	74.21	(13.19)	3.60 (0.00)
Final Examination	60.93	(19.51)	70.81	(12.39)	2.21 (0.03)
All Exams Score	203.63	(48.86)	235.52	(36.60)	2.66 (0.01)
Participation	62.27	(12.98)	58.63	(14.21)	0.94 (0.35)
Exams & Participation	265.90	(52.24)	294.15	(47.21)	2.02 (0.049)

* Means, with standard deviations in parentheses.

The key aspects of the course designs are presented in Table 3, with differences highlighted. The hybrid course involved face-to-face weekly lectures for about one hour and 45 minutes, and hands-on computer lab assignments for roughly another 45 to 50 minutes per week. The instructor maintained a Website for class announcements, and to post grades, review exams, assignments, etc. Students used the Internet to access online study guide problems, as well as various other Internet resources to complete the lab assignments. Email was used to communicate with the entire class and with individual students.

The online group met in person only for an introductory, orientation session, and three other times for two in-class midterm examinations and the final comprehensive exam. Delivery of the course content took place entirely in the virtual environment.

For synchronous interaction, students and instructor met weekly in a virtual chat room for one hour and a half. Attendance to the weekly chat was mandatory. Asynchronous interaction took place via email and a threaded bulletin board. The online students supplemented their standard textbook readings with lecture modules that we prepared and posted in advance. The modules were Microsoft Word documents that provided additional analysis and discussion of the most important and/or difficult topics of the week. The main purpose of the lecture modules was to provide the

Table 6. Scores by gender and instruction mode

Variable	Men*	Women*	Test Statistics t-test (p value)
All Exams Score/Online	204.80	202.96	0.08 (0.94) df = 20
All Exams Score/Hybrid	231.27	241.53	0.74 (0.47) df = 27

* Means, with standard deviations in parentheses.

online students with a close substitute for the more traditional face-to-face lecture, in the sense that the information content delivered to the online students through the modules reflected the information content provided in the live lectures to the hybrid group.

Table 4 lists the evaluation instruments used in this experiment. Two in-class examinations and a comprehensive in-class, final exam were administered to both groups, and they contained the same set of questions for both the online and the hybrid course. In all three cases, students had to work on a combination of basic definition and true/false questions, short worked problems, and multiple-choice questions. All answers were graded from common keys, and we used the same point allocation across questions. Three short quizzes (multiple-choice questions only) were also administered. The online students took the quizzes on the Internet, while the traditional group was presented with the same questions in class, and was allowed to consult books and lecture notes.

Finally, the online learners were evaluated on their online class participation, particularly to the weekly chat, while the hybrid group was evaluated on weekly lab assignments. Since only those students who came to class in person received the lab assignments, lab work counted as class participation/attendance for the students in the hybrid course.

Does Online Learning Improve Performance?

The summary statistics for the performance measures are presented in Table 5 below. The most startling outcome we observed was the lower performance of the online learners in their total exam results; this score represented the weighted sum of points earned in the quizzes and in the three exams, with a maximum possible score of 325. The measure that includes class participation (maximum total score in this case was 400) is also significantly different between the two groups, with online students again performing worse than the hybrid group. The final grade distribution also mirrored this trend. The differences are statistically significant at the 5% level, with the performance gap on the second midterm and on the overall exam score being statistically significant at the 1% level.

Although the online students began the semester with indications of stronger math background, higher Cal State Fullerton GPA, more academic experience with economics, and lower job-related demand on their time, they performed significantly worse than the students enrolled in the live section of the course. These results contradict those of Navarro and Shoemaker (2000a, 2000b) regarding student performance in economic principles, but they lend support to the outcome observed in Brown and Liedholm (2002).

Our finding of poorer online performance was most polarized for midterms and comprehensive final exam results. All three exams included written, essay-type questions, which required deeper understanding of the material, and the ability to apply economic concepts and methods to real-world situations. The second midterm, which incorporates analysis of consumer theory and production costs, is usually the most conceptually difficult exam of the semester, and here the online learners performed the worst. On the other hand, the virtual class did not score as poorly on simple multiple-choice quiz questions. This trend in performance outcomes seems to parallel that observed by Brown and Liedholm (2002), with the performance gap between online and traditional learners increasing with the growing sophistication of the test questions.

A review of the summary statistics presented in Table 1 and Table 2 might help to shed some light into why the online learners performed so poorly.

As previously discussed, students enrolled in the virtual class on average only a week before instruction began, while students in the hybrid course enrolled almost 20 days before the beginning of instruction. This difference in enrollment dates may be important and indicative of selection bias in the online sample. Both instructors noted that some of the students enrolled in the online class expressed that they could not 'get into' other closed sections of Economics Principles. Thus, the online method of delivery may not have been their first, preferred choice. In statistical terms, these students may not have been correctly sorted into the teaching and delivery modes best suited to their learning styles, and a form of negative selection bias may have occurred.

Other important differences in student background characteristics were the higher female ratio and the higher percentage of students with children in the online group. In fact, unlike Brown and Liedholm, we found that online female students did worse than their male counterparts, and they performed much worse than the female population in the face-to-face lecture group. We also found that female students in the more traditional setting perform better than their male counterparts.

Table 6 summarizes these findings. Although the t-test statistics indicate that the differences in scores were not statistically significant, the raw data clearly suggest the possibility of the distance-learning environment being especially unfavorable to female students.

Female students, especially working mothers, have traditionally more pressing family needs to attend to. They might have initially thought that the online learning mode would be more flexible and adaptable to their busy schedules. Our results suggest that ultimately the heavy demands on working mothers' time did not allow them to dedicate the effort needed for a successful online experience. On the other hand, for the hybrid section of the class, the data show better female performance.

To conclude, our results concerning gender-performance relationship in economics courses contradict the usual findings that women do worse than men in economics and that the performance gap could be reduced with more intensive and comprehensive use of information technology in the course.

Concluding Remarks and Suggestions for Future Research

This study finds that the virtual classroom environment, when compared to a more traditional setting, has a negative impact on the performance of students taking introductory economics classes. We find that the use of information technology beyond the now pervasive supporting role that such technology has acquired in higher education, has negative effects on student academic performance as measured by traditional evaluation instruments. Furthermore, our data show that female students are potentially at a greater disadvantage than their male counterpart when choosing the online option. This result is at odds with previous research that indicates how online delivery of course content might facilitate female learning and retention of economic concepts.

In designing our study, we chose to limit ourselves to easy-to-use, accessible, and relatively simple Internet tools, while other studies included multimedia presentations that used video, digital sound, animated photo images, and interactive graphs, for highly sophisticated content delivery. We think that the development of such multimedia and interactive tools still requires more professional expertise and support than what many small colleges and universities might be able to provide to their faculty and their students.

Our experimental design suffers from two limitations, both of which might have affected our findings. On one hand, because different instructors taught the two courses, there is the possibility of significant instructor bias. We feel quite confident that we addressed this problem as much as possible under the circumstances, controlling for about everything (related to course content and teaching style) that could reasonably be controlled for. Nevertheless, to eliminate any possibility of instructor bias, in future research we will collect data on two groups of students for each delivery mode, and we will have the same instructor teach both a test and a control section of the course each semester.

The second potential source of bias in the data comes from students self-selecting the type of course. It is not clear to us whether in the future it will be possible to randomly assign students to each class without violating university rules, and without artificially restricting the students' enrollment options. The second-best approach to addressing the self-selection problem is the one we took in our experiment. It involves collecting as much information as possible on student background characteristics so as to be able to control for factors different from the specifics of the course design, which might influence performance.

Finally, the authors are fully aware of a more general, pedagogical issue, concerning whether the traditional performance evaluation tools are altogether obsolete and inadequate to evaluate teaching and learning in the virtual environment.

References

Agarwal, R., & Day, A. E. (1998, Spring). "The Impact of the Internet on Economic Education." *Journal of Economic Education*, 99–110.

Blackley, J. A., & Curran-Smith, J. (1998). "Teaching Community Health Nursing by Distance Methods: Devlopment, Process, and Evaluation." *Journal of Continuing Education for Nurses, 29*, 148–153.

Bonca, C. (1998, September 4–10). "Welcome to Virtual U." *OC Weekly*.

Brewer, S., & Erickson, D. (1997). "A Tale of Two Classrooms." *Journal of Computing in Teacher Education, 13*, 20–22.

Brown, B. W. , & Liedholm, C. E. (Spring 2002). "Can Web Courses Replace the Classroom in Principles of Microeconomics?" *American Economic Review*.

California State University Fullerton. (2001, March 12). "Springtime Blossom With Record Crop of Students." *Public Affairs.* Retrieved July 5, 2002 from http://www.fullerton.edu

Carnevale, C. (2001, February 21). "What Matters in Judging Distance Teaching? Not How Much It's Like a Classroom Course." *The Chronicle of Higher Education*.

Case, K. E., & Fair, R. C. (2001). *Principles of Microeconomics* (6th ed.). Prentice Hall.

Gagne, M., & Shepherd, M. "Distance Learning in Accounting: A Comparison Between a Distance and Traditional Graduate Accounting Class." *T.H.E. Journal, 28*, 58–65, 2001.

Green, R., & Gentemann, K. (2001). "Technology in the Curriculum: An Assessment of the Impact of On-Line Courses." *George Mason University,* .

Goldberg, D. (1998, April 5). "Teaching Online-Education Review," *The Washington Post*.

Johnson, S. D., Aragon, S. R., Shaik, N., & Palma-Rivas, N. (2000). "Comparative Analysis of Learner Satisfaction and Learning Outcomes in

Online and Face-to-Face Learning Environments." *Journal of Interactive Learning Research,* 11, 29–49.

Kane, J., & Spizman, L. (1999–01). "Determinants of Student Retention of Microeconomics Principles Concepts." *Working Paper,* SUNY-Oswego.

Kashy, D. A., Albertelli, G., Kashy, E., & Thoennessen, M. (October 2001). "Teaching with ALN Technology: Benefits and Costs." *Journal of Engineering Education.*

Maki, R. H., Maki, W. S., Patterson, M., & Whittaker, P. D. (2000)."Evaluation of a Web-based Introductory Psychology Course: Learning and Satisfaction in On-line versus Lecture Courses." *Behavior Research Methods, Instruments, & Computers,* 32, 230–239.

McCollum, K. (1997, February 21). "In Test, Students Taught on Line Outdo Those Taught in Class." *The Chronicle of Higher Education.*

Morrissey, C. A. (1998)."The Impact of the Internet on Management Education: What the Research Shows." *Pepperdine University.*

Navarro, P. (Spring 2000). "Economics in the Cyberclassroom." *Journal of Economic Perspectives,* 14, 119–1332.

Navarro, P., & Shoemaker, J. "Economics in Cyberspace: A Comparison Study." *Mimeo,* University of California-Irvine.

Navarro, P. , & Shoemaker, J. (Fall 1999). "The Power of Cyberlearning: An Empirical Test." *Journal of Computing in Higher Education,* 11, 29–54.

Navarro, P., & Shoemaker, J. (July 2000a). "Policy Issues in the Teaching of Economics in Cyberspace: Research Design, Course Design, and Research Results." *Contemporary Economic Policy,* 18, 359–366.

Navarro, P., & Shoemaker, J. (2000b). "Performance and Perceptions of Distance Learners in Cyberspace.' *The American Journal of Distance Education,* 14, 15–35.

Sherry, A. C., Fulford C. P., & Zhang, S. (1998). "Assessing Distance Learners' Satisfaction with Instruction: A Quantitative and a Qualitative Measure.', *The American Journal of Distance Education,* 12, 4–28.

Simkins, S. (1999, Summer)."Promoting Active-Student Learning Using the World Wide Web in Economics Courses." *Journal of Economic Education,* 278–291.

Smeaton, A., & Keogh, G. (1999). "An Analysis of the Use of Virtual Delivery of Undergraduate Lectures." *Computers and Education,* 32, 83–94.

Stinson, B. M., & Claus, K. (2000, February)."The Effects of Electronic Classrooms on Learning English Composition." *T.H.E. Journal* 27-7.

Twigg, C. A. (2001)."Innovation in Online Learning: Moving Beyond No Significant Difference." *Center for Academic Transformation,* The Pew

Learning and Technology Program, Rensselaer Polytechnic Institute.

Vachris, M.A. (September 1997). "Teaching Economics in a Virtual Classroom." *Virginia Economic Journal.*

Vachris, M.A. (1999, Summer). "Teaching Principles of Economics without 'Chalk and Talk': The Experience of CNU Online." *Journal of Economic Education*, 30, 292–303.

Vasarhelyi, M., & Graham, L. (1997, August). "Cybersmart: Education and the Internet." Management Accounting, 32–36.

Virginia Tech. (1998). "Course Restructuring and the Instructional Development Initiative at Virginia Polytechnic Institute: A Benefit Cost Study." Virginia Tech.

Zhang, P. (1998, Summer). "A Case Study on Technology Use in Distance Learning." *Journal of Research on Computing in Education*, 30, 398–416.

Assessing Differences in Instructional Methods: Uncovering How Students Learn Best

Nancy Ostiguy
The Pennsylvania State University
Ann Haffer
California State University, Sacramento

Abstract

After assessing student outcomes in a general education science course using distributed learning environments (e.g., traditional classroom, television, or Web environment), the authors found no significant differences in achievement. Even though television and Web students reported greater levels of interaction with the instructor, they were more likely to report dissatisfaction with the level of interaction.

Colleges and universities are under pressure from many sides to offer courses using distributed learning environments, e.g., Web-based, televised, and video-conferencing courses (Allen 1998). Faculty are reviewing the potential benefits and detriments afforded in these environments, especially to students' learning outcomes. Little data assessing outcomes, however, have been published (Windschitl 1998).

As teachers, we believe we know what current classroom learning outcomes are, and we want to know if they are as good in distributed learning environments. Most of the information we have concerning learning outcomes, either in the distributed learning or classroom environment, is anecdotal. Comparing assessments of student learning outcomes and student perceptions of learning in different environments would add to our knowledge about the influence of these environments.

To determine if there were differences related to learning environments, an introductory environmental science course was taught using three different environments: an on-campus studio classroom, a simultaneous cable broadcast from the studio, and a separate Web-based class approach. We –

Course Structure

In the fall of 1994, the Environmental Studies department at California State University, Sacramento began offering Introductory Environmental Science, a one-semester life science general education classroom-based course for nonscience majors, on the community cable education channel. Then, in the spring of 1998, a Web-based option to Introductory Environmental Science was added.

As the course instructor (Ostiguy), I established three goals before offering it in the distributed learning format. The first was to teach students with different learning styles. By including computer-based illustrations focused on the specific concepts taught, animations slowed to show individual frames, and photographs of various organisms, systems, and pollution problems, I was better able to accommodate various learning styles. An active-learning environment provided through online self-assessment quizzes helped students to determine if they understood the concepts and principles outlined in the course goals and objectives. In addition, I increased the number of focused discussions on class material during and after class (electronic communication).

The second goal was to provide a context for the scientific information to be learned. I have observed during my years teaching this course in the classroom, as did Labianca (1998) with his nonchemistry major students, that students want a context for the scientific information they are learning. For example, students come to class curious about or at least having heard about environmental problems, e.g., species extinction, air and water pollution. As a result of student curiosity about environmental topics, it is possible to motivate students to learn scientific concepts, e.g., food webs, habitats, and niches, using environmental issues as a starting point because these issues can be better understood when the scientific concepts are understood.

The last goal was to increase students' communication with their peers and the instructor. To facilitate this goal, students were required to obtain and use their university-provided e-mail accounts. Students also had to participate in an asynchronous (not simultaneous) threaded discussion group.

During the spring of 1998, students registered for one of three different instructional environments of Introductory Environmental Science, either classroom, cable, or Web. It was impossible to randomly assign a student to a particular section of the course because some courses required cable access or a home computer, neither of which some students had. And other students were unable to attend the classroom lectures because they worked during those hours. Therefore, students were allowed to vary how they attended the course.

Students in the classroom or television course had to complete the class at the pace that I set, while the students learning on the Web proceeded at their own pace. All students received the same syllabus containing the reading assignments; exams; online, nongraded interactive self-assessment quizzes; and other course information. Students also all used the same textbook.

Classroom and television students participated in online discussions with their classmates using a listserv while Web students used the asynchronous threaded discussion software Conferencing on the Web (COW was developed by Kevin Klavins at San Francisco State University). The Listserv and COW stimulated conversations and allowed me to give them constant feedback. Students were encouraged to interact with me by e-mail, telephone, or by visiting in person. The assignments were the same for the students in all three learning environments.

Methods

To determine if instructional approaches caused a difference in student learning outcomes, we conducted pre- and post-tests to assess students' knowledge of biological concepts. On the first day of class, we sent students in the Web-based section an e-mail message asking them to complete a 26-question test. The pretest was also located on the course Webpage. We asked students in the cable television section during the live broadcast on the first day to obtain a copy of the pretest by contacting the instructor or by downloading it from the class Web site. Students in the studio section received the pretest in class. All students had to return the assessment by the end of the first week. Ten extra credit points were offered as an incentive to each student to complete the pretest.

The post-test was administered, using the same pretest questions, as part of the final examination. To decrease the likelihood that familiarity with the questions would affect the post-test answers, the questions were scattered among the other questions and noncontent-wording changes were made (e.g., changing the wording of a question from false to true).

At the end of the semester, we surveyed students on learning styles, faculty/student interaction, use of technology, and influence of learning environment to determine if instructional methods caused differences in students' perceptions of learning. All students received the survey and a self-addressed, stamped envelope with their final exams. They were asked to return the survey as soon as possible and were awarded 10 extra-credit points if they completed the survey within a week of the final exam. (A copy of the survey questions can be obtained from the authors.)

Results and Discussion

Forty-three students registered for the studio section, 54 registered for the cable television section, and 19 signed up for the Web-based section. Response rates differed between the surveys and the pre- and post-tests. No significant difference was observed between the sections in their response rates for the surveys. Eighty-eight percent of the classroom students, 83% of the cable students, and 79% of the Web students returned the surveys. We observed a significant difference among the sections in the completion rate of the pretest and post-test ($p < .001$). Only 17% of the students attending via television completed both tests, while 72% of the classroom students and 42% of the Web students completed both tests. We did not observe significant demographic differences between the students by course

Table 1. Selected demographic characteristics by section

Initial Enrollment Options Course	Sex Female Male		Age (Mean)	Ethnicity White Non-white		Previously Distant Enrolled in Education
Classroom ($n = 38$)	60.5%	39.5%	24	54.3%	45.7%	29%
Television ($n = 44$)	53.3%	44.4%	23	41.9%	58.1%	33%
Web ($n = 15$)	60%	40%	24	53.3%	46.7%	33%

section. Sex, age, ethnicity, class level, course grade, previous enrollment in a distributed learning course, or number of enrolled units did not differ (Table 1).

A significant difference in attendance behavior was observed ($p < .0001$). Classroom students were most likely to attend in the classroom, television students attended by watching videotapes or the live television broadcast, and Web students completed the course on the Web (Table 2). Though it was possible to predict a student's preferred learning environment based upon his or her section enrollment, some students chose to attend classes using all available environments—studio, cable, and Web. Forty-three percent of the students registered in the studio section and 26% of the students registered in the Web section watched lectures on television or by videotape.

Table 2. Percentage of lectures attended by section

Initial Enrollment Options	Percentage of Lectures Attended			
	Classroom	Television*	Web	Did Not Attend
Classroom ($n = 38$)	54%	43%	1%	2%
Television ($n = 44$)	9%	85%	1%	5%
Web ($n = 15$)	1%	26%	65%	8%

* Watched live broadcast or videotape at home or in the library.

Students frequently commented in the survey that their ability to select and vary the instructional environment was one of the strengths of the course. Many students felt the ability to choose the learning environment allowed them to "attend" all class sessions. The videotapes were also reported to be useful when studying for exams. Students commented positively concerning the availability of lectures via television or videotape because these alternative formats allowed them to keep up with their course work when either they or their children were ill.

There were no differences in student self-reported learning styles. Most of the students indicated that they preferred to work with others or to work actively with the concepts while learning (63%). This learning preference presents a challenge for the distributed learning environment because it is an environment that does not demand that students work synchronously, and asynchronous group work is new for many students. In fact, one attribute of the television or Web-based learning environment is the ability of students to complete work independently of other students and their instructor. Seventy-three percent of Web students indicated the most significant aid to learning was the asynchronous, flexible nature of the Web instructional method. These students reported that proceeding at their own pace was very important to their success. Asynchronous interactions such as COW and student-to-student and instructor-to-student e-mail need to be incorporated into Web course design.

Nearly all the students used e-mail to interact with the instructor (Table 3). Only one student out of the 116 students surveyed indicated that e-mail had not been used. The majority of students (84%) reported that they were moderately or very skilled using e-mail while almost three-quarters (74%)

Table 3. Student/faculty interaction ouside classroom

Initial Enrollment Options	Mode of Interaction				
	E-mail	Faculty Office	Phone	After Class	Fax
Classroom ($n = 38$)	100%	18%	16%	8%	3%
Television ($n = 44$)	98%	47%	29%	0%	13%
Web ($n = 15$)	100%	27%	40%	0%	27%

stated that they were moderately or very skilled using the Web. Today's student can be expected to know, or be quick to learn, the skills necessary to communicate and work via the Internet. We found, as did Hedges and Mania-Farnell (1998/1999), e-mail to be an excellent tool for increasing communication.

We asked students to provide information about student and instructor interactions. Students in the three learning environments interacted with the instructor outside the classroom very differently ($p = .027$). The level of interaction reported by the television and Web students was greater in several areas than that reported by classroom students. Thirty-nine percent of the television students, 21% of the Web students, and only 16% of the classroom students reported speaking with the instructor in her office. The television students were more apt to speak to the instructor in her office ($p = .047$). Twenty-four percent of the television students and 32% of the Web students, but only 14% of the classroom students reported talking with the instructor on the phone. No differences were reported in e-mail interaction.

A small number of television (33%) and Web (20%) students indicated that the lack of interaction between themselves and the instructor interfered with their ability to learn. Web and television students frequently commented that it was hard to ask questions because they had to wait for an e-mail reply from the instructor. (All e-mail messages were responded to within 24 hours of receipt, and over 90% of the messages received replies less then four hours after receipt.) The classroom students did not express dissatisfaction with the faculty and student interaction.

The conclusions of Wegner et al. (1999) on student attitudes toward learning experiences differed from our study. They wrote that students in the Internet-based section of the course had more positive feelings about their learning experiences than students had in the in-class section, though the data were not statistically significant. Our study indicated that Web and television students tended to interact more with the instructor than classroom students, but the Web and television students perceived themselves to have fewer interactions than they desired. This perception needs to be explored. It may be that the more physically distant student needs more interaction, or it is possible that the traditional classroom facilitates interaction, whether used or not, and the distant student is reacting to the lost opportunity to interact.

We did not gather data about the quantity or quality of interaction during class, nor did we obtain accurate information about the quantity or quality of interaction out of class. It would be useful to gather these data, e.g., e-mail messages between students and between students and instructor, to see if the type and quantity of interaction is correlated to learning outcome or to type of instruction.

We noted a significant difference in student use of the online self-assessment quizzes ($p < .005$). Seventy-three percent of the Web students, 45% of the classroom students, and 27% of the television students used the Web-based quizzes. Thirty-three percent of the students reported that the quizzes were useful when studying for exams. We spent over a year developing interactive self-assessment quizzes, and it was encouraging that a substantial proportion of the students used them. Several students commented that they found the quizzes to be "well arranged and interesting" and "extremely useful" because they helped them "extract the main ideas and concepts." As we gain more experience with the software, and the hardware requirements become less difficult for our students to meet, this instructional tool could be even more beneficial in creating an interactive environment that connects students to the material.

Learning Assessment

Wegner et al. (1999) found no significant difference in achievement between students in different sections of an Internet-based and in-class course while Schutte (1996) found students who were randomly assigned to a Web-based social statistics course averaged scores 20% higher than the randomly assigned classroom students. In our study, no significant difference in the mean pre- or post-test scores was observed between students enrolled in the three learning environments. Student use of all three learning environments, irrespective of the learning environment the student selected at the time of registration, may have produced these results.

Within each of the learning environments, we observed significant differences in the mean pretest and mean post-test scores (Table 4). The Web students increased their final score by 2.7 ($p = .04$) points, while the television students increased by 4.0 ($p = .036$), and the classroom students by 4.6 ($p = .001$). Again these results differ from Schutte (1996), who found significantly better scores by the Web-based students. While the difference between the post-test scores for the students in the three environments is not statistically significant, the improvement in the post-test score was greatest for the classroom students.

Significant differences between the pretest and post-test scores for all students were observed for 17 of the 26 questions. These responses were more likely to differ significantly among classroom students than among students in the television and Web environments; the classroom students improved

Table 4. Mean and standard deviation of pretest and posttest scores by learning environment

| | Learning Environments | | |
	Classroom[*]	Television[**]	Web[***]
Pretest	16.2 (4.48)	15.33 (2.87)	17.9 (2.53)
Posttest	20.8 (3.07)	19.3 (3.37)	20.6 (1.68)

[*] Classroom mean pretest score versus mean posttest score ($p = .0001$)
[**] Television mean pretest score versus mean posttest score ($p = .036$)
[***] Web mean pretest score versus mean posttest score ($p = .040$)

their correct response rate for fifteen questions, while the television and Web students improved their correct response rate for three and two questions, respectively.

Outcome

Our inability to randomly assign learning environment may have affected the study results and reduced the ability to generalize this study. If students selected learning environments in a way that resulted in different types of students being enrolled in each of the course sections, then the results of the study would be biased. We do not believe that self-selection by the students would have resulted in the best (or worst) students enrolled in one type of learning environment rather than another. Therefore, the effect of self-selection on learning outcome should be minimal as all levels of ability and self-motivation should be present in each section.

It is possible that self-selection could have influenced student perception of the learning environment. Students would be most likely to select the environment best liked, and each learning environment would have shown high satisfaction levels; the error would have been toward no significant difference. This was not the case. Students in the Web and cable television sections of the course reported lower levels of course satisfaction than did the students in the studio section. The last reason why we do not believe that allowing students to select their learning environment had an impact on our results is because the students in each section did not differ demographically.

Overall, the students in the Web and television learning environments learned less than we would have preferred. There were fewer positive changes in their responses from the pretest to the post-test than the classroom students and more dissatisfaction expressed with their learning environments. Ehrmann (1997) asserts that differences observed between learning in the classroom and the distributed learning environment can be explained by the teaching methods used in each environment. While the course material and assignments were identical for the students in this study, and every effort was made to ensure that the teaching methods were identical, the way the student experienced the course differed. When a student perceives an instructor to be less accessible, as a substantial minority of the Web and television students did, the teaching method is not identical. It would be interesting to determine if correlations exist between learning style, type of learning environment, course satisfaction, and learning outcome. It is possible that learning style interacts with learning environment to influence course satisfaction. We are currently designing a study to collect data on each of these variables to explore this issue.

We learned several things from this study that have helped us to improve this and other courses we teach. Students appreciate the availability of alternative methods of instruction. For example, a course taught in a classroom can be videotaped and the videotapes made available to students for use when they wish to review material, study for an exam, or watch a missed class. We have found it useful to establish asynchronous threaded discussion groups among the students to foster learning outside the classroom. Beginning an asynchronous discussion with a focused question or questions and evaluating student contributions for quality have improved the depth of the discussions. Interactive online quizzes have proven to be very popular. We believe that the higher-order thinking questions asked on exams are answered successfully more often because the students are challenged to think at this level with the online quizzes. It is always possible to improve one's courses, and the results from this study have been useful in directing our changes.

References

Allen, R. D. (1998). Distance learning: Meeting our education responsibilities with technology. *Journal of College Science Teaching*, 27, 393.

Chickering, A. W., & Ehrmann, S. C. (1997). Implementing the seven principles: Technology as lever. *American Association for Higher Education*. Online at: *www.aahe.org/technology/ehrmann.htm*.

Ehrmann, S. C. (1997). Asking the right question: What does research tell us about technology and higher learning? Online at: *www.learner.org/edtech/rscheval/rightquestion.html*.

Hedges, K., & Mania-Farnell, B. (1998). Using e-mail to improve communication in the introductory science classroom. *Journal of College Science Teaching, 28*, 198–202.

Labianca, D. A. (1998). How to make nonscience majors more receptive to organic chemistry. *Journal of College Science Teaching, 27*, 397–400.

Schutte, J. G. (1996). Virtual teaching in higher education: The new intellectual superhighway or just another traffic jam? Online at: *www.csun.edu/sociology/virexp.htm*.

Wegner, S. G., Halloway, K. C. , & Garton, E. M. (1999). The effect of internet-based instruction on student learning. *Journal of Asynchronous Learning Network, 3*(2), 98–106.

Windschitl, M. (1998). The www and classroom research: What path should we take? *Educational Researcher, 27*(1), 28–33.

Constructing and Implementing a Web-Based Social Policy Course: A Pilot Test in Cyberspace

Maria Roberts-DeGennaro
San Diego State University

Abstract

This article reports on the construction and implementation of a Web-based graduate social policy course. In developing the online teaching strategy, the framework of a constructivist model of computer-mediated instruction was used to conceptualize the design of the course. The author used formative and summative approaches in pilot testing this course in cyberspace, with the intent of teaching it online later as a regularly scheduled semester course. The author contends that careful planning and critical thinking are paramount in computer-mediated instruction, if this method of delivering courses in higher education is to be successful and meaningful.

Computer-mediated education has existed in a limited form since the 1980s in the United States. The evolution of distance education has expanded the reality of an individual's undeniable right to learn (Sherow & Wedemeyer, 1990). In reviewing this evolutionary process, Sherron and Boettcher (1997) suggest correspondence courses, and educational radio and television were generations one and two, respectively. The third generation, between 1985 and 1995, to use computers for instruction were systems that were located on a single campus or in a single classroom. However, the tools and technical expertise required to support multimedia presentations, such as streaming audio and video, were expensive and time consuming. Currently, the fourth generation, 1995 to 2005, of users of computer-mediated education is characterized by the extensive use of the Internet as a primary transport mechanism.

This latter generation has created an explosion in the use of information- and computer-based technologies. Present trends indicate that future students will get their education on three campuses:

1. residential college community,

2. global electronic campus, and

3. continuing education and training provided at their workplace by employers and community organizations (Rossman, 1992).

The fallout from this explosion is that the investment in the use of technology in higher education is time consuming and expensive. The entire digital plant infrastructure of the educational institution needs to support online learning, as well as prepare faculty, students, and staff for this new format (Boettcher, 2001). Administrators need to be supported in their efforts to design, develop, and deliver online degrees and courses. Faculty need to learn how to use the technology, and subsequently, to implement and integrate it into courseware appropriate for online learning (Gilbert, 2001). This investment will ultimately create opportunities for enriching the course learning, enhancing instructional methods, and transforming how, when, and where people learn. Lambert (2000) envisions a day when the academic environment will use a variety of media and employ a variety of teaching styles.

Seaberg's (2001) national survey on the use of the Internet in graduate social work education suggests that little is known about the experiences of social work faculty with the use of computer-based instruction and that some social work faculty appear to be moving beyond the beginning stages of using computer-based instructional technology. He advocates that more should be done to facilitate the convergence of using technology in social work education. Likewise, McNutt (1996; 2000) supports the position that social work educators must use the new technologies to prepare students for practice in the information age.

Tracy and Pine (2000) contend that it is critical for social work students and faculty to use the Internet for obtaining information on model social welfare policies and programs, and research studies, as well as information from electronic databases. These activities will stimulate an interest in policy practice and an increase in the transfer of information to and from sites around the world.

Faculty teaching social policy courses could offer creative learning opportunities for students to analyze proposed legislation or changes to existing legislation through the Internet and then develop advocacy strategies by using the electronic media to politically influence the direction of this legislation. Hamilton and Fauri's (2001) survey found that the strongest predictor of political participation by social workers was their sense of efficacy. This suggests the importance of teaching the principles of policy practice and developing learning activities in which students can see the results from exercising their political voice.

Raymond, Ginsberg, and Gohagan (1998) contend that social work educators are struggling to keep pace with the impact of this technology explosion in preparing students for practice in a technology-enhanced environment. They suggest that the profession of social work needs models for training social work educators to use technology across the curriculum, as the interest in methods for using the Internet to teach social work courses increases.

Seaberg (1999) who has taught clinical research courses completely via the Internet, believes that social work education needs to increase the experiential base of a variety of faculty testing the virtual classroom as a teaching medium on a variety of content areas with a variety of students. Descriptions of these experiences could then lead to refinements in identifying what seems to work and why. His position is not that social work education is on the cusp of a paradigm shift in teaching models, but rather that the virtual classroom may add to our repertoire of teaching models.

This article reports on the construction and implementation of a Web-based social policy course section in the School of Social Work at San Diego State University. In addition to this Web-based section, six on-campus sections of this course were taught in the fall 2000 semester. This social policy course is a required course for all first-year students in the first semester of their graduate program. In developing the online teaching strategy, the framework of a constructivist model of computer-mediated instruction was used to conceptualize the design of the course. The author used formative and summative approaches to evaluate the course, particularly the planning and instructional processes. The pilot testing of this Web-based course was conducted in order to produce some useful information for refining the course before it is taught as a regularly scheduled semester course. The author contends that careful planning and critical thinking are paramount in computer-mediated instruction, if this method of delivering social work education is to be successful and meaningful.

Constructivist Model of Computer-Mediated Instruction

Distance education courses support learner-centered environments that accommodate both the learners' various needs and motivations for enrolling in these courses (Hodes, 1997–98). Royse (2000) who taught a Web-based social work research course, asserts that online learning has advantages. Students can participate in an online course at any hour of the day or night. This provides greater accessibility for students who work or who need to be at home after work to care for children or elders. Likewise, students who have a difficult time traveling due to distance can easily access online courses. Bricout (2001) suggests students with disabilities can benefit from computer-mediated education, if accommodations support online learning.

Thus, in a Web-based learning environment, students can set their own pace and interact with prepared materials as often as they choose. However, online learning goes beyond simply accessing information and control. Anderson and Garrison (1998, p.100) believe that the key issue in distance education is the quality of the learning experience, that is, the ability to critically judge information and construct knowledge and action. They support the position that educational theory is shifting to a collaborative constructivist conception of learning. This orientation assumes that shared control is the prerequisite to online learning if students are expected to assume responsibility for constructing meaning.

The constructivist perspective rejects the view that knowledge can be transmitted in whole from the instructor to the learner. This perspective focuses on the individual's responsibility to construct meaning as well as authentic reciprocal communication for the purposes of confirming understanding and generating worthwhile knowledge. Prawat (1992) suggests that curriculum should be viewed as a matrix of ideas to be explored over a period of time rather than as a road map.

Learning in a Web-based environment then becomes an active process in which both the instructor and the students participate. In this process, a "web of learning" is created (Palloff & Pratt, 1999, p. 6). Learning through a computer-mediated course is not a passive experience. Besides logging on to the course, students are expected to contribute to the learning process by posting their thoughts and ideas to online discussions, and participating in online chats with the instructor and other students.

Palloff and Pratt (1999, p. 82) suggest the learner is responsible for using the guidance from the instructor in a meaningful way in a Web-based course. This means that learners are responsible for actively seeking solutions to problems contained within the knowledge area being studied and raising the level of those solutions to one of more complexity. Learners are expected to view problems and questions from a number of perspectives and to question the assumptions underlying these perspectives. Thus, the learner is constructing new forms of knowledge and meaning. However, ". . . we must guard against 'naive constructivism' where educators have a blind faith in the ability of students to construct meaningful knowledge on their own" (Garrison, 1995, p. 138).

The challenge for distance educators is to set up a cognitively rich learning environment to facilitate the distant students' construction processes (Zhang, 1998). Raymond and Pike (1997, p. 282) suggest this new educational paradigm of using technology for teaching purposes necessitates a rethinking of the nature of higher education, the roles of teachers and students, the learning environment, and the ownership of intellectual property. In distance education, students do become active participants in the learning process and are more accountable for the learning outcomes. Through electronically supported instruction, students can access information independently with the instructor serving more as a facilitator and less as a purveyor of information. Therefore, students will embark on an active process that increases their chances for a lifetime of learning (Chamberlin, 2001).

Even though the instructor should be concerned with all aspects of the educational transaction in a Web-based course, the role best performed by the instructor is monitoring and guiding the cognitive aspects of the students educational experience. Garrison (1989) believes, "It is the challenging of perspectives and the presentation of alternative viewpoints that the student is not likely to perform adequately by him or herself independently. In all of this, however, it must be remembered that it is the communication process that facilitates such interactions and that presents a special challenge to the distance educator" (p. 35).

Planning the Development of a Web-Based Social Policy Course

In designing any Web-based course, the primary concerns should focus on the general aims of the curriculum content and how it is to be structured and delivered. Careful and comprehensive planning of a Web-based course requires a systematic, organized method. The instructor (author) was provided course release time of three semester units (20%) in the spring 2000 semester to draft a set of course modules for a graduate social policy course through a grant funded by the California State University Commission on Extended Education through the Chancellor's Office. However, a second semester of course release time would have been useful in refining the courseware materials. The transformation of these courseware materials to Blackboard, which is a software platform for e-learning, required some additional time during the summer before the course was pilot tested in the fall 2000 semester.

Schieman (1990, pp. 67–68) suggests several guidelines for developing an online course. These guidelines were adapted by the author in constructing the Web-based course including:

- Articulate a rationale for designing a Web-based course that incorporates the expected outcomes of the course.

- Articulate a set of learning objectives listing the values/ethics, skills, and knowledge areas that students are expected to achieve in the course.

- Develop the teaching strategies to be employed and the courseware materials that are appropriate for the number of course units and the intended learning outcomes of the course.

- Develop an evaluation plan, certainly of a formative type that includes a summative component. The intent of the evaluation must be to evaluate not only the performance of the learners but also the check and balance of the course with the focus on improving the method of online instruction.

- Re-examine the entry behaviors of the learners as an on-going activity in order to understand the analyses later of the learning outcomes and changes needed for the course.

The instructor considered each of these guidelines in formulating the course syllabus. Since the instructor had delivered the curriculum content of this graduate social policy course in a traditional on-campus setting for several years, there was a history of teaching experience which was valuable in developing the courseware materials for this online course. Using this history, the instructor conceptualized the transformation of the course content to a different method of delivering the course.

A critical component in constructing a Web-based course is to create an effective syllabus. The instructor (author) followed five basic steps in creating the course syllabus for the Web-based course:

1. define purpose, outcomes and objectives for the course,

2. choose appropriate reading materials,

3. select a set of course assignments with clear guidelines for grading,

4. develop policies for grade distribution, and

5. establish a topic-driven course outline with readings. Palloff and Pratt (1999) suggest that the most successful online courses are guided by a syllabus that is topic driven.

An example is to create a weekly schedule that includes a discussion topic for the week with readings geared to spark discussion of that topic. Another example is to structure the course around the required readings allowing the material in the readings to create the discussion.

The instructor basically used the same syllabus for teaching the two on-campus sections and the Web-based section of this social policy course. Chamberlin (2001, p. 32) recommends a "one-course-for-all approach" in which the instructor uses the same syllabus and course guidelines for all students, regardless of whether they are enrolled on-campus or online.

Course assignments should be designed to support and guide the online learning process. These assignments are crucial in providing feedback to the instructor as to what the students are learning and how they are applying what they are learning in the virtual classroom. The following assignments were created to sustain this learning process.

1. Three quizzes were administered on the Blackboard course site on prescheduled days between 8 a.m. and 9 p.m. Each quiz was timed so

that the students had a specific number of minutes to complete it. The timer on Blackboard starts recording the minutes after the student accesses the quiz. Each quiz was accessible under "Course Documents" as Quiz I, Quiz II, and Quiz III on the Blackboard course site. The quizzes were scheduled about a month apart during the semester.

2. Students were required to prepare a social policy analysis using a specific framework provided by the instructor to analyze a bill that would either affect existing social policy or propose new social policy legislation. This bill was expected to be under debate either at the state or federal level of government. It was expected to have a direct impact on the provision, planning and/or evaluation of health and human services in the U.S. The students were expected to seek approval from the instructor as to the appropriateness of the bill for the assignment before conducting the social policy analysis. The instructor provided over 20 World Wide Web sites as "External Links" within the Blackboard course site to assist the students in researching a bill being debated at the federal or state level of government. References consisting of government documents, refereed publications, World Wide Web sites, and other sources were expected in preparing the social policy analysis. By a specific due date, the social policy analysis was sent as an attachment in an e-mail message to the instructor.

3. Students were required to add a discussion thread to ten Forums on the "Discussion Board" on Blackboard. The student's participation on the "Discussion Board" was important in facilitating interaction among the students enrolled in the online course. Students were required to either express their viewpoint or raise a question and then discuss the issues related to a particular Forum. The students were required to document the ten Forums in which they started a discussion thread and then e- this list to the instructor. The instructor confirmed this list by checking the online record of discussion threads to each Forum.

4. After preparing the social policy analysis, students were required to send an e-mail message to their elected representative(s) to support or oppose the proposed social policy legislation. To assist the students in identifying their elected state/district representative, the instructor provided a set of Websites as "External Links" on Blackboard that located the representatives according to the student's zip code. A framework was provided by the instructor for the students in preparing this electronic advocacy assignment. A copy of the e-mail message, when it was sent to the representative, was required to be sent to the instructor as evidence of completing the assignment.

5. Students were required to create a Homepage on the Blackboard course site. These Homepages provided an avenue for the students to provide some information about themselves, including photographs. In addition, students posted information related to the proposed piece of legislation that they were analyzing. A Homepage is a resource that offers an opportunity for students to learn about other students in the virtual classroom, which is comparable to learning about other students in a traditional on-campus classroom.

The instructor recruited first-year graduate social work students to participate in the pilot testing of the Web-based course by providing an orientation to the course at the first class session of two on-campus social policy course sections taught by the instructor in the fall 2000 semester. Five students volunteered to participate in the pilot testing after observing the demonstration of the course on Blackboard at this orientation. Thus, after this initial face-to-face orientation, the instructor and the five students only met in cyberspace.

Instructional Process in Delivering a Web-Based Social Policy Course

The instructional process in delivering any Web-based course involves a sustained dialogue between the instructor and the students. The instructor must be committed to supporting and guiding the learning process through feedback on an ongoing basis during the delivery of the Web-based course. Through the learning process, the instructor facilitates the flow of the course and evaluates learning outcomes.

In performing these functions, the instructor needs to be competent enough in the use of the technology to assist the students to work through technical dilemmas. This requires the availability of sufficient administrative and technical support, as well as adequate equipment and software. Most important, the instructor needs to exhibit a positive attitude towards using the technology.

As mentioned previously, Blackboard was used to deliver this Web-based course through cyberspace. This e-learning software platform provided the organizational structure through which participants (instructor and students) could engage with the course material and with one another. Making the virtual classroom real for the students involves a high degree of feedback and reinforcement in cyberspace. Hantula (1998) suggests this can be facilitated through posting messages, asking questions, and raising points of discussion. Blackboard records each "hit" made by either the students or the instructor. Therefore, the instructor could closely monitor the students' virtual attendance. Using the "Communication" feature on the Blackboard course site, the instructor sent weekly e-mail messages to the students, such as reminders of assignments that were due in the near future. In addition, the instructor used the "Announcements" feature on Blackboard to post messages.

It is important to list the terms of service (netiquette) for the students who are enrolled in an online course site. These terms could include:

1. Vulgar, obscene or indecent language or images are prohibited on the course site;

2. All information entered on the course site by any student user can be viewed by the instructor;

3. The number and type of "hits" by student users are monitored by the instructor on the course site; and

4. Names and e-mail addresses of student users are available to all students enrolled in the Web-based course.

Besides posting a set of terms under "Announcements" on the Blackboard course site, the instructor posted the software requirements for accessing the courseware materials, including the graphics and multimedia presentations. In addition, it is crucial to emphasize to the students the importance of installing antivirus software on their computers.

The instructor created a survey to gather data from students on their use of computers. It was posted as a survey under "Course Documents" on the Blackboard course site. The students were asked to complete it on Blackboard during the first week of the course. The survey data were useful to the instructor in understanding the computer equipment and software used by the students. For example, the data provided information on the word processing software used by the students for submitting written course assignments, the type of connection the students were using to access the Internet, the capacity of the computer used by the students, etc. Overall, this small group of students had a diverse background in their use of computers.

The instructor used the format of a topic-driven course outline. This format provided the students with a weekly schedule that included a discussion topic for the week with readings geared to spark discussion. Based on this schedule, a PowerPoint presentation of lecture materials with graphics was created by the instructor for each week. At the beginning of each presentation, the weekly readings were posted along with reminders of assignments that were due in the near future. Then a set of PowerPoint lecture materials was presented that addressed topics in the required readings, as well as related topics. In each weekly presentation, there was a list of study questions covering the required readings. These weekly PowerPoint presentations were accessible under "Course Documents" on the Blackboard course site. Seaberg's (2001) survey of the use of the Internet in graduate social education found that the most commonly used computer-based teaching tool was PowerPoint presentations of lecture outlines and other course materials.

For the pilot test of this Web-based course, the instructor produced four video clips with the assistance of staff from the University's Instructional Technology Services. In these video clips, the instructor was taped while giving an oral presentation based on a written script prepared by the instructor. This script was displayed through a teleprompter so that the instructor could read the script while being filmed. The purpose of these video clips was to provide a personal message from the instructor. The first video clip was an orientation to the course. The other video clips were instructions for completing the course assignments that reinforced the written information in the online courseware materials. Thus, these video clips served the function of providing an audio-visual message to the students from the instructor to remind them of the guidelines for completing the assignments comparable to an instructor in a traditional on-campus course setting. These video clips were accessible under "Course Documents" in the Blackboard course site. Written transcripts of these video clips were also accessible under "Course Documents" if the students experienced technical problems in playing the video clips.

The instructor posted Forums on the "Discussion Board" on the Blackboard course site. Students were then expected to add discussion threads to these Forums. For example, one Forum was related to the National Association of Social Worker's Code of Ethics, with an "External Link" connecting the students to this Website. The students were expected to critically reflect on these ethics and then discuss some ethical issues and policy implications related to social work practice. The use of this "Discussion Board" is referred to as asynchronous discussion, that is, students can read and comment on a topic under discussion at their leisure. Online discussions help students understand that they are communicating with real people in cyberspace. They become part of an educational cyber-community of learners (Knowlton, Knowlton & Davis, 2000).

In contrast, synchronous discussion or chat is used where the students log on to a course site at once and interact with each other in real time. The instructor used the "Virtual Classroom" (Chat Room) feature on the Blackboard course site several times during the semester. These sessions can be stimulating and challenging when used as office hours in cyberspace. If group projects are assigned, the Chat Room can be used by the groups to chat about tasks related to their project.

Evaluating the Pilot Testing of the Web-Based Social Policy Course

An ongoing process of planning and review occurred while pilot testing the Web-based course so that it could be refined, before the instructor taught a regularly scheduled section of this online social policy course in the fall 2001 semester. The more we can identify the processes that lead to good student outcomes, the more likely we will be able to replicate effective teaching strategies for online learning. In gathering data, a formative approach was used to evaluate the content, structure, and delivery of the course at various points throughout the course. This information was especially important for the instructor, who was learning how to teach an online course while teaching the course. In addition, a summative approach was used to determine whether the expected learning outcomes were achieved, as well as the level of student satisfaction with the course (Stocks & Freddolino, 1998).

Formative Approach to Evaluate a Pilot Testing of a Web-Based Course

Palloff and Pratt (1999) suggest that a formative evaluation can surface gaps in the course material or in the learners' ability to grasp the material. This latter approach to evaluation is particularly meaningful when it asks how students are experiencing the course, the mode of instruction, and the online environment. One of the most effective methods of gathering the evaluative data from this pilot test was through electronic communications. In e-mail messages, the instructor requested feedback from the students as the Web-based course progressed throughout the semester. Sustaining dialogue between the instructor and the students is critical to the success of online learning and teaching.

In addition, students provided feedback on the course during prearranged chat sessions that occurred every few weeks during the semester. Originally, a specified time each week was established for the one-hour chat session, but the instructor discovered that the best time for the instructor was not necessarily convenient for the students. After conducting a brief survey of the students' preferred days and times, the instructor rescheduled a different set of one-hour chat sessions. Since this was a pilot test of the course with only five students, it was fairly easy to manage the sessions. However, if there are more than 25–30 students in a Web-based course section, it might be advantageous on a few occasions to organize several small group sessions in the Chat Room with specific students participating in a session.

Overall, the administration of the timed quizzes was effective. However, technical problems occurred if a student attempted to perform some other function while completing a timed quiz as the quiz would close before the student completed it. As a result, warnings were then posted in e-mail messages to the students regarding technical difficulties that could occur if they performed other functions while completing the timed quizzes.

The discussion threads added by the students on the Forums reflected critical thinking. It is important to state guidelines for the students in starting these threads, such as establishing a specific number of threads to a specific number of Forums. The instructor provided positive feedback to the students when they started a thread of discussion. This is similar to a traditional classroom where the instructor says, "Good question".

Stating specific requirements for completing the social policy analysis assignment was critical in ensuring that the students understood the expectations for the assignment. Also, by having the students investigate a bill that was currently in debate at the federal or state level of government, it prevented potential problems with students possibly purchasing or using previous papers. After completing the social policy analysis, the students sent it as an attachment as a word processor file in an email message to the instructor. The instructor made comments on the analysis. After grading it, the instructor returned it to the student.

In completing the electronic advocacy assignment, the students e-mailed their elected state/district representative a position statement related to a proposed piece of legislation that they investigated. The instructor provided a framework for the students in constructing the e-mail message to their representative.

The weekly PowerPoint presentations were posted on the Blackboard course site at least two weeks in advance, This gave the students a few weeks to read and review these lectures. Previous weekly lectures were not removed from the Blackboard course site so that students could refer back to these when preparing for the quizzes.

Data collected from this formative evaluation will be used to fine-tune the course before it is taught as a regularly scheduled semester course. The primary purpose of implementing a monitoring evaluation system is to provide ongoing and useful feedback (Grinnell, 2001). The next section describes the data collected through the pilot testing of an assessment tool, which was administered and completed online.

Summative Approach to Evaluate a Pilot Testing of a Web-Based Course

All five of the students who participated in the pilot testing of the Web-based course successfully completed the course. In order to gather some summative data on the students' experiences in the online learning environment, the instructor developed a tool, Assessment of Computer-Mediated Instruction Form. The instructor intends to use this tool as one of the instruments to assess the Web-based course when it is taught as a regularly scheduled semester course. Royse, Thyer, Padgett, and Logan (2001) stress the importance of pilot testing a newly drafted questionnaire on a small group of subjects who represent the study population.

Overall, the five students in the pilot testing of the Web-based course reported that they devoted about three hours each week to the online course. This included the time used to view the weekly PowerPoint lecture materials and to interact online with the instructor or other students in the course, but excluded the time spent reading the chapters in the textbooks. Since students in a comparable on-campus course would spend about three hours attending a weekly class session, it appears that the time the students devoted to online learning was comparable to traditional pedagogical learning.

Four of the five students suggested they were satisfied either to a great or some extent with the level of online interaction with the instructor. All of the five students suggested they were satisfied to some extent with the level of online interaction between the students. Overall, the primary problem or frustration reported by the students in completing the online course was not having weekly direct face-to-face contact with the instructor or the other students. These findings stress the importance of working to create sustained dialogue in a virtual classroom. In the future when existing technology is affordable and/or accessible, it will be possible to have face-to face cyberspace interactions with students in a virtual classroom.

Four of the five students accessed the Chat Room and suggested it was useful to some extent. The most useful feature of the Chat Room was that it provided an opportunity for the students to "talk" to the instructor and the other students. Four of the five students suggested that the Discussion Board was useful to a great or some extent. Likewise, the most useful feature of the Discussion Board was that it offered the students an opportunity to discuss topics, receive feedback, and express opinions. Both the Chat Room and the Discussion Board appeared to serve an important function in creating a virtual classroom.

There were varied opinions regarding the usefulness of the video clips. Three of the five students suggested that these clips were useful to a great or some extent. The other two students suggested that reading the written scripts of the video clips was just as useful as viewing or listening to the clip.

Four of the five students suggested that the PowerPoint lecture notes were useful to a great or some extent. These PowerPoint presentations:

1. served to organize the course content,

2. provided a focus to the weekly topics, and

3. augmented the readings.

Students suggested that the course assignments, including the quizzes, social policy analysis, and electronic advocacy, increased their understanding of social policy. Thus, these assignments seem appropriate in assessing student learning related to the curriculum content of this Web-based course.

The students unanimously reported that they would enroll in another online course, primarily, because it provided them more-control of the learning process. They could decide when it was the best time to access the course and review the courseware materials. Also, the students agreed that they would recommend this online course to another student. Even though the students suggested the course offered a convenient way to learn the courseware material, they also reported that they had to be responsible for keeping up with the readings and weekly lecture notes, as well as staying on task to complete the assignments.

Recommendations for Teaching a Web-Based Course

Based on the construction and implementation of this Web-based social policy course, the author suggests the following strategies might be useful in developing an online course and delivering it in cyberspace.

- Provide an orientation to the Web-based course that provides information about the dynamics of participating in the learning environment of computer-mediated instruction.

- Construct a course syllabus that reflects an organized and systematic structure for presenting the curriculum content in cyberspace.

- Establish clear guidelines in the course assignments and identify how online participation is figured into the grading policy.

- Build a course site that does not require a high level of technical skills to navigate.

- Create a virtual classroom environment in which there is sustained dialogue between the participants in the Web-based course.

In planning and implementing any technology change, Lick (2001) suggests the following is the first question to be addressed: "What learning must take place before this change effort can be successfully implemented?" (p. 24). For social work educators to use technology in their classrooms, they must be trained to use it. The pursuit of technology competence is warranted, but it requires a commitment of time and motivation from the instructor (Zhao, 1998). In turn, this requires resources, such as equipment with the capacity to perform the technical functions, and appropriate software to create the courseware materials. Likewise, administrative support is required if the institution "walks the talk" about its perceived role in transforming distance education and collaborating in the global electronic campus.

However, technology simply provides only an alternative method for delivering a course. Hantula (1998) suggests that it is not the technology alone that enables the virtual classroom, but rather the networking of technologies and participants in the online learning environment. As virtual classrooms proliferate, it is increasingly important to equip students with positive attitudes toward the use of computers and a level of technical skills that will enable them to use digital tools in the information age.

Contracting with course developers who lack both teaching experience and a history of building curriculum content in a particular area should be avoided. The author firmly believes that the inputs to each Web-based course in social work education are unique so the course cannot be canned or packaged. Pre-packaged self-instructional materials are essentially designed for a mass market and do not support the assessment of student learning in a professional school.

Social work educators should be encouraged to be innovative and to experiment with this medium of online teaching. The author's experience in pilot testing a Web-based course for one full semester has laid a strong foundation for the author to refine the course and to offer it as a regularly scheduled semester course in the fall 2001 semester. When it is offered, the author will be conducting a comparative research study investigating the differences and similarities between two Web-based sections and an on-campus section of this social policy course exploring: (a) student attitudes toward computers, (b) demographic profiles of online and on-campus students, and (c) summative data related to the Web-based course.

Note

Since pilot testing this Web-based course, the author has taught it three additioanl times as a regularly scheduled course. A comparative research study was conducted to analyze the outcomes between on-campus sections and online sections of this course. See Roberts-DeGennaro, M., & Clapp, J. (in press). Assessing the Virtual Classroom of a Graduate Social Policy Course. *Journal of Teaching in Social Work*.

References

Anderson, T., & Garrison, D. R. (1998). Learning in a networked world: New roles and responsibilities. In C. Campbell Gibson (Ed.), *Distance learners in higher education: Institutional responses for quality outcomes* (pp. 97–112). Madison, WI: Atwood Publishing.

Boettcher, J. (2001). New classics and personal favorites: An annotated bibliography for online teaching and learning. *Syllabus, 14*(7), 36–38.

Bricout, J. (2001). Making computer-mediated education responsive to the accommodation needs of students with disabilities. *Journal of Social Work Education, 37*(2), 267–281.

Chamberlin, W. S. (2001). Face-to-face vs. cyberspace: Finding the middle ground. *Syllabus, 15*(5), 10–11 & 32.

Garrison, D. R. (1989). Understanding distance education: A framework for the future. New York: Routledge.

Garrison, D. R. (1995). Constructivism and the role of self-instructional course materials: A reply. *Distance Education, 16,*(1), 136–140.

Gilbert, S. W. (2001). Sacrifice time to integrate technology? Why bother? *Syllabus, 15*(4), 24.

Grinnell, R. (2001). *Social work research and evaluation: Quantitative & qualitative approaches.* Itasca, IL: F. E. Peacock Publishers.

Hamilton, D., & Fauri, D. (2001). Social workers' political participation: Strengthening the political confidence of social work students. *Journal of Social Work Education, 37*(2) 321–332.

Hantula, D. (1998). The virtual industrial/organizational psychology class: Learning and teaching in cyberspace in three iterations. *Behavior Research Methods, Instruments, & Computers, 30*(2), 205–216.

Hodes, C. (1997–98). Developing a rationale for technology integration. *Journal of Educational Technology Systems, 26*(3), 225–234.

Knowlton, D., Knowlton, H., & Davis, C. (2000). The whys and hows of online discussion. *Syllabus, 13*(10), 54–58.

Lambert, M. (2000). Context versus content—A fresh look at the ongoing debate over place-based vs. distance education. *Syllabus, 13*(10), 24.

Lick, D. (2001). Leading change: Creating the future for education technology. *Syllabus, 15*(5) 22–24.

McNutt, J. (1996). National information infrastructure policy and the future of the American welfare state: Implications for the social welfare policy curriculum. *Journal of Social Work Education, 6*(3) 375–388.

McNutt, J. (2000). Organizing cyberspace: Strategies for teaching about community practice and technology. *Journal of Community Practice, 7*(1), 95–109.

Palloff, R., & Pratt, K. (1999). *Building learning communities in cyberspace: Effective strategies for the online classroom.* San Francisco: Jossey-Bass.

Prawat, R. S. (1992). Teachers' beliefs about teaching and learning: A constructivist perspective. *American Journal of Education, 100*(3), 354–395.

Raymond, F., Ginsberg, L., & Gohagan, D. (1998). Introduction. In F. Raymond, L. Ginsberg, & D. Gohagan (Eds.), *Information technologies:*

Teaching to use—Using to teach (pp. 1–5). New York: Haworth Press.

Raymond, F., & Pike, C. (1997). Social work education: Electronic technologies. In R. Edwards (Ed.), *Encyclopedia of social work*, 19th edition, 1997 supplement (pp. 281–299). Washington DC: National Association of Social Workers Press.

Rossman, P. (1992). *The emerging worldwide electronic university: Information age global higher education.* Westport, CT: Greenwood Press.

Royse, D. (2000). Teaching research online: A process evaluation. *Journal of Teaching in Social Work, 20*(1/2), 145–158.

Royse, D., Thyer, B., Padgett, D., & Logan. T. K. (2001). *Program evaluation.* Belmont, CA: Wadsworth.

Schieman, E. (1990). Instructional development concerns. In D. R. Garrison, & D. Shale (Eds.), *Education at a distance* (pp. 67–76). Malabar, Florida: Robert Krieger Publishing.

Seaberg, J. (1999). *The virtual classroom, asynchronous teaching via the Internet.* [Online] Available: http://www.people.vcu.edu/~jseaberg/virtom.htm

Seaberg, J. (2001). *Use of the Internet and other teaching tools in graduate social work education.* [Online] Available: http://www.people.vcu.edu/~jseaberg/teaching-survey.htm

Sherow, S., & Wedemeyer, C. (1990). Origins of distance education in the United States. In D. R. Garrison, & D. Shale (Eds.), *Education at a distance* (pp. 7–22). Malabar, Florida: Robert Krieger Publishing.

Sherron, G., & Boettcher, J. (1997). *Distance learning: The shift to interactivity.* CAUSE Professional Paper Series #17. Boulder, CO: CAUSE. [Online] Available: http://www.educause.edu/ir/library/pdf/PUB3017.pdf

Stocks, J., & Freddolino, P. (1998). Evaluation of a World Wide Web-based graduate social work research methods course. In F. Raymond, L. Ginsberg, & D. Gohagan (Eds.), *Information technologies: Teaching to use—Using to teach* (pp. 51–69). New York: Haworth Press.

Tracy, E., & Pine, B. (2000). Child welfare education and training: Future trends and influences. *Child Welfare, 79*(1) January/February, 93–113.

Zhang, P. (1998). A case study on technology use in distance learning. *Journal of Research on Computing in Education, 30*, 398–416.

Zhao, Y. (1998). Design for adoption: The development of an integrated Web-based education environment. *Journal of Research on Computing in Education, 30*, 307–327.

Utility of Course Web Resources for Students with Learning Disabilities

Charles M. Slem and Steven T. Kane
California Polytechnic State University, San Luis Obispo

Abstract

One way to cope with the unprecedented influx of college students with learning disabilities is to develop individual course management tools that are designed for all students but would be especially helpful for students with learning disabilities. An example of this approach capitalizes on the common medium of the Internet to provide 24-hour access to Web resources which support an introductory psychology class. In addition to wide use and high evaluations by students in general, these resources were more heavily used by students with learning disabilities. Compared to students who did not report a learning disability, these students rated the usefulness of the resources more highly and believed that the resources gave them more control over their course work.

According to a 1999 study by the American Council on Education, students with learning disorders are attending college in unprecedented numbers (Henderson, 1999). In fact, as many as 4% of college students and 10% of adults nationwide suffer from a learning disorder (American Psychiatric Association, 1994). Although recent research has explored the usefulness of assistive technologies for learning disabled students (e.g. speech recognition software, computerized text readers, etc.), few studies have investigated the utility of Web-based course support materials (Raskind and Higgens, 1998). Given the nature of college-level instruction, a significant challenge to universities is to develop and provide effective resources to assist these students in achieving their academic goals.

Traditionally, "extra-course" assistance, e.g. note takers, books on tape, tutors, etc. have been used to help students master course content. Another strategy is to develop general course-management tools that are designed to help all students master the course material but would be especially useful for students with learning disabilities. The emerging use of the World Wide Web offers a common medium providing students with 24-hour access

Charles M. Slem and Steven T. Kane, *Utility of Course Web Resources for Students with Learning Disabilities.* (2001, August). Paper presented at the Annual Conference of the American Psychological Association, San Francisco, CA (ERIC Document Reproduction Service No. ED346082). Reprinted by permission of the authors.

to such resources. One example of this approach as it pertains to students with learning disabilities can be seen in the implementation of supporting Web resources for a large introductory psychology course.

The course Web resources were designed to integrate the lecture component of the introductory course with the accompanying textbook resources. Special design considerations were made for simplicity, functionality, and a student-oriented perspective that linked course resources with student goals. The lecture component of the course Web resources contained lecture outlines, links to library resources, related campus resources, sample exams, instructor-based resources, and relevant World Wide Web links. The textbook component included chapter outlines, concept synopses, graphs and figures, definitions of key terms, links to related concepts in other chapters, sample test questions, World Wide Web sites, access points to Web-based tutorials, and additional commentary. Students could seamlessly navigate from the instructor developed lecture resources to the supporting textbook resources. A particular topic covered in the lecture portion of the course was linked to the Web resources developed to support the textbook's treatment of the same topic. supporting resources, e.g. sample test questions, links to library components, etc. were also conveniently linked to the text and lecture components.

While not designed specifically for students with learning disabilities, it is possible that the highly integrated structure and content of these Web resources could provide students with learning disabilities an additional tool to master course concepts. It was predicted that compared to students who did not report any known or suspected learning disabilities, students with learning disabilities would report more frequent use of the Web resources and more highly rate the utility of the Web resources. In addition, these students were predicted to more likely believe that the Web resources gave them more personal control over the course, increased their learning, and enhanced their educational experience.

Method

Routine surveys evaluating the Web resources surveys were administered to 240 students during fall quarter, 1999, and winter quarter, 2000. In addition to the standard evaluation questions, students were asked if they knew or suspected they had some sort of learning disability. On a six-point scale, the degree of severity ranged from "very minor and does not affect my college performance" to "a significant disruption that may force me to leave the university." Other questions included a rating of increased personal control, increased learning, and the belief that Web pages would enhance their educational experience ("strongly agree" to "strongly disagree").

Results

Of the 227 students responding to the survey question, 54 (25.8%) reported a suspected or known learning disability (Table 1). Table 2 summarizes use patterns of the students enrolled in the introductory course. The Web resources were used to some degree by over 95% of the students. While approximately 67% of the students who did not report learning disabilities were heavy or moderate users, 83% of the students reporting learning disabilities reported heavy or moderate use. Table 3 summarizes the differences between the two groups on rating items. The students reporting learning

Table 1. Perceived severity of learning disability in respondents indicating a learning disability ($n = 53$)

Number	Percentage	Perceived Severity
12	22.2	"Very Minor and does not affect college performance."
20	37.0	"A disruption that requires extra effort in some classes but does not affect my overall performance."
10	18.5	"A significant disruption that requires great effort to get the grades I want."
9	16.7	"A significant disruption that has forced me to settle for grades that are lower than I know I am capable of."
2	3	"A significant disruption that may force me to leave Cal Poly."

Table 2. Use patterns of Web resources in percentages

Usage	Total Percentage of Respondents	Learning Disabled Respondents	Non-Learning Disabled Respondents
Heavy	25.6	39.6	22.1
Moderate	43.2	43.4	44.8
Light	28.6	17.0	30.5
Little/None	2.6	0.0	2.6

$N = 240$

Table 3. Summary of the differences between learning disabled and non-learning disabled

Item	Mean of LD	Mean of Non-LD	DF	t value	rob.
Usefulness	1.75	2.13	190	3.26	.001
Increased Control	1.72	2.06	102	2.59	.01
Increased Learning	1.83	2.02	102	1.28	.20
Enhanced Educ.	1.69	1.89	102	1.96	.12

$N = 240$

Note: LD = learning disabled respondents.

disabilities significantly used the Web resources more heavily than the other students (z = -2.9 [corrected for ties] p = .004, Mann-Whitney nonparametric test). On a seven-point scale rating usefulness (Figure 1), students in general rated the Web resources as being useful, mean = 2.06. In comparing the students who identified themselves as having a known or suspected learning disability versus those who did not, the learning disabled students rated the usefulness of the Web resources significantly higher, t = 3.26, df = 190, p <. 001.

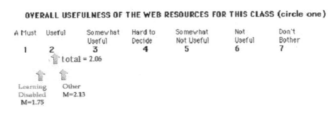

Figure 1. Overall usefulness rating

Most students generally agreed that the Web resources increased their sense of control, increased their learning of course material, and enhanced their education. The group identified as possessing some learning disability reported significantly stronger agreement with a sense of increased control, t = 2.59, df 204, p <. 01. There were no significant relationships between perceived severity and any other variable.

Discussion

The course Web resources were widely used and rated highly by students. This supports the notion that well designed and task-relevant Web resources will be perceived as helpful by students in general. As predicted, students reporting known or suspected learning disabilities found the Web resources even more helpful and used them more heavily.

There may be a concern that because of their information processing deficits, learning-disabled students would be less likely to use computer and Web-based course support systems. This is not likely the case in general, as research by Suthakaran and Sedlacek (1999) found that learning disabled students were just as efficacious in their computer use as their non-disabled peers.

It is speculated that in addition to the underlying model which drove the overall logic and design of the Web resource platform, there may be specific characteristics that are key to their perceived success by students with learning disabilities:

- The structure of the Web resources is highly organized and mirrors the organization of the course.

- Key concepts are clearly identified and concisely explained in small, more manageable chunks within the context of the actual text structure.

- There are multiple interactive sample examinations that not only identify the most likely concepts to be tested in the format in which they will be tested, but also have interactive links back to the appropriate text material.

- The platform is organized so that relevant resources are immediately accessible when the student is likely to need them.

It must be pointed out that the Web resources described here are not similar to the current Web course-management platforms offered by most universities or the major publishers. Those platforms appear to be designed for efficient data storage rather than flexible and interactive Web tools. Their organization is not set up to closely mirror the course, and it is not clear that they would provide the kind of assistance the Web resources described in this study offered. Greater attention to the needs of students and course goals is necessary to fulfill the potential of Web-based learning tools.

References

American Psychiatric Association. (1994). *Diagnostic and statistical manual of mental disorders* (4th ed.). Washington, DC: Author.

Henderson, Cathy (1999). *College freshman with disabilities: A biennial statistical profile*. Washington, DC: American Council on Education.

Raskind, M. H. & Higgins, E.L. (1998). Assistive technologies for post-secondary students with disabilities: An overview. *Journal of Learning Disabilities, 31*, 27–40.

Suthakaran, V. & Sedlacek, W.E. (1999). Computer aversion among students with and without learning disabilities. *Journal of College Student Development, 40*, 428–431.

Student Participation in a Discussion-Oriented Online Course: A Case Study

Dawn Poole
California State University, Stanislaus

Distance learning has been around for centuries. It has evolved from primarily text-based correspondence courses to videotape-based instruction and now compressed video transmission that allows for two-way audio and video connections between the teacher and the learner (Schlosser & Anderson, 1994). Because of advances in hardware and software, the Internet also can be an effective distance-learning medium.

Computer-mediated communication has the potential to transform education by creating learner-centered instructional environments (Van Gorp, 1998). Van Gorp continues, "The Web is now more than an area to access and post information: It is a place to interactively communicate and construct knowledge" (p. 12). Computer conferencing can be used to foster intellectual development, learner autonomy, and equal opportunities for students to participate in discussion (Cifuentes, Murphy, Segur, & Kodali, 1997). Furthermore, "computer conferencing provides students with opportunities to elaborate on and defend their positions to other students and to negotiate meaning with teachers and fellow students" (p. 186).

The body of knowledge about how students engage in learning in online courses is rather modest at this time. Because the use of telecommunications tools in higher education coursework has the potential to address teaching and learning in ways that are different from traditional instruction, it is critical to develop a solid understanding of what transpires during courses offered through this delivery medium.

This study examined the nature of student participation in an online course. Several research questions were examined:

- In what ways did students choose to access and engage in course materials?
- How did students participate during the week in which they moderated the discussion?
- What were the contents of the students' bulletin board posts?
- How did student participation contribute to the class as a community of learners?

Reprinted with permission from the *Journal of Research on Computing in Education*, vol. 27, no. 3, copyright © 1995, ISTE (International Society for Technology in Education), 800.336.5191 (U.S. & Canada) or 541.302.3777 (International), iste@iste.org, www.iste.org. All rights reserved.

Method

The Course

EDIT 5110, Social Perspectives of Technology in Education, was a 2-unit graduate course offered in fall 1998 at California State University Stanislaus. It was a required course for students pursuing a Master of Arts in Education with emphasis in Educational Technology. There were no face-to-face class meetings; however, it was not an independent study course. Collaboration and discussion were incorporated into the online course design.

Each week, students read articles dealing with social, ethical, or legal perspectives of technology and they completed an online quiz designed to assess their understanding of the articles' content. Students were required to post at least two messages per week to the online bulletin board. Each class member moderated or co-moderated one of the weekly discussions, which took place after the quiz on the topic had been completed. In addition, students wrote a position paper and a midterm examination with a partner and they completed an individual project dealing with a social issue regarding technology in education. For class purposes, the week began at 12:01 a.m. Sunday and ended at midnight Saturday. EDIT 5110 was the only course in the master's program offered entirely online.

The first requirement of the semester was for students to post a biography to the course bulletin board, an exercise to acquaint them with class members and also to familiarize them with the Website's features. Social, ethical, and legal topics were selected for their timeliness and discussion potential. Several controversial topics were purposely included so that multiple perspectives could be shared and understood. Some examples included the neutrality of technology, gender and technology, and filtering in relation to the First Amendment.

All online interaction was controlled through a course Website that students accessed using a browser and a password. The software, WebCT, allowed for threaded discussions (asynchronous), live chats (synchronous), quizzes, and more. All communications and contributions were stored and tracked for analysis after the semester had concluded.

Participants

Fourteen graduate students were enrolled in the course, 10 females and 4 males. All were K-12 teachers, with experience varying from less than 1 year to over 20 years. All students were interested in obtaining a Master of Arts in Education with emphasis in Educational Technology. EDIT 5110 was the first online course taken by each of the students, though some had engaged in other Web-based activities prior to their enrollment.

Data Collection and Analysis

The study was primarily a qualitative analysis of student participation in the course. Statistical analyses were performed on some of the data as well to gain a more comprehensive understanding of what transpired. The purpose of the study was to understand how students chose to engage themselves with the course materials and with each other.

All of the bulletin board contributions during the semester were collected and coded. E-mail messages sent to the course instructor were saved and tabulated. Surveys were sent to all class members at the end of the semester to gather information regarding student perception of the online course experience, and three students chose to write a follow-up analysis of their participation.

Observations and Interpretations

Accessing Course Materials

One of the reasons online courses have become popular is that students can participate when it is convenient for them to do so. In this course, bulletin board posts and quizzes needed to be completed by midnight each Saturday, providing flexibility based on individuals' schedules and preferences. Most of the students in the course accessed the class Website several times each week and contributed far more messages to the bulletin board than were required. Over a 15-week time period, students posted a total of 1,025 messages to the bulletin board. More posts were made on Saturdays than any other day; however, other than a midweek lull on Tuesdays, students participated in the discussions throughout the week (Figure 1). Computer conferencing systems extend class time, which may lengthen the time students spend engaged in course content (Cifuentes, Murphy, Segur, & Kodali, 1997).

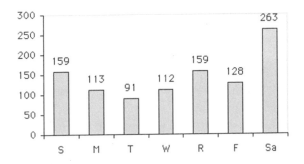

Figure 1. Number of student posts to the bulletin board by day of the week

As varied as the day of the week in which students posted messages was the time of day in which they participated. Most of the students were teaching during daytime hours on weekdays; this resulted in fewer posted messages during daytime hours than evening hours on weekdays. This pattern continued during the weekends as well (Figure 2).

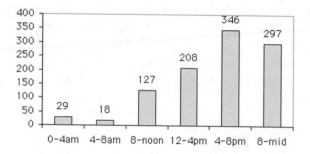

Figure 2. Time of day in which student posts were made to the bulletin board.

Students primarily accessed course materials from their home computers. Access from their school computers or campus computers was relatively minimal (Figure 3). Campus computers were the primary access option for two students who did not have access to the Web at home. These two students checked the course Website fewer times than other students throughout the week.

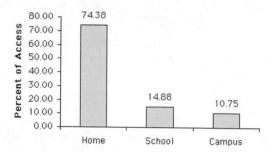

Figure 3. Location of computers used to access course materials, by percent of total access.

Students became very active participants in the class. They were required to post a total of 27 messages during the semester. Table 1 indicates that the average number of posts per student was nearly 73 messages. The table also indicates how many of the 1,458 total posts (which included student posts, instructor posts, and visitor posts) each student read. The Number of Total

Table 1. Summary of involvement in the class bulletin board, by student

Gender	Number of Posts	Average Number of Lines Per Post	Number of Articles Read	Number of Total Hits
F	35	14	1156	1347
F	27	12	499	576
M	78	19	1356	1746
M	37	8	682	827
F	59	13	1406	1584
F	121	15	1394	1649
F	221	10	1695	1999
M	63	12	1009	1160
F	109	14	1441	1792
F	42	13	522	624
F	38	20	471	648
F	20	16	409	486
M	41	18	1022	1151
F	125	10	1508	1817
AVG	72.6	13.9	1040.7	1243.3

Hits column indicates the combined total of number of articles read, the number of posts made, and the number of course home page accesses (which linked them to the bulletin board, synchronous chat, quiz section, and course calendar).

Student participation varied from person to person, which happens in all classroom settings, but the online medium gave each of them a voice (Piburn & Middleton, 1998; Schlagal, Trathen, & Blanton, 1996; Thomas, Clift, & Sugimoto, 1996). Some of the students chose not to read all of the posts. In a traditional class format, students are less likely to ignore verbal responses from students than they were in the online class. In EDIT 5110, students were unaware that the number of posts that they read could be tracked. It is possible that some of them may have read a higher percentage of the posts had they known this. On the other hand, the number of posts became quite large, one of the possible dangers of online learning (Kimball, 1995). There was no direct relationship between course grade and reading each message, so students may have completed other tasks in lieu of reading the messages.

The correlation between the number of posts a student contributed and the average number of lines per his/her posts was $r = -0.318$, a moderately negative relationship between the two factors. The students who were the most frequent contributors to the class bulletin board had somewhat shorter messages than did the students who made fewer posts. The students who were very active in the discussion often wrote one- or two-line reactions to other messages. Those who were less active did not tend to exhibit this behavior as frequently.

WebCT includes a synchronous chat feature, which can be tracked by the instructor. Although students were encouraged to use this option as they worked with their partner on the position paper and midterm essay, only two chat room conversations were initiated for this purpose. Most of the students visited the chat rooms early in the semester to see how they were designed but did not view the feature as an appealing option for course communication. Instead, most pairs collaborated via e-mail only, while a handful of face-to-face meetings and phone conversations facilitated the development of these projects.

Involvement as a Moderator

A review of the literature regarding online learning indicated that students became more involved and responsible for their participation when the entire course was not instructor-driven (Cifuentes, Murphy, Segur, & Kodali, 1997; Rohfeld & Hiemstra, 1995). For this reason, each class member was responsible for moderating or co-moderating the discussion for one week. Moderator duties were assigned based on student topic preferences.

Early in the semester, students read two articles outlining the responsibility of the moderator to prepare them for their role. It was up to individual students, however, to decide how to fulfill the position. Table 2 indicates

Table 2. Comparison of student participation during moderator and non-moderator weeks

Student	Number of posts during moderator week	Average number of posts per week during non-moderator weeks	Average number of lines per post for moderator week	Average number of lines per post during non-moderator weeks
1	7	2.33	20	12
2	6	1.75	13	12
3	17	5.08	25	18
4	9	2.33	7	8
5	12	3.92	14	13
6	35	7.17	18	13
7	15	17.17	16	9
8	21	3.50	13	11
9	28	6.75	19	12
10	4	3.17	19	12
11	11	2.25	22	19
12	N/A*	N/A*	N/A*	16
13	9	1.67	20	17
14	19	8.83	12	9
AVG	14.50	4.76	16.8	12.9

*This student's participation was affected by personal matters not related to the class, and she eventually withdrew.

that students' participation in the class changed during the week of their moderator obligation. The number of posts made by moderators during their assigned weeks averaged 14.5, whereas students each posted an average of only 4.76 messages per week during periods when they were not moderating the discussion. This was a highly significant difference ($t = 4.261$, $p < .0011$). In addition, students' posts were significantly longer during weeks when they were moderating the discussion ($t = 5.019$, $p < .0003$).

The student moderators provided "the intellectual impetus, the ideological framework from which the discussion would progress" (Tagg, 1994, p. 43). Students took their role very seriously, as indicated by these differences in participation. Upon completion of the course, one student reflected, "The duties of the moderator really allowed us to follow one discussion so carefully that we literally behaved as the instructor. I enjoyed the fact that the instructor had enough confidence in students to engage [us] in this process." The moderator role not only facilitated a learner-centered environment, it also served as an empowering opportunity for students.

Content of Posts

There were several ways to examine the contents of the bulletin board messages. One analysis was based upon the work of Thomas, Clift, and Sugimoto (1996), who coded computer-mediated conversations into several focus areas. Based on their model, EDIT 5110 messages were coded as one or more of the following:

> *Article.* Material that specifically mentioned one of the article authors or content directly from one of the readings.

> *Content.* Information that related to the course readings, but was not directly elicited by the article.

> *Technical.* Messages related to the Website.

> *Procedural.* Announcements, logistics, and course requirements.

> *Non-Academic.* Messages that did not directly relate to the class; generally social in nature.

The bulletin board messages were, overall, very focused on course content (Table 3). Student posts that were related to the content of the readings or to the articles themselves comprised 85% of the total student messages.

Table 3. Percentage of instructor and student posts by category

	Article	Content	Technical	Procedural	Non-Academic
Instructor	12.7	62.5	7.0	9.7	8.1
Students	14.9	69.7	4.4	1.9	9.1

The content of the bulletin board messages was more focused on academics than the messages that were sent to a listserv used in a science and mathematics teaching methods course (Piburn & Middleton, 1998). However, the online medium was used only as a supplement to instruction in that study rather than as the sole delivery mechanism, as in EDIT 5110. The degree to which student contributions relate to actual content may depend highly on the purpose of the computer-mediated communication.

There were relatively few posts related to technical issues, partly because of student experience with technology, and also because WebCT was relatively easy to use. The bulk of the technical posts related to America Online disconnections during quizzes, bulletin board features, and occasional server problems. The other main technical thread was a student-initiated request to eliminate old bulletin board messages in an effort to decrease the number of listed messages.

Procedural posts were almost entirely made by the instructor. Each week a post was made outlining the tasks to accomplish during that week. Other procedural posts dealt with completion of the course questionnaire, suggestions for final project topics, and information dealing with the Master's program in general.

The bulk of posts in the non-academic category related to the scheduling of two social gatherings: one at a conference and one after the semester ended. Other posts in this category dealt with information about the Miller Analogies Test, an exam required for acceptance into the Master's program, and ride sharing to another class that many of the students were taking.

An additional coding system was used to analyze the verbal interactions included in the messages. Bellack, Kliebard, Hyman, and Smith conducted a three-year study of the teaching process through an analysis of the verbal interaction between teachers and students (1966). They examined what the speakers said, and how that dialog contributed to the class. Although the study was done over three decades ago, their observations serve as a basis for language patterns in classrooms. It is possible that the shift to more student-centered learning has changed the interactions between teachers and students since the 1966 observations. Many college courses, however, are still delivered via lecture, and would likely yield similar findings.

The authors categorized the verbal interactions into four categories, called pedagogical moves:

Structuring: Setting the context for behavior by initiating or stopping interaction. An example is to begin class by focusing on a topic or problem.

Soliciting: Verbal prompts designed to elicit a verbal response. Questions, commands, imperatives, and requests fall under this category.

Responding: Addressing soliciting moves.

Reacting: Responses caused indirectly by structuring, soliciting, or responding. Clarification, synthesis, and expanding on ideas serve as reacting moves, while a responding move is always elicited by a solicitation.

Each bulletin board message was coded with one or more of the pedagogical moves. In the 1966 study, teachers performed 61.7% of the moves. In this online course, the teacher performed only 29.6% of the moves, while students performed the remaining 70.4%. This mirrored Piburn & Middleton's (1998) findings regarding the ratio of faculty to student contributions to their listserv, indicating the potential of Web-based instructional media to change the role of the teacher.

Table 4 depicts a comparison of the conversation that occurred in the three instructional environments: the online course (bulletin board), the listserv (as a class supplement), and the traditional classroom. In traditional classrooms, teachers solicit and react, whereas the teachers' role in the two online media environments included only a small percent of soliciting moves. In the online course, teacher moves were balanced between structuring, soliciting, and responding, a difference

Table 4. Percentage of move types by instructor and students in the bulletin board, on the listserv and in traditional classrooms

	Instructor				Students			
	Structure	Solicit	Respond	React	Structure	Solicit	Respond	React
Online	4.6	5.4	5.7	13.9	4.9	14.7	7.9	42.9
Listserv[1]	0.0	3.6	15.2	10.9	7.6	23.9	15.2	23.9
Classroom[2]	4.8	22.8	3.5	22.6	0.4	4.4	25.0	5.7

[1] Piburn & Middleton (1998).
[2] Bellack, Kliebard, Hyman, & Smith (1966).

from the other two studies. Among students, the online group generated a much higher percentage of reacting moves than in the other two groups. In the online course, each structuring and soliciting move often elicited responses or reactions from multiple students.

An online setting often provides less restrained communication between students than in a more traditional setting, and it allows students to function without the influence of a dominant point of view such as that of the teacher or other class member (Buckley, 1997). The difference in moves made by teachers and students in the various class settings supports this position. Students seem to take control more in electronic conversations, consistent with constructivist approaches where teachers and students take on different classroom roles (Piburn & Middleton, 1998).

Class as Community

Because online students do not share a physical connection to their class-mates, community building needs to occur differently than it does in traditional classes. However, studies indicate that communities do develop among students involved in computer-mediated conferencing systems (Herrmann, 1998; McDonald & Gibson, 1998; McGinnis, 1996; Schlagal, Trathen, & Blanton, 1996). An examination of what contributes to a sense of community can help to strengthen online course design.

One measure of the sense of community among the students is the use of class members' names in bulletin board messages. Of the 1,025 student posts, 448 messages (44.1% of the student posts) included the mention of 500 class-member names (some messages contained more than one name). Referring to other class members is a strong indicator that students felt connected with their classmates, and it is a successful technique in online courses (Paulsen, 1995). It is likely that students repeatedly included others' names because of the unified atmosphere it created among and between class members.

Because visual and verbal cues are absent from online learning environments, it is common for groups to develop some way of expressing their emotions and feelings (Cifuentes, Murphy, Segur, & Kodali, 1997). In some cases, students may use emoticons, computer keystrokes that resemble things like smiley faces, to help convey meaning. In EDIT 5110, emoticons were used in only 5.3% of the posts. It is possible that this was due to the large percentage of posts related to the course content. When students did use emoticons, it was mostly to lighten the tone. Some people believe that the use of emoticons has a "flattening" effect on the emotional content of a message (Buckley, 1997), illustrated in the following post. "I enjoy having the opportunity to think things through before writing to an audience of "peers". However, I am finding it challenging to not have the opportunity to interact with you face-to-face. I find that I miss the "humanity" of it all... the real laughs and chuckles vs :)."

The "humanity" component, as in the above quote, came up repeatedly in discussions. One student wrote, "I agree that the in-depth level of inter-action between us can not occur in spontaneous classroom debate or dialogue. (But I still miss not hearing the emotion in the voices, and especially not being able to put faces with the opinions!)." Students appreciated the passionate messages that were made possible because of the reflection time facilitated through the medium. Conversely, the physical presence of others could not fully be replicated online. Related to how physical presence contributes to class community, one student observed:

As I was sitting waiting for the famous Tuesday night class to begin, I was struck by the fact that many of us who had engaged in some rather serious discourse online were just sitting and chatting about rather innocuous topics when we came face to face. Now granted, the class had not begun, and we were not in a formal seminar, but it seemed rather ironic, or interesting, that when we did get in a setting where we could read each others faces, and hear sarcasm, etc (all the things that we said were missing from posted messages) that not much was happening on an intellectual level.

It appeared that though the students felt they were missing out on a human component in traditional classes, their perception of the interactions that take place in them did not necessarily parallel the reality.

The author of one of the required readings suggested posting messages using a pen name to provoke discussion in online courses (Paulsen, 1995). After reading the article, a female student requested the creation of an account for "Darren Smith," which she would manage. A biography was posted for this fictitious class member, a conservative, somewhat chauvinistic male who was thinking about becoming a teacher. Messages under his name were posted throughout the semester, often containing content that generated lots of discussion among class members. Though Darren's name was never listed on the course Website where completed partner products were posted, the possibility that he was fictitious did not occur to students. Darren's real identity was revealed at a social gathering after the semester had ended. Several students were amused, especially in light of some of Darren's opinions. This feeling was not shared by all, however. One male student was offended to find out that Darren was not a real person. In a reflective analysis after the completion of the class, he wrote:

> When I learned that a fictitious character had been added to our class, I understood the motivation of expanded perspective for group discussion, but felt duped. I expended considerable personal energy trying to help restore this make-believe person's place or credibility in the group. (I truly sweat over the comments I posted in attempt to reconcile this wayward sheep, though I wondered how he could have been so "stupid" or unaware.) I was not amused to learn that I had befriended or come to the aid of a figment of someone's imagination.

Because online communities are based largely on trust between and among students and instructors (Cifuentes, Murphy, Segur, & Kodali, 1997), the process of introducing false identities to provoke discussion is questionable. In this case, the discussion was very rich without the introduction of a "provoker." Other techniques suggested by Paulsen, such as the use of student moderators and visiting experts, might be more conducive to community building. If fictitious students are created to spur discussion, it is suggested that they be announced to class members.

Two topics during the course generated a fair amount of disagreement and friction between students: gender issues related to technology, and filtering. These disagreements actually contributed to the development of the class community. The gender discussion unfolded over approximately a three-week period. The first week was a discussion of the neutrality of computers/technology, and included several gender-related items. The next set of articles dealt with gender from a critical theory perspective. The third week focused on equity in general, and certainly gender was one aspect included with this topic.

The critical theory articles, in particular, addressed societal issues that went beyond the use and creation of technology. Many students contributed passionate messages to the bulletin board during this discussion, some of which were uncomfortable for others to read. A post from the "imposter" student suggesting that the natural role of the female is to be in the home initiated one controversial discussion thread. Another male student responded, "I was afraid that you'd "started something" here! Now, I'm wanting to come to your aid – I think it's that "male-bonding" thing!?!" He went on to gingerly but effectively infuse his opinion with that of the imposter and three female students who had previously reacted to the message. This student did not defend the initial post, but rather offered another interpretation of the discussion that had transpired. He concluded the message by suggesting that the males in the class wear "heavy armor" for the next few days.

Ironically, in a long-term study of community building on a listserv, conflict occurred during a gender-related discussion of invited speakers to a conference (Herrmann, 1998). The tone on the listserv was different during this part of the discussion than it was at other times. It took a suggestion to disband the listserv to resolve the conflict. Although EDIT 5110 would not have ended because of disagreements, students' willingness to participate in future discussions may have been compromised by the dissenting ideas. Instead, it created a stronger bond between class members, as they negotiated meaning and understanding with each other. Comments such as, "Sorry, DC, I respectfully disagree..." were common.

The class became enough of a community for class members to inform others when they would be away from the discussion. One student wrote, "Oh, by the way, I'm signing off for a few days. I'm moving (ugh!) and my telephone service won't be connected. . . ." Another wrote, "I'm off on a deer-hunting trip, so I will miss all of the chatter for the next four or five days. . . . Students apologized for technical or other difficulties which limited their participation. It is unlikely that they would have felt compelled to share this information if they had not felt a sense of community, or if students believed their posts were merely perfunctory.

McDonald & Gibson explored group dynamics and development in a computer conferencing course (1998). Their results showed that specific criteria could be identified regarding group dynamics, and that these patterns are manifested in both face-to-face and computer conferencing environments. Though the study here did not focus on these patterns specifically, it was clear that a community of learners developed among and between class members.

Discussion

The proliferation of online courses requires an understanding of the unique learning environment that computer-mediated communication facilitates. Awareness of student participation patterns can help online course designers capitalize upon the strengths of the medium.

Access to course materials varied widely from student to student, but indicated an overall commitment to learning. The number of student posts to the bulletin board far exceeded expectations. Students checked in throughout each week to more effectively follow the discussion threads. Readily available Web access is an obvious consideration in such courses; in fact home computers are almost a necessity for students to participate to the extent that they did in EDIT 5110. In traditional class settings, students sometimes are reluctant to contribute, either because they do not want to lengthen the class or because they feel their response will not reflect what they want to say. The flexible participation schedule afforded by computer-mediated communication tools can lengthen class time, while the reflection time may encourage more widespread participation by all students.

Despite the availability of a synchronous chat feature, students did not choose to arrange live conversations with their classmates. They preferred the more time-independent communication facilitated through the bulletin board and through e-mail. Synchronous chats should be scheduled only when they are necessary to build student understanding.

Requiring student participation as a moderator, after providing students with a foundation regarding what the role entails, can have a positive impact on discussions. Moderators posted more and longer messages than when these students were not moderators. The use of student moderators eliminated the need for the instructor to assume the leadership role alone.

It is likely that moderator responsibilities also contributed to students' sense of community, since it was a common experience for all class members.

Online courses can certainly foster discussion related to course content. A very high percentage of posted messages dealt directly with the required readings. The online medium facilitated a shift in the traditional student and teacher functions in the class. The students took an active role in the course. The medium may not only facilitate student participation; it may also encourage instructors to change their role as the teacher.

The Web-based delivery medium did not inhibit the development of the class as a community. In many ways, it actually contributed to the formation of a cohesive group. Students referred to each other in their bulletin board posts, indicating an effort to maintain the dialogue as conversation rather than as distinct and unconnected messages. Though they could not read facial expressions or gestures, students' written responses were such that class members could interpret meaning, emotion, and sarcasm. Because the development of online communities is based largely on trust, care must be taken to maintain this atmosphere throughout the course. In EDIT 5110, this trust may have been breached through the introduction of a fictitious student.

One of the best examples of community development surfaced during an extended discussion of gender issues related to technology. Though student positions were often in opposition, class members were very respectful of each other and made an effort to at least understand the alternative view. Traditional class structures sometimes encourage emotional outbursts, whereas the online medium enabled students to respond with passionate but well-supported positions. All voices were heard, not just those of the most vocal students.

There is still much to learn about the impact of online courses on student learning. Course designs that allow for flexible student-centered participation may effectively take advantage of the learning environments that can be facilitated through online course tools.

References

Bellack, A. A., Kliebard, H. M., Hyman, R. T., & Smith, F. L. (1966). *The language of the classroom*. New York: Teachers College Press.

Buckley, J. (1997). The invisible audience and the disembodied voice: Online teaching and the loss of body image. *Computers and Composition, 14*(2), 179–88.

Cifuentes, L., Murphy, K. L., Segur, R., & Kodali, S. (1997). Design considerations for computer conferences. *Journal of Research on Computing in Education, 30*(2) 177–201.

Herrmann, F. (1998). Building on-line communities of practice: An example and implications. *Educational Technology, 38*(1), 16–23.

Kimball, L. (1995). Ten ways to make online learning groups work. *Educational Leadership, 53*(2), 54–56.

McDonald, J., & Gibson, C. C. (1998). Interpersonal dynamics and group development in computer conferencing. *The American Journal of Distance Education, 12*(1), 7–25.

McGinnis, J. R. (1996). Promoting an electronic community with the use of communication technology in a graduate elementary science methods class. *Journal of Elementary Science Education, 8*(1), 39–63.

Paulsen, M. F. (1995). Moderating educational computing conferences. In Z. L. Berge & M. P. Collins (Eds.) *Computer mediated communication and the online classroom, Volume III: Distance Learning* (pp. 81-89). Cresskill, NJ: Hampton Press.

Piburn, M. D. & Middleton, J. A. (1998). Patterns of faculty and student conversation in listserv and traditional journals in a program for preservice mathematics and science teachers. *Journal of Research on Computing in Education, 31*(1), 62–77.

Rohfeld, R. W., & Hiemstra, R. (1995). Moderating discussions in the electronic classroom. In Z. L. Berge & M. P. Collins (Eds.) *Computer mediated communication and the online classroom, Volume III: Distance Learning* (pp. 91-104). Cresskill, NJ: Hampton Press.

Schlagal, B., Trathen, W., & Blanton, W. (1996). Structuring telecommunications to create instructional conversations about student teaching. *Journal of Teacher Education, 47*(3), 175–183.

Schlosser, C. & Anderson, M. (1994). *Distance Education: Review of the Literature.* Washington, DC: Association for Educational Communications and Technology.

Tagg, A. C. (1994). Leadership from within: Student moderation of computer conferences. *The American Journal of Distance Education, 8*(3), 40–50.

Thomas, L., Clift, R., & Sugimoto, T. (1996). Telecommunication, student teaching, and methods instruction. An exploratory investigation. *Journal of Teacher Education, 47*(3), 165–174.

Van Gorp, M. J. (1998). Computer-mediated communication in preservice teacher education: Surveying research, identifying problems, and considering needs. *Journal of Computing in Teacher Education, 14*(2), 8–14.

WebCT [Computer Software]. (1996–1999). Vancouver, British Columbia: WebCT Educational Technologies.

Critical Examination of the Use of Online Technologies in Diverse Courses at a Large Comprehensive University

James M. Monaghan and Rowena S. Santiago
California State University, San Bernardino

Abstract

We explore cases of three classes that implemented online teaching/learning technologies as part of a university wide faculty development grant program. We examined students' satisfaction with key components of the learning experience. Instruments included students' pre-assessments and post-assessments, an instructors' post survey, course syllabi, grant proposals, and instructors ' end-of-grant reports. We present implications for campus wide implementation of online teaching/learning technologies. We include discussion of a model for implementing innovative technologies campus wide (online teaching support model).

Background

In 1997, faculty interest in online teaching at California State University, San Bernardino (CSUSB) started increasing. By 1999, the number of faculty who wanted to do online teaching had grown significantly. Faculty faced many questions and issues as they embarked to do online teaching. The Teaching Resource Center (TRC), the faculty development unit that supports teaching and innovative instruction, also faced the task of helping in faculty's new role as online teachers.

To address these needs, TRC drew upon instructional design and evaluation models (Van Slyke, Kittner & Belanger, 1998; Belanger & Jordan, 2000; Dick & Carey, 1996; Salisbury, 1996; Seels & Glasgow, 1998) and identified the major steps involved in course development as applied to online teaching. TRC developed a systematic and holistic plan that serves both as the map and the glue that holds the various phases and players together (Santiago, 2001). This systematic plan has seven major steps

Planning and Preparation. The instructor studies the big picture and the instructional and non-instructional issues that will have an impact on successful online teaching. Addressing issues up front gives a good estimate of how much time and effort need to be invested, and helps determine one's readiness for online teaching.

Funding. Faculty are encouraged to seek funding through grant programs that lead to a course buyout, money for resources and/or hiring a student assistant

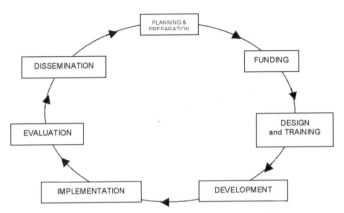

Figure 1. Online teaching support model: Seven major steps

Instructional Design and Training. Designing lessons for online teaching is not simply converting existing materials into digitized format. Skills and training for goal analysis, task analysis, assessment, instructional materials development, and the use of hardware and software are addressed in this step.

Instructional Materials Development and Testing. This step involves developing instructional materials, testing them, and making sure that they can be delivered successfully online and that users will be able to access them with minimal instructional and technological glitches.

Implementation. The course is actually taught online. The instructional design is put into action, the instructional materials are used, and technology is relied upon to deliver instruction, all towards the achievement of learning goals.

Evaluation. Evaluation identifies the strengths and weaknesses of the instructional design, instructional materials, and delivery medium. Most importantly, it measures the extent to which goals were met.

Dissemination. Innovation and change that is well planned and appropriately evaluated also results in lessons learned and quality products. When reported to a professional community, this leads to further validation, peer evaluation, and replication, which then leads to scholarship of teaching (Hutchings and Schulman, 1999).

Description of Grant Program

To support online teaching, TRC sponsors the Web-based Course Development Grant program that awards summer stipends ($5,000) to faculty. The course redesign or development can range from using a significant combination of online features as teaching enhancement to delivering the whole course online. When first offered in 1999, 12 faculty proposals were funded. The Course Development Grant Program was funded by the Office of the Provost. Administrative support for online teaching also resulted in student support through the Student Technology Support Center, the establishment of an Office for Distributed Learning and the hiring of a librarian to support distance courses.

Analysis of the Efficacy of the Grant Program

To inform our analysis of the efficacy of the online components of the courses, we utilized a variety of assessment tools including pre and post surveys of students, a post survey of faculty, and an analysis of course syllabi, grant proposals and final reports.

Comparison data from the three classes in which we had sufficient data from both the student pretest and posttest are listed below. We report results from a comparison of the uses of online technologies in the three courses. We examined student data (pretest and posttest), faculty data (free response and multiple-choice questions), course syllabi, and the course development proposal. Our intention was to utilize triangulation in an attempt to ascertain factors that led to successful and efficacious uses of online technologies from both the faculty and the student perspectives.

Three classes that were offered in the 1999-2000 academic year were examined. The description of each course is listed as it appeared in the course syllabi and/or the catalog of programs:

1. English as a Second Language (EESL)—Research in English as a Second Language: Covers various perspectives used to guide research in TESOL. Includes analysis, discussion, reflection and writing about key issues and concepts in research. Students will design and carry out literature review working towards a theoretical framework to gain foundation as expert practitioner or future researcher.

2. Criminal Justice (CJUS)—Research Methods in Criminal Justice: Introduction to scientific methodology and research designs used to conduct basic and applied research in the criminal justice field.

Emphasis on scientific operationalization, survey methodology, and concepts of evaluation design.

3. Information Sciences (INFO)—Decision Support Systems: Formal information systems that support organizational decision-making. Topics include the strategy, framework, design, implementation and evaluation of decision support systems. Students will create and apply decision support systems to planning, coordinating, organizing, controlling and/or directing tasks.

Pre-Survey

Table 1. Student demographics

Demographics		CJUS	EESL	INFO
Level	Graduate	3%	91%	5%
	Senior	40%		90%
	Junior	47%		5%
Degree sought	Masters	10%	100%	15%
	Bachelors	90%		75%
Age	40s & 50s		27%	20%
	30s	7%	45%	15%
	20s	87%	27%	65%
Gender	Male	43%	18%	45%
	Female	53%	82%	55%
Miles from campus	> 50 mi.	10%	18%	5%
	40-49 mi.	3%	9%	10%
	30-39 mi.	17%	0%	20%
	20-29 mi.	17%	9%	5%
	10-19 mi.	20%	0%	15%
	< 9 mi.	27%	55%	40%

In the student pre-survey, we obtained data on three categories: student demographics, student background, and student experience on the use of technology. A summary of demographic data for 61 students who took the pretest in the 3 classes is listed in Table 1.

As shown in Table 1, the majority of the students were in upper division working for a bachelor's degree except for the Education masters students (EESL). Most of the students were in their 20's and 30's. Female students were in the majority, especially in the Education course. Almost half of the students live close to campus (< 9 miles) except for the CJUS students who are distributed in various distances from campus.

Table 2. Student background

Background		CJSU	EESL	INFO
Reason for taking course	Recommended	27%	9%	25%
	Required	83%	100%	70%
	Interesting	17%	18%	30%
	Fits schedule	37%	18%	60%
Hours to spend on course	>= 17 hrs	3%	36%	0%
	13-16 hrs	3%	9%	0%
	9-12 hrs	23%	36%	10%
	5-8 hrs	57%	18%	75%
	0-4 hrs	13%	0%	15%
Same instructor before	Yes	37%	73%	10%

For background data, we surveyed students' reasons for taking the course, the number of hours that they intended to spend on the course per week, and whether they had had the instructor before. Data from this component of the survey is listed in Table 2.

In general, students were taking the course because it was required. A secondary reason was that it fit their schedule. The majority of the undergraduate students planned to spend 5-12 hours per week on the course, with graduate students planning to spend more than 17 hours per week on their course. Most of these graduate students had had a course with the instructor before.

We also surveyed students' use of and comfort level with online technologies. A summary of students' use of technology is given in Table 3.

Based on the data, student access to computers and Internet at home is very high (87–100%). Of the three groups, the graduate students had the most experience in the use of online technology in a course. Online experience is high for research and email use in all three courses. Students are most comfortable in the use of computers, Internet and email.

Post Survey

In the student post survey we coupled the internally developed and tested Student Evaluation of Learning Effectiveness (or SELE, a self report measure of learning that utilized a five-point Likert scale and which had been approved for use in evaluation of teaching by the Faculty Senate), with a self-report instrument concerning technology use in the course.

One particularly striking result involves the post survey item concerning how well the online learning experiences fostered interaction and teamwork among class members. In INFO, this was unmistakably the most highly

JAMES M. MONAGHAN · ROWENA S. SANTIAGO

Table 3. Student use of technology

Use of technology		CJUS	EESL	INFO
Access at home				
	Computer	93%	91%	100%
	Internet	87%	91%	90%
Used in previous course				
	Online syllabus	47%	73%	40%
	Online lectures	33%	73%	30%
	Online tests	7%	82%	20%
	Online research	70%	91%	80%
	Online discussion	10%	36%	20%
	Email	77%	91%	80%
	Chat rooms	23%	9%	25%
Comfort level				
(5=highest)	Using computers	4.3	4.0	4.8
	Using internet	4.3	3.9	4.7
	Using chat rooms	3.2	3.4	4.1
	Using email	4.1	4.6	4.6
	Taking online course	3.2	3.8	3.6
	Joining online discussion	2.8	3.5	3.7

rated item (mean = 4.5 of 5). In the other two courses, EESL and CJUS, this was clearly the lowest rated item (mean = 3.1 of 5, mean = 2.9 of 5, respectively). In comparing scores of both EESL and CJUS with INFO, two tailed t-tests indicated significance with $p <. 01$.

We found the highest mean posttest scores in the answers to three questions that related to the structure of the courses and to the involvement of the teacher in the learning process.

To the question: "The course matched objectives with assessment", the mean for CJUS was 4.2, for EESL, it was 3.9, and for INFO, it was 4.3. "Utilizing clear grading criteria was also rated high by all three courses, with INFO mean at 4.4, CJUS at 4.1 and EESL at 3.9. All three courses had almost the same means for the question "Instructor contributed to learning"

Table 4. Online components of course fostered interaction and teamwork

Course fostered interaction and teamwork			
	CJUS	EESL	INFO
5=Excellent	29%	18%	59%
4=Very Good	0 %	9%	35%
3=Satisfactory	21%	45%	6%
2=Poor	29%	18%	0%
1 =N/A	21%	9%	0%
Mean	2.9	3.1	4.5

Table 5. Satisfaction with course items controlled by instructor

	CJUS	EESL	INFO
Matched objectives with assessment			
5 = Excellent	50%	27%	41%
4 = Very Good	36%	36%	47%
3 = Satisfactory	7%	36%	12%
2 = Poor	0%	0%	0%
1 = N/A	7%	0%	0%
Mean	4.2	3.9	4.3
Utilized clear grading criteria			
5 = Excellent	43%	55%	47%
4 = Very Good	36%	0%	41%
3 = Satisfactory	14%	27%	12%
2 = Poor	0%	18%	0%
1 = N/A	7%	0%	0%
Mean	4.1	3.9	4.4
Instructor contributed to learning			
5 = Excellent	43%	36%	35%
4 = Very Good	50%	36%	53%
3 = Satisfactory	0%	27%	12%
2 = Poor	0%	0%	0%
1 = N/A	7%	0%	0%
Mean	4.2	4.1	4.2

(CJUS = 4.2, EESL = 4.1, INFO = 4.2). In tandem, this data would be an indicator of clear grading criteria that connected with stated objectives of the courses.

The lowest means reflected responses to whether the online components of the course "Fostered discussion on multicultural and diversity issues".

When it came to identifying who contributed to the learning experience, the instructor was ranked highest, based on the mean scores. EESL ranked "self" equally with the instructor, while CJUS ranked "self" as second and other students as lowest. Interestingly, concerning who contributed to their

Table 6. Did online components foster discussion on multicultural and diversity issues?

Fostered discussion on multicultural and diversity issues			
	CJUS	EESL	INFO
5 = Excellent	29%	27%	18%
4 = Very Good	14%	18%	35%
3 = Satisfactory	21%	36%	29%
2 = Poor	14%	18%	18%
1 = N/A	21%	0%	0%

learning, INFO ranked "Other student/s" equally with the instructor. For both CJUS and EESL this was the lowest rated item of the three.

We also surveyed how satisfied students were with online course materials. Satisfaction was rated high by all three courses. However, when asked if online materials helped facilitate learning, means for all three courses were low.

Table 7. Rating for how well the instructor, the student, and other students contributed to the learning experience

Contributed to learning experience	CJUS	EESL	INFO
Instructor	4.2	4.1	4.2
Self	3.6	4.0	4.0
Other Student/s	3.4	3.5	4.2

Table 8. Online materials survey results

	CJUS	EESL	INFO
Satisfied with online materials	4.7	4.1	4.2
Online materials facilitated learning	2.3	3.4	3.5

For all three courses examined, online materials were reported to have saved students time. However, in the EESL class, students reported spending more time on the online tests but saving time through use of discussion board.

Table 9. Time spent/saved using online components

Time Spent	CJUS	EESL	INFO
Online Materials			
Saved time	36%	64%	69%
Spent more time	0%	9%	6%
No answer	64%	27%	13%
Online Tests			
Saved time	0%	27%	0%
Spent more time	0%	55%	0%
No answer	100%	27%	100%
Discussion Board			
Saved time	7%	64%	0%
Spent more time	0%	9%	0%
No answer	93%	27%	100%

Faculty Syllabi, Proposals, Grant Reports, and Post Surveys

The faculty post survey was composed of items concerning their needs and uses of online technologies, coupled with an evaluation of students' learning that paralleled the student post survey. We also examined how the use of online technologies impacted faculty workload.

In our ongoing analysis we are considering the factors that led to successful and efficacious use of online technologies for both faculty and students. We are currently conducting our analysis via triangulation where we compare student data, faculty data (composed of free response and multiple-choice questions), information provided in the course syllabi, the grant proposals, and the end of grant reports.

We were not able to directly correlate the faculty post data with the student post data for individual courses due to the anonymity of the faculty post surveys. However, we were able to glean some data in the aggregate for professors' general satisfaction with the use of online technologies in their classes. Based on that data it was clear that faculty appreciated the support that was given to them.

Two of the three instructors provided access to syllabus information. Based on this information, in the INFO class, students were required to work in teams to complete projects. The professor used online materials but did not list use of the discussion board in his syllabus. By contrast, in the EESL class, students were not required to work in teams. The instructor required the use of the discussion board, online materials and online tests.

In the grant proposals, teaching was to be enhanced with the posting of online materials and links to relevant websites (see Table 10). EESL also incorporated the use of online tests and discussion board. INFO proposed to implement more technologies than were actually incorporated into the course.

Discussion

Based on the data presented above, it appears clear that in all three courses, students were satisfied with the connections made between the objectives of the course and the assessments used. This would imply that the courses were relatively well designed.

However, though the courses were relatively well received, it appears that improvements could have been made in the effective use of online technologies. For instance, the INFO course did not, according to the syllabus, the final report and the students' post surveys, use a discussion board for collaboration and file sharing. This was the case even though extensive collaboration was necessary for successful completion of course projects and even though at least 40% of the students lived 20 or more miles from campus.

Myer (2001) indicated that a fundamental problem with much research on online instruction is that it has failed to disaggregate the effects of the instructional design from the effects attributable to the technology. This appears to be the case in the courses that we examined above, as each could be shown to have been efficacious (based on student post survey data).

It is striking that two of the three courses did not reflect good scores on online learning activities fostering interaction and teamwork. This is striking as online technologies such as threaded discussion boards and chat rooms can be very powerful tools for collaboration (see Jonassen, et al., 1999). This would suggest that the full power of the technologies available through the WebCT tools to the instructors had not been utilized. In the third course, the INFO course, it is not clear whether chat rooms were utilized by students (see table 10). However, the structure of the course required extensive collaboration on projects (according to the course syllabus).

Similarly, for all three classes, the mean scores on facilitating discussions concerning diversity were low. Online technologies have the potential to enable ready access to global perspectives (see Papert, 1998), yet it would appear that this characteristic of the technology was not utilized effectively.

The fact that students in all three classes generally believed that using online technologies saved time would suggest improved instructional efficiency for all classes. With a population composed of commuters who often hold full time jobs, this result is weighty.

Though we asked students to rate how well the online learning experiences (using 5=excellent; 4=very good; 3=satisfactory; 2=poor; 1=not applicable), contributed to the effectiveness of the class (as measured by multiple items detailed in the above tables of results), respondents may not have read the items with respect to online technologies but rather with respect to the entire class. For instance, in the INFO class, students identified online components of the class to have contributed to fostering interaction and teamwork, yet a discussion board was not utilized in the course, according to the proposal, the syllabus, the final report, and student post surveys. We are also concerned that in some cases, students may not have understood the terms used and may have therefore answered questions erroneously (e.g. some students rated discussion boards and chat rooms that did not appear to have been implemented in a particular course).

Given our data analysis, several implications are suggested for implementation of the Online Teaching Support Model at our university. In examining the seven components of the model, there is evidence that several of the components may require substantial additional support. Specifically, the instructional design and training area may need additional attention to enable faculty to best integrate online technologies into their

Table 10. Online components of course design

	Course Design				
	Online Materials	Online Tests	Online Research	Online Discussion, Email, Chat Rooms	Bulletin Board
Based on Proposal:					
CJUS	All course notes, exercises	Practice quizzes, assessment			
EESL	Information modules/ tutorials using PowerPoint and audio	Part of tutorial			
INFO	Course content, glossary, site links for articles	Online quizzes and surveys		Mentioned in the justification but not part of project description	
Based on syllabus:					
CJUS					
EESL	Assignment descriptions	100-point quiz set, review quizzes	Accessing TESOL research via technology		Weekly announcements
INFO					
Based on final report:					
CJUS					
EESL	Course materials	Quizzes			Used extensively
INFO	Course content			Mentioned it affords students to interact but was not reported to have been done	

course design. We are concerned that our evidence suggests that instructors may not use the most powerful or appropriate technologies to assist with learning outcomes for their class or that they may use technologies in ways that are not effective. Additionally, in the evaluation area, several flaws were present. Faculty did not administer the instruments consistently in their courses (even though evaluation was a critical component of the grant). Thus, of the twelve funded projects, we were able to realize comparison data from only three classes in which we had sufficient data from both the student pretest and posttest.

We surmise that, in general, there is a tendency for faculty to focus on innovation and on technology and not on evaluation of the online course components. In order to better collect data from faculty, and to encourage them to have students participate fully in pretest and posttest administration, additional faculty incentives and reminders are likely to be necessary. Engaging faculty in a post-course interview would also likely assist analysis of the efficacy of the online course components.

We will apply the lessons learned from this analysis to future faculty development grant projects. This will assist us in serving the educational needs of our students through the use of technologies that can bridge barriers to access. We believe that the Online Teaching Support Model can be effectively applied at other institutions that would internally fund faculty development efforts. Based on our experience, special attention should be applied to the instructional design and evaluative components of such efforts.

References

Belanger, F. & Jordan, D. H. (2000). *Evaluation and implementation of distance learning: Technologies, tools, and techniques.* Hershey, PA and London, UK: Idea Group Publishing.

Dick, W. & Carey, L. (1996). *Systematic design of instruction.* New York: Addison-Wesley Publishing Company.

Hutchings, P. and Shulman, L. (1999). The Scholarship of Teaching. *Change: The Magazine of Higher Learning, 31*(5), 10–15.

Jonassen, D., Prevish, T., Christy, D. & Stavrulaki, E. (1999). Learning to solve problems on the web: Aggregate planning in a business management course. *Distance-Education; 20*(1), 49–63.

Myer, K. (2001, November). *Review of research on quality in distance education (web).* Paper presented at the 13th annual conference of the Western Cooperative for Educational Telecommunications (WCET), Coeur d'Alene, Idaho.

Papert, S. (1998). Let's tie the digital knot. *Technos, 7*(4), 10–12.

Salisbury, D. (1996). *Five technologies for educational change: Systems thinking, systems design, quality science, change management instructional technology.* Englewood Cliffs, New Jersey: Educational Technology Publications.

Santiago, R. (2001). Systematic planning for online teaching to support faculty's new role. In C. Montgomerie & J. Viteli (Eds). *Proceedings of Ed-Media 2001* (pp. 100–101). Tampere, Finland: Association for the Advancement of Computing in Education.

Seels, B. & Glasgow, Z. (1998). *Making instructional design decisions.* New Jersey: Prentice-Hall.

Van Slyke, C., Kittner, M. & Belanger, F. (1998). Identifying candidates for distance education: A telecommuting perspective. In *Proceedings of the Americas Conference on Information Systems* (pp. 666–668).

List of Contributors

Chris Aberson is an assistant professor at Humboldt State University who specializes in quantitative and social psychology.

Christina A. Bailey is Professor of Chemistry and Biochemistry at California Polytechnic State University, San Luis Obispo and chair-elect of the department.

Jean-Pierre R. Bayard is a Professor of Electrical and Electronic Engineering at California State University, Sacramento, where he chairs the CTL Teaching Using Technology Committee. He also serves as a Peer Reviewer on the MERLOT Engineering Editorial Board.

Jeffrey Bell is Professor of Biology at California State University, Chico, a co-developer of the Biolabs simulations, and the co-editor of the biology section of MERLOT.

Rina Benmayor is a professor in the Department of New Humanities for Social Justice at California State University, Monterey Bay. She teaches oral history, life stories and new media, Latina/o Studies, and literature.

Frances F. Berdan is Professor of Anthropology at California State University, San Bernardino.

Dale Berger is a Professor of Psychology at Claremont Graduate University and Director of the W.I.S.E. Project.

Beth Chance is Associate Professor of Statistics at California Polytechnic State University, San Luis Obispo and 2002 recipient of the American Statistical Association's Waller Education Award.

Phyllis M. Connolly, Ph.D., APRN, BC, CS, is a full professor and graduate coordinator in the School of Nursing at San José State University and Project Director for the FITNE Nightingale Tracker Project.

Gail Corbitt is department chair and Professor of Management Information Systems at California State University, Chico and a SAP Distinguished Scholar.

Suellen Cox is Head of Instruction and Information Services at the Pollak Library, California State University, Fullerton.

Gladys Deniz, a Technology Resource Teacher at West Fresno Elementary School District, created the photograph used on the cover when she was a participant in the 2002 CSU Summer Arts program at California State University, Fresno.

Victoria L. Elfrink, Ph.D., RNBC, is an adjunct professor in Health Care Informatics for UNITEC Polytechnic Institute, Auckland, New Zealand and Senior Associate of iTelehealth Inc., in Frederick, Maryland. She is a member of the American Nurses Association Committee for Nursing Practice Information Infrastructure and the former project director for the FITNE Nightingale Tracker Project.

William C. Epstein is a full professor in the Construction Management Department at California Polytechnic State University, San Luis Obispo.

Bret Eynon is a Professor of History and Director of the Center for Teaching and Learning at LaGuardia Community College, CUNY.

Joan Garfield is Professor of Educational Psychology, University of Minnesota, and currently directs the ARTIST project on assessment in introductory statistics.

Bijan B. Gillani, who received his doctorate from the University of Southern California in Educational Technology, is currently a professor and the coordinator of the Graduate Program in Educational Technology Leadership at the California State University, Hayward. His most recent publication is a book entitled *Learning Theories and the Design of E-Learning Environments.*

Neil Granitz is an Associate Professor of Marketing at California State University, Fullerton. He has published research in the *Journal of Business Ethics*, the *Journal of Marketing Education*, and other journals.

Courtney Granner is a professor in the School of Art and Design and the Animation/Illustration Program Co-coordinator at San José State University.

Chiara Gratton-Lavoie, a full-time Lecturer of Economics and Director of the Center for Economic Education at California State University, Fullerton, earned her Ph.D. in Economics from Virginia Polytechnic Institute and State University, Virginia. She teaches principles of microeconomics and intermediate microeconomics courses.

C. Scott Greene is a Professor of Marketing at California State University, Fullerton. He has published research in the *Journal of Business Ethics*, the *Journal of Marketing Education*, and other journals.

Ann Haffer is Professor of Nursing, California State University, Sacramento.

Mike Healy is a graduate student at Claremont Graduate University studying cognitive psychology.

Laura Henriques is an Associate Professor of Science Education and serves as the Science Single Subject Credential Advisor at California State University, Long Beach.

Elizabeth Housewright is Acting Associate University Librarian at the Pollak Library, California State University, Fullerton.

Steven T. Kane is a psychologist and Coordinator of Assessment with the Disability Resource Center and a Lecturer in the Psychology and Child Development Department at California Polytechnic State University, San Luis Obispo.

Kevin Kingsbury is an Associate Professor of Chemistry at California Polytechnic State University, San Luis Obispo.

Kristen Kulinowski, Ph.D. is Executive Director for Education and Public Policy for the NSF-funded Center for Biological and Environmental Nanotechnology and a Faculty Fellow in the Department of Chemistry at Rice University. Dr. Kulinowski contributed to the development of the innovative "studio chemistry" curriculum while on the faculty at California Polytechnic State University, San Luis Obispo.

James Mensching is a Professor of Management Information Systems and former Technical Director of SAP at California State University, Chico.

James M. Monaghan is the Director of the Office of Distributed Learning and Associate Professor of Instructional Technology at California State University, San Bernardino.

Terri Nelson is an Associate Professor of French at California State University, San Bernardino, where she is currently working on a new Web-based teaching tool.

Gary Novak is Associate Dean of the College of Natural and Social Sciences and Professor of Geological Sciences at California State University, Los Angeles.

Cecilia O' Leary is a Professor of Cultural History and chair of the Senate University Learning Requirements Policy Committee at California State University, Monterey Bay.

Walter Oliver is Professor Emeritus at California State University, San Bernardino and former director of the CSU Strategic Language Initiative.

Nancy Ostiguy is an Associate Professor of Entomology at The Pennsylvania State University.

Jeffrey Paradis, after cutting his teeth in the Cal Poly Studio classroom, went on to teach in the studio format at the University of Central Florida. Jeff currently is focussed on working with preservice K-8 teachers at California State University, Sacramento.

Dawn Poole is an Associate Professor of Educational Technology and is chair of the Advanced Studies in Education Department at California State University, Stanislaus.

Maria Roberts-DeGennaro is a professor in the School of Social Work, College of Health and Human Services, at San Diego State University.

Victoria Romero is a graduate student at Claremont Graduate University studying category learning in infancy.

Rowena S. Santiago is the Director of the Teaching Resource Center and Professor of Instructional Technology at California State University, San Bernardino.

Rod Schoonover is an associate professor at California Polytechnic State University, San Luis Obispo. He specializes in mathematical biology and biophysical and general chemistry, and he is an unrepentant Mac user.

Charles M. Slem is Professor of Psychology at California Polytechnic State University, San Luis Obispo and studies the impact of technological change in the workplace.

J. Laurie Snell is Emeritus Professor of Mathematics, Dartmouth College and developer of the CHANCE course and CHANCE newsletter.

Denise Stanley, an Assistant Professor of Economics at California State University, Fullerton, earned her Ph.D. in Economics from the University of Wisconsin-Madison. She teaches principles of microeconomics and economics of Latin America.

Edward Stark is a History/Social Sciences Teacher at Redlands East Valley High School in Redlands, California.

Carey Van Loon is Information Technology Consultant at California State University, San Bernardino.

Paul A. Weber is an assistant professor in the Construction Management Department at California Polytechnic State University, San Luis Obispo.

Tracey M. Weis is a Professor of African-American History and director of three interrelated Underground Railroad initiatives at Millersville University.

Randy Yerrick is a research associate and science methods instructor for the Center for Research of Math and Science Education at San Diego State University. As an Apple Distinguished Educator, Randy spends much of his time volunteering in K-6 environments teaching science content and processes through state-of-the-art technologies and innovative strategies.

List of Reviewers

Roberta Ambrosino is Acting Director and Instructional Technology Specialist at the Center for Teaching and Learning, California State University, Dominguez Hills.

Terry Ballman is Associate Professor of Spanish and Chair of Multiple Programs at California State University, Channel Islands.

Kimberly Bellah is currently pursuing a doctoral degree in agricultural education at the University of Florida. Previously, she served as a teacher educator in agricultural education at California Polytechnic State University, San Luis Obispo for seven years.

Bob Bleicher is Assistant Professor of Science Education at California State University, Channel Islands and an advocate of preparing future teachers to feel comfortable with using technology in their classrooms.

C. Kaye Bragg is chairwoman of Political Science and Director of the Faculty Teaching and Learning Center at California State University, Bakersfield.

Merri Lynn Casem is an Assistant Professor of Biology at California State University, Fullerton, where she is actively involved in curricular reform and innovation in teaching biology.

Marshall Cates is a Professor of Mathematics at California State University, Los Angeles and a consultant on Early Assessment for the Chancellor's Office.

Catheryn Cheal runs the Office of Online Instruction at California State University, Northridge and teaches art history online.

Doris Christopher is Associate Dean of Student Services at California State University, Los Angeles, and a professor in the Information Systems Department.

Cynthia Desrochers is Professor of Education at California State University, Northridge, and founding director of the campus faculty development center.

Liliane Fucaloro is Professor of French and department chair of the English and Foreign Languages Department at California State Polytechnic University, Pomona.

Paivi Hoikkala teaches in the History Department at California State Polytechenic University, Pomona, using technology to manage all her courses.

Bob Hurt is Professor of Accounting and Accounting Department Assessment Coordinator at California State Polytechenic University, Pomona.

Shahnaz Lotfipour is Professor of Educational Technology and the Director of the Joint Ed.D. and Educational Multimedia Program at California State Polytechenic University, Pomona.

Rick Luttmann has been a Professor of Mathematics at Sonoma State University since 1970; he recently served a three-year term as Chair of the Faculty, and he is an Associate Editor for the *American Mathematical Monthly.*

Susan Rogers is a lecturer in the English and Foreign Languages Department at California State Polytechnic University, Pomona, where she both develops and teaches Online Freshman Composition Courses.

C. E. Tapie Rohm, Jr. is Professor of Information and Decision Sciences at California State University, San Bernardino.

Coleen Saylor is a Professor of Nursing and the Director of the Center for Faculty Development and Support at San José State University.

Armin Schulz is a Professor of Reading in the College of Education at California State University, Stanislaus and also serves as the Director of the Faculty Center for Excellence in Teaching and Learning on that campus.

Bethany Shifflett is a professor at San José State University in the Human Performance Department and presently the WASC Accreditation Review Coordinator for the campus.

Alayne Sullivan is an Associate Professor of Literacy Education at California State University, San Bernardino, where she coordinates the Master's Degree Program in Reading and Literacy Education.

Sandra Sutphen is currently serving as interim coordinator for the California State University, Fullerton Faculty Development Center, but in real life she is a political scientist who teaches public administration with a specialization in emergency management.

Mark Thompson is Professor of English at CSU Stanislaus.

Louise Timmer is Professor of Nursing at California State University, Sacramento, and a member of the CSU Institute for Teaching and Learning Advisory Board and of the Academic Senate CSU.

Luis A. Vega is an Associate Professor of Psychology at California State University, Bakersfield specializing in intergroup relations and perceived discrimination issues as well as mentoring of first-generation college students.

James Wheeler is a Professor of Chemistry at California Maritime Academy, CSU and an Education Specialist in Undergraduate Science Instruction.

Nicole Wickler is an assistant professor at California State Polytechnic University, Pomona and Science Educator for the Center for Education Equity in Mathematics, Science, and Technology in the College of Science.

Marilyn Winzenz is Associate Provost and Director of the Center for Excellence in Learning and Teaching (CELT) at California State University, Chico.

William J. Wolfe is Associate Professor of Computer Science at California State University, Channel Islands.